RES GESTAE DIVI AUGUSTI

At the end of his life the emperor Augustus wrote an account of his achievements in which he reviewed his rise to power, his conquest of the world, and his unparalleled generosity towards his subjects. This edition provides a new text, translation and detailed commentary – the first substantial one in English for more than four decades – which is suitable for use by students of all levels. The commentary deals with linguistic, stylistic, and historical matters. It elucidates how Augustus understood his role in Roman society, and how he wished to be remembered by posterity; and it sets this picture that emerges from the *Res Gestae* into the context of the emergence both of a new visual language and of an official set of expressions. The book also includes illustrations in order to demonstrate how the Augustan era witnessed the rise of a whole new visual language.

ALISON E. COOLEY is Senior Lecturer in Classics and Ancient History at the University of Warwick. Recent books include *Becoming Roman, Writing Latin? Literacy and Epigraphy in the Roman West* (2002, edited), and *Pompeii* (2004).

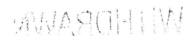

RES GESTAE DIVI AUGUSTI

Text, Translation, and Commentary

ALISON E. COOLEY

CAMBRIDGE
UNIVERSITY PRESS

CAMBRIDGE
UNIVERSITY PRESS

University Printing House, Cambridge CB2 8BS, United Kingdom

Cambridge University Press is part of the University of Cambridge.

It furthers the University's mission by disseminating knowledge in the pursuit of
education, learning and research at the highest international levels of excellence.

www.cambridge.org
Information on this title: www.cambridge.org/9780521601283

First published 2009
Reprinted 2015
3rd printing 2016

Printed in the United Kingdom by Clays, St Ives plc

A catalogue record for this publication is available from the British Library

Library of Congress Cataloguing in Publication data
Augustus, Emperor of Rome, 63 BC–14 AD
[Res gestae divi Augusti. English and Latin]
Res gestae divi Augusti / text, translation, and commentary,
Alison E. Cooley.
p.   cm.
Includes bibliographical references and indexes.
ISBN 978-0-521-84152-8 (hbk.) – ISBN 978-0-521-60128-3 (pbk.)
1. Rome – History – Augustus, 30 BC–14 AD   2. Augustus, Emperor of Rome,
63 BC–14 AD   I. Cooley, Alison.   II. Title.
DG279.A413 2009
937'.07 – dc22
2008055927

ISBN 978-0-521-84152-8 hardback
ISBN 978-0-521-60128-3 paperback

For Paul

Contents

vii

Illustrations

ACKNOWLEDGEMENTS FOR ILLUSTRATIONS

Fig. 1: by kind permission of Prof. H. von Hesberg; Figs. 2, 4–5: photos by Prof. S. Mitchell; Figs. 8, 14, 17, 34: photos by A. E. Cooley, reproduced by kind permission of Prof. E. La Rocca, Sovraintendenza ai Beni Culturali del Comune di Roma, and Dr C. Sintès, Musée Archéologique d'Arles; Figs. 9, 13, 15, 19, 20, 27, 28, 30, 32, 33, 37: by kind permission of Richard Abdy, British Museum, London; Figs. 10, 11, 21, 25: © The Trustees of the British Museum; Figs. 18, 24, 31, 38: © The Trustees of the British Museum; Figs. 12, 26, 35, 36: photographs courtesy of the Syndics of the Cambridge University Library.

Preface

I'm glad to be able to take this opportunity to thank Graham Oliver, whose enthusiastic and congenial collaboration over a paper for the Triennial Conference on the *RGDA* initially inspired the idea of undertaking this project. I'd also like to acknowledge the role played by my students at Warwick, notably the three cohorts who have grappled the Augustan age with me, who often make me clarify my ideas, and generally help inspire me by their enthusiasm for the subject. Michael Sharp has been supportive of the book from start to finish, offering invaluable practical help. Three Cambridge University Press assessors made helpful suggestions in planning the shape of the book in its infancy; Stephen Mitchell and the other Cambridge University Press reader provided copious suggestions for guiding the original typescript towards maturity; I hope that they like what they find now. Any faults in the book remain the result of my oversight or stubbornness. For help in compiling the illustrations I'm indebted to Michael Sharp, Stephen Mitchell, and my father. I'm grateful to Richard Abdy of the British Museum for permission to reproduce some of the images of coins already to be found in the LACTOR sourcebook, *The Age of Augustus*, ed. M. G. L. Cooley. Family support has been crucial, and I'm incredibly fortunate to have such tolerant children, husband, parents, and mother-in-law. Among other things, I'd single out the constructive criticism and practical help from Melvin and my parents, and the innumerable hours of childcare undertaken by my mother-in-law. The children have been wonderfully patient when I disappear, so I thank Emma for letting me get on with 'pretend work' whilst at home. Finally, I dedicate the book to Paul; if he hadn't been such a good baby and toddler, it simply would not have been possible to write this book.

February 2008
Warwick

Abbreviations

AE	*Année Epigraphique*
BM Coins, Rom. Emp. I	*Coins of the Roman Empire in the British Museum* = Mattingly (1923)
BM Coins, Rom. Emp. II	*Coins of the Roman Empire in the British Museum* = Mattingly (1930)
BM Coins, Rom. Rep.	*Coins of the Roman Republic in the British Museum* = Grueber (1910)
CIL	*Corpus Inscriptionum Latinarum*
EJ	Ehrenberg and Jones (1976, 2nd edn.)
FGrH	F. Jacoby, *Fragmente der griechischen Historiker*
FIRA²	*Fontes Iuris Romani Antejustiniani* = Riccobono (1941)
HRRel	*Historicorum Romanorum Reliquiae* = Peter (1906)
IGRom	*Inscriptiones Graecae ad res Romanas pertinentes*
ILLRP	*Inscriptiones Latinae Liberae Rei Publicae* = Degrassi (1957)
ILS	*Inscriptiones Latinae Selectae*
Inscr. Ital.	*Inscriptiones Italiae* XIII.i = Degrassi (1947); XIII.ii = Degrassi (1963); XIII.iii = Degrassi (1937)
LACTOR	LACTOR 17, *The Age of Augustus* = Cooley (2003)
LTUR I	*Lexicon Topographicum Urbis Romae* I. *A–C* = Steinby (1993)
LTUR II	*Lexicon Topographicum Urbis Romae* II. *D–G* = Steinby (1995)
LTUR III	*Lexicon Topographicum Urbis Romae* III. *H–O* = Steinby (1996)
LTUR IV	*Lexicon Topographicum Urbis Romae* IV. *P–S* = Steinby (1999a)

LTUR V	*Lexicon Topographicum Urbis Romae* V. *T–Z* = Steinby (1999b)
MAMA	*Monumenta Asiae Minoris Antiqua* IV = Buckler, Calder, and Guthrie (1933)
*OCD*³	*Oxford Classical Dictionary* = Hornblower and Spawforth (1996, 3rd edn.)
OGI	*Orientis Graeci Inscriptiones Selectae*
PECS	*Princeton Encyclopaedia of Classical Sites* = Stillwell (1976)
PIR	*Prosopographia Imperii Romani* = Klebs et al. (1897/8)
*PIR*²	*Prosopographia Imperii Romani* = Groag et al. (1933–)
RE	*Real-Encyclopädie d. klassischen Altertumswissenschaft*, eds. A. Pauly, G. Wissowa, and W. Kroll (1893–)
RDGE	*Roman Documents from the Greek East* = Sherk (1969)
RGE	*Rome and the Greek East* = Sherk (1984)
RIC I²	*Roman Imperial Coinage* = Sutherland (1984, 2nd rev. ed.)
RIC II	*Roman Imperial Coinage* = Mattingly and Sydenham (1926)
RRC	*Roman Republican Coinage* I = Crawford (1974)
SCPP	*Senatus consultum de Cn. Pisone patre* = Eck et al. (1996)
SEG	*Supplementum Epigraphicum Graecum*
Suppl. It.	*Supplementa Italica*
*Syll.*³	*Sylloge Inscriptionum Graecarum*

Journal abbreviations follow those in *Année Philologique*; abbreviated references to classical authors follow the conventions in the *Oxford Classical Dictionary* (3rd edn.)

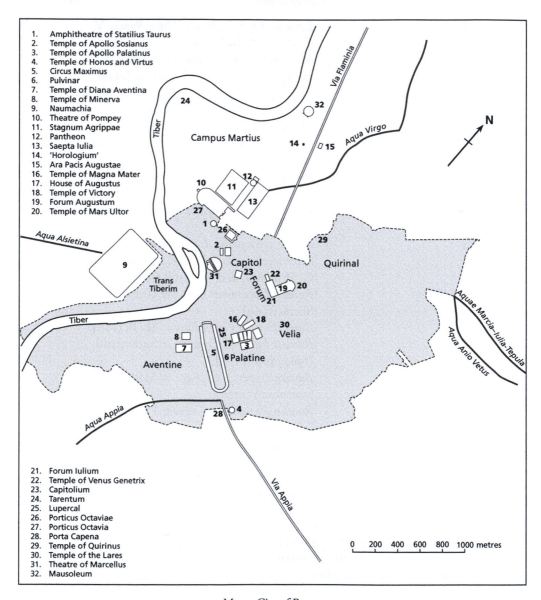

1. Amphitheatre of Statilius Taurus
2. Temple of Apollo Sosianus
3. Temple of Apollo Palatinus
4. Temple of Honos and Virtus
5. Circus Maximus
6. Pulvinar
7. Temple of Diana Aventina
8. Temple of Minerva
9. Naumachia
10. Theatre of Pompey
11. Stagnum Agrippae
12. Pantheon
13. Saepta Iulia
14. 'Horologium'
15. Ara Pacis Augustae
16. Temple of Magna Mater
17. House of Augustus
18. Temple of Victory
19. Forum Augustum
20. Temple of Mars Ultor

Via Flaminia

24

32

Tiber

Campus Martius

Aqua Virgo

14 •   15

10   11   12

13

27

Aqua Alsietina

1   26

2

9   Capitol

31   23   22

19   20

Trans
Tiberim

Forum

21

29

Quirinal

Tiber

16   18

8   25   30

7   17   3   Velia

Aquae Marcia–Iulia–Tepula

Aqua Anio Vetus

5   6 Palatine

Aventine

Aqua Appia   28   4

21. Forum Iulium
22. Temple of Venus Genetrix
23. Capitolium
24. Tarentum
25. Lupercal
26. Porticus Octaviae
27. Porticus Octavia
28. Porta Capena
29. Temple of Quirinus
30. Temple of the Lares
31. Theatre of Marcellus
32. Mausoleum

Via Appia

0   200 400 600 800 1000 metres

Map 1 City of Rome.

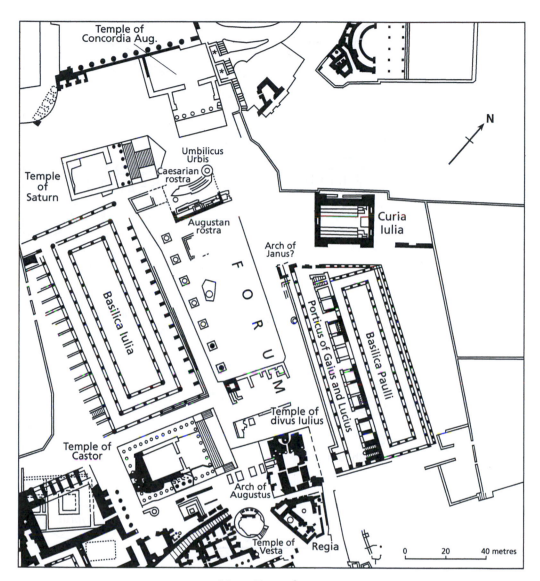

N

Temple of
Concordia Aug.

Umbilicus
Urbis

Caesarian
rostra

Temple
of
Saturn

Augustan
rostra

Curia
Iulia

Arch of
Janus?

F
O
R
U
M

Basilica Iulia

Porticus of Gaius and Lucius

Basilica Paulli

Temple of
divus Iulius

Temple of
Castor

Arch of
Augustus

Temple of
Vesta

Regia

0   20   40 metres

Map 2 Roman forum.

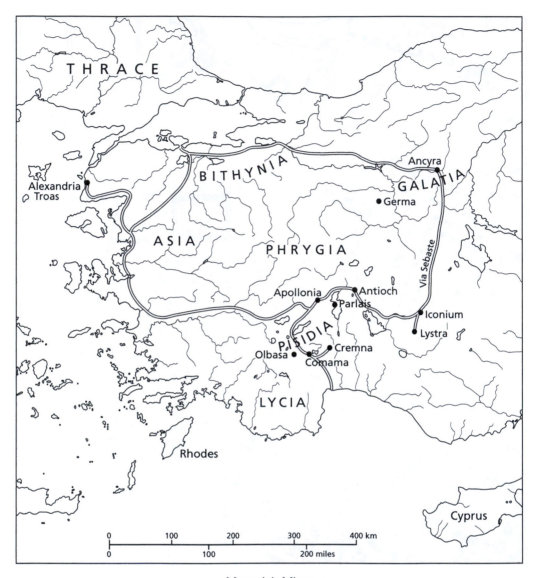

THRACE

BITHYNIA

Ancyra

GALATIA

Alexandria
Troas

Germa

ASIA

PHRYGIA

Via Sebaste

Apollonia

Antioch

Parlais

Iconium

PISIDIA

Lystra

Olbasa

Cremna

Comama

LYCIA

Rhodes

Cyprus

0   100   200   300   400 km
0   100   200 miles

Map 3 Asia Minor.

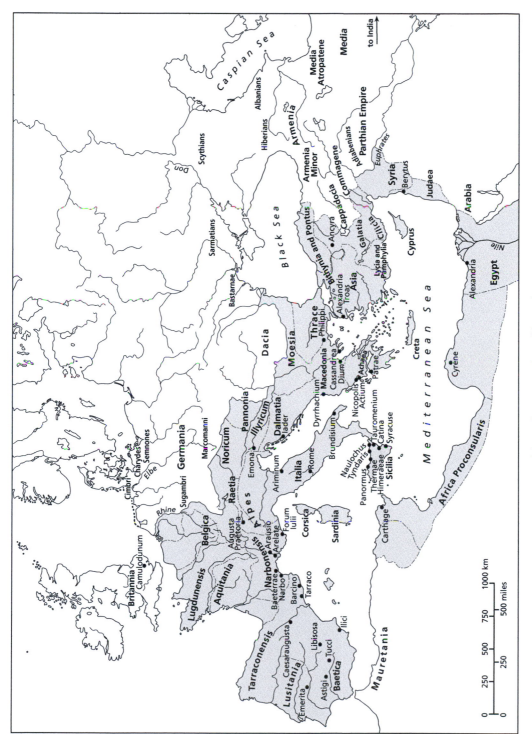

Map 4 Roman empire and beyond.

Introduction

I 'QUEEN OF INSCRIPTIONS'

In the opening chapter of his *Annals*, Tacitus briefly outlines the changes in political structure that Rome experienced from the regal period onwards, and maps onto these changes the ways in which history has been written. He comments, 'But the successes and failures of the Roman people of old have been recorded by famous writers, and there was no lack of people of fair talent for telling of the times of Augustus, until they were scared off by the flattery that was swelling up' (*sed veteris populi Romani prospera vel adversa claris scriptoribus memorata sunt, temporibusque Augusti dicendis non defuere decora ingenia, donec gliscente adulatione deterrerentur*).[1] Although we cannot be sure which authors Tacitus had in mind here, we do know of histories about the civil wars and the earlier years of Augustus' era written by Asinius Pollio, Livy, Cremutius Cordus, Seneca the Elder, and Titus Labienus.[2] It is unlikely that these were unduly influenced by flattery: Horace remarked upon the hazardous nature of Pollio's undertaking to write about the civil wars between 60 BC and 42 BC,[3] whilst Cremutius Cordus praised Brutus and Cassius in his histories that covered the period from the civil wars down to at least 18 BC, and was later condemned under Tiberius;[4] Labienus was otherwise known as 'Rabienus' because of his violent style, and his books were burned for their libellous content during Augustus' later years.[5] Indeed, the Elder Seneca recalls how even the fiercely independent Labienus himself interrupted one of his recitations from his history with the comment, 'the sections which I am passing over will be read after my death'.

None of these works survives in its entirety. Instead, our main historical literary works are those by Dio Cassius and Suetonius. Suetonius' biography is particularly useful in its recording of sources hostile to Augustus, such as letters and taunts composed by Antony, and in preserving some verbatim quotations and letters from Augustus himself, but the biography is not intended to offer a historical narrative, and any attempt to

---

[1] Tac. *Ann.* 1.1.2.   [2] Cf. Goodyear (1972) 95 ad loc.   [3] Hor. *Carm.* 2.1.
[4] Suet. *Aug.* 35.2; Tac. *Ann.* 4.34–5.   [5] Sen. *Controv.* 10, praef. 5–8 = LACTOR P24.

create one from it is doomed to failure.[6] Similarly, although without Dio Cassius we would lack any major narrative of the period, Dio's history is full of pitfalls, where he has been over-influenced by his third-century perspective and by his desire to portray Augustus as a model ruler, or has indulged in a degree of licence in structuring his annalistic account.[7] All this makes the task of constructing a chronological political narrative of the age of Augustus incredibly tricky. Even major crises, like the 'conspiracy of Murena', remain impenetrable to the modern historian.[8] The *Res Gestae Divi Augusti* (*RGDA*) further complicates this problem, since it too is not designed to offer an accurate narrative of the Augustan era. Why, then, did the great German ancient historian Theodore Mommsen call it the 'queen of inscriptions', and in what respects does it illuminate the age of Augustus?[9]

Above all, the *RGDA* offers an invaluable insight into the political ideology of the Augustan era, in the words of Augustus himself. Comparison with other inscriptions, coins, poetry, and art and architecture reveal how key themes upon which Augustus focuses in his retrospective on his whole career, the things for which he wished to be remembered, are strikingly present in a variety of contemporary literary, material, and visual media. This is not to imply that we can detect the workings of Augustan 'propaganda', but rather the development of a consensus that is reflected in the emergence both of a 'new visual language' and of an official set of expressions.[10] These were not imposed by Augustus, but the ideology was adopted by many different groups, including the senate, equestrians, and people at Rome, as well as by others beyond Italy, notably colonists in the provinces.

Coins, inscriptions, art and architecture, and literature share themes with the *RGDA*, and use common language to describe them. For example, the theme of world conquest was proclaimed in the prominent heading to the *RGDA*, celebrated in Horace's *Carmen Saeculare*, and symbolically represented on coins. It was also expressed through art and architecture in Rome by means of the *porticus ad nationes*, and Agrippa's Map.[11] Other major themes include the importance of restoring constitutional government at Rome after the long years of civil disorder, and the priority that should be

---

[6] Hostile remarks by Antony in Suetonius: *Aug.* 2, 4, 7, 10, 16, 68–9, 70; cf. other traces of hostile traditions in *Aug.* 4 (Cassius Parmensis); 11 (Aquilius Niger); 13 (Marcus Favonius); 35 (Cremutius Cordus); 51 (Iunius Novatus and Cassius Patavinus); 54 (Antistius Labeo). Quotations from Augustus: *Aug.* 31.5, 40.5, 42, 51, 58, 64.2, 65.2, 65.4, 71.2–4, 74, 76, 85, 86–7, 98.4, 99.1.

[7] Swan (2004) 13–26; Rich (1990) 17; Reinhold (1988) 5–6, 9–11, 12–15.

[8] Cf. Dio Cass. 54.3, with Rich (1990) 174–6.   [9] Mommsen (1906) 247.

[10] Zanker (1988) v–vi; Wallace-Hadrill (1986).

[11] Hor. *Carm. Saec.* vv. 53–6; *RIC* I² 59 no. 255; *BM Coins, Rom. Emp.* I 99 no. 604; Simon (1993) 91 no. 49; cf. *RIC* I² 59 no. 254, 60 no. 268; *BM Coins, Rom. Emp.* I 42 no. 217, 99 nos. 602–3, 101 nos. 622–3; Simon (1993) 91 nos. 50–1. Cf. commentary on heading **orbem terrarum imperio populi Romani subiecit**.

given to restoring traditional religious practices and buildings in the city
(see further section 5, below).

2 *RES GESTAE DIVI AUGUSTI* (*RGDA*) AT ROME

At the first meeting of the senate after Augustus' death in AD 14, Tiberius'
son, the Younger Drusus, read out to the senate the deceased's will and
three further documents.[12] The first of these issued instructions about his
funeral, the second was a 'summary of his achievements' (*index rerum a se
gestarum*), and the third contained a 'brief account of the whole empire'
(*breviarium totius imperii*).[13] Augustus requested that his *Res Gestae* be
inscribed and displayed on bronze in front of his Mausoleum on the Field
of Mars (*Campus Martius*) (see Map 1). The use of bronze set the *RGDA* on
a par with Roman legal and other important official documents, and evoked
ideals of sacrosanctity and durability.[14] By choosing bronze, Augustus was
implicitly elevating his account of his achievements, evoking the moral
authority usually enjoyed by texts inscribed on bronze, in accordance with
his ambition to act as a role model for the rest of society (see pp. 40–1).[15] At
the same time he could allude to ideas of religious sanctity that underlay
his authority in Roman society.

The Mausoleum was completed in 28 BC, several decades before his death
(Figure 1).[16] Given its size and complexity, work on the monument must
have begun some years earlier, perhaps in 32 BC, with the tomb playing
an important role in the final propaganda battle against Antony, leading
up to the naval battle at Actium in 31 BC. By building such a massive
tomb for himself at Rome, the young Caesar was eager to highlight the
contrast between himself and Antony. Whereas he was demonstrating his
commitment to the city, Antony's will (which Octavian illegally seized
and made public) revealed that he wished to be buried at Alexandria with
Cleopatra.[17] Rumours suggested that he was even contemplating shifting
the capital away from Rome to Egypt.[18] Augustus' tomb was unsurpassed in
size by any other, and it dominated the approach to Rome from the north
along the Flaminian Way (*via Flaminia*) or river Tiber.[19] It impressed at least
one contemporary, Strabo, whose account of Rome describes it in some
detail: 'The so-called Mausoleum is most noteworthy: a huge mound set
on a lofty plinth of white marble near the river, thickly shaded by a covering
of evergreen trees right up to the summit. On the top is a bronze statue
of Caesar Augustus while below the mound are the tombs of Augustus
himself, his close relatives and family.'[20] The location of the Mausoleum

---

[12] Dio Cass. 56.33.1.   [13] Suet. *Aug.* 101.4.   [14] Nissen (1886) 483; cf. Williamson (1987).
[15] Cf. 8.5; cf. Suet. *Aug.* 31.3, 31.5, 34.2.   [16] Suet. *Aug.* 100.4.
[17] Plut. *Vit. Ant.* 58.4–8; Dio Cass. 50.3.5.   [18] Dio Cass. 50.4.1; Kraft (1967).
[19] Von Hesberg (1996); Zanker (1988) 73–6.
[20] Strabo *Geography* 5.3.8 = LACTOR K29: ἀξιολογώτατον δὲ τὸ Μαυσώλειον καλούμενον, ἐπὶ
κρηπῖδος ὑψηλῆς λευκολίθου πρὸς τῷ ποταμῷ χῶμα μέγα, ἄχρι κορυφῆς τοῖς ἀειθαλέσι τῶν

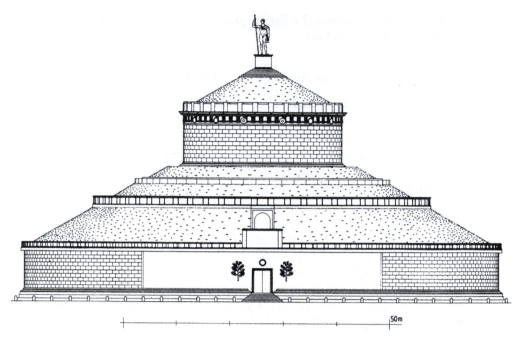

Fig. 1 Mausoleum of Augustus, reconstruction drawing by H. von Hesberg.

on the Field of Mars (*Campus Martius*) set it in proximity to several other monuments of significance to Augustus' self-image, including the altar of Augustan Peace (*ara Pacis Augustae*) and the meridian instrument.[21] Its south-facing entrance may have presented viewers with a sight line to the door of the Pantheon, perhaps linking in this way the two circular buildings which marked Augustus' progression from mortal to immortal status.[22] Consequently, some of the main themes in the *RGDA* – notably Augustus' peaceful settlement of the world, and his defeat of Antony and annexation of Egypt – were shared with distinctive monuments nearby.[23]

Known as the 'Mausoleum' or *tumulus* in contemporary sources, Augustus' tomb became a powerful dynastic statement, implicitly rivalling the original Mausoleum at Halicarnassos of King Mausolus of Caria, which ranked as one of the seven wonders of the ancient world.[24] It may also have been intended to evoke the burial mounds of Trojan princes, who were the legendary ancestors of the Julian family, and perhaps the tomb of Alexander the Great.[25] The idea that it drew its inspiration from the tumuli of Etruscan towns such as Caere (Cerveteri) stumbles against the

δένδρων συνηρεφές· ἐπ' ἄκρῳ μὲν οὖν εἰκών ἐστι χαλκῆ τοῦ Σεβαστοῦ Καίσαρος, ὑπὸ δὲ τῷ χώματι θῆκαί εἰσιν αὐτοῦ καὶ τῶν συγγενῶν καὶ οἰκείων.

[21] See 12.2n. **ad campum Martium**.   [22] Davies (2000) 137–42, espec. fig. 94.
[23] Elsner (1996) 39.   [24] Vitr. *De Arch.* 2.8.10–11.
[25] Holloway (1966); Reeder (1992); Zanker (1988) 72–7.

unlikelihood that Augustus wished to be seen as heir of the Etruscan kings of Rome, the expulsion of the last of whom, Tarquinius Superbus, had marked the beginning of the Republic.[26] The tomb provided resting places for several members of his family before the ashes of Augustus himself were eventually interred there in AD 14.[27] His nephew and son-in-law Marcellus was the first to be buried there in 23 BC,[28] followed by his sister (also Marcellus' mother) Octavia in 11/10 BC.[29] Augustus' close collaborator and next son-in-law Agrippa was buried there in 12 BC, at Augustus' express wish, despite his having a tomb elsewhere on the Field of Mars (*Campus Martius*).[30] His stepson Drusus (the Elder) followed in 9 BC,[31] and his grandsons, who were also his adopted sons, Lucius in AD 2[32] and Gaius in AD 4.[33] Augustus forbade either his disgraced daughter Julia or his granddaughter Julia from being buried there.[34] Those buried there were not simply members of the Julian family, therefore, suggesting that another principle of selection was at work. Indeed, the dynastic message of the tomb became clearer and clearer during Augustus' lifetime.

Before the *RGDA* was put on display outside the Mausoleum, some time after Augustus' death in AD 14, a marble copy was set up of the 'shield of virtue' (*clupeus virtutis*) bestowed upon Augustus in 26 BC.[35] Representations in stone of the laurels set up outside Augustus' house on the Palatine have also been found, suggesting that the entrance to his tomb may have mirrored that to his house, in this way adopting the common Roman perception that tomb and house were parallel homes for the dead and the living.[36]

Augustus' achievements were not the only ones presented outside his Mausoleum. A whole sequence of inscriptions displayed the achievements, or *res gestae*, of other members of the family too, some set up before the *RGDA*, others afterwards. On the premature death in AD 19 of Germanicus, Tiberius' heir presumptive, the senate decreed that bronze pillars displaying the senatorial decree which had been passed in his honour should be displayed in front of the Mausoleum next to the similar decrees which had been passed earlier in honour of Gaius and Lucius, who had also died prematurely.[37] Although we do not have these decrees, a decree passed at Pisa in honour of Gaius appears to have followed the senate's lead closely. The Pisan inscription referred to his achievements in the service of the state: 'after a consulship which he had completed while successfully waging war beyond the furthest boundaries of the Roman people, after

---

[26] Davies (2000) 13–19, 49–67.   [27] Macciocca (1996).

[28] Virg. *Aen.* 6 869–74 = LACTOR G37; Dio Cass. 53.30.5.

[29] *CIL* VI 40356, 40357 = LACTOR J32.   [30] *CIL* VI 40358; Dio Cass. 54.28.5.

[31] *CIL* VI 40359; Dio Cass. 55.2.3.   [32] *CIL* VI 40360, 40364.   [33] *CIL* VI 40361–3.

[34] Suet. *Aug.* 101.3.   [35] See 34.2n. **clupeus**; for a surviving fragment, see *CIL* VI 40365.

[36] See 34.2; von Hesberg and Panciera (1994) 113–18. Cf. Petron. *Sat.* 71 for a humorous representation of this idea.

[37] *Tabula Siarensis* fr. ii, col. a, ll. 5–7 = Crawford (1996) 518 no. 37.

he had carried out his state duties properly, with the most warlike and greatest peoples subdued or brought into alliance'.[38] This is very similar to Augustus' emphasis on foreign conquest in the *RGDA*, as well as at his funeral ceremony, where his effigy was displayed wearing the garb of a triumphal general, and during which the display of images of the nations subdued by Pompey the Great implicitly invited (presumably favourable) comparison with Augustus' martial deeds.[39] Further hints of the contents of these honorific decrees come from some inscribed fragments belonging to the monument's exterior, which appear to record the deeds of Agrippa, Drusus, Lucius, Gaius, and Germanicus.[40] Enough survives of the fragments to show that they share the common theme of foreign conquest. We might further surmise that the Younger Drusus, who died in AD 23 and was buried in the Mausoleum, and who was granted honours which were closely modelled upon those awarded to Germanicus, Gaius, and Lucius, may also have been honoured in a similar way. It is likely that imperial funerals provided occasions on which the crowds in attendance had their attention drawn to the inscriptions recording the achievements of Augustus and other members of his family. It may also be the case that the inscriptions came into the foreground more often than this, at annual sacrifices at the Mausoleum by the *Augustales* on the anniversaries of the deaths of these individuals.[41] Strabo's reference to 'wonderful promenades' in the sacred precinct behind the Mausoleum even evokes the everyday strolls which the inhabitants of Rome could enjoy in its vicinity.[42]

In short, the text of the *RGDA* should not be thought of in isolation. Rather, it joined other inscriptions already displayed on the exterior of the Mausoleum, which outlined the achievements of Augustus' potential heirs. It was also juxtaposed with two obelisks brought back from Egypt, booty which made clear his triumph over Cleopatra (and Antony). Naturally enough, Augustus' achievements and inscriptions surpassed all others, but together they presented the 'Achievements of the Augustan family', the *Res Gestae domus Augustae*. In this way, the epigraphic display of the Mausoleum contributed to its dynastic intent, offering to the viewer exemplary lives, which justified the privileged place in society of Augustus' family.

3 *RGDA* IN ITS PROVINCIAL CONTEXTS

No physical trace remains of the *RGDA* in Rome, since the bronze tablets on which it was inscribed must have been melted down many centuries

---

[38] *post consulatum quem ultra finis extremas populi [Ro]mani bellum gerens feliciter peregerat, bene gesta re publica, devicteis aut in [fid]em receptis bellicosissimis ac maxsimis gentibus*: ILS 140 lines 9–11 = EJ no. 69 = LACTOR J61.
[39] Dio Cass. 56.34.   [40] *CIL* VI 40358–60, 40363, 40367.
[41] *Tabula Siarensis* fr. ii, col. a, 1–5 = Crawford (1996) 518 no. 37.
[42] Strabo *Geography* 5.3.8 = LACTOR K29.

ago. Instead, we rely for a text upon three copies set up in the province of Galatia in central Asia Minor (Turkey) (see Map 3, Asia Minor). Galatia had only recently become a province, being annexed by Rome in *c.* 25 BC upon the sudden death of Amyntas, a client king of Rome, when he was captured on campaign and killed by the Homanadenses.[43] The region had, however, been dominated by Rome for much of the first century BC; its Gallic chieftains shared Rome's hatred for Mithridates VI of Pontus and, after the latter's defeat, Pompey the Great had installed three tetrarchs in Galatia (one for each tribe), as part of his reorganization of the whole region.[44] Amyntas had succeeded Deiotarus in 40 BC, and shortly afterwards received from Antony control of Pisidia and Phrygia Paroreius, an area which included Apollonia and Antioch near Pisidia.[45] Antony then made Amyntas king of Galatia, Lycaonia, and part of Pamphylia at around the turn of 37/36 BC.[46] By this time, the Celtic Galatian élite had adopted the trappings of Hellenistic culture; Amyntas himself was the first Galatian leader not to bear a Celtic name. The kingdom was of strategic importance to Rome, since it served as a buffer zone against incursions from mountain tribes and from the Parthians further east.[47]

At Ancyra (Ankara), the *RGDA* is inscribed in both Latin and Greek upon the temple of Rome and Augustus, and so it is known as the *Monumentum Ancyranum*, the 'queen' of all inscriptions, in Mommsen's view.[48] From Pisidian Antioch (Yalvaç) we have a Latin copy, the *Monumentum Antiochenum*, which was probably displayed on a monumental gateway leading to a temple to Augustus. At Apollonia (Uluborlu) a Greek version, the *Monumentum Apolloniense*, was inscribed on a large base that supported several statues. All three copies were probably associated with sanctuaries for emperor worship.[49]

a Ancyra

Ancyra was the provincial capital of Galatia, a new city founded by Augustus himself in around 25 BC for the *Sebasteni Tectosages Ancyrani*. It was an obvious location for the new capital, since there had previously been a stronghold occupying the same strategic geographical position.[50] Along with Pessinus and Tavium, it was assigned one of the three Galatian tribes, and its territory was expanded.[51]

The text of the *RGDA* was inscribed twice on the temple of Rome and Augustus (see Figures 2 and 3). This temple served as the headquarters for the centrally regulated provincial cult, administered by the provincial

---

[43] Strabo *Geography* 12.6.3; Dio Cass. 53.26.3.   [44] Strabo *Geography* 12.3.1.
[45] Strabo *Geography* 12.5.1, 12.6.4.   [46] Dio Cass. 49.32.3.
[47] Levick (1967) ch. 4; Mitchell (1993) ch. 3.   [48] Mommsen (1906) 247.
[49] Elsner (1996); Güven (1998); Botteri (2003b).   [50] Strabo *Geography* 12.5.2.
[51] Mitchell (1993) 86–91, 101–12.

Fig. 2 Temple of Rome and Augustus, Ancyra.

council (*koinon*) of the Galatians.[52] The *RGDA* was not, however, part of the original design for the temple, which was begun during Augustus' lifetime. Indeed, the temple itself may have been consecrated during the years between about 5 BC and AD 5, given the character of its architectural decoration. Originally, therefore, there was no space left empty for the

---

[52] Burrell (2004) 166.

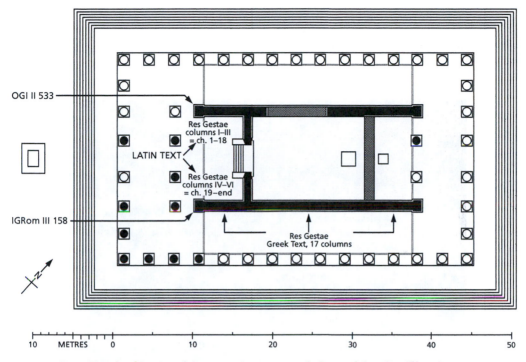

OGI II 533

Res Gestae
columns I–III
= ch. 1–18

LATIN TEXT

Res Gestae
columns IV–VI
= ch. 19–end

IGRom III 158

Res Gestae
Greek Text, 17 columns

10   METRES   0   10   20   30   40   50

Fig. 3 Temple of Rome and Augustus, Ancyra: ground-plan, with location of inscriptions (based on Schede and Schultz (1937) 9 fig. 5).

inscription: when the decision was made to add it, a substantial area of the temple's surface, which consisted of rectangular blocks of squared masonry with distinct margins, had to be smoothed over.[53] In this way, the inscription was added to the temple after Augustus' death in AD 14, possibly in about AD 19.[54]

The Latin text, derived from the prototype at Rome, was inscribed in two parts inside the temple, to the left and right on the *antae* inside the *pronaos*, starting next to the entrance (Figure 4). Each of the two parts contained three columns of writing, each one *c.* 1.17 m wide, containing 43–54 lines of text. The first part ran from chapter 1 to chapter 18, the second from chapters 19 to 35, followed by the Appendix. The heading ran in larger letters in three lines over the top of the first three columns.[55] The letters were brought out by red paint, which still remained in many places in the nineteenth century.[56] The Greek version was carved upon the outside face of the southern *cella* wall (Figure 5). It extended over a width of 20.5 m, and comprised nineteen columns of writing, each one *c.* 95 cm wide, containing twenty to twenty-five lines of text. The last column of

[53] Krencker and Schede (1936) 51.   [54] Mitchell (1986) 29–30.
[55] Krencker and Schede (1936) 51; Kornemann (1933) 214.   [56] Perrot and Guillaume (1862) 261.

Fig. 4 *RGDA*, Latin version at Ancyra.

Fig. 5 *RGDA*, Greek version at Ancyra.

Greek text, however, is only about 9 lines long. Here too, the heading was presented in larger letters above the rest of the text.

The inscription was an impressive sight: the temple provided a golden background for its crimson lettering, traces of which are still visible today.[57]

[57] Pers. comm., Stephen Mitchell, Nov. 2006. Pococke's remark (1745) 88 that 'the letters appear to have been gilt on a ground of vermilion' inadvertently reversed the colour scheme.

In addition to its striking colour scheme, the temple appears to have dominated Ancyra during the town's early years, when it was apparently the only classical-style building to be constructed there. The decision to display this text on this monument was a good one: the prominent title of the inscription confirmed the apotheosis of the ruler who was worshipped at the temple, whilst the details following it demonstrated why he had been deified (see p. 41). As at Antioch (see pp. 14–16), the imperialist message of the *RGDA* chimed in with its architectural context, since a personification of Victory, or *Nike*, was represented on the right-hand rear *anta*. Its acanthus frieze may also have summoned up images of peace and prosperity to complement those in the inscription.[58]

The *RGDA* was not the only text inscribed upon the temple. On the projecting end of the left-hand *anta* of the temple's *pronaos* was inscribed a list of the names of the annually appointed priests of Rome and Augustus during the Julio-Claudian era, giving details of their benefactions. These names include members of the former royal families of the three Galatian tribes. Their benefactions include gladiatorial spectacles, athletic displays, chariot races, beast hunts, sacrifices at the temple, public feasts, and distributions of olive oil.[59] Until recently, the list had been thought to date from between about AD 19 and AD 30. Careful re-examination of the inscription by Altay Coşkun within the context of new and revised numismatic and epigraphic evidence now points to its first eighty-two lines having been inscribed in AD 14, but recording the benefactions of priests in post from 5/4 BC.[60] A similar text on the end of the right-hand *anta* listed benefactions from the early second century AD, by which date the cult had become more closely focused upon the figure of the emperor, to the exclusion of the goddess Rome, and was by then not so much in honour of Augustus himself as a generic ruler cult for the figure of the Roman emperor.[61] As at Rome, viewers were invited, at least implicitly, to compare the benefits granted by Augustus with those granted by other people, in this case benefactions given to Ancyra by foremost members of the local élite. Such a comparison was encouraged by the distinctively Roman character of some of the benefactions, such as gladiatorial spectacles. In particular, the grain distribution by Amyntas son of Gaizatodiastes in AD 25/26 recalls Augustus' distribution of grain to the *plebs* of Rome,[62] not least since the Greek inscription uses the Latin word *modius* rather than the Greek μέδιμνος to describe the measures of grain. Furthermore, Pylaemenes sponsored athletic contests along with chariot and horse racing, a combination

---

[58] Krencker and Schede (1936) taf. 31b, 47c.

[59] *OGI* II 533 = *IGRom* III 157 = EJ no. 109 = Braund (1985) no. 137; but the most accurate text is in Krencker and Schede (1936) 52–7, with taf. 43–4, espec. 44a.

[60] Halfmann (1986), Mitchell (1986); Burrell (2004) 167–8. Stephen Mitchell has kindly informed me about the important work of Dr Coşkun, which will be published shortly; cf. Mitchell (2008), Mitchell and French, *The Inscriptions of Ancyra* I (forthcoming).

[61] *IGRom* III 158; Burrell (2004) 168.   [62] See 15.1.

of spectacles that appears to have been first adopted for the games at Rome in 28 BC celebrating Actium (see p. 145), and so he appears to have been imitating a model of benefaction specific to Augustan Rome. Other benefactions, however, were typically Greek and Celtic.[63] From this inscription, therefore, we see how members of the former ruling families of Galatia spent considerable sums of money upon benefactions made as part of the worship of Augustus and Rome, and in doing so consolidated their high status within the new social structure established under Augustus. Naturally, their expenditure was nothing when compared with the sums spent by Augustus, recorded in the *RGDA*.

The temple was converted into a church in around the sixth century, and then in the fifteenth century a mosque was added alongside it. These transformations helped to secure the text's survival. (For its rediscovery, see pp. 43–4).

b Antioch near Pisidia

Antioch had been founded by the Seleucids in the third century BC before it was re-founded as a colony of Roman citizens (*colonia Caesarea Antiochia*) by Augustus for veterans of the fifth and seventh legions in 25 BC, when the new province of Galatia was established (see p. 7). Alongside the veteran inhabitants were indigenous Anatolians, as well as families that derived their roots from the Seleucid settlement.[64] Situated on a strong site in the foothills of Sultan Dağ, the town occupied a pivotal position on the road system based around the *via Sebaste*, the new road (named after Augustus) built to consolidate Roman control over the new province, and whose milestones were numbered from Antioch.[65] It was just one of a sequence of *coloniae* founded by Augustus, including Cremna, Comama, and Olbasa, which were linked together by the *via Sebaste*.[66] (See Map 3, Asia Minor.) These towns and their inhabitants were expected to make a contribution to the consolidation of the new province, protecting southern Galatia from the tribes of the Taurus mountains.[67] The veteran colonists who formed the élite of Antioch (whose names show that most were born in Italy)[68] took pains to foster close contacts with Rome during the Augustan period, perhaps precisely because they were so isolated geographically. The town elected prominent members of Rome's élite as honorary magistrates, including P. Sulpicius Quirinius (who probably served as governor of Galatia *c.* 12 BC–7 BC) and Drusus the Elder (Augustus' stepson and Tiberius' brother).[69] Situated, like Rome, upon seven hills, the town even

[63] Mitchell (1993) 107–10.   [64] Levick (1967) ch. 6; Mitchell and Waelkens (1998) 5, 8.
[65] Ramsay (1916) 87–8; Ehrenberg (1925) 197–200; Mitchell and Waelkens (1998) 4.
[66] Cf. 28.1 n. **Pisidia**.
[67] Ramsay (1916) 83–4; Levick (1967) 38–40; Mitchell and Waelkens (1998) 9.
[68] Levick (1967) ch. 6.   [69] *ILS* 9502, 7201.

presented itself as a miniature Rome, naming some of its districts (*vici*) after landmarks in the capital.[70] The setting up of the *Res Gestae* here, therefore, is symptomatic of a desire to imitate Rome, and to forge close ties to the capital.

The *RGDA* (in Latin only) was inscribed upon slabs of limestone revetment in ten columns of text, with the heading inscribed in four lines above the first two columns. The heading was in larger lettering (1.9–4.0 cm) than the rest of the text, which is rather variable (1.2–1.8 cm).[71] Four different stonecutters appear to have contributed to the work.[72] The lettering was picked out with red dye.[73] About 270 small fragments have been published.[74] From the marks of chisel and hammer upon many of the fragments, D. M. Robinson deduced that the inscription had been deliberately smashed into tiny pieces at some time before the town was destroyed by Arabs in AD 713.[75] The fragments were discovered widely scattered near the steps of an impressive triple-arched gateway, which joined together a colonnaded street, the *Tiberia plateia*, and a large colonnaded square, perhaps called the *Augusta plateia*, via a monumental staircase (Figure 6).[76] The upper square led to a large temple, which was most probably dedicated to Augustus, if, as seems likely, the area was known as the *Augusta plateia*.[77] Other possibilities include Iuppiter Optimus Maximus, Roma and *divus* Augustus, or the local deity Men. On the temple *cella*, a frieze with acanthus foliage, garlands, and bulls' heads provided variations on themes from Rome's altar of Augustan Peace.[78] There is some debate about the inscription's original architectural context (see p. 47), but the most likely suggestion is that it was displayed on the central, inner faces of the monumental gateway.[79] The precise location of the inscription, however, is less important for our purposes than the certainty that it was generally associated with the gateway and temple.

The decorative scheme of the gateway commemorated Roman victories over barbarians and the outbreak of Augustan peace. Draped winged Victories accompanied images of fruitful peace (such as garlands with

[70] Levick (1967) 76–8; Mitchell and Waelkens (1998) 8–10.

[71] Ramsay and von Premerstein (1927a) 17.   [72] Ramsay and von Premerstein (1927a) 19.

[73] Robinson (1926a) 26; Ramsay and von Premerstein (1927a) 18.

[74] Ramsay (1916) 108–29; Ehrenberg (1925) 189–97; Robinson (1926a) 7–20; Ramsay and von Premerstein (1927a); Drew-Bear and Scheid (2005).

[75] Robinson (1926a) 2.

[76] Robinson (1924) 438, 440; Ramsay and von Premerstein (1927a) 1–2; Mitchell and Waelkens (1998) ch. 2, 146–9, pl. 12.

[77] Ramsay (1916) 108.

[78] Robinson (1924) 441–2; Mitchell and Waelkens (1998) 123, 157, 165, pls. 14–15.

[79] Ramsay and von Premerstein (1927a) 4, 10, 13–16, followed by Mitchell and Waelkens (1998) 146, 164. For other possibilities, summarized by Kornemann (1933) 214–15, see Robinson (1926a) 22–4, with pl. VIIb (on the front of four pedestals roughly halfway up on the staircase); von Premerstein (1932) 202, 224–5 (on the four sides of a base bearing a lifesize equestrian statue of Augustus); Botteri (2003a) 246–7 (the temple). Ramsay (1916) 107 n. 3 pointed out that the fragments did not belong to the exterior of the temple, since they were of limestone, whereas its facing was of marble. Robinson (1926a) 22 was correct to state, however, that the temple was of limestone (pers. comm., Stephen Mitchell, Nov. 2007).

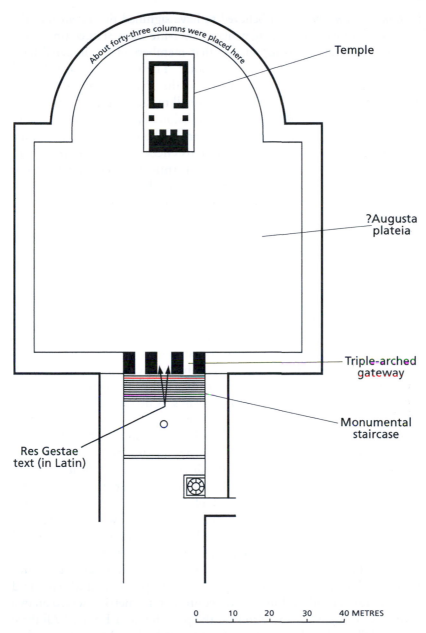

Fig. 6 Architectural context of *RGDA* at Pisidian Antioch (based on Mitchell and
Waelkens (1998) 153 fig. 31).

flowers, fruits, and ribbons), and defeated barbarians were depicted on
either side of the central arch. Images of Poseidon flanked by dolphins,
tritons with trophies, and ships' prows and rams reminded the viewer of
naval victories too. A representation of his birth sign, Capricorn, alluded
to Augustus himself, and his divine descent was recalled by an image of

the *sidus Iulium*, the comet believed to have signified the ascent into the heavens of Julius Caesar. Fragments of over-life-sized statues (including a colossal head of Augustus) suggest that members of the imperial family peered down from the gateway's roof.[80] The gateway was dedicated to Augustus in 2/1 BC,[81] and so predated the *RGDA*, but the addition of the *RGDA* strikingly reinforced the overall message of the monumental ensemble, emphasizing Rome's imperial mission in general[82] and Augustus' victories by both land and sea in particular.[83] Whereas the imperialist tone of the *RGDA* was mitigated somewhat in its Greek versions (see pp. 28–9), the triumphalist tone of the original text at Antioch, where only the Latin text was on display, was entirely appropriate both to its general context – a *colonia* of veterans, established in a newly conquered region – and to its specific monumental context.

c Apollonia

Not much is known about Apollonia (Uluborlu), but it was a Greek foundation probably dating back to the third century BC. It only became part of Galatia under Amyntas (see p. 7), and some colonists were added to its community under Augustus. Our main source of information is its inscriptions, largely found in reused contexts, and a few physical remains.[84] The inscriptions reveal that members of the local élite justified their own status via their involvement in emperor worship. One family stands out in particular. Apollonios, son of Olympichos, is described in an honorific decree issued by the council (βουλή) and people (δῆμος) as priest of Rome, 'friend of the emperor and friend of his country' (φιλοσέβαστον καὶ φιλόπατριν). The same inscription reveals that he had set up three equestrian statues in the sanctuary (ἐν τῶι τεμένει) of the *Sebastoi* (perhaps in honour of Tiberius, Germanicus, and Drusus), had represented the city on an embassy to Germanicus (presumably in AD 18, when Germanicus was on his tour of duty in the East), and had served the town as gymnasiarch and priest of Rome.[85] Apollonios shared his enthusiasm for the imperial family with his brother, Olympichos, whom the people (δῆμος) honoured as 'friend of the emperor' (φιλοσέβαστον) and for his 'reverence towards the *Sebastoi*' (ἐπί τε τῆι εἰς τοὺς Σεβαστοὺς εὐσεβείαι), and who received a grant of Roman citizenship.[86] Another brother, Demetrios, served on two embassies to Augustus, and also held the priesthood of Rome.[87] All three brothers followed in the footsteps of their grandfather, Artemon, who had

---

[80] Robinson (1924) 437–9, (1926b) 25, 26, 41–5, with figs. 34, 38–9, 41–50, 60, 62; (1926c) 125, 129–36, pl. V; Mitchell and Waelkens (1998) 160–4, pls. 112–15.
[81] Mitchell and Waelkens (1998) 146–7.   [82] See heading, 3.1–2, 4.1–3, 13, 26–33.
[83] See 3.1–2, 3.4, 4.2, 13.   [84] *PECS* 72.   [85] *MAMA* IV no. 142.
[86] *MAMA* IV no. 161.   [87] *IGRom* III no. 320.

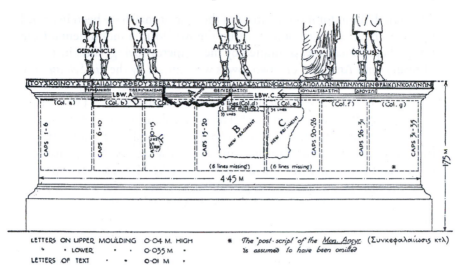

Fig. 7 Context of *RGDA* at Apollonia (*MAMA* fig. 17).

served as priest of Zeus some time earlier in the first century BC, and was honoured with a decree of the people.[88]

The *RGDA* was inscribed at Apollonia upon a large base (*c.* 4.45 m long), which probably bore five statues of members of the imperial family. It would be entirely appropriate if these statues originally stood in the sanctuary of the *Sebastoi* mentioned above (see Figure 7).[89] Fragments of the names of Germanicus, Tiberius, and Augustus have been found, to which Julia Augusta and Drusus are highly probable additions. Gaius and Lucius have also sometimes been included in reconstructions of the text. The crucial phrase at the start of the dedicatory inscription on the base is usually restored as referring to the city of Apollonia, as follows: [τοὺς κοινούς τε καὶ ἰδίους θεοὺς Σε]βαστοὺς καὶ τοὺς π[αῖδας αὐτῶν ὁ δῆμος Ἀπολλωνιατῶν Λυκίων Θραικῶν κολώνων.] / [Γερμανικῶι. Τιβερίωι Καίσαρι.] θέῷ Σε[βαστῶι. Ἰουλίαι Σεβαστῆι. Δρούσωι.] ('[The people of the Apollonian, Lycian, and Thracian colonists (honour) the public] and private Augustan gods and their children. To Germanicus. Tiberius Caesar. God Augustus. [Julia Augusta. Drusus]').[90] Other restorations would also be possible, perhaps including the names of prominent members of the élite involved in emperor worship. The dedicatory formula and the imperial names occupy the top two lines, and are inscribed in much larger lettering than the text of the *RGDA*, which follows beneath them, below the mouldings which carried the larger letters, spread out over seven columns. It is unclear whether or not the Appendix was included; even if there was

---

[88] *MAMA* IV 141.   [89] Mitchell (1993) 104.

[90] *MAMA* IV no. 143/*IGRom* III no. 312. This text follows *MAMA*, underlining letters for which the editors had to rely upon earlier travellers.

not enough room for it on the front of the base, it may have been inscribed upon its end.[91] The decision to set up the *RGDA* in a monumental form was perhaps a local one, prompted by the 'emperor-loving' élite, in a spirit of rivalry with Antioch. The two towns were linked by the *via Sebaste* and, whereas Antioch was a full Roman colony, Apollonia had simply received a settlement of colonists (*coloni*) into its existing community.[92] The unusual formula 'Apollonian, Lycian, and Thracian colonists' (Ἀπολλωνιατῶν Λυκίων καὶ Θρακῶν κολωνῶν) found on its coins and inscriptions appears to be inspired by a sense of rivalry with the nearby colony.[93] It seems most likely that the base inscribed with the *RGDA* at Apollonia was set up some time between AD 14 and AD 20, given that a statue to Germanicus stood upon it. This timeframe would fit closely with the probable date of its inscribing at Ancyra (see p. 9).

d Mechanisms for publication

The presence of three copies of the *RGDA* in Galatia invites discussion of how the text was distributed from Rome.[94] It makes a great deal of difference to our picture of the relationship between Rome and its provinces whether a central authority such as the senate issued instructions requiring the *RGDA* to be displayed in an inscribed form throughout the empire or whether provincial communities themselves took the initiative to create monuments incorporating the *RGDA*. These are not the only possibilities, however, since another model of how the *RGDA* came to be inscribed in provincial cities might attribute the move to the provincial governor and, given the survival of copies of the *RGDA* from just a single province, Galatia, this last possibility might initially seem the most attractive.

The heading of the Latin inscriptions – 'Below is a copy of the achievements of the deified Augustus . . . as inscribed upon two bronze pillars which have been set up at Rome' – indicates that the monuments self-consciously presented the text as being copied from the exemplar at Rome. It is often assumed that a central instruction was issued from Rome requiring universal publication of the *RGDA* throughout the Roman empire.[95] In part, this assumption is influenced by the perception that the text of the *RGDA* was of no interest to an audience outside Rome: 'No one in Ancyra, Apollonia, or Antioch could possibly have been interested in the boring enumeration of *largitiones* and *congiaria*, of games and of mimes performed in Rome.'[96] It is commonplace to point out that Rome's provinces are

---

[91] Harrer (1937) 248 challenged the view in *MAMA* that there was not sufficient space on the front.
[92] Mitchell (1993) 77.   [93] Ramsay (1922) 185.   [94] Cooley (2007).
[95] Recently, Scheid (2007) xvii; Eck (2003) 1–2.
[96] Yavetz (1984) 8; cf. Levi (1947) 189, 'un documento destinato soltanto al popolo romano'. In this, as in other matters, Mommsen set the tone (1883) vi, arguing that Augustus shrewdly wrote what he wanted the *plebs Romana* to know or believe about him.

normally mentioned only as part of Rome's imperial mission, when they are conquered or become allies of Rome, and that Augustus' focus upon the benefits he had given to the city of Rome and Roman citizens would have held little of interest for provincial readers.[97] It would then simply be a curious coincidence that the three copies of the text that happen to survive have done so in a single province.[98] As I shall explore in more detail below (see pp. 26–30), this assumption is largely based upon a consideration of the Latin text alone, since a close reading of the Greek version shows that it skilfully adapted Augustus' words for an audience far from Rome.

Furthermore, the final Appendix may even have been composed precisely for the benefit of provincial readers.[99] It is clearly not part of Augustus' own composition since the verbs change from first to third person. Besides, in contrast to the rest of the *RGDA*, sums of money in the Appendix are calculated in *denarii* rather than in *sestertii*, in other words, in the unit of currency in use in the Greek east rather than in that used at Rome.[100] The content of the Appendix is also suggestive of a shift in focus away from Rome. Although most of the expenditure listed is still of relevance solely to Rome, section 4 mentions towns in receipt of financial aid following earthquakes and fire. This detail is absent from the main text of the *RGDA*, and it may be worth noting that towns in the Greek east are known to have received financial help from Augustus on several occasions following earthquakes.[101]

Another problem with assuming that the *RGDA* was once a common sight throughout the empire is that documents were not generally disseminated in that way. On the whole, the state did not issue empire-wide orders for documents to be set up as monumental inscriptions. Instead, publication of a document in the form of an epigraphic monument occurred most often at the instigation of individuals, both Roman and provincial, and of provincial communities. The commonest type of publication was when a document was aimed at a specific audience, and was set up as an inscription on the initiative of members of the local élite. Less often did the senate or emperor issue instructions for publishing a document in an inscribed form.

In a very few cases, however, the Roman senate did issue instructions for the universal publication of a document, notably the *Tabula Siarensis* and the senate's decree concerning Gnaeus Calpurnius Piso (*senatus consultum de Cn. Pisone patre* = *SCPP*), both of AD 20. The former contained a record of the honours given to Germanicus on his untimely death, and was published since the senate wished

[97] Brunt and Moore (1967) 4; cf. Hoffmann (1969) 21.
[98] Cf. Yavetz (1984) 29 n. 49: 'I have no explanation for the strange coincidence that the only three known copies of the *Res Gestae* were found in different districts of a single province.'
[99] Kornemann (1933) 217.   [100] Viereck (1888) 85.
[101] Dio Cass. 54.23.7, Paphos; Dio Cass. 54.30.3, province of Asia; Dittenberger and Purgold (1896) no. 53, Cos; cf. Suet. *Tib.* 8, for an appeal for help from Laodicea, Thyatira, and Chios.

the more readily to show the respect of every order towards the Augustan household and the agreement of all citizens in honouring the memory of Germanicus Caesar, that the consuls should publish this decree of the senate beneath their edict, and that they should order the magistrates and ambassadors of the municipalities and colonies to send a written copy to the municipalities and colonies of Italy and to those colonies which were in the provinces, and that those who were in command in the provinces would be acting properly and correctly if they took pains to see that this decree of the senate were fixed in as prominent a place as possible.[102]

The latter, an account of the trial of Calpurnius Piso, who was widely rumoured to have murdered Germanicus, was published

> so that the course of the proceedings as a whole may be handed down more easily to the memory of future generations, and so that they may know what the senate's judgement was concerning the unique self-control of Germanicus Caesar and the crimes of Gnaeus Piso Senior, the senate has decided that . . . this decree of the senate should be inscribed on bronze and set up in the busiest city of each province, in the busiest place of the city, and that likewise this decree of the senate should be set up beside the standards in each legion's permanent headquarters.[103]

These two examples of universal publication, however, are exceptional, and belong to a very specific historical context, when the senate was trying to consolidate Tiberius' position as the first imperial successor at a time of crisis early in his reign, and when it was also seeking to find a role for itself in the new order of the principate.[104] At this time, the senate was becoming aware of the importance of distributing its decrees as a means of promoting the new dynastic ideology, and as a way of boosting its own status, since it presented itself as second in importance only to the imperial family in teaching Roman society how to behave.[105] Furthermore, by publishing its decrees, the senate effectively appropriated for itself the legislative function which more properly belonged to popular assemblies.[106] This was in stark contrast to the character of senatorial decrees up to this point, which were not thought of as having a universal relevance because they contained the senate's advice to a particular magistrate in response to a specific query posed to it by that magistrate.[107]

---

[102] *item senatum velle atque aequom censere, quo facilius pietas omnium ordinum erga domum Augustam et consensu\<s\> universorum civium memoria honoranda Germanici Caesaris appareret, uti co(n)s(ules) hoc s(enatus) c(onsultum) sub edicto suo proponerent iuberentque mag(istratus) et legatos municipiorum et coloniarum descriptum mittere in municipia et colonias Italiae et in eas colonias quae essent in \<p\>rovinciis; eos quoque qui in provinci\<i\>s praessent recte atque ordine facturos si hoc s(enatus) c(onsultum) dedisse\<n\>t operam ut quam celeberrumo loco figeretur.* Tab. Siarensis frag. II, col. B ll. 21–7 = Crawford (1996) 518 no. 37.

[103] *et quo facilius totius actae rei ordo posterorum memoriae tradi posset atque hi scire\<nt\>, quid et de singulari moderatione Germ(anici) Caes(aris) et de sceleribus Cn. Pisonis patris senatus iudicasset, placere uti . . . hoc s(enatus) c(onsultum) {hic} in cuiusque provinciae celeberruma{e} urbe eiusque i\<n\> urbis ipsius celeberrimo loco in aere incisum figeretur, itemq(ue) hoc s(enatus) c(onsultum) in hibernis cuiusq(ue) legionis at signa figeretur:* SCPP lines 165–72 = Eck et al. (1996) 50.

[104] Rowe (2002) 8.   [105] Cooley (1998).   [106] Rowe (2002) 43, 64–6.
[107] Mommsen (1907) 300.

In the case of the *RGDA*, it is more plausible to suggest that the provincial governor saw to the publication of the *RGDA* within his province than that some central authority at Rome ordered the publication of the *RGDA* throughout the empire.[108] We do not know the identity of the governor in Galatia at this date, but a useful parallel comes from the publication of the *SCPP* in Baetica. There the name of the governor Numerius Vibius Serenus features prominently in the heading of one of the major copies of the decree, implying that he was personally involved in disseminating the decree. He evidently arranged for the *SCPP* to be published even more widely than the senate had instructed, since the copies that survive from Baetica cannot be traced to 'the busiest city of each province', but were displayed in relatively minor towns too, such as Irni, which, as it was neither municipality nor colony at the time, was not required by the senate to publish its decree.[109] Vibius Serenus had offended Tiberius, according to Tacitus, when, having helped to convict Libo Drusus in AD 16, he subsequently complained that he had been insufficiently rewarded by the emperor.[110] He may have judged (in the event, wrongly, since he was subsequently exiled) that he might win back the emperor's favour by proclaiming his enthusiasm for the imperial family in this way.[111] Even in the case of the *SCPP*, therefore, local factors were important in determining the extent to which the publication clause was actually fulfilled.[112]

A further possibility is that the decision to publish the *RGDA* was made by the provincial council (τὸ κοινόν), which oversaw the development of emperor worship on a provincial level. Governor and provincial council might also work towards the same ends. A suggestive parallel may be found in the publication of instructions throughout the province of Asia for implementing its new calendar in honour of Augustus in 9 BC. The provincial governor Paullus Fabius Maximus issued instructions for the publication of his edict ('I shall order the decree inscribed upon a slab to be set up in the temple, having ordered that the edict be written in both languages'), to which the provincial council added extra instructions in its decree ('that the official rescript of the proconsul and the decree of Asia be inscribed on a slab of white marble, and that this be set up in the sanctuary of Rome and Augustus. And also that the public advocates for the year take care that both the official rescript of Maximus and the decree of Asia be inscribed on white marble slabs in the main cities of the assize districts, and that these slabs be set up in the shrines of

---

[108] Gordon (1968) 129–30, 137.

[109] Eck *et al.* (1996) 279–87; Potter (1998); Stylow and Corzo Pérez (1999). Similarly in the case of the *Tabula Siarensis*, Siarum was not a *colonia*, and so fell outside the remit of the senate's publication clause: Crawford *et al.* (1996) 536.

[110] Tac. *Ann.* 4.29.   [111] Eck *et al.* (1996) 101–3; Cooley (1998) 209.

[112] Compare too the publication of Diocletian's Edict on Maximum Prices: Cooley (2007) 207–8, and the Customs Law from Ephesus: Rowe (in press).

Caesar').[113] Inscribed copies found in Priene, Apamea Kibotos, Dorylaion, Maionia, and Eumeneia suggest that this demand for province-wide publication was indeed executed.

Even if it was the case that the publication of the *RGDA* in Galatia was prompted at a provincial level by governor and/or provincial council, our earlier discussion of the local contexts of the three copies that do survive demonstrates how the document was transformed into three distinctive local monuments, and that the local élite may well have played a significant part in setting up the *RGDA* in their towns. This is not to claim that Roman officials were not involved at any stage, since it appears that the texts were subject to Roman approval. The fact that the Greek versions at Ancyra and Apollonia share the same prototype (even to the extent that they display some common errors) suggests that an approved official Greek translation of the *RGDA* may have been generated in the province.[114] Nor should we exclude the possibility that other copies of the *RGDA* may at some point be found in a different province; I simply suggest that it is not safe to assume that the *RGDA* was universally published, and that it is worthwhile exploring local contexts in order to understand why it was set up.

4 THE LANGUAGE OF THE *RGDA*

a *Stylistic characteristics of the Latin text*

On the whole, the *RGDA* lacks literary elegance; instead, as is appropriate for an inscribed text, it is notable for the conciseness and apparent simplicity with which Augustus expresses himself.[115] Even though the style of the inscription is unexceptional, it is possible to trace how the ways in which language is used in the Latin text complements its meaning, reinforcing the messages Augustus wished to convey in the *RGDA* about his achievements and position in the state (see pp. 34–41). Augustus generally adopts a striking economy of expression in a number of ways. Whilst this is of course only suitable for an inscribed text, it throws into relief the occasions when he is marginally more expansive. Participle clauses, especially ablative absolutes, produce a more pithy style on many occasions than if he had used subordinate clauses, right from the opening statement *annos*

---

[113] *OGI* II 458; *RDGE* no. 65 = *SEG* 4.490 = EJ no. 98 = *RGE* 101 = LACTOR H34. Cited passages: προστάξω δὲ χαραχθὲν <ἐν> τῇ στήλῃ τὸ ψήφισμα ἐν τῷ ναῷ ἀνατεθῆναι, προστάξας τὸ διάταγμα ἑκατέρως γραφέν – IV lines 28–30; ἀναγραφῆναι δὲ τὸ δελτογράφημα τοῦ ἀνθυπάτου καὶ τὸ ψήφισμα τῆς Ἀσίας ἐν στήλῃ λευκολίθῳ, ἣν καὶ τεθῆναι ἐν τῷ τῆς Ῥώμης καὶ τοῦ Σεβαστοῦ τεμένει. προνοῆσαι δὲ καὶ τοὺς καθ' ἔτος ἐκδίκους ὅπως ἐν ταῖς ἀφηγουμέναις τῶν διοικήσεων πόλεσιν ἐν στήλαις λευκολίθοις ἐνχαραχθῇ τό τε δελτογράφημα τοῦ Μαξίμου καὶ τὸ τῆς Ἀσίας ψήφισμα, αὐταί τε αἱ στῆλαι τεθῶσιν ἐν τοῖς Καισαρήοις – VI lines 62–7.

[114] The two versions are compared by Scheid (2007) lxviii–lxxi.

[115] Lauton (1949); Gordon (1968) 127, 137–8; Bardon (1968) 54, 55–6. Scheid (2007) xxvi–xxviii adopts an extreme view that distances Augustus from the compositional process altogether.

undeviginti natus ('aged nineteen years old').[116] He uses adjectives sparingly, usually only where they are essential to a word's meaning, such as in cases like *equester ordo* ('equestrian order') or *pontifex maximus* ('chief priest').[117] When he does use adjectives elsewhere, they draw our attention to particular achievements and emphasize their importance. Adjectives show us how impressive his contributions to Rome have been (*impensa grandi* – 'incurring great expense', 20.1; *bestiarum Africarum* – 'of African wild beasts', 22.3), and how extensive the empire he has established (*complura oppida* – 'many towns', 26.5; *plurimae aliae gentes* – 'very many other tribes', 32.3).[118] One of the most prominent messages of the *RGDA* is that Augustus enjoyed unanimous support (*equites Romani universi* – 'the Roman equestrians all together', 14.2; *tota Italia* – 'the whole of Italy', 25.2; *senatus et equester ordo populusque Romanus universus* – 'the Roman senate and equestrian order and people all together', 35.1). Adjectives in the first two chapters of the *RGDA* encourage a positive interpretation of his early career (e.g. *decretis honorificis* – 'honorific decrees', 1.2; *iudiciis legitimis* – 'by way of the courts of law', 2). Above all, the repetition of *privato consilio et privata impensa* ('at my personal decision and at my personal expense', 1.1) makes clear that his earliest interventions on behalf of the state were as a private citizen, and invites us to make comparisons with other great Romans who had acted in a similar capacity. His use of asyndeton is another example of his conciseness, but it also emphasizes significant lists and lends them an air of factual objectivity.[119]

According to Suetonius, Augustus 'took especial care to express his meaning as clearly as possible',[120] and, although the particular example given by Suetonius (of his including prepositions in front of the names of towns) only occurs once in the *RGDA* (26.2), we can see how Augustus makes use of repetition for clarity (for example, *dedi meo nomine et quinquiens filiorum meorum aut nepotum nomine* – 'I gave in my name and five times in the names of my sons or grandsons', 22.1).[121] Another stylistic characteristic is his use of repetition and word order for emphasis.[122] This cannot always be captured in an idiomatic English translation. Whereas the main verb generally occurs at the end of a sentence, it is sometimes followed by a further statement, which receives extra emphasis in this way (for example, *Capitolium et Pompeium theatrum utrumque opus impensa grandi refeci **sine ulla inscriptione nominis mei*** – 'I restored the Capitoline temple and theatre

---

[116] 1.1; cf. 26.3, 29.1, 31.1, 32.2; Lauton (1949) 111.   [117] Lauton (1949) 108–9.

[118] Cf. 26.1, 27.3.

[119] For example, see lists of priesthoods held by Augustus, 7.3; buildings in Rome, 19; provinces swearing loyalty to him, 25.2; provinces where he has founded colonies, 28.1; foreign kings seeking refuge with him, 32.1. Lauton (1949) 112.

[120] Suet. *Aug.* 86.1, *praecipuam curam duxit sensum animi quam apertissime exprimere.* Cf. Mart. 11.20.10 for Augustus speaking *Romana simplicitate*, 'with Roman plainness'.

[121] Cf. *lustrum . . . quo lustro*, 8.2–4. Lauton (1949) 114; Bardon (1968) 57.

[122] Bardon (1968) 57–9.

of Pompey, incurring great expense for both buildings, **without inscribing my name anywhere on them**', 20.1).[123] Postponing a word until the end of its clause results in a similar effect (for example, *cum . . . esset parta victoriis **pax*** – 'when **peace** had been achieved by victories', 13).[124] Postponing the numbers of men and beasts participating in his shows highlights their spectacular character (*hominum circiter **decem millia*** – 'about **10,000** men', 22.1).[125] Conversely, starting a sentence with the verb is very striking, especially combined with anaphora, as it is when Augustus turns to the oath of loyalty sworn in his favour: ***iuravit** in mea verba tota Italia sponte sua . . . **iuraverunt** in eadem verba provinciae*' ('The whole of Italy of its own accord **swore an oath of allegiance** to me . . . The . . . provinces **swore the same oath of allegiance**', 25.2).[126] Some ideas are also emphasized by postponing the conjunction in subordinate clauses, for example highlighting the critical situation of the state in the case of *res publica **ne** quid detrimenti caperet* ('**to prevent** the state from suffering harm', 1.3).[127] Elsewhere, Augustus draws attention to a relative clause by making it precede the main clause (for example, *qui parentem meum interfecerunt* – 'those who murdered my father', 2).[128]

Another feature which the *RGDA* shares in common with his other public pronouncements is that Augustus avoids Greek words, except where they have become fully integrated into the Latin language.[129] For example, in referring to a mock naval battle, instead of using the single word *naumachia* ('mock sea fight'), derived from Greek, he adopts a more wordy, purely Latinate expression *navalis proeli spectaculum* ('spectacle of a naval battle').[130] This feature probably reflects Augustus' sense of propriety, a perception that a Latin unadulterated by Greek influences was most fitting to a text of such weighty significance as the *RGDA*. This sentiment corresponds to the picture of Roman language nationalism under Tiberius that prompted him to banish the use of Greek in the Roman senate.[131]

The syntax of the *RGDA* conveys the unambiguous message that Augustus is central to the state. The fact that the whole text is written in the first person makes this clear on a basic level, and this is reinforced by the repetition and emphatic positioning of the adjective *meus*. This possessive pronoun occurs again and again in the *RGDA*, and is often delayed for effect until after the noun it qualifies (for example, *impensa et cura*

---

[123] Cf. 7.1–2, 20.2, 31.1.

[124] Cf. *bis acie*, 2; *imperator*, 4.1; *senatus*, 14.1; *exercitus ad oppidum Mariba*, 26.5; *per eius clupei inscriptionem*, 34.2; *patrem patriae*, 35.1.

[125] Cf. *bestiarum circiter tria millia et quingentae*, 22.3; *millia hominum tria circiter*, 23.

[126] Cf. 5.2.

[127] Cf. *sacrosanctus in perpetuum ut essem*, 10.1; *pontifex maximus ne fierem*, 10.2; *tertium decimum consulatum cum gerebam*, 35.1. Lauton (1949) 115.

[128] Cf. *quae tum per me geri senatus voluit*, 6.2; *qui sub signis meis tum militaverint*, 25.3. Lauton (1949) 115.

[129] Gelsomino (1958), especially 149–52.   [130] 23; Gelsomino (1958) 149. Cf. 25.1; 26.3, 27.3.

[131] Suet. *Tib.* 71; Kaimio (1979) 96, 132–3, 325–6.

mea – 'through **my** expenditure and supervision', 5.2).[132] In just one case, it is thrown into particular relief when the words *meo iussu et auspicio* ('under my command and auspices') are placed right at the start of an entire phrase.[133] The personal tone of the whole inscription masks the revolutionary novelty involved in Augustus talking of 'my army' (*exercitus meus*, 30.2) and 'my fleet' (*classis mea*, 26.4). His description of his veterans as being 'my soldiers' (*militum meorum*, 15.3) would have been unobjectionable, given the personal relationship between troops and their commander, but to extend this to the whole army and fleet of the Roman state was an astounding sign of how successfully Augustus had taken over control of the military forces of Rome.[134] In the course of a single chapter, we see how the unique achievements of the army under Augustus in conquering new areas of the world actually result in its changing from 'the army of the Roman people', *populi Romani exercitus* (30.1), to 'my army', *exercitus meus* (30.2). This metamorphosis is smoothly effected via an intermediate step of the army acting *meis auspicis*, 'under my auspices', a conventional expression that masks the radical shift whereby Augustus assumes authority over the whole Roman army. Similarly, Augustus' personal relationship with foreign kings and envoys gradually creeps into the text. In speaking of the friendship enjoyed by foreign kings and envoys with Rome, Augustus first describes it as 'friendship with me and the Roman people', *amicitiam meam et populi Romani* (26.4). He then uses a more traditional expression, 'friendship of the Roman people', *amicitiam populi Romani* (29.2), before alluding to 'our friendship', *amicitiam nostram* (32.2), perhaps in a deliberately vague fashion. The traditional role of the senate in dealing with foreign envoys is usurped in this way, and even the *populus Romanus* implicitly plays only a supporting role to the main actor, Augustus.[135]

Lastly, Augustus chooses his words carefully in order to create a positive impression of his position in the state. By precisely reproducing official formulae in referring to political institutions, such as the *senatus consultum ultimum* (1.3), or the triumvirate (7.1), he inserts his political career into the traditional framework of the state.[136] By contrast, at the grand climax of the whole text, Augustus surprises us with an unexpected variation on a traditional theme. The customary formula 'senate and people of Rome', *senatus populusque Romanus*, occurs four times in the text,[137] paving the way for the phrase 'senate and equestrian order and people of Rome', *senatus et equester ordo populusque Romanus universus* (35.1), to make an impact on the reader, conveying how extensively Roman society has been restructured under the guidance of Augustus in his guise as their 'father', *pater patriae*.

---

[132] Cf. 3.3, 4.3 (x2), 9.2, 10.1, 11, 14.1, 15.1, 16.1 (x2), 17.1, 17.2 (x2), 18, 20.1, 20.3 (x3), 21.1, 21.3, 24.2, 34.2 (x3).
[133] 26.5.   [134] Cf. Raaflaub (1987) 266–9.   [135] Braunert (1975) 46–7.
[136] Bardon (1968) 56.   [137] 6.1, 14.1, 34.1, 34.2.

b Features of the Greek translation

It is likely that an official version of the *RGDA* in Greek was distributed on request to Ancyra and Apollonia (see p. 22). I use the term 'version' rather than 'translation' to emphasize the fact that the Greek text is not simply a word-for-word rendering of the Latin original into Greek.[138] In the past, this Greek version has been condemned by scholars as the poor quality work of a Roman whose primary language was Latin, the botched product of a translation service based at Rome.[139] This attitude, however, largely resulted from judging it by the standards of classical Attic Greek rather than those of *koine* Greek used under the Roman empire.[140] More recently, it has been suggested that the *RGDA* was not translated in Rome at all, but in the Greek east.[141] Admittedly, some aspects of the translation are highly influenced by its Latin model, but this may be deliberate rather than a mistake, with the aim of making the Greek text sound Roman.[142] Certainly, its use of Greek is strikingly more proficient than that found in translations of senatorial decrees, and it differs from them in its choice of vocabulary.[143] For example, whereas the Latin phrase *res publica* ('the state') is usually rendered in Greek translations of senatorial decrees as τὰ δημόσια πράγματα ('the state affairs'), the *RGDA* gives us τὰ κοινὰ πράγματα ('the public affairs') and ἡ πατρίς ('the fatherland') as well. In the latter case, this choice of expression serves a distinct purpose, of heightening the emotional tone in alluding to the struggle against Brutus and Cassius.[144] On occasion, the Greek version even improves upon the Latin original. For example, it uses ἔθνος ('nation') rather than δῆμος ('citizenry'), where the Latin uses *populus*, in order to distinguish between the *populus Romanus* and a non-Roman nation.[145] Far from being a word-for-word translation (like the senatorial decrees), the Greek text is a version designed to be comprehensible to a provincial audience, and in some cases even tailored to its sentiment.[146]

For an audience unfamiliar with the topography and institutions of the city of Rome, specific references are simplified, or explanatory paraphrases provided, or sometimes even details are omitted. For example, instead of repeating Augustus' statement about his bridge repairs word-for-word, referring to the Mulvian and Minucian bridges by name, the Greek simply

---

[138] Cf. useful tables of differences between Latin and Greek versions in Scheid (2007) xxx–xxxiv.
[139] Viereck (1888) 88.   [140] Meuwese (1920), (1926); Regard (1924) 148.
[141] Meuwese (1920) 2, 54, 62–3; Wigtil (1982b); Adams (2003) 471.
[142] Meuwese (1920) 117; Wigtil (1982a) 628–31, (1982b) 190; Adams (2003) 469–71, 504.
[143] Reichmann (1943) 18–19, 21–6; Wigtil (1982b) 193. Overall, it bears a greater resemblance to an edict on the requisitioning of transport issued by the governor of Galatia early in Tiberius' reign: Mitchell (1976) 109–10.
[144] τὰ δημόσια πράγματα, 1.3, 1.4; τὰ κοινὰ πράγματα, 1.1; ἡ πατρίς, 2.1; Vanotti (1975) 308–9.
[145] 26.4; Wigtil (1982a) 633. Cf. 30.2.
[146] Reichmann (1943) 21–6; Vanotti (1975); Wigtil (1982a), (1982b); Cooley (2007) 210–13.

refers to 'all the bridges on it except for two which were not in need of repair' (γεφύρας τε τὰς ἐν αὐτῆι πάσας ἔξω δυεῖν τῶν μὴ ἐπιδεομένων ἐπισκευῆς).[147] Even the *curia Iulia* becomes simply the βουλευτήριον, or council chamber.[148] In a further simplification, *pontifices* become 'priests' and the Vestal Virgins 'priestesses'.[149] The names of Roman deities are either explained by parenthesis or given a Greek equivalent, with the usual correspondences such as Jupiter and Zeus, Juno and Hera, as well as more unexpected ones, such as the 'shrine of Pan' for the Lupercal, and describing the Lares as 'heroes'.[150] Similarly, the distinctiveness of Rome's festival of the *ludi saeculares* ('centennial games') and the significance of bestowing the *corona civica* ('civic crown') upon Augustus are both made clear in the Greek.[151] In dealing with the *ludi saeculares*, the translator both transliterates the Latin word into Greek, and also provides an explanation of the word's meaning: θέας τὰς διὰ ἑκατὸν ἐτῶν γεινομένας ὀνομαζομένας σαικλάρεις ('the spectacles that occur after 100 years called *saeclares*').[152] Likewise, the provincial Greek reader is not assumed to appreciate the honour and achievement symbolized by the civic crown: ὅ τε δρύινος στέφανος ὁ διδόμενος ἐπὶ σωτηρίαι τῶν πολειτῶν ('the oak wreath which is given for saving fellow citizens').[153]

Political expressions in Latin are not always translated by the same word in Greek, but the translator instead varies the Greek in order to explain them fully. The Latin word *imperium* provides a good example of this.[154] It is first translated by the Greek word for 'rods' (ῥάβδους), as the equivalent of *fasces*, the symbols of magisterial authority at Rome, in a context where Augustus is talking of the recognition given to him by the senate in 43 BC.[155] Later, however, when Augustus mentions that he had carried out the census by virtue of his consular *imperium* (*tum iterum consulari cum imperio lustrum solus feci* – 'Then for a second time I conducted a census on my own with consular power'), the Latin term is translated as ὑπατικῆι ἐξουσίαι (εἶτα δεύτερον ὑπατικῆι ἐξουσίαι μόνος . . . τὴν ἀποτείμησιν ἔλαβον).[156] Elsewhere, the idea of *imperium* as power exercised by the Roman people is translated as ἡγεμονία ('political supremacy') or as προστάγματα ('commands').[157] On a single occasion, Augustus even uses the word to signify 'territorial empire' in speaking of the closure of the gates of Janus in celebration of peace throughout the Roman empire (*cum per totum imperium populi Romani terra marique esset*

---

[147] 20.5; cf. 11.1. Reichmann (1943) 22; Vanotti (1975) 313; Marrone (1977) 319; Wigtil (1982b) 192.

[148] 34.2, 35.1; Marrone (1977) 319.

[149] 11, 12.2; for other simplifications, see 4.2, 17.1, 22.2. Reichmann (1943) 23; Vanotti (1975) 313; Marrone (1977) 326.

[150] 11.1, 13.1, 19.1, 19.2, Appendix 2. Reichmann (1943) 21–2.

[151] 22.2, 34.2; cf. 4.1. Reichmann (1943) 22; Vanotti (1975) 315, 320; Marrone (1977) 321–2; Wigtil (1982a) 634.

[152] 22.2.   [153] 34.2.   [154] Vanotti (1975) 308; cf. *princeps*: 13n., *ter me principe*; Vanotti (1997).

[155] 1.2.   [156] 8.3.   [157] ἡγεμονία 27.1; cf. 26.1, 30.1; προστάγματα 30.2.

parta victoriis pax). This was a new meaning for the word that had only just developed at that time, and in this case the Greek adopts a paraphrase (εἰρηνευομένης τῆς ὑπὸ Ῥωμαίοις πάσης γῆς τε καὶ θαλάσσης – 'once all land and sea was at peace under the Romans').[158] Similarly, the word *congiaria* ('distributions') presented the translator with a challenge, since no equivalent institution existed in the Greek world. As a result, he translates the Latin word differently even when it recurs in the course of a single chapter.[159]

The Greek also adapts the Latin original to its new cultural context. On a basic level, for instance, it converts sums from Roman (sesterces) into Greek denominations (*denarii*). Other modifications reflect differences between Rome and the Greek east. For example, Augustus draws attention to the fact that games were performed at Rome in fulfilment of vows for his welfare in his lifetime (*vivo me*), not, as would normally be the case there, as funerary games after his death. The translator, however, omits the words *vivo me*, because the exceptional character of having games performed in one's lifetime at Rome was not applicable in the Greek world, where, on the contrary, such games were far from exceptional.[160] Similarly, the translator omits the phrase *apud omnia pulvinaria* ('at all public feasts'), since no equivalent was readily available to his audience.[161]

The most striking difference between the two texts, however, comes straight away in the heading. The subordinate clauses in the Latin title emphasize Augustus' world conquest and his benefactions to the people of Rome (*rerum gestarum divi Augusti, quibus orbem terrarum imperio populi Romani subiecit et impensarum, quas in rem publicam populumque Romanum fecit* – 'the achievements of the deified Augustus, by which he made the world subject to the rule of the Roman people, and of the expenses which he incurred for the state and people of Rome'), and this imperialist tone permeates the rest of the *RGDA*.[162] By contrast, the heading in Greek is much shorter and makes no mention of Augustus' conquests, even perhaps leaving open the possibility that his gifts were as much directed towards the provinces as towards Rome: 'Translated and inscribed below are the deeds and gifts of the god Augustus' (μεθηρμηνευμέναι ὑπεγράφησαν πράξεις τε καὶ δωρεαὶ Σεβαστοῦ θεοῦ).[163] In this way, the most prominent part of the Greek inscription directs its readers towards a rather different interpretation of the text as a whole, and is perhaps designed not to offend the sensibilities of a community such as that of Ancyra, which had only recently been brought under direct Roman control. The imperialist tone is also softened elsewhere. Where Augustus explains the meaning of the closing of the gates of Janus, his explanation reflects the regime's ideology of *pax Augusta* in the sense of 'pacification after military victory'.[164] By contrast, the Greek version omits the explicitly militaristic phrase *parta*

---

[158] 13. Richardson (2003) 141–2.   [159] 15.1, 15.3; Vanotti (1975) 314.
[160] 9.1. Scott (1932); Vanotti (1975) 311.   [161] 9.2.   [162] Nenci (1958) 293–4.
[163] Vanotti (1975) 314; Botteri (2003a) 244.   [164] Rich (2003) 333.

victoriis pax ('when peace had been achieved by victories').[165] References to Roman triumphs are also omitted in two other passages.[166] Overall, therefore, we can see how minor changes introduced into the translation substantially modify the tone of the inscription, perhaps making it more acceptable to a provincial audience under Roman rule.

Other changes in the Greek version reflect a willingness to acknowledge the monarchical nature of Augustus' position at Rome, which would perhaps be less openly acceptable at Rome itself.[167] At the high point of the whole text, where, having reviewed Rome's position as a world power, he returns to the subject of the greatest honours granted to him by the senate, Augustus presents an assessment of his authority in Rome in 28/27 BC. His concluding statement, *post id tempus auctoritate omnibus praestiti* ('after this time I excelled everyone in influence'), implies that he achieved overwhelming *auctoritas* only after the senate had granted him the exceptional honours listed. The Greek version, however, does not translate *post id tempus* ('after this time') at all, removing in this way any sense of chronological or causal relationship between Augustus' primacy and honours granted to him by the senate, simply stating 'I excelled everyone in reputation' (ἀξιώματι πάντων διήνεγκα).[168] The Greek version also underplays the role of the *plebs* at Rome. Whereas Augustus is keen to acknowledge the importance of the *plebs* in supporting him, the Greek is more dismissive of the *plebs*, even referring to it as ὄχλος, which usually bears a pejorative meaning ('rabble') in a somewhat misguided attempt to distinguish the *plebs urbana* from the *populus Romanus*, as well as using the more usual word δῆμος ('citizenry').[169]

Finally, the fact that a few errors of interpretation creep into the translation reinforces the view that the translator was based in the Greek east, and not at Rome. In reporting the census figures, the Greek version inadvertently ruins Augustus' proud claim that the number of Roman citizens increased steadily from 4,063,000 through 4,233,000 up to 4,937,000 by giving the first figure as 4,603,000.[170] Some errors in dealing with more technical sides of the Latin text suggest that the translator was not completely au fait with Roman institutions. For example, the translator misinterprets Augustus' reference to the four major colleges of priests at Rome as instead referring to the college of the four priests. This seems to be the result of a potential ambiguity in the Latin word order, but it would not have presented a problem had the translator appreciated that Augustus was referring to the traditional system of religious colleges at Rome (consisting of the *pontifices, augures, quindecimviri,* and *septemviri*).[171]

---

[165] 13.1. Reichmann (1943) 22; Vanotti (1975) 313.
[166] 21.3, *ad triumphos meos*; 15.3, *triumphale congiarium*. Wigtil (1982a) 634.
[167] Vanotti (1975) 323; Wigtil (1982a) 636.   [168] 34.3. Vanotti (1975) 320–31.
[169] 15.2; Wigtil (1982a) 636, (1982b) 192.   [170] 8.2–8.4. Wigtil (1982b) 192.
[171] 9.1. Marrone (1977) 317 n. 2; Wigtil (1982b) 190–1. For other mistakes, see 15.3, 20.3, 31.2.

In short, rather than attempting to replicate Augustus' words as closely as possible as the result of a perception that the deified emperor's words held a special status,[172] the translator makes a fair number of what might appear at first glance to be inconsequential modifications, but which together add up to offering a substantially different view of Augustus' achievements and expenses for the benefit of a provincial audience from that intended for its original audience at Rome. Not only does the translator simplify and explain the Latin text for its new audience, he even softens its imperialist tone, emphasizing instead Augustus' role as a donor and benefactor, and playing down his role as a conqueror. At the same time, it offers a less subtle picture of Augustus' supremacy at Rome than the one developed by Augustus himself, and as such is typical of the wider response within the Greek east to his emergence as de facto monarch.[173]

5 THE MESSAGES OF THE *RGDA*

Much ink has been expended upon the question of what type of document the *RGDA* is and why Augustus produced it.[174] It has been variously described as an epitaph, a political testament, a rendering of accounts for the reign, a description of his new political system, and a bid for deification. Given that one of the most prominent messages of the *RGDA* is the uniqueness of Augustus, it should come as no surprise that the text does not follow in others' steps in a straightforward way.

We can trace many possible influences upon the *RGDA*, ranging from inscriptions set up in Rome and Latium to monuments in the Greek east and even beyond. The most obvious place to start is with funerary inscriptions at Rome which advertise the deceased's achievements and which are, at least in part, written in the first person.[175] This is not to imply that the *RGDA* is in any straightforward way an epitaph, even though it was displayed outside Augustus' tomb – clearly it goes far beyond the normal scope of such a text – but we can trace some similarities between Augustus' autobiographical account of his achievements and some unusual funerary inscriptions at Rome. The *elogia* set up in the tomb of the Scipios on the *via Appia* are often cited in this context, especially that of Cn. Cornelius Scipio Hispanus from the late second century BC.[176] It starts with a conventional career inscription, listing his various magistracies and priesthoods: 'Gnaeus Cornelius Scipio Hispanus, son of Gnaeus, praetor, curule aedile, quaestor, tribune of the soldiers twice, member of the Board

---

[172] Cf. Adams (2003) 470–1.   [173] Cf. Millar (1984).

[174] Von Wilamowitz-Möllendorff (1886); Mommsen (1906); Dessau (1928) 265–83; Kornemann (1933) 223–9; Gagé (1935) 25–34; Brunt and Moore (1967) 2–3; Hoffmann (1969) 20–1; Ramage (1987) 111–16; Simon (1993) 22–4, 182–5; Scheid (2007) xliii–lxii.

[175] Cf. Ridley (2003) 55–6.

[176] *CIL* VI 1293 = *ILLRP* 316, *Cn. Cornelius Cn. f. Scipio Hispanus, pr., aid. cur., q., tr. mil. ii, xvir sl. iudik., xvir sacr. fac.*

of Ten for judging law suits, member of the Board of Ten for making sacrifices.' This is followed by a four-verse poem written in the first person: 'I have heaped up virtues on my family through my conduct, I have produced children, I have emulated the deeds of my father. I won the praise of my ancestors so that they rejoice that I have been created by them; my official honour has ennobled my race.'[177] In this case, however, the facts and the subjective interpretation of the facts are separated from each other by appearing in prose and verse respectively. Augustus, by contrast, juxtaposes facts and interpretation right from the start of his inscription in such a way that he disguises the subjectivity of his account, and makes what is really interpretation appear as fact.

Other epitaphs set up by Rome's most high-ranking men allude to the same sort of achievements as those listed in the *RGDA*. For example, Munatius Plancus (consul in 42 BC) listed on his tomb at Gaeta his magistracies, triumph and associated temple building, and involvement in establishing colonies: 'Lucius Munatius Plancus, son of Lucius, grandson of Lucius, great-grandson of Lucius, consul, censor, hailed as victorious general twice, one of the Seven in charge of feasts, having triumphed over the Raetians built the temple of Saturn from the spoils, divided up lands in Italy at Beneventum, in Gaul established the colonies of Lugdunum and Raurica,' but his list is of course nowhere near as extensive as Augustus', and is presented in the third person.[178]

Another Republican inscription often discussed as a precedent for the *RGDA* is an unusual building inscription set up by P. Popillius Laenas (consul in 132 BC), in which, contrary to the norm, he proclaims his achievements in the first person, starting 'I [Publius Popillius son of Gaius, consul] built the road', and is concerned with emphasizing that he has been the first to sort out the use of public lands, 'I was the first to see to it that herdsmen yielded to ploughmen on public land'.[179] A more intriguing parallel, and one that is more likely to have been known to Augustus, is the inscription set up at Philae by his first prefect of Egypt, Cornelius Gallus, a close collaborator who fell into disgrace and was compelled to commit suicide.[180] This monument offers three versions of Gallus' accomplishments in three different languages, Latin, Greek, and hieroglyphs, composed in the first person. Gallus proudly claims to have been the first to penetrate deep into the Nile Valley, to have sacked five cities and subdued the Thebaid (a region which he alleges was previously feared by all the

---

[177] *virtutes generis mieis moribus accumulavi, / progeniem genui, facta patris petiei. / maiorum optenui laudem ut sibei me esse creatum / laetentur; stirpem nobilitavit honor.*

[178] CIL X 6087 = ILS 886, *L. Munatius L. f., L. n., L. pron. / Plancus cos., cens., imp. iter., viivir / epulon., triump. ex Raetis aedem Saturni / fecit de manibis, agros divisit in Italia / Beneventi, in Gallia colonias deduxit / Lugudunum et Rauricam.*

[179] *[P. Popillius C. f. cos.] viam fecei . . . primus fecei ut de agro poplico aratoribus cederent pastores*: ILS 23 = ILLRP 454; cf. Ridley (2003) 59.

[180] EJ no. 21 = *ILS* 8995 = LACTOR P5. Gallus' fall: Suet. *Aug.* 66.2; Dio Cass. 53.23.5–24.1.

kings of Egypt), and to have received envoys from the king of Aethiopia to
whom he extended his protection. Like the *RGDA*, it offers statistics to give
an objective, factual appearance to what is really a subjective account. Not
only is Gallus' inscription similar in tone and theme to some of the proud
claims of the *RGDA*, but it also displays striking similarities in the wording in Latin.[181] The impression that Gallus and Augustus shared similar
ideas about how to exploit epigraphic monuments also emerges from their
shared habit of commemorating their achievements by inscribing in Latin
beneath Egyptian obelisks.[182] Like the *RGDA*, the two texts of Popillius
and Gallus stand out because of their singular character.

In general, however, laudatory inscriptions known as *elogia*, which are
in turn influenced by the custom of delivering funeral orations, provide
the closest epigraphic parallels to the *RGDA* at Rome. An inscription upon
the column of C. Duilius, on display in the Roman forum and decorated
with the prows of captured ships, gave a detailed account of his military
victories.[183] Duilius defeated the Carthaginians at Mylae in 260 BC, the
first Roman to win a victory at sea. Like the *RGDA*, the *elogium* is not
composed in chronological order, but adopts a thematic structure, listing
first his engagements by sea and then by land. In a phrase reminiscent of
those composed by Augustus, Duilius receives honour for being the first to
have engaged in naval warfare successfully.[184] Given its prominent location
in the heart of Rome and its apparent fame during the imperial period,[185]
it is tempting to consider this as one possible role model for Augustus. The
most famous set of *elogia* was on display in the Augustan forum (21.1n.
forumque Augustum).[186] Augustus issued a proclamation declaring that
he wanted his own achievements to be judged by comparison with those
of the great Romans of the past, represented by the statues and inscriptions
in his forum.[187] What the *RGDA* makes clear, of course, is how thoroughly
Augustus excelled all his predecessors.

Two passages of literature offer further paradigms. The first is an account
in Diodorus Siculus of an inscription dedicating spoils to a goddess (perhaps Venus), which was set up by Pompey the Great in 61 BC on the day
of his triumph.[188] He describes it as a record of Pompey's achievements in
Asia, and gives what purports to be a copy of its text (albeit in Greek).

---

[181] Adams (2003) 641.
[182] Gallus' inscription on the 'Vatican obelisk': EJ no. 374 = *AE* 1964.255, 1968.521 = LACTOR M10.
Cf. Dio Cass. 53.23.5, who states that one reason for his downfall was that he had inscribed his
achievements upon the pyramids.
[183] *ILLRP* 319; cf. Ridley (2003) 58–9.
[184] Lines 6–7 *[r]em navebos marid consol primos c[eset copiasque c]lasesque navales primos ornavet
pa[ravetque]*.
[185] Plin. *HN* 34.11.20; Quint. *Inst.* 1.7.12. It appears to have been reinscribed in the early imperial
period: Frank (1919).
[186] Ridley (2003) 61–3 considers these to provide the 'closest parallels' to the *RGDA*.
[187] Suet. *Aug.* 31.5.
[188] Diod. Sic. 40.4., cf. Plin. *HN* 7.97–8. Nicolet (1991b) 31–3; Heuss (1975) 72–5; Ridley (2003) 60–1.

This is arguably the closest parallel to Augustus' *RGDA*, since it not only presents details of his conquests, but also ends with a statement of the sum of money being dedicated to the goddess, along with valuables captured from the enemy. Augustus' theme of *impensae* is also foreshadowed in Pompey's claim to have increased the revenues of the Roman people. Other claims made by Pompey in this inscription find echoes in the *RGDA*, such as liberating the seas from pirates (25.1) and extending the frontiers of the empire to the ends of the inhabited world (26). A conscious rivalry with Pompey on Augustus' part in choosing to compose the *RGDA* would fit well with the pattern of emulation of Pompey in the *RGDA* as a whole (see heading, 1.1, 3.1, 5.2, 20.1, 25.1, 27.2, 31.2).

A less obvious comparison is one of Propertius' poems, 4.11.[189] Composed in 16 BC, it presents a speech in the first person by the newly deceased Cornelia (perhaps not coincidentally a daughter of Augustus' first wife Scribonia). The poem plays on the idea that it is a verse epitaph with the words 'on this stone' (*in lapide hoc*, v. 36). Cornelia, like Augustus in the *RGDA*, claims that she is providing a model of behaviour for others to copy. Cornelia states that she is 'an element in a great house which ought to be copied' (*magnae pars imitanda domus*, v. 44), and she instructs her daughter to copy her: 'see to it that you copy me in holding a single husband' (*fac teneas unum nos imitata virum*, v. 68). This is echoed in the *RGDA* (8.5) by Augustus' claim that 'I myself handed down to later generations exemplary practices for them to imitate' (see pp. 40–1).

Moving away from Rome, grandiose inscriptions set up by monarchs in the Hellenistic world and in the Near East offer accounts of their achievements that at first consideration appear similar in tone to the *RGDA*. The trilingual Bisitun inscription, rendered in Old Persian, Babylonian, and Elamite, of Darius I, King of Persia, who reigned 522–486 BC, is even more impressive in scale than the *RGDA*.[190] The text runs to many hundreds of lines, with the cuneiform version in Old Persian alone occupying over 500 lines. It is carved high up above the Royal Road on a cliff face of Mount Bisitun (north-west Iran), so high as to be illegible from below, but it is accompanied by a large relief depicting Darius, with his foot upon the usurper Gaumata, facing nine rebels bound as captives, whose defeats are described in the inscriptions. These give a detailed narrative account written in the first person of the civil war by which Darius came to power and of his further military exploits, quashing revolts at home and conquering enemies abroad. Although it would be rash to suggest that Augustus was directly influenced by this particular inscription, some echo of it may have filtered down through the grandiose inscription set up by his near-contemporary Antiochus I of Commagene, a client king of Rome, who himself claimed descent from Darius I. Antiochus had a text

---

[189] Hallett (1985).   [190] Brosius (2000) 27–40 no. 44; Ridley (2003) 53.

inscribed in *c.* 40 BC on the backs of the sculpted thrones of huge seated figures incorporated into his tomb at Nemrud-Dağ. It recorded the 'works of his own benevolence for all eternity' and prescribed cult in his own honour, and so, like the *RGDA*, it was not an epitaph as such, despite its location.[191] The main problem with suggesting a close connection between such inscriptions and the *RGDA* is that Augustus would not have wanted to appear as a monarch.[192]

A more common sight in the Hellenistic Greek east were the ubiquitous honorific decrees, many of which narrated the honorand's achievements and career in some detail.[193] These decrees were intended not only to reward a benefactor, but also to encourage others to emulate him. Like Augustus, the honorand was regarded as the community's notable benefactor, but of course the crucial difference between these decrees and the *RGDA* lies in the fact that the latter was not the result of a decision taken by some civic institution to honour Augustus: it was composed by Augustus himself.

What all this amounts to is that Augustus did not imitate a single model in composing his work, but created a composition that was *sui generis*. In doing so, Augustus allowed himself the freedom to compose something that offered insights into how he perceived his role in politics and society. In terms of precedents, the most attractive notion is of rivalry with Pompey, given that this sentiment can be traced elsewhere in the *RGDA*, and since *impensae* ('expenses') as well as *res gestae* ('achievements') are in evidence in both cases. Indeed, Augustus created something distinctively Roman in its outlook, which connected *res gestae*/success in warfare and *impensae*/expenditure funded by the spoils of war, *ex manubiis*.[194] A victorious general would produce an account of his accomplishments in various forms: firstly, as a report to the senate justifying his claim to a triumph, secondly on placards displayed during the triumphal procession, and lastly as a monument commemorating the triumph, whether in the form of a votive inscription or an arch decorated with reliefs.[195] The structure of the *RGDA* has often been outlined as falling into three sections: *honores* ('honours', 1–14), *impensae* ('expenses', 15–24), and *res gestae* ('achievements', 25–35).[196] Instead of imposing an 'either *res gestae* or *impensae*' structure upon the work, we should consider how the two themes are intertwined. This has the advantage of avoiding the necessity of labelling the first section as *honores*; rather, the inscription relates both *res gestae* and *impensae* right from the start, with the statement 'I mustered an army on my personal instigation and at my personal expense' (*exercitum privato consilio et privata impensa*

---

[191] *OGI* I 383 – Burstein (1985) 63–6 no. 48. Mommsen (1906) 256; Ridley (2003) 53–5.

[192] Gagé (1935) 32; Simon (1993) 23.

[193] For a flavour of some of these, see Chaniotis (2005) 32–4, 38–9; Bagnall and Derow (2004) 13 and 76 = *Syll.*³ 374 and *SEG* 1.366.

[194] Gagé (1935) 31, (1939).   [195] Gagé (1939).

[196] Gagé (1935) 13–14; Levi (1947) 193–4; with elaborations in Ramage (1987) 17–20, Scheid (2007) xxxvi–xliii.

comparavi). Augustus then continues to weave the two motifs together. For example, he mentions in the same breath his foundation of veteran colonies and his funding of them (3.3). He also explains how he could restore ornaments to temples in Asia because of the successful outcome of his military endeavours (24.1). The two themes also receive equal weight on the occasions when he specifies that expenditure was funded by the spoils of war (15.1; 15.3; 21.1–3). Rather than having to explain away what appears to be a reversion to the first theme of *honores* in the final two chapters (34–5), these chapters can be seen as the proper culmination of the whole work, recording the ultimate accolade given to Augustus in virtue of his *res gestae* and *impensae*.[197]

What Augustus hoped to achieve in composing this work and ordering it to be displayed outside his Mausoleum is similarly complex. Tendencies to characterize it in a straightforward manner, such as Mommsen's description of the work as a 'Rechenschaftsbericht', a 'rendering of accounts', are too single-faceted.[198] Furthermore, although Mommsen also set the trend in considering its intended audience to have been the *plebs* of the capital, even the question of whom Augustus wanted to address in his *RGDA* is open to question.[199]

The *RGDA* is clearly a political document; this is not the place to look for an objective account of Augustus' career, least of all in its early stages.[200] Augustus' claim to have won two victories at Philippi in 42 BC, for example, overlooks the fact that the victory over Brutus and Cassius was actually the work of Antony (2.1). Sextus Pompey is dismissed as a pirate involved in a slave war, without actually being named (25.1). It is possible to detect many such deliberate distortions of the truth, but the lack of an alternative contemporary narrative history of the Augustan age is keenly felt. For example, the claim repeated until relatively recently that Augustus deliberately omitted to mention his *proconsulare imperium maius*, hiding what was in fact a key element in his power, has turned out to be a modern mirage, ultimately derived from a confused and exaggerated account in Dio Cassius (53.32.5) of Augustus' powers in 23 BC.[201] This turn of phrase would not have seemed familiar to Augustus nor to his contemporaries, since 'the very expression *proconsulare imperium* was itself an imperial invention, first attested under Tiberius'.[202] Nor is this the place to look for disappointments in Augustus' lifetime: it would be unreasonable to expect reference to the exiles of the two Julias or the Varian disaster in a work celebrating his achievements.

---

[197] Nicolet (1991b) 19; cf. Levi (1947) 207.   [198] Mommsen (1906).   [199] Mommsen (1883) vi.

[200] Ridley (2003) 25–50, 159–227, 234–41 offers a critical overview of the lack of perspicacity often shown by modern scholars dealing with the *RGDA*, not least the tendency to assume that Augustus cannot lie in the text because it was publicly displayed.

[201] Heuss (1975) 68; cf. Yavetz (1984) 8–11; Ridley (2003) 90–2. Contra, Brunt and Moore (1967) 84; Girardet (2000); Ferrary (2001) 109, 116.

[202] Cotton and Yakobson (2002) 196–7, with n. 16.

A number of political messages are propagated by the *RGDA*: 'constitutional change was really continuity'; 'military *potestas* was less important as a basis for rule than was *auctoritas*'; 'the impulse towards autocracy . . . was actually based on popular consensus'; 'public and private interests could in fact coincide, at least in the person of the *princeps*'; 'vengeance was displaced by *clementia*'; 'civil wars were really fights with foreign foes'; 'war itself was effectively peace'.[203] The *RGDA* conveys the implicit message that the Roman empire was in the best possible condition, through the actions of one man, Augustus, who had solved all the problems, and who ruled in the interests of all through his *auctoritas* and virtues, without infringing sovereignty of the senate and people of Rome.[204] It was, in effect, a demonstration that Augustus had achieved his avowed intent of becoming the 'originator of the best order' (*optimi status auctor*), and had fulfilled his hope of laying lasting 'foundations for the state' (*fundamenta rei p.*). This echoes a motif on coins minted at Rome by L. Mescinius Rufus in 16 BC, which depicted on their obverse an inscription within an oak wreath, commemorating the fulfilment of a vow to Jupiter for the health of Augustus because 'through him, the state is in a greater and more peaceful condition'.[205]

In addition, the *RGDA* promotes a claim of world conquest (see 25–33). The text evokes the ends of the known world, including fifty-five geographical names, many of which must have sounded distinctly exotic to a Roman audience, especially those referring to distant peoples. This claim is encapsulated in the prominent heading to the Latin inscription: 'Below is a copy of the achievements of the deified Augustus by which he made the world subject to the rule of the Roman people' (see p. 28; commentary on heading **orbem terrarum imperio populi Romani subiecit**).[206] In putting forward such a claim, Augustus not only emulated Pompey the Great (see pp. 32–3), but also brought to mind the conquests of Alexander the Great, who had won lasting fame for subduing new areas of the world, notably India. Augustus further invites comparison of his achievements and those of Alexander in a more detailed way. Whereas Alexander had died before mounting a campaign in the furthest west at the Pillars of Hercules, Augustus proclaims that his conquests extended from that same place – Gades (Cádiz) – to the mouth of the River Elbe (26.2). Furthermore, the embassy to Augustus from India, which reached him at Tarraco, offered a mirror image of the embassy of envoys who travelled from the West to Alexander whilst he was in the East (see 31.1n. **ad me ex India**). By such implicit comparisons, the *RGDA* makes clear that Augustus surpassed even

---

[203] Santirocco (1995) 230. [204] Diesner (1985) 41.

[205] Suet. *Aug.* 28.2, revealing Augustus' aim of putting into practice what Cicero had explored in theory, according to Schäfer (1957) 325, 332. *BM Coins, Rom. Emp.* I 17–18 nos. 91–4: *quod per eu(m) r(es) p(ublica) in amp(liore) atq(ue) tran(quilliore) s(tatu) e(st)* = LACTOR L10 (illustrated).

[206] Nicolet (1991b) 15–27.

Alexander in extending Roman influence to the ends of the known world and completed his unfinished project of conquering the West.[207]

Augustus himself is at the centre of attention throughout the inscription, literally because of the work's grammatical structure (first person verbs and possessive pronouns abound, cf. pp. 24–5), and thematically.[208] No Roman outside the imperial family is mentioned by name, except for consuls, whose names appear in dating clauses in an implicit claim that ordered government, with its regular appointment of annual consuls, has returned.[209] By contrast, the exotic personal names of kings from both East and West abound in the later chapters, adding local colour and apparent exactitude to Augustus' account of his relationships with foreign potentates (27.2, 32.1–2, 33). Only a few members of Augustus' family appear – Agrippa, Marcellus, Gaius and Lucius, and Tiberius – and even then (with the exception of Agrippa) they are defined in relation to Augustus, Marcellus as his son-in-law, Gaius and Lucius as his sons, Tiberius as his stepson and later son. Even the reason for their appearance is focused on Augustus: Gaius and Lucius are honoured on Augustus' account (14.1), whilst both Tiberius and Gaius act as Augustus' representative (27.2, 30.1), and Marcellus is mentioned only because of the theatre Augustus builds in his name (21.1). Agrippa is the notable exception to this rule, and he alone is accorded equal status to Augustus in the *RGDA*. He appears as his colleague on two occasions, in conducting the census of 28 BC (8.2) and in organizing the *ludi saeculares* ('centennial games') of 17 BC (22.2). By the time of the second event, he had become Augustus' son-in-law, having married Julia in 21 BC, but this is not mentioned. Imperial women are conspicuous by their absence.[210]

One of the recurring motifs of the work is of Augustus being the first to accomplish certain achievements or to receive particular honours.[211] This is stated explicitly for a very wide range of *res gestae* ('achievements') and *impensae* ('expenses'). New areas of the world were opened up under his leadership, as his fleet explored the northern expanses of Ocean (26.4), and the Pannonians were subdued, a people whom the Roman army had never previously even approached (30.1). Envoys came from India for the first time, and Rome enjoyed friendly exchanges with new peoples (31.1, 32.3). Augustus was the first Roman to receive the honour of being met by a delegation of senior magistrates in Campania (12.1).[212] The fact of his being first is repeated often enough for it to be understood without having to be stated explicitly elsewhere.

The idea of Augustus breaking new ground justifies the implicit claim that his birth marked a new era in Roman history: the gates of Janus had been opened only twice 'before I was born' (*priusquam nascerer*, 13).

---

[207] Levi (1947) 206; Nenci (1958) especially 290–8. Cf. 24.1.   [208] Ramage (1987) 21–8.
[209] Ramage (1987) 26–8, 88.   [210] Ridley (2003) 69–70.
[211] Nenci (1958) 291–2; Ramage (1987) 31–2.   [212] Cf. 10.2.

Similarly, he can speak of 'my era' as heralding a new level of generosity in paying for land used for settling colonies in Italy and the provinces (*id primus et solus omnium . . . ad memoriam aetatis meae* – 'I was the first and only one to have done this . . . as far as people living in my era recall', 16.1). All this innovation, however, is balanced by due consideration of ancestral custom. Augustus specifically invokes the ancestors, or *maiores*, on several occasions.[213] His opening of the gates of Janus was in accordance with the wishes of the *maiores* (13), whilst his decision not to make Armenia a province is represented as being in accordance with ancestral precedent (*malui maiorum nostrorum exemplo* – 'I preferred, in accordance with the example set by our ancestors', 27.2). His statement that he accepted no magistracy contrary to ancestral custom (*nullum magistratum contra morem maiorum*, 6.1) serves to influence the reader's interpretation not just of his rejection of the post of guardian of laws and customs (*curator legum et morum*, 6.1), but also of the dictatorship and perpetual consulship mentioned in the previous chapter (5.1, 5.3).[214] At other times he implies that he has had due regard for tradition, such as in refusing to become *pontifex maximus* ('chief priest') in Lepidus' lifetime (10.2). It is indicative of Augustus' skill in projecting his self-image that he can successfully represent himself both as guardian of tradition and as bold innovator.[215] This balancing act emerges most clearly in his claim to be reintroducing exemplary ancestral practices through his new laws (*legibus novis me auctore latis multa exempla maiorum exolescentia iam ex nostro saeculo reduxi* – 'By means of new laws brought in under my sponsorship I revived many exemplary ancestral practices which were by then dying out in our generation', 8.5).

The distinctive character of the *RGDA* emerges clearly by comparing it with Augustus' earlier (mostly lost) autobiography.[216] Augustus wrote thirteen books of autobiography down to the end of the Cantabrian War (26/25 BC).[217] As far as we can tell from fragmentary sources, and from the biography composed by Nicolaus of Damascus, which was probably based on it, the autobiography was polemical in tone, aiming to counteract common criticisms being levelled at Augustus in the early years of his dominance at Rome. Augustus countered aspersions cast against his family background by stating that his ancestors may only have been of equestrian rank until his father became a senator, but his family was old and wealthy.[218] He also invoked a dream by Cicero which allegedly forecast his future greatness.[219] In response to comments about his rather undistinguished performances in battle, he focused upon his successes in Illyria.[220]

---

[213] Nenci (1958) 292; Hoffmann (1969).
[214] For discussion of Augustus' apparent observance of constitutional proprieties see Burian (1991).
[215] Cf. Ridley (2003) 233–4.   [216] Peter *HRRel.* II 54–64; Malcovati (1944) 84–97.
[217] Suet. *Aug.* 85.1.   [218] Peter *HRRel.* II 54 fr. 1/Malcovati (1944) fr. 3.
[219] Peter *HRRel.* II 54 fr. 2/Malcovati (1944) fr. 4.
[220] Peter *HRRel.* II 61–2 fr. 13/Malcovati (1944) fr. 15.

He defended his actions against men who had once been his allies by representing his behaviour as motivated by the need for vengeance for the death of Julius Caesar.[221] Augustus' primary audience for his autobiography was his contemporaries, as he aimed to justify his rise to power; the *RGDA* addresses itself just as much to posterity as to contemporaries.

This is not to say that Augustus was unconcerned with contemporary audiences. We may assume that his primary audience was in the city of Rome, given that he instructed the *RGDA* to be set up outside his Mausoleum. Augustus did not, however, address himself to a single audience, but wrote for the benefit of the senate and people of Rome, the equestrian order, and perhaps even other members of the imperial family. It seems surprising, given the striking rise to prominence of freedmen under Augustus, that they form one constituency which is steadfastly ignored throughout the *RGDA*.[222] Augustus also pays scant regard to a provincial audience, and it is left to the translator to make amends for this to some degree (see pp. 26–30). By contrast, the population of Italy features several times (9.2, 10.2, 16.1, 21.3, 25.2) since its support was of particular importance to him; it had been crucial in bringing about his rise to power and in securing his position in the long term.[223]

Augustus gives the impression that he valued the traditional instruments of government at Rome, the *senatus populusque Romanus*. The senate and people of Rome are often portrayed as the initiators of significant actions or as expressing their support for Augustus. Together, they offer him the posts of dictator (5.1) and guardian of laws and customs (6.1), they authorize him to increase the number of patricians (8.1), vote honours for Gaius and Lucius (14.1), dedicate the shield of virtue in his honour (34.2), and (in a significant deviation from the usual formula) together with the equestrian order, hail him as father of the fatherland (35.1). Decrees of the senate are mentioned explicitly eleven times in the course of the *RGDA* and on other occasions the senate is described as instigating actions; Augustus presents himself as subordinate to the senate, simply as an agent carrying out its wishes.[224] By contrast, some of the same actions are attributed in Suetonius' biography to Augustus himself. For example, whereas in the *RGDA* the closing of the gates of Janus is by senatorial decree (13), Suetonius simply states 'he closed Janus Quirinus three times' (*Ianum Quirinum . . . ter clusit*, Suet. *Aug.* 22). Similarly, in the case of his restoration of temples, Suetonius omits to mention what Augustus states in the *RGDA*, that he did so on the authority of the senate (20.4; Suet. *Aug.* 30.2). By choosing to focus upon senate and people as active agents, Augustus projects an

---

[221] Yavetz (1984) 1–3.

[222] For Augustus' selective depiction of Roman society, see Braunert (1975).

[223] Syme (1939) 276–93; Zanker (1988) 307–11, 316–23.

[224] Senatorial decrees: 1.2, 4.1, 4.2, 9.1, 10.1, 12.1, 12.2, 13, 14.1, 34.2, 35.1; senate as instigator: 5.1, 6.1, 6.2, 8.1, 11, 14.1, 20.4, 34.2, 35.1; Augustus as agent of the senate: 6.2, 8.1.

impression of constitutional propriety, which reaches a climax in his claim to have transferred 'the state from my power into the control of the Roman senate and people' (34.1).[225] Augustus wanted to be seen as the people's champion in a broader sense too. Much of the expenditure detailed in the *RGDA* – games (22–3), distributions (15), corn dole (5.2, 15.1, 18), and building works (19–21) – was calculated to benefit the *plebs* of Rome. The perspective that the *plebs* was primarily interested in 'bread and circuses' was far from unique to Juvenal's time.[226] Finally, Augustus' emphasis upon his tribunician power (4.4, 6.2, 15.1–2) could be a way of representing himself as concerned with protecting the interests of the common man at Rome.

Another of Augustus' aims may have been to offer himself and his achievements to an audience made up of younger members of the imperial family, senators, and equestrians as a model of how to behave; the virtues for which he was awarded the shield of virtue are themselves illustrated in the course of the *RGDA*.[227] Augustus was not alone in championing the principle of teaching the right way to behave through offering exemplary behaviour (8.5). The idea that great men and women from the past could provide moral examples, *exempla*, to the rest of society was deeply ingrained in Roman culture, from the didactic purpose of funeral eulogies to Livy's history.[228] At roughly the same time as the publication of the *RGDA* in Galatia, the senate was actively promoting the idea that members of the imperial family could teach the rest of Roman society how to behave through their own virtuous behaviour. Documents dealing with the death of Germanicus and subsequent trial of Cn. Calpurnius Piso in AD 20 were disseminated by the senate, one of whose aims was to inform the Roman world of Germanicus' exemplary character and of Piso's nefarious behaviour (see p. 20).[229] Nor was it only the upper classes at Rome who were being addressed, but the senate outlined how the whole of society, right down to the *plebs*, could follow the lead given by the imperial family in its reaction to Germanicus' death.[230] In passing sentence upon Piso, the senate claimed that its own collective behaviour was closely modelled upon that of Augustus: 'Likewise the senate, mindful of its own clemency, justice, and great-heartedness – virtues which it has inherited from its ancestors, and especially learnt from its leaders, the deified Augustus and Tiberius Caesar Augustus.'[231] The idea that Augustus himself had fulfilled a didactic role

[225] Burian (1991); Eder (2005) 14.   [226] Juv. 10.81.
[227] Yavetz (1984); Ramage (1987) 74–100.   [228] Polyb. 6.54; Livy *praef.* 10 = LACTOR D1.
[229] *SCPP* 165–7 = Eck *et al.* (1996) 50; Cooley (1998).   [230] *SCPP* 132–62 = Eck *et al.* (1996) 46–8.
[231] *SCPP* 90–2 = Eck *et al.* (1996) 44, *item senatum, memorem clementiae suae iustitiaeq(ue) <atq(ue)> animi magnitudinisque, quas virtutes {quas} a maioribus suis accepisset, tum praecipue ab divo Aug(usto) et Ti. Caesare Aug(usto) principibus suis didicisset*; cf. *Tab. Siar.* fr. ii col. b 13–17 = Crawford (1996) 518 no. 37 for the idea that recording in an inscription the eulogy for Germanicus delivered by Tiberius might be 'useful' for successive generations of youngsters.

in teaching the senate how to behave is in accordance with his own view of his role in Roman society, as expressed in the *RGDA*.

It is probably misleading to look for a single overriding message in such a complex text. Nevertheless, consideration of the text's very first audience suggests that Augustus may have written the work as a way of justifying his deification and of encouraging the senate to expedite the process. This takes us back to a time even before the text assumed an inscribed form at Rome, since its very first 'publication' was when it was read out at the first meeting of the senate after Augustus' death.[232] There are strong resonances in the *RGDA* of the Hellenistic doctrine that someone might earn apotheosis because of his outstanding conquests and benefactions, and in particular the *RGDA* echoes Euhemerus' *Sacred Record*, which had been translated from Greek into Latin by Ennius.[233] Several parallels can be traced between Euhemerus' description of Zeus and Augustus' account of himself in the *RGDA*. For example, we find a golden inscription set up by Zeus: 'on this column he wrote out his deeds so that there might be a monument of his achievements for posterity'.[234] In addition, it is suggested that Zeus intended to serve as a role model to others: 'he gave an example for others to copy', which finds a close echo in the *RGDA*.[235] Zeus, like Augustus, also wins the support of kings through friendship, not just through force.[236] Such comparisons between Zeus and Augustus had been foreshadowed in the way that parallels had already been drawn between Augustus and Jupiter in poetry, especially by Ovid.[237] As Bosworth points out, 'There are two sets of *res gestae*, both inscribed on monumental stelae by mortal dynasts who achieved godhead. In both cases world empire is achieved by conquest and conciliation, and it is accompanied by unparalleled benefactions: peace, civilization and internal concord.'[238] The very first audience of the *RGDA* was the senate, a group of educated Romans who would have been awake to literary allusions, and its response to the text a few days later, after the funeral, was to vote state cult for Augustus.[239] If it was Augustus' intention to appeal for deification through the *RGDA*, he would have been well satisfied with the locations of the copies set up in Galatia in monumental complexes concerned with emperor worship (see pp. 7–18).

---

[232] Dio Cass. 56.33.1; Suet. *Aug.* 101.1, 4.

[233] Bosworth (1999); cf. von Wilamowitz-Möllendorff (1886) 624–5.

[234] Lactant. *Div. Inst.* 1.11.33 = *FGrH* 63 F3, *in qua columna sua gesta perscripsit ut monumentum posteris esset rerum suarum.*

[235] Lactant. *Div. Inst.* 1.22.26 = *FGrH* 63 F23, *exemplum ceteris ad imitandum dedit.* Cf. 8.5.

[236] Cf. 31–3.

[237] Ov. *Met.*1.199–205 = LACTOR G53, *Tr.* 2.33–40, 215–18 = LACTOR G56, *Fast.* 1.650 = LACTOR K41, *Fast.* 2.131–2 = LACTOR H38.

[238] Bosworth (1999) 16. Cf. also Hor. *Epist.* 1.17.33–5 for the sentiment that *res gestae* could bring someone close to the throne of Jupiter: *res gerere et captos ostendere civibus hostis / attingit solium Iovis et caelestia temptat: / principibus placuisse viris non ultima laus est.*

[239] Tac. *Ann.* 1.10.8; Bosworth (1999) 12.

6 DATE OF COMPOSITION

Augustus ends the *RGDA* with the words 'When I wrote this I was in my seventy-sixth year' (*cum scripsi haec, annum agebam septuagensumum sextum*),[240] in other words, the last year of his life, from his birthday on 23 September AD 13 to his death on 19 August AD 14. Despite this clear statement, most scholars have assumed that this is not accurate, and that the *RGDA* was composed before that time and updated by Tiberius after Augustus' death.[241] The hand of Tiberius is assumed to have contributed up-to-date information relating to AD 13 and 14 in particular, of which the most recent statistic is the thirty-seventh grant of tribunician power to Augustus on 26 June AD 14.[242] Various proposals have been put forward in support of the idea that it is possible to trace compositional layers in the text, with the most popular argument being that the *RGDA* was substantially completed by 2 BC, but with other drafts and emendations perhaps occurring in 23, 12, and 4 BC, AD 1, 6, and 14.[243]

The main reasons for this tendency to complicate a straightforward matter are incredulity at the coincidence that Augustus should choose to compose the *RGDA* in the final weeks of his life, and a misreading of Suetonius. As regards the first of these, this coincidence becomes more credible if we take account of Augustus' superstitious character.[244] Suetonius records two omens from AD 14, which were interpreted as predicting Augustus' imminent demise. Augustus is supposed to have reacted to the first omen by asking Tiberius to recite the vows relating to the next census period of five years on the assumption that he himself would not outlive this period. In addition, damage to an inscription by a thunderbolt was thought to herald his final 100 days. It is therefore entirely plausible that Augustus reacted to these omens by composing the *RGDA*, perhaps between 26 June and his final departure from Rome on 24 July. It would not have been an impossible feat for Augustus to compose the work so quickly, with all the help that would have been available to him from imperial freedmen in assembling the impressive array of facts and figures. The fact that Augustus could be prompted by an omen to embark upon a major undertaking is clearly shown by his construction of the temple of Jupiter the Thunderer on the Capitol, after he had narrowly escaped being struck by lightning when on campaign in Cantabria (see 19.2n. ***Iovis Tonantis***). Secondly, it

---

[240] 35.2.

[241] This is with the notable exception of Ramage (1988), who champions the simple view that we should accept what is written at face value, and that the *RGDA* was composed in the summer of AD 14. Cf. Ramage (1987) 13.

[242] 4.4; Mommsen (1906) 257; Brunt and Moore (1967) 6, 44.

[243] Debate about compositional layers summarized by Kornemann (1933) 217–23; reviewed by Gagé (1935) 16–23, Scheid (2007) xxii–xxvi. Cf. Robinson (1926a) 1; Hohl (1937) 338; Braccesi (1973); Nicolet (1991b) 19; Simon (1993) 8.

[244] Suet. *Aug.* 90–2.

is worth citing in full what Suetonius has to say about Augustus depositing his will: 'The Vestal virgins brought forth a will which had been deposited with them, along with three documents, which had also been sealed. He had composed the will on 3 April in the consulship of Lucius Plancus and Gaius Silius [i.e. AD 13], a year and four months before he died, and it was written in two copies, one in his own hand, the other in the hands of his freedmen Polybius and Hilario. All of these were opened in the senate and read out.'[245] From this, we can make a distinction between the format of the will, written on wax tablets, and the other documents on papyrus rolls (*volumina*).[246] This argues against the hypothesis that the rolls were simply codicils to the will.[247] All of the documents are produced by the Vestals, and so presumably had been deposited with them, but only the will is given a precise date of composition.[248] In conclusion, therefore, there seems every reason to believe that the *RGDA* was composed towards the end of Augustus' lifetime. Consequently, it offers a personal, final summing-up statement by Augustus of what he thought he had achieved, presented in accordance with his vision both of his own role as *princeps* and of Rome's place within the world.

7 TRANSMISSION OF THE TEXT AND PREVIOUS STUDY OF THE MONUMENTS

a Ancyra

The Latin text of the *RGDA* was first identified and transcribed in 1555 by the circle of Augier [Ogier] Ghiselin de Busbecq, ambassador of the Holy Roman Emperor Ferdinand I to Sultan Süleyman the Magnificent. In pursuing his diplomatic mission, Busbecq was accompanied by a large retinue, several members of which were interested in exploring the lands controlled by the Ottomans. They included fellow ambassadors Ferenc Zay and Hungarian bishop Anton Verancsics, together with the latter's secretary Janos Belsius, a German–Hungarian merchant Hans Dernschwam, and physician William Quackelbeen. As they travelled about, they made a point of looking for and recording ancient monuments, coins, Latin and Greek inscriptions, popular customs recalling ancient ones, as well as plants and flowers. Busbecq wrote some lively letters about his diplomatic mission, which were published between 1581 and 1589. His account of their discovery at Ancyra shows that he immediately appreciated its significance:

---

[245] *testamentum L. Planco C. Silio cons. III. Non. Apriles, ante annum et quattuor menses quam decederet, factum ab eo ac duobus codicibus partim ipsius partim libertorum Polybi et Hilarionis manu scriptum depositumque apud se virgines Vestales cum tribus signatis aeque voluminibus protulerunt. quae omnia in senatu aperta atque recitata sunt,* Suet. *Aug.* 101.1.

[246] Hohl (1937) 323.   [247] Contra Champlin (1989) 163–4.

[248] Ramage (1988) 79; contra Brunt and Moore (1967) 6.

Here we saw a very beautiful inscription, containing a copy of the tablets in which Augustus gave a summary of his achievements. We made our people copy as much as was legible. It is engraved on the marble walls of a building now ruinous and roofless, which formerly may have formed the official residence of the governor. As you enter the building one half of the inscription is on the right, and the other on the left. The top lines are nearly perfect; in the middle the gaps begin to present difficulties; the lowest lines are so mutilated with blows of clubs and axes as to be illegible. This is indeed a great literary loss, and one which scholars have much reason to regret; the more so as it is an ascertained fact that Ancyra was dedicated to Augustus as the common gift of Asia.[249]

One of his companions, Hans Dernschwam, executed the earliest drawing of the building with the *RGDA* in his diary,[250] and Janos Belsius copied out the inscription for him at the back of it. Its first edition was produced in 1579, appended to a commentary on Aurelius Victor's work *On the Caesars*, by the Flemish Jesuit scholar Andreas Schott, who had become a close friend of Busbecq, and who received a copy of the text from him. It was later published in a revised edition by Joost Lips (Justus Lipsius) in 1588.[251]

Following a century during which the inscription was strangely neglected, distinguished travellers began to be drawn to the monument, including Josephe Pitton de Tournefort and Paul Lucas, sent by Louis XIV in 1701 and 1705.[252] Lucas' account of his visit summons up a vivid picture of the obstacles he had to surmount in order to be allowed to spend time copying both the Latin and Greek inscriptions: he resorted to claiming that the inscription contained important medical notes of use to him in an assumed guise of a doctor, and trying to copy the texts outside prayer hours at the adjacent mosque, so as to minimize being observed.[253] He comments that he had to climb up onto the mosque in order to be able to read the Greek inscription, and notes that another part of it remained hidden by a house.[254] A few years later, the English clergyman Richard Pocoke spent almost a whole month in Ancyra, in the course of his extensive travels through Egypt, Palestine, Cyprus, Crete, Asia Minor, and Greece between

---

[249] *hic pulcherrimam vidimus inscriptionem et tabularum illarum quibus indicem rerum a se gestarum complexus est Augustus exemplum. id, quatenus legi potuit, per nostros homines transcribendum curavimus. exstat incisum aedificii, quod olim fortasse praetorium fuerat, diruti et tecto carentis marmoreis parietibus, ita ut dimidia pars intrantibus ad dextram dimidia ad sinistram occurrat. suprema capita fere integra sunt. media lacunis laborare incipiunt. infima vero clavarum et securium ictibus ita lacerata, ut legi non possint. quod sane rei literariae non mediocre damnum est a doctis merito deplorandum: idque eo magis quod urbem illam ab Asiae communitate Augusto dicatam fuisse constet.* Trans. von Martels (1991) 149–50.

[250] Krencker and Schede (1936) 3 Abb. 2.   [251] Von Martels (1991); Ridley (2003) 3–8.

[252] Ridley (2003) 9–15.

[253] Lucas (1712) I 137–8 ('Ainsi un jour en me promenant avec lui auprès de l'Inscription, je lui dis que j'en avois lû les premiers mots; qu'elle contenoit quelques remarques sur l'ancienne Medecine, que j'y pourrois trouver quelques bons remedes pour sa santé, s'il vouloit me la laisser copier'), 142, 145; 393–4 (transcription of Latin inscription).

[254] Lucas (1712) 148–9.

1737 and 1742. He offered a verbal description of the temple (see p. 11), but did not publish a text of the inscription, even though he claimed to have copied a part of it.[255]

These travellers were succeeded in the first half of the nineteenth century by the diplomat Sir John Macdonald Kinneir (1813)[256] and by the distinguished geologist and Member of Parliament W. J. Hamilton (1836), who negotiated with the owner of an unoccupied house to demolish the wall which was obscuring the Greek text. This done, he could read and transcribe five more columns of the Greek text, which he found well preserved, but he realized that two-thirds of the inscription were still concealed by two further houses. On gaining access to one of these, he found that 'the inscription was not protected by a mud wall as in the former case, but that the bare wall of the temple was exposed in the interior of the house, so that the inscription has been in many places obliterated'.[257]

The next important turning point came in 1861, when Napoleon III commissioned a detailed study of the monument by the archaeologist Georges Perrot and architect Edmond Guillaume. As well as describing its current state and sketching a reconstruction of the temple, they made careful drawings of the inscription and translated it into French.[258] Their drawings provided the foundation for Theodor Mommsen's first edition of the inscription (1865), which also incorporated the fragments from Apollonia, but they had not been able to see the whole of the Greek text. A few years later, the Berlin Academy commissioned Karl Humann to travel to Ankara in order to make a plaster-cast of both inscriptions, as an aid to Mommsen in producing a second edition of the text. Over several days in July 1882, he produced a cast in 194 pieces, and this provided Mommsen with more accurate information from which to produce his second edition of the text (1883).[259] Humann was accompanied by Alfred von Domaszewski, then a young student, who examined in person parts of the Latin inscription, which had weathered badly, and whose notes aided Mommsen who was working only from the plaster-of-Paris copy. Unfortunately the Greek version did not receive the same attention, since von Domaszewski was struck down by typhus fever, and Humann encountered difficulties in gaining access to the Greek inscription because of the houses still built against the exterior temple wall.[260] A copy of the temple's *pronaos* was created in 1910 for display in the archaeological exhibition of 1911 in Diocletian's Baths at Rome, marking the fiftieth anniversary of Italian unification (see pp. 53–4).

---

[255] Pococke (1745); Ridley (2003) 16–17. [256] Kinneir (1818) 69–71, 72; Ridley (2003) 17.
[257] Hamilton (1842) I 420–2, citation from 422; Ridley (2003) 18.
[258] Perrot and Guillaume (1862) I 247–55, 295–312, pls. 13–31, espec. pls. 25–9; Krencker and Schede (1936) 8; Ridley (2003) 19–20.
[259] Dessau (1928) 261–5. [260] Humann and Puchstein (1890) 40–4; Ridley (2003) 20–1.

The foundation of the modern Republic of Turkey marked an important moment in the monument's history, as a new sense of national consciousness emerged, along with an eagerness to promote the country's cultural heritage. The Turkish Historical Society was founded in 1931, and benefited from the personal interest of the first president of Turkey, Mustafà Kemal Atatürk. Such renewed interest in the monument was reinforced by the publication by the German architect Daniel Krencker and archaeologist Martin Schede in 1936 of their fieldwork carried out a decade earlier. In response to the international celebrations in 1937/8 to mark the two thousandth anniversary of Augustus' birth, Atatürk ordered the demolition of houses built onto the temple's exterior wall (which had covered, but also protected part of the inscription). Further excavations and clearance directed by H. Koşay in 1938–9 revealed parts of the foundations.[261] More recently, since 1997, the Dipartimento di Scienze dell'Antichità "Leonardo Ferrero", Università degli Studi di Trieste has been engaged in a programme of work at the temple, one of whose main aims has been to produce a detailed photographic record of the inscriptions.[262] Finally, Stephen Mitchell, David French, and Graham Oliver also recorded the inscriptions during 2005/6, making a full hand copy and taking new photographs of the texts, which will be included in the new corpus of the inscriptions of Ancyra currently being prepared.[263]

b Pisidian Antioch

Excavations by Sir William and Lady Ramsay in 1914 revealed some fifty or sixty fragments of the *RGDA*. At first, the small size of the fragments meant that most of them had to be recovered from spoil heaps, and the help of local boys had to be enlisted in the search for inscribed fragments.[264] Their investigations were curtailed by the outbreak of World War I and by a sudden intervention by the Pasha of Konia, who put an end to the work.[265]

In 1924, permission was given to Ramsay for a further programme of excavation led by Prof. D. M. Robinson and funded by the University of Michigan. This uncovered another 215 fragments.[266] The partnership of Ramsay and Robinson, however, was a doomed one, as revealed by a report by Prof. F. W. Kelsey dated 16 August 1924, and made public by Robinson:

The causes of the friction were chiefly two. Mr Robinson, in accordance with sound scientific procedure, sought out a place for the dump where the bed rock was exposed and no archaeological remains could possibly be covered; but the first time he left the excavations for a day to go to the Bank at Ak-Shehir to draw money

---

[261] Güterbock (1989).   [262] Botteri (2001).
[263] S. Mitchell and D. French, *The Inscriptions of Ankara* vol. I (in preparation).
[264] Ramsay (1916) 112–13.   [265] Ramsay and von Premerstein (1927a) 2.
[266] Robinson (1926a); Mitchell and Waelkens (1998) 28–30.

for the payroll, Mr Ramsay ordered the men to dump the excavated earth nearer the dig, precisely where Mr Robinson reasoned that the principal monument should lie, and afterwards Mr Ramsay would listen to no argument on the matter. After Mr Ramsay left, Mr Robinson's surmise was proved to be correct and the dump ordered by Mr Ramsay has all had to be removed, at considerable extra cost . . . Mr Ramsay, having no interest in sculpture or architecture, was willing to permit the natives to carry off cut stones, and even parts of entablatures, all of which Mr Robinson insisted should be reserved for the study of the architect.[267]

The editors of the journal *Klio* were even driven to publish a brief notice stating that, in future, they would only publish issues relating to the historical context of the *RGDA*.[268] As a consequence of their personal differences, Ramsay and Robinson indulged in a bad-tempered race to publish the fragments, and hostile exchanges were published between Ramsay, Ramsay's collaborator Anton von Premerstein, and Robinson.[269] Unfortunately, excavations at Antioch also came to an abrupt halt.

These circumstances may also have encouraged them to pursue their different interpretations of how the text was originally displayed at Antioch. Ramsay favoured the view that the text had been inscribed in two parts on the facing walls of the central archway of the triple-arched *propylon*. This would have been similar in effect to its layout at Ancyra, with five columns of text on each side, with chapter 19 marking the start of the second section, as at Ancyra. By contrast, Robinson argued that the text had been inscribed upon four pedestal bases, which projected in front of the pilasters of the *propylon*. Neither scholar was likely to agree with his rival.[270]

After their excavation, the fragments were embedded in heavy plaques of concrete surrounded by metal frames, and taken to Ankara, where they languished in the environs of the temple of Rome and Augustus until they were rescued by Mehmet Taşlıalan and taken back to the museum at Yalvaç.[271] The fragments have recently been photographed by Charles Crowther and republished by Thomas Drew-Bear and John Scheid.

c Apollonia

When William Buckler, William Calder, and William Guthrie visited Uluborlu in 1930, they could find and read only three of the six blocks to have been seen and recorded in the last 200 years, and had to rely on earlier nineteenth-century travellers for a record of the missing three blocks in

---

[267] Robinson (1928) 170–1, with response by Ramsay (1928).
[268] 'Schlusswort der Redaktion', *Klio* 22 (1928) 173.
[269] Robinson (1927); von Premerstein (1927a, 1927b); Ramsay and von Premerstein (1927a) 7–8, (1927b); Robinson (1928); Ramsay (1928).
[270] This is typical of the whole discussion of the monument at the time. Compare the dismissal of Robinson's suggestion ('Doch hat Robinson schwerlich recht') that the inscription had been deliberately broken up: Ramsay and von Premerstein (1927a) 9.
[271] Drew-Bear and Scheid (2005) 217–18.

publishing their version of the monument in *MAMA* IV, part of a series published by the American Society for Archaeological Research in Asia Minor. This is not surprising, given the earlier reports, which record that three pieces of a fine cornice or architrave, with large lettering above, and four or five columns of small writing below, formed paving stones in one of the streets on the Acropolis. In 1842, Hamilton observed that they had deteriorated by his day from when they had been seen in 1833, only a few years before, by the Rev. F. V. J. Arundell, British Chaplain at Smyrna, and commented prophetically 'in a few more years, if not removed, the whole will be obliterated'.[272] What remains of the *RGDA* from Apollonia is now housed in Afyon Museum.

8 REINTERPRETATIONS OF THE *RGDA*

a Roman responses

Near the beginning of his *Annals*, which start with the death of Augustus and first imperial succession, Tacitus presents two conflicting assessments of Augustus' rule, one apparently favourable, the other openly hostile. These are not attributed to specific speakers,[273] but reputedly reflected what was commonly being said at the time by discerning onlookers,[274] and are reported in indirect speech. Before turning to these, however, he first reports how the majority (by implication, the undiscerning) marvelled at inconsequential things.[275] He starts his list of things of no consequence with the coincidences that Augustus died on the same day as he was first elected consul, in the same bedroom as his father, but he then goes on to list other things which Augustus proudly includes in his *RGDA*, namely the number of his consulships, his thirty-seven continuous years of tribunician power (4.4), the number of times he had been hailed as victorious general (4.1), 'and other honours multiplied or new' (4, 9–12, 34–5).[276] The clear implication of this is that the very things of which Augustus was so proud were nothing more than trivialities.[277]

Turning then to what discerning men had to say about their late leader, he starts with a positive assessment, which echoes the *RGDA*.[278] Close verbal and thematic similarities suggest that Tacitus is consciously responding to Augustus' own words. There are four main themes which occur in both texts. Firstly, Octavian's participation in the civil wars is justified: both texts excuse him on grounds of his *pietas* towards Caesar and the dire needs of the state.[279] Secondly, they present a picture of Augustus' impact on the

---

[272] Hamilton (1842) II 362, with 491 no. 455; cf. Arundell (1834) I 241, II 426–7.
[273] Tac. *Ann.* 1.9.1: 'much talk then about Augustus himself', *multus hinc ipso de Augusto sermo.*
[274] Tac. *Ann.* 1.9.3, *apud prudentes.*   [275] Tac. *Ann.* 1.9.1, *plerisque vana mirantibus.*
[276] Tac. *Ann.* 1.9.2, *aliaque honorum multiplicata aut nova.*   [277] Goodyear (1972) 154–5.
[278] Davis (1999) espec. 3–6.
[279] Tac. *Ann.* 1.9.3, *pietate erga parentem et necessitudine rei publicae*; cf 2.1, 1.1.

state. Thirdly, they celebrate his foreign conquests, praising the extent of the empire and its peacefulness, with both accounts alluding to it being bounded only by Ocean and by far-off rivers (26, 30).[280] Finally, they both deal with his transformation of the city of Rome (19–21). This thematic similarity is intensified by linguistic echoes. For example, Tacitus' report describes Augustus' position in the state as that of *princeps*, which is the description adopted by Augustus in the *RGDA*.[281] Even in what appears to be a positive review, however (and, taken at face value, it is obviously intended to contrast with the subsequent openly critical assessment), Tacitus subtly subverts Augustus' self-representation. For example, in dealing with Octavian's plunge into civil war, Tacitus first mentions his *pietas* towards Caesar, and the needs of the state only second.[282] By reversing the order of *RGDA* 1–2 and emphasizing Octavian's personal motivations in avenging Caesar's death, he undermines the rationale of Octavian's fight against Antony, even whilst repeating Augustus' own justifications for his actions.[283]

By contrast, the much lengthier hostile assessment more openly brings into question claims put forward in the *RGDA*, and *Annals* 1.10.1–4 closely imitates and refutes *RGDA* 1–3.[284] It offers a critical view of things which Augustus had presented in a positive way by questioning his motivations and by stating what had remained unstated. It represents Octavian's raising of a private army after Caesar's death in the worst possible light,[285] and explains how Octavian probably had a hand in the deaths of the consuls Hirtius and Pansa.[286] In his account of how he came to acquire his first consulship, Augustus focuses on his election by the people, not mentioning opposition from the senate.[287] This emphasis is now inverted in Tacitus: 'the consulship was extorted against the senate's will'.[288] Similarly, whereas Augustus had claimed that the 'liberators' had been exiled according to due judicial process, Tacitus' version undermines this by describing the fate of Brutus and Cassius as *exitus*, not *exilium*.[289] As for the triumvirate, Tacitus draws attention to the unsavoury activities of this alliance, the land

---

[280] Tac. *Ann.* 1.9.5, *mari Oceano aut amnibus longinquis saeptum imperium*; cf. 26.2, *qua includit Oceanus a Gadibus ad ostium Albis fluminis*.

[281] Tac. *Ann.*1.9.5, *non regno tamen neque dictatura, sed principis nomine constitutam rem publicam*; cf. 5.1 for Augustus' rejection of the dictatorship; 13, 30.1, 32.3 for Augustus as *princeps*.

[282] Tac. *Ann.* 1.9.3.   [283] Urban (1979) 61.

[284] For detailed analysis of Tacitus' (ab)use of the *RGDA*, see Urban (1979), especially 62–4.

[285] Tac. *Ann.* 1.10.1, 'but because of his desire to rule, veterans were mustered through bribery, an army was prepared by a youngster acting in a private capacity, the consul's legions were corrupted, and favour towards Pompeians feigned', *ceterum cupidine dominandi concitos per largitionem veteranos, paratum ab adulescente privato exercitum, corruptas consulis legiones, simulatam Pompeianarum gratiam partium*. Cf. 1.1.

[286] Tac. *Ann.* 1.10.2, *caesis Hirtio et Pansa, sive hostis illos, seu Pansam venenum vulneri adfusum, sui milites Hirtium et machinator doli Caesar abstulerat*. Cf. 1.4, *cum cos. uterque in bello cecidisset*.

[287] 1.4, *populus autem eodem anno me consulem . . . creavit*.

[288] Tac. *Ann.* 1.10.2, *extortum invito senatu consulatum*.

[289] Tac. *Ann.* 1.10.3; cf. 2; Urban (1979) 64.

confiscations and proscriptions, without mentioning at all the existence of the triumvirate as a legal framework for power.[290] Finally, Augustus' boast to have conquered the world is called into question by Tacitus reminding us of 'disasters like those of Lollius and Varus', a choice of expression which implies that these disasters were typical of a wider picture rather than exceptional.[291]

Given the historical context of this passage, providing a retrospective on Augustus' reign in the days following his death, it is entirely appropriate for Tacitus to have taken his inspiration from the *RGDA*, which was actually published at that time. The anonymous assessments which he purports to record provide an alternative to Augustus' own self-representation. Although we cannot prove that Tacitus worked directly from a text of the *RGDA*, the close correspondences make it seem likely. Echoes of the *RGDA* are also found in Velleius Paterculus and Suetonius. In the case of Velleius, some echoes appear to relate directly to the *RGDA*, especially allusions to its opening chapter at 2.61.1, but other echoes may instead be the result of a shared linguistic repertoire, reflecting the official versions of events.[292] A handful of echoes in Suetonius are close enough to suggest a deliberate imitation, as appropriate to a biography of Augustus.[293] Even earlier the *RGDA* had notably attracted one other ironical literary imitator already by the mid-first century AD. In Seneca's *Apocolocyntosis*, composed shortly after Claudius' death and the accession of Nero, the scenario of Claudius' admittance among the gods upon his deification is given a humorous treatment. The author depicts a 'senate' of the gods, at which various gods give their opinion as to whether or not Claudius should be admitted to their body, until the deified Augustus intervenes at some length with his maiden speech to the house, tipping the balance of the debate against Claudius. His speech begins with a statement that effectively summarizes the *RGDA*. 'Then the deified Augustus got to his feet to declare his opinion in turn . . . "Was it for this that I achieved peace on land and sea? Was it for this reason that I put an end to civil wars? For this that I gave the city a foundation on laws, adorned it with public buildings, so that – I am at a loss for words, conscript fathers: all words fall short of my indignation."'[294] Clearly, part of the humour here is by attributing a potted version of the *RGDA* to Augustus at the gods' senate. It seems apparent, therefore, that the text of the *RGDA* was common currency among writers dealing with the age of Augustus, and that Augustus' own account of his achievements

---

[290] Tac. *Ann.* 1.10.2.   [291] Tac. *Ann.* 1.10.4, *Lollianas Varianasque clades.*

[292] See 1.1n. **annos undeviginti natus** and 1.1n. **a dominatione factionis oppressam**; for further echoes in 2.89.2–3, see 34.1n. **postquam bella civilia exstinxeram.**

[293] Scheid (2007) lxiii–iv tabulates five clear correspondences between Suetonius and the *RGDA*.

[294] Sen. *Apocol.* 10.1, *tunc divus Augustus surrexit sententiae suae loco dicendae . . . 'in hoc terra marique pacem peperi? ideo civilia bella compescui? ideo legibus urbem fundavi, operibus ornavi, ut – quid dicam p. c. non invenio: omnia infra indignationem verba sunt.'*

served as a point of reference for later authors in moulding their accounts of his era.

Finally, two other possible echoes of the *RGDA* from the early second century AD when Tacitus was writing support the idea that Augustus' composition held a prominent place in the cultural consciousness of the élite at the time. The reliefs carved upon Trajan's column not only present a narrative of the Dacian Wars but also, like the *RGDA*, encapsulate the emperor's virtues, albeit in pictorial form. Furthermore, their monumental context, at the emperor's burial place, which was surmounted by his statue, recalls that of Augustus' *RGDA*.[295] Hadrian imitated the *RGDA* rather more closely, but details are obscured by the fact that we have to rely for information upon a brief note in Pausanias. In explaining why a tribe at Athens had been named after the current emperor, Pausanias briefly lists his main benefactions and achievements, ending with the comment that all these were recorded in an inscription upon the Pantheon at Athens.[296] Clearly, the little we have from Pausanias is very valuable, since he is writing from personal experience about contemporary Athens, and it is enough to intimate strongly that Hadrian's Athenian inscription emulated Augustus' earlier one in several respects. Like Augustus, he includes military achievements (suppression of the Jewish revolt), adornment and building of sanctuaries old and new, and benefactions to Greeks and foreigners alike. In particular, Hadrian's claim never to have entered upon a war voluntarily recalls a similar claim by Augustus, that he had 'attacked no people unjustly'.[297] Appropriately for such a philhellene emperor, Hadrian's benefactions were primarily intended and recorded for the benefit of Greeks, not Romans, and so balanced the focus upon the city of Rome so evident in Augustus' account.[298]

b Mussolini and the RGDA

Under Mussolini's fascist regime, the *RGDA* won favour as a monument to imperialism. In 1938, a copy of the *RGDA* was set in bronze lettering on the podium supporting the recently excavated altar of Augustan Peace, which was regarded at the time as being the other outstanding expression of Rome's imperial rule (Figure 8).[299] Fragments of the altar had first surfaced in 1568 from the foundations of the Palazzo Peretti-Ottoboni (Fiano), but recovery of the substantial parts of the altar of Augustan Peace remaining underground had to wait nearly 400 years for the necessary technical knowledge and political interest to emerge. The altar was reconstructed at a new location, in a glass pavilion designed by Vittorio Ballio Morpurgo

---

[295] Huet (1996) 21–4.   [296] Paus. 1.5.5.   [297] 26.3, *nulli genti bello per iniuriam inlato.*
[298] Von Wilamowitz-Möllendorff (1886) 623–4; Mommsen (1906) 254.
[299] Kostof (1978) 304, fig. 36; Cecchelli (1925/6) 69.

Fig. 8 *Res Gestae*, as reinscribed for Mussolini on the outer wall of the Ara Pacis museum, Rome.

alongside the Mausoleum, overlooking the Tiber.[300] There was considerable debate at the time as to where the monument should be relocated, with the Capitol appearing to some to be the best place (as preserving 'l'essenza più pura dello spirito romano'), but Mussolini decided on juxtaposing it with the Mausoleum.[301] A photograph taken on 7 May 1938 of Mussolini and Hitler viewing a processional panel of the altar of Augustan Peace on display in the Museo Nazionale at Diocletian's Baths, even before the reconstruction of the monument had been completed, illustrates the importance of the altar to the image of Mussolini's new empire.[302] When the altar of Augustan Peace was formally opened on 23 September of the same year, the ceremony attended by Mussolini himself formed the culmination of celebrations for the bimillenium of Augustus' birth (see pp. 53–4).[303]

The claims to world conquest in the *RGDA* fitted nicely with the ambitions of the fascist regime to establish a new Italian empire, as expressed by Mussolini in his speech delivered to mark the installation of Rome's first fascist governor on 31 December 1925: 'Within five years Rome must appear amazing to all the peoples of the world; huge, ordered, powerful,

[300] Moretti (1938); Ridley (1986) 37–8; Kostof (1978) 304.
[301] Cecchelli (1925/6), quotation from 70, supported by another article in the first issue of *Capitolium* by Cremonesi (1925/6) 396; see also Kostof (1978) 303.
[302] Medina Lasansky (2004) 83 fig. 76 (photograph: Istituto LUCE, Rome); Scobie (1990) 30, 31 fig. 6.
[303] Photograph in Zeri (2006) 14; cf. Muñoz (1938) 505.

as it was at the time of the first empire of Augustus.'[304] These ambitions peaked during the second decade of fascist rule, 1932–42, with Rome's ancient empire being frequently invoked in the hope of inspiring and justifying the modern policy of expansion. Mussolini consistently appealed to ancient precedent to justify his regime's imperialist project, above all its invasion of Ethiopia.[305] Four large marble maps were set up along the Via dell'Impero (now the Via dei Fori Imperiali) in 1934, showing the stages in the expansion of the Roman empire, with a fifth map being added after the campaign in Ethiopia of 1935–6.[306] These ambitions were realized with the proclamation of the Italian empire on 10 May 1936.[307]

Augustus was represented as the perfect forerunner for many of the regime's policies, and above all as the precedent for establishing a Roman empire.[308] Mussolini associated himself with the image of Rome's first emperor and his empire in a variety of ways.[309] The year-long Mostra augustea della romanità (Augustan Exhibition of Romanness), which opened on Augustus' birthday, 23 September 1937, was a key component in the elaborate celebrations marking the bimillennium of Augustus' birth.[310] It promoted the identification of Augustus with Mussolini, both leaders being represented as having brought peace and imperial rule to Italy.[311] This was made most explicit by the pairing of monumental statues of the two leaders at the entrance to the exhibition, but was also reinforced by the way in which, on the same day, Mussolini opened the Augustan exhibition just an hour before he reopened the Mostra della rivoluzione fascista (Exhibition of the Fascist Revolution), which had first opened in celebration of ten years of fascist government in 1932.[312]

In Room 2 of the Augustan exhibition, which illustrated the theme of empire, was displayed the plaster cast of the *pronaos* of the temple of Rome and Augustus at Ancyra,[313] which had been fashioned in 1911 for the archaeological exhibition in the Baths of Diocletian marking the fiftieth anniversary of the unification of Italy.[314] That earlier exhibition had foreshadowed the fascist one.[315] By illustrating the spread of Roman civilization and military power, the exhibition generated hopes that it would inspire the youth of Italy to imitate the virtues 'which made Rome morally and materially the ruler of the world', in the words of Rodolfo

---

[304] 'Tra cinque anni Roma deve apparire meravigliosa a tutte le genti del mondo; vasta, ordinata, potente, come fu ai tempi del primo impero di Augusto': Mussolini (1942) 92; Ridley (1986) 19; Scobie (1990) 9–10.

[305] Stone (1999) 207.   [306] Bondanella (1987) 183–7.

[307] Kostof (1978) 302.   [308] Cagnetta (1976) 154–67.

[309] Cagnetta (1976) especially 141–4; Scobie (1990) 10–11.   [310] Pallottino (1937).

[311] Cagnetta (1976) especially 147–51; Silverio (1983); Ridley (1986) 36–7; Bondanella (1987) 189–91; Benton (2000) 175–83. Cf. Stone (1999) 208, 209.

[312] Cagnetta (1976) 148; Stone (1999) 215–16.   [313] *Mostra augustea della romanità* (1938) 17–20.

[314] *Catalogo della mostra archeologica* (1911) 10 (Lanciani's opening speech), 174–80; Kostof (1978) 304.

[315] Giglioli (1928/9).

Lanciani's opening speech.[316] In fact, these very words are quoted favourably by Giglioli in his article from 1927/8 published in the regime's populist magazine for Rome, *Capitolium*, promoting the idea of creating a Museo dell'impero romano.[317] The cast was subsequently transferred to the Museo dell'impero (Museum of the Empire), which was re-arranged in 1952–5 as the Museo della civiltà romana (Museum of Roman Civilization) in EUR, where it may still be viewed.[318]

The exhibition was not just for the benefit of a home audience. Reports of Hitler's hour-long visit to the exhibition on 6 May as part of his state visit to Rome mention the *RGDA* as one of the exhibits particularly admired by the Führer. In fact, Hitler was so impressed with the exhibition as a whole that he requested to revisit it the next day.[319] A translation of the *RGDA* was also displayed alongside a model of the altar of Augustan Peace in Room 8, which focused on the theme of poets and writers of the Augustan age.[320] The overall aim of the exhibition was to demonstrate the widespread extent of Roman rule in antiquity, and to suggest that Mussolini's imperial designs were simply a return to Roman birthright to rule over others.[321] A book written by the Minister of Education, Giuseppe Bottai, who had also acted as Governor of Rome from 1935 to 1937, entitled *L'Italia di Augusto e l'Italia di oggi* (*The Italy of Augustus and the Italy of Today*), was published to coincide with the bimillennium, and it ensured that the implicit parallels between emperor and Duce did not go unnoticed.[322] Even more blatantly, a report in Rome's newspaper *Corriere della Sera*, published on the exhibition's opening day, observed that '*Romanità* and Fascism are manifestations of the same spirit. The two great historical phenomena which led to the creation of the Empire of Augustus and to our Empire represent two moments in the millennial life of a people who have rediscovered their own virtues and reconquered their youth.'[323]

Several archaeological projects also brought Augustus into focus, including excavation of the Augustan forum in 1924–30, one of the earliest fascist excavations in Rome, and the 'Liberation' of Augustus' Mausoleum in 1936–8. Mussolini's personal patronage of this project is graphically realized in a staged photograph of 22 October 1934 showing him wielding a pickaxe atop the Mausoleum's roof, ready to start clearing away the auditorium which had been built on top of the monument, having ended his speech with

---

[316] *Catalogo della mostra archeologica* (1911) 11: 'che resero Roma moralmente e materialmente la dominatrice del mondo'.

[317] Giglioli (1927/8) 9.   [318] Benton (2000) 184 fig. 12.12.   [319] Scobie (1990) 28–9.

[320] *Mostra augustea della romanità* (1938) 105; Benton (2000) 183.

[321] Kostof (1978) 287, 303; Stone (1999) 215–16.

[322] Bondanella (1987) 202. For discussion of other similar publications, see Cagnetta (1976) 151–4; Quartermaine (1995) 207–9.

[323] 'La fiamma sacra della rivoluzione' *Corriere della Sera* (23 Sept. 1937), cited by Stone (1999) 216. Similar sentiments were expressed in the Nazi party's newspaper of 25 September: Scobie (1990) 27–8.

the words 'ed ora, la parola al piccone' ('and now, words give way to the pickaxe').[324] Six streets surrounding the Mausoleum were demolished in 1934–40, and a new piazza juxtaposing symbols of the ancient and modern empires was completed in 1941.[325] The east and north sides of the Piazzale Augusto Imperatore housed the Istituto Nazionale Fascista della Previdenza Sociale, which was responsible for social welfare programmes, and which funded the construction of the piazza. Other buildings were decorated by both Roman and fascist emblems.[326] A brief Latin inscription flanked by two winged victories holding up *fasces* on the façade of Fabbricato B even presented a modest *Res Gestae* for Mussolini, echoing some of Augustus' claims:

This place, where the departed spirit of Augustus flies through the air, after the emperor's mausoleum had been rescued from the darkness of centuries, and the dispersed parts of the Altar of Peace had been restored, Mussolini *Dux* demolished the old congested places and decreed that it should be decorated with more splendid streets, buildings, and houses suitable for a civilized form of life. In the year 1940; fascist era 18.[327]

The whole ensemble was completed by displaying the altar of Augustan Peace on a high platform between the Mausoleum and the Tiber. In this way, an inscription of the *RGDA* was displayed once again near to where Augustus had originally intended. Impressive though it was as a visual spectacle, especially when floodlit at night, the micro-environment of the glass pavilion and the increased levels of traffic pollution conspired to damage the monument, and recently on the same site a new museum designed by the American architect Richard Meier opened on 21 April 2006 (Rome's birthday). The only element preserved from Ballio Murpurgo's design is the bronze letters of the *RGDA* on the podium.[328]

---

[324] Kostof (1978) fig. 1; Mulè (1934) 465.
[325] Kostof (1978); Ridley (1986) 24–5; Bondanella (1987) 201–2.
[326] Kostof (1978) 304–16; Ridley (1986) 20; Bondanella (1987) 202.
[327] *hunc locum ubi Augusti manes volitant per auras postquam imperatoris mausoleum ex saeculorum tenebris est extractum araeque pacis disiecta membra refecta Musso[[lini dux]] veteribus angustiis deletis splendidioribus viis aedificiis aedibus ad humanitatis mores aptis ornandum censuit anno MDCCCCXL [[ae. f. XVIII]]*: Kostof (1978) 325 n. 65, fig. 38; Benton (2000) 183, 185 fig. 12.13.
[328] Zeri (2006).

RES GESTAE DIVI AUGUSTI

Text and translation

EXPLANATORY NOTE

This edition provides a composite text of both Latin and Greek versions, as derived from the inscriptions surviving from Ancyra, Pisidian Antioch, and Apollonia. The aim is to provide as full a text as possible, sometimes including letters that are no longer extant on the inscriptions but that have been read in the past, indicating editorial supplements where the letters have never been legible to modern eyes. In cases where letters have been faintly discerned by only a single modern viewer, but appear secure from the context or by comparison with the version in the other language, these letters have not been bracketed. These composite texts are indebted to the exemplary recent edition by John Scheid (2007), to which the reader is directed for a full presentation of the epigraphic texts, with apparatus criticus. See Appendix for a list of readings that diverge from Scheid's composite text (Scheid (2007) 4–25).

The following standard symbols are used:

[abc]   Letters which have been lost where the inscription has been damaged, but which the editor has supplied.

<abc> Letters omitted by mistake from the original inscription, which the editor has added.

{abc}   Letters included by mistake in the original inscription, and which should be deleted.

⌜abc⌝   Letters corrected by the editor, in place of an error in the original inscription.

a(bc)   An abbreviated word, which the editor has written out in full.

HEADING

rerum gestarum divi Augusti, quibus orbem terra[rum] imperio populi
Rom[a]ni subiecit, et inpensarum, quas in rem publicam populumque
Romanum fecit, incisarum in duabus aheneis pilis, quae su[n]t Romae
positae, exemplar sub[i]ectum.

Below is a copy of the achievements of the deified Augustus, by which
he made the world subject to the rule of the Roman people, and of the
expenses which he incurred for the state and people of Rome, as inscribed
upon two bronze columns which have been set up at Rome.

CHAPTER I

1. annos undeviginti natus exercitum privato consilio et privata impensa
comparavi, per quem rem publicam a dominatione factionis oppressam
in libertatem vindicavi. **2.** eo [nomi]ne senatus decretis honorif[i]cis in
ordinem suum m[e adlegit C(aio) Pansa et A(ulo) Hirti]o consulibus
con[sula]rem locum s[ententiae dicendae simu]l [dans et i]mperium mihi
dedit. **3.** res publica n[e quid detrimenti caperet], me pro praetore simul
cum consulibus pro[videre iussit. **4.** p]opulus autem eodem anno me consulem, cum [consul uterqu]e in bel[lo ceci]disset, et triumvirum rei publicae
constituend[ae creavit].

1. Aged nineteen years old [44 BC] I mustered an army at my personal
decision and at my personal expense, and with it I liberated the state,
which had been oppressed by a despotic faction. **2.** For this reason the
senate passed honorific decrees admitting me to its body in the consulship of
Gaius Pansa and Aulus Hirtius [43 BC], at the same time giving me consular
precedence in stating my opinion, and it gave me supreme command. **3.**
To prevent the state from suffering harm, it ordered me as *propraetor* to
take precautions together with the consuls. **4.** In this same year [43 BC],
moreover, the people appointed me consul, after both consuls had fallen
in war, and triumvir for settling the state.

HEADING

μεθηρμηνευμέναι ὑπεγράφησαν πράξεις τε καὶ δωρεαὶ Σεβαστοῦ θεοῦ,
ἃς ἀπέλιπεν ἐπὶ Ῥώμης ἐνκεχαραγμένας χαλκαῖς στήλαις δυσίν.

Translated and inscribed below are the achievements and gifts of the god
Augustus, which he left engraved at Rome upon two bronze tablets.

CHAPTER I

1. ἐτῶν δεκαε[ν]νέα ὢν τὸ στράτευμα ἐμῆι γνώμηι καὶ ἐμοῖς
ἀν[αλ]ώμασιν ἡτοί[μασα], δι᾽ οὗ τὰ κοινὰ πράγματα [ἐκ τῆ]ς τ[ῶ]ν
συνο[μοσα]μένων δουλήας [ἠλευ]θέ[ρωσα. **2.** ἐφ᾽ ο]ἷς ἡ σύνκλητος ἐπαινέσασά με [ψη]φίσ[μασ]ι προσκατέλεξε τῆι βουλῆι Γαΐωι
Πά[νσ]α<ι> καὶ [Αὔλωι Ἱρτίω]ι ὑπ[ά]το[ι]ς ἐν τῆι τάξει τῶν ὑπα-
τευσάντων τὸ σ[υ]μ[β]ουλεύειν δοῦσα, ῥάβδους τέ μοι ἔδωκεν. **3.** [περ]ὶ
τὰ δημόσια πράγματα μή τι βλαβῆι, ἐμοὶ με[τὰ] τῶ[ν] ὑ[π]άτων
προνοεῖν ἐπέτρεψεν ἀντιστρατήγωι ὄντ[ι. **4.** ὁ δ]ὲ δ[ῆ]μος τῶι αὐτῶι
ἐνιαυτῶι ἀμφοτέρων [τῶν ὑπάτων ἐν π]ολέμωι πεπτω[κ]ό[τ]ων ἐμὲ
ὕπατον ἀπ[έδειξ]εν καὶ τὴν τῶν τριῶν ἀνδρῶν ἔχοντα ἀρχὴν ἐπὶ τῆι
καταστάσει τῶν δ[η]μοσίων πραγμάτ[ων] ε[ἵ]λατο.

1. When I was nineteen years old, I got ready on my own initiative and
at my own expense the army by means of which I set the state free from
the slavery imposed by the conspirators. **2.** On account of these things the
senate passed decrees in praise of me and enrolled me into the senate in the
consulship of Gaius Pansa and Aulus Hirtius, giving me the status of an
ex-consul in offering advice and it gave me rods of office. **3.** It entrusted to
me as *propraetor* together with the consuls the task of taking precautions
that nothing should harm the state. **4.** In the same year, when both consuls
had fallen in war, the people appointed me consul and chose me for the
office of triumvir in charge of the settled order of the state.

CHAPTER 2

qui parentem meum [interfecer]un[t, eo]s in exilium expuli iudiciis legitimis ultus eorum [fa]cin[us, e]t postea bellum inferentis rei publicae vici
b[is a]cie.

Those who killed my father I drove into exile by way of the courts of law,
exacting retribution for their crime and afterwards I defeated them twice
in battle while they were making war upon the state.

CHAPTER 3

1. [b]ella terra et mari c[ivilia ex]ternaque toto in orbe terrarum s[aepe
gessi], victorque omnibus v[eniam petentib]us civibus peperci. **2.** exte[rnas]
gentes, quibus tuto [ignosci pot]ui[t, co]nservare quam excidere ma[lui].
3. millia civium Roma[no]rum [sub] sacramento meo fuerunt circiter
[quingen]ta. ex quibus dedu[xi in coloni]as aut remisi in municipia sua
stipen[dis emeri]tis millia aliquant[o plura qu]am trecenta, et iis omnibus
agros a[dsignavi] aut pecuniam pro p[raemis mil]itiae dedi. **4.** naves cepi
sescen[tas praeter] eas, si quae minore[s quam trir]emes fuerunt.

1. I have often conducted wars by land and sea, civil and foreign, across
the whole world, and as victor I was merciful to all citizens who asked for
pardon. **2.** As for foreign peoples, those whom I could safely pardon, I
preferred to preserve than to destroy. **3.** There have been roughly 500,000
Roman citizens under oath of allegiance to me. Considerably more than
300,000 of these I have settled in colonies or sent back to their towns after
they had completed their terms of service, and to all of them I allotted
pieces of land or else gave them money as the rewards for their service. **4.**
I have captured 600 ships excluding those smaller than triremes.

CHAPTER 2

[τοὺς τὸν πατέρα μου] φονεύσαντ[α]ς ἐξώρισα κρί[σεσιν ἐνδί]κοις τειμω[ρ]ησάμε[ν]ος αὐτῶν τὸ [ἀσέβημα κ]αὶ [με]τὰ ταῦτα αὐτοὺς πόλεμον ἐ[πιφέροντας τῆι πα]τ[ρ]ίδι δὶς ἐνείκησα παρατάξει.

Those who killed my father I banished through legitimate trials, exacting vengeance for their sacrilege and after that I twice defeated them in battle when they waged war on the fatherland.

CHAPTER 3

1. [πολέμους καὶ κατὰ γῆ]ν καὶ κατὰ θάλασσαν ἐμφυ[λίους καὶ ὀθνείου]ς ἐν ὅληι τῆι οἰκουμένηι πολλ[άκις ἐποίησα, νει]κήσας τε πάντων ἐφεισάμην [τῶν ἱκετῶν πολειτῶν. **2.** τ]ὰ ἔθνη, οἷς ἀσφαλὲς ἦν συν[γνώμην ἔχειν, ἔσωσα μ]ᾶλ[λον] ἢ ἐξέκοψα. **3.** μυριάδες Ρωμαίων στρατ[εύ]σ[ασ]αι ὑπ[ὸ τὸ]ν ὅρκον τὸν ἐμὸν ἐγένοντ[ο] ἐγγὺς π[εντήκ]ο[ντ]α· [ἐ]ξ ὧν κατή[γ]αγον εἰς τὰς ἀποικίας ἢ ἀπ[έπεμψα εἰς τὰ]ς ἰδίας π[ό]λεις ἐκπλ[ηρωθέντων τῶν] ἐνι[αυτῶν τῆς] στρατε[ίας] μυριάδας ὀλ[ίγω]ι π[λείους ἢ τριάκοντα καὶ] αὐτο[ῖ]ς πᾶσ[ιν ἀγροὺς] ἐμ[έρισ]α ἢ [χρήματα ἀντὶ δωρεῶν στρατείας] ἔδωκ[α]. **4.** ναῦς εἷ[λον ἐξακοσίας ἐ]κτὸ[ς τούτων, εἴτινες ἥσσονες] ἢ τ[ριήρεις ἐγένοντο].

1. I often waged wars both by land and by sea, civil and foreign, in the whole of the inhabited world, and having won I spared all citizens who sought my protection. **2.** Tribes whom it was safe to pardon, I kept alive rather than eradicated. **3.** There came nearly 500,000 Romans to serve in the army under my oath. Of these, once their years of military service had been completed, I settled in colonies or I sent back to their own towns a few more than 300,000, and to all of them I distributed lands or I gave them cash in place of the bounty of military service. **4.** I captured 600 ships excluding those which were smaller than triremes.

CHAPTER 4

1. [bis] ovans triumphavi et tri[s egi] curulis triumphos et appella[tus sum v]iciens et semel imperator, [decernente pl]uris triumphos mihi sena[t]u, qu[ibus omnibus su]persedi. l[aurum de f]asc[i]bus deposui in Capi[tolio, votis quae] quoque bello nuncupaveram [sol]utis. **2.** ob res a [me aut per legatos] meos auspicis meis terra ma[riqu]e pr[o]spere gestas qui[nquagiens et q]uinquiens decrevit senatus supp[lica]ndum esse dis immortalibus. dies a[utem, pe]r quos ex senatus consulto [s]upplicatum est, fuere DC[CCLXXXX. **3.** in triumphis meis] ducti sunt ante currum meum reges aut r[eg]um lib[eri novem. **4.** consul f]ueram terdeciens cum [scribeb]a[m] haec, [et eram se]p[timum et t]ricen[simu]m tribuniciae potestatis.

1. Twice I have celebrated triumphal ovations and three times I have driven triumphal chariots and I have been hailed twenty-one times as victorious general, although the senate voted me more triumphs, from all of which I abstained. I deposited the laurel from my *fasces* in the Capitoline temple, in fulfilment of the vows which I had taken in each war. **2.** On account of affairs successfully accomplished by land and sea by me or through my deputies under my auspices the senate fifty-five times decreed that thanksgiving should be offered to the immortal gods. Moreover the days during which thanksgiving has been offered by decree of the senate have amounted to 890. **3.** In my triumphs nine kings or kings' children have been led in front of my chariot. **4.** I had been consul thirteen times at the time of writing, and I was the holder of tribunician power thirty-seven times [AD 14].

CHAPTER 5

1. [dic]tat[ura]m et apsent[i e]t praesent[i mihi delatam et a popu]lo et a se[na]tu, [M(arco) Marce]llo e[t] L(ucio) Arruntio [co(n)s(ulibus),] non rec[epi. **2.** non sum] depreca[tus] in s[umma f]rum[enti p]enuria curationem an[non]ae, [qu]am ita ad[min]ist[ravi, ut intra] die[s] paucos metu et periclo praesenti civitatem univ[ersam liberarim impensa et] cura mea. **3.** consul[atum] quoqu[e] tum annuum e[t perpetuum mihi] dela[tum non recepi].

1. Even though the post of dictator was conferred upon me both when I was absent and when I was present by both people and senate in the consulship of Marcus Marcellus and Lucius Arruntius [22 BC], I did not accept it. **2.** I did not decline to manage the corn supply during a very severe grain shortage, and I administered it in such a way that within a few days I freed the entire community from pressing fear and danger through my expenditure and supervision. **3.** When the consulship too was conferred upon me at that time for a year and in perpetuity, I did not accept it.

CHAPTER 4

1. δὶς ἐ[φ'ἵππου ἐθριάμβευσα καὶ] τρὶς [ἐ]φ'ἅρματος, εἰκοσά[κις καὶ ἅπαξ προσηγορεύθην αὐτο]κράτωρ, τῆς [συνκλήτου ἐμοὶ πλείους θριάμ-βου]ς ψηφισσ[αμένης, ὧν πάντων ἀπεσχόμην. ἀ]πὸ τ[ῶ]ν ῥ[ά]βδων τὴν δάφνην ἀπ[έθηκα ἐν τῶι Καπιτωλίωι], τὰς εὐχάς, ἃς ἐν τῶ[ι] πολέμωι ἑκάστωι ἐποιησάμην, ἀποδούς. **2.** διὰ τὰς ἐμὰς πράξεις [ἢ] τὰς τῶν [πρεσβευτῶν] μ[ου, ἃς αἰσίοις οἰωνοῖς καὶ κατὰ γῆν καὶ κατ]ὰ θά[λασσα]ν κατώρθωσα, π[εντ]ηκοντάκις [καὶ] πεντά[κις ἐψ]ηφίσατο ἡ σύ[νκλητ]ος θεοῖς δεῖ[ν] θύεσθαι. [ἡμ]έραι οὖν αὐ[τα]ὶ ἐ[κ συ]ν[κλήτου] δ[ό]γματ[ο]ς ἐγένοντο ὀκτα[κ]όσιαι ἐνενή[κοντα]. **3.** ἐν [τ]οῖς ἐμοῖς [θριάμ]βοις [πρὸ το]ῦ ἐμοῦ ἅρμ[ατος βασι]λεῖς ἢ [βασιλέων παῖ]δες [πρ]οήχθησαν ἐννέα. **4.** ὑπάτευον τρὶς καὶ δέκ[ατο]ν, ὅτε τ[αῦ]τα ἔγραφον, καὶ ἤμη[ν τρια]κ[οστὸ]ν καὶ ἔβδομ[ον δημαρχ]ικῆς ἐξουσίας.

1. Twice I triumphed on horseback and three times in a chariot, twenty-one times I was hailed as victorious general; when the senate voted me more triumphs, I abstained from them all. I put aside in the Capitolium the laurel from the rods of office, paying back the prayers which I undertook in each war. **2.** Because of my achievements or those of my deputies, which I successfully accomplished with auspicious omens both by land and by sea, the senate voted fifty-five times that sacrifices ought to be made to the gods. In fact, there were 890 of these days in accordance with senatorial decree. **3.** In my triumphs nine kings or children of kings were led in front of my chariot. **4.** I was consul for the thirteenth time, when I wrote this, and I was in my thirty-seventh year of tribunician power.

CHAPTER 5

1. αὐτεξούσιόν μοι ἀρχὴν καὶ ἀπόντι καὶ παρόντι διδομένην ὑπό τε τοῦ δήμου καὶ τῆς συνκλήτου Μ[άρκ]ωι [Μ]αρκέλλωι καὶ Λευκίωι Ἀρρουντίωι ὑπάτοις ο[ὐκ ἐδ]εξάμην. **2.** οὐ παρη<ι>τησάμην ἐν τῆι μεγίστηι [τοῦ] σ[είτ]ου σπάνει τὴν ἐπιμέλειαν τῆς ἀγορᾶς, ἣν οὕ[τως ἐπετήδευ]σα ὥστ' ἐν ὀλίγαις ἡμέρα[ις το]ῦ παρόντος φόβου καὶ κι[νδ]ύνου ταῖς ἐμαῖς δαπάναις τὸν δῆμον ἐλευθερῶσα[ι]. **3.** ὑπατείαν τέ μοι τότε δι[δ]ομένην καὶ ἐ[ν]ιαύσιον κα[ὶ δ]ι[ὰ] βίου οὐκ ἐδεξάμην.

1. I did not accept absolute power that was offered to me when I was both absent and present by both the people and the senate in the consulship of Marcus Marcellus and Lucius Arruntius. **2.** I did not decline to take on the supervision of the market during the worst grain shortage, which I took care of in such a way so as to free the people from the present fear and danger at my own expense in a few days. **3.** I did not accept the annual and lifetime consulship being offered to me at that time.

CHAPTER 6

1. [consulibus M(arco) V]in[icio et Q(uinto) Lucretio] et postea P(ublio) Lentulo et Cn(aeo) L[entulo et terti]um [Paullo Fabio Maximo] e[t Q(uinto) Tuberone senatu populoq]u[e Romano consentientibus] ut cu[rator legum et morum summa potestate solus crearer, nullum magistratum contra morem maiorum delatum recepi. **2.** quae tum per me geri senatus] v[o]luit, per trib[un]ici[a]m p[otestatem perfeci, cuius potes]tatis conlegam et [ips]e ultro [quinquiens a sena]tu [de]poposci et accepi.

1. In the consulship of Marcus Vinicius and Quintus Lucretius [19 BC], and later of Publius Lentulus and Gnaeus Lentulus [18 BC], and thirdly of Paullus Fabius Maximus and Quintus Tubero [11 BC], even though the senate and people of Rome were in agreement that I should be appointed on my own as guardian of laws and customs with supreme power, I accepted no magistracy conferred upon me that contravened ancestral custom. **2.** The things which the senate wanted to be accomplished by me at that time, I executed by virtue of my tribunician power, for which power I myself, of my own accord, five times demanded and received a colleague from the senate.

CHAPTER 7

1. [tri]umv[i]rum rei pu[blicae c]on[s]ti[tuendae fui per continuos an]nos [decem. **2.** p]rinceps s[enatus fui usque ad e]um d[iem quo scrip]seram [haec per annos] quadra[ginta. **3.** pon]tifex [maximus, augur, XVvir]um sacris fac[iundis, VIIvirum ep]ulon[um, frater arvalis, sodalis Titius,] fetialis fui.

1. I was one of the triumvirs for settling the state for ten consecutive years. **2.** I have been the highest ranking member of the senate right until the very day on which I wrote this, for forty years. **3.** I have been chief priest, augur, one of the Fifteen for conducting sacred rites, one of the Seven in charge of feasts, Arval brother, member of the fraternity of Titus, and fetial priest.

CHAPTER 6

1. ὑπάτοις Μάρκωι Οὐινουκίωι καὶ Κοΐντωι Λ[ουκρ]ητ[ίωι] καὶ μετὰ τα[ῦ]τα Ποπλίωι καὶ Ναΐωι Λέντλοις καὶ τρίτον Παύλλωι Φαβίωι Μαξίμωι καὶ Κοΐν[τωι] Τουβέρωνι τῆς [τε σ]υνκλήτου καὶ τοῦ δήμου τῶν Ῥωμαίων ὁμολογ[ο]ύντων, ἵνα ἐπιμελητὴς τῶν τε νόμων καὶ τῶν τρόπων ἐ[πὶ μ]εγίστηι ἐ[ξ]ουσίαι μόνος χειροτονηθῶ{ι}, ἀρχὴν οὐδεμ[ία]ν πα[ρὰ τὰ πά]τρ[ια] ἔ[θ]η διδομένην ἀνεδεξάμην. **2.** ἃ δὲ τότε δι᾽ ἐμοῦ ἡ σύνκλητος οἰκονομεῖσθαι ἐβούλετο, τῆς δημαρχικῆς ἐξο[υ]σίας ὢν ἐτέλε[σα. κ]αὶ ταύτης αὐτῆς τῆς ἀρχῆς συνάρχοντα [αὐτ]ὸς ἀπὸ τῆς συνκλήτου π[εν]τάκις αἰτήσας [ἔλ]αβον.

1. In the consulship of Marcus Vinucius and Quintus Lucretius, and after that of Publius and Gnaeus Lentulus, and thirdly of Paullus Fabius Maximus and Quintus Tubero, when both the senate and the people of Rome were in agreement that I alone should be appointed supervisor of both laws and customs possessing the greatest authority, I adopted no power that was being offered contrary to ancestral customs. **2.** But whatever at that time the senate wanted to be regulated by me, I accomplished by virtue of tribunician power. And I myself requested and received from the senate five times a colleague in this same power.

CHAPTER 7

1. τριῶν ἀνδρῶν ἐγενόμην δημοσίων πραγμάτων κατορθωτὴς συνεχέσιν ἔτεσιν δέκα. **2.** πρῶτον ἀξιώματος τόπον ἔσχον τῆς συνκλήτου ἄχρι ταύτης τῆς ἡμέρας ἧς ταῦτα ἔγραφον, ἐπὶ ἔτη τεσσαράκοντα. **3.** ἀρχιερεύς, αὔγουρ, τῶν δεκαπέντε ἀνδρῶν τῶν ἱεροποιῶν, τῶν ἑπτὰ ἀνδρῶν ἱεροποιῶν, ἀ[δε]λφὸς ἀρουᾶλις, ἑταῖρος Τίτιος, φητιᾶλις.

1. I was one of the triumvirs in charge of settling the state for ten continuous years. **2.** I held first place for expressing my opinion in the senate up until this day on which I wrote this, for forty years. **3.** Chief priest, augur, one of the Fifteen in charge of sacred rites, one of the Seven in charge of sacred rites, Arval brother, Titian companion, fetial.

CHAPTER 8

1. patriciorum numerum auxi consul quintum iussu populi et senatus. **2.** senatum ter legi, et in consulatu sexto censum populi conlega M(arco) Agrippa egi. lustrum post annum alterum et quadragensimum fec[i], quo lustro civium Romanorum censa sunt capita quadragiens centum millia et sexag[i]nta tria millia. **3.** tum [iteru]m consulari cum imperio lustrum [s]olus feci C(aio) Censorino [et C(aio)] Asinio co(n)s(ulibus), quo lustro censa sunt civium Romanorum [capit]a quadragiens centum millia et ducenta triginta tria m[illia. **4.** et te]rtium consulari cum imperio lustrum conlega Tib(erio) Cae[sare filio] m[eo feci], Sex(to) Pompeio et Sex(to) Appuleio co(n)s(ulibus), quo lustro ce[nsa sunt] civ[ium Ro]manorum capitum quadragiens centum mill[ia et n]onge[nta tr]iginta septem millia. **5.** legibus novi[s] m[e auctore l]atis m[ulta e]xempla maiorum exolescentia iam ex nostro [saecul]o red[uxi et ipse] multarum rer[um exe]mpla imitanda pos[teris tradidi].

1. I increased the number of patricians by command of the people and senate when consul for the fifth time [29 BC]. **2.** I revised the membership of the senate three times, and in my sixth consulship [28 BC] I conducted a census of the population with Marcus Agrippa as my colleague. I performed the ceremony of purification forty-two years after the last one; in this census 4,063,000 individual Roman citizens were registered. **3.** Then for a second time I conducted a census on my own with consular power in the consulship of Gaius Censorinus and Gaius Asinius [8 BC]; in this census were registered 4,233,000 individual Roman citizens. **4.** And for a third time I conducted a census with consular power with Tiberius Caesar my son as colleague in the consulship of Sextus Pompeius and Sextus Appuleius [AD 14]; in this census were registered 4,937,000 individual Roman citizens. **5.** By means of new laws brought in under my sponsorship I revived many exemplary ancestral practices which were by then dying out in our generation, and I myself handed down to later generations exemplary practices for them to imitate.

CHAPTER 8

1. τῶν [πατ]ρικίων τὸν ἀριθμὸν εὔξησα πέμπτον ὕπατ[ος ἐπιτ]αγῆι τοῦ τε δήμου καὶ τῆς συνκλήτου. **2.** [τ]ὴ[ν σύ]νκλητον τρὶς ἐπέλεξα. ἕκτον ὕπατος τὴν ἀπ[ο]τείμησιν τοῦ δήμου συνάρχον[τ]α ἔχων Μᾶρκον Ἀγρίππαν ἔλαβον, ἥτις ἀπο[τείμη]σις μετὰ [δύο καὶ] τεσσαρακοστὸν ἐνιαυτὸν [σ]υνε[κ]λείσθη. ἐν ἧι ἀποτειμήσει Ῥωμαίων ἐτει[μήσ]α[ντο] κεφαλαὶ τετρακόσια[ι] ἑξήκοντα μυρ[ι]άδες [καὶ] τρισχίλιαι. **3.** [εἶτα δεύτερον ὑ]πατικῆι ἐξ[ουσίαι μόνος Γαΐωι Κηνσωρίνωι καὶ] Γαΐωι [Ἀσινίωι ὑπάτοις τὴν ἀποτείμησιν ἔλαβον]· ἐν [ἧ]ι ἀπ[οτειμήσει ἐτειμήσαντο Ῥωμαί]ων τετ[ρακόσιαι εἴκοσι τρεῖς μυριάδες καὶ τ]ρι[σ]χίλιοι. **4.** κ[αὶ] τρίτον ὑπατικῆι ἐξουσίαι τὰς ἀποτειμή]σε[ι]ς ἔλα[βο]ν, [ἔχω]ν [συνάρχοντα Τιβέριον] Καίσαρα τὸν υἱόν μο[υ Σέξτωι Πομπηΐωι καὶ] Σέξτωι Ἀππουληΐωι ὑπάτοις, ἐν ἧι ἀποτειμήσει ἐτειμήσαντο Ῥωμαίων τετρακόσιαι ἐνενήκοντα τρεῖς μυριάδες καὶ ἑπτακισχείλιοι. **5.** εἰσαγαγὼν καίνους νόμους πολλὰ ἤδη τῶν ἀρχαίων ἐθῶν καταλυόμενα διωρθωσάμην καὶ αὐτὸς πολλῶν πραγμάτων μείμημα ἐμαυτὸν τοῖς μετέπειτα παρέδωκα.

1. I increased the number of patricians when consul for the fifth time by order of both the people and the senate. **2.** I selected the senate three times. When consul for the sixth time I conducted the census of the people, having Marcus Agrippa as colleague; this census was completed after a 42-year period. In this census of Romans 4,603,000 individuals were assessed. **3.** Then for a second time with consular power on my own in the consulship of Gaius Censorinus and Gaius Asinius I conducted the census. In this census 4,233,000 Romans were assessed. **4.** And for a third time with consular power I conducted the censuses, having Tiberius Caesar my son as colleague, in the consulship of Sextus Pompeius and Sextus Appuleius; in this census 4,937,000 Romans were assessed. **5.** Introducing new laws I restored many ancient customs that were already becoming obsolete and I myself handed myself down as a model of many things to future generations.

CHAPTER 9

1. vota p[ro salute mea susc]ipi p[er con]sules et sacerdotes qu[in]to qu[oque anno senatus decrevit. ex iis] votis s[ae]pe fecerunt vivo me [ludos aliquotiens sacerdotu]m quattuor amplissima colle[gia, aliquotiens consules. **2.** pr]iva[ti]m etiam et municipatim universi [cives unanimite]r con[tinente]r apud omnia pulvinaria pro vale[tu]din[e mea s]upp[licaverunt].

1. The senate decreed that vows for my good health be performed by consuls and priests every four years. In accordance with these vows, games have often been celebrated in my lifetime, sometimes by the four most eminent colleges of priests and sometimes by the consuls. **2.** Moreover all citizens in private and as a municipality have, with one accord, repeatedly offered prayers for my good health at all public feasts.

CHAPTER 10

1. nom[en me]um [sena]tus c[onsulto inc]lusum est in saliare carmen, et sacrosanctu[s in perp]etu<u>m [ut essem et q]uoad viverem tribunicia potestas mihi e[sset per lege]m st[atutum est. **2.** pontif]ex maximus ne fierem in vivi [c]onle[gae mei l]ocum, [populo id sace]rdotium deferente mihi, quod pater meu[s habuer]at, r[ecusavi. qu]od sacerdotium aliquo⌐t⌐ post annos, eo mor[t]uo d[emum qui civilis tu]m[ultus] occasione occupaverat, cuncta ex Italia [ad comitia mea] confluen[te mu]ltitudine, quanta Romae nun[q]uam [fertur ante i]d temp[us fuisse], recep[i], P(ublio) Sulpicio C(aio) Valgio consulibu[s].

1. My name was incorporated into the hymn of the Salii by decree of the senate, and it was ratified by law that I should be permanently sacrosanct and that I should hold tribunician power for as long as I live. **2.** I rejected the idea that I should become chief priest as a replacement for my colleague during his lifetime, even though the people were offering me this priesthood, which my father had held. After several years, on the eventual death of the man who had taken the opportunity of civil unrest to appropriate it, I did accept this priesthood; from the whole of Italy a crowd, such as it is said had never before this time been at Rome, flooded together for my election, in the consulship of Publius Sulpicius and Gaius Valgius [12 BC].

CHAPTER 9

1. εὐχὰς ὑπὲρ τῆς ἐμῆς σωτηρίας ἀναλαμβάνειν διὰ τῶν ὑπάτων καὶ ἱερέων καθ᾽ ἑκάστην πεντετηρίδα ἐψηφίσατο ἡ σύνκλητος. ἐκ τούτων τῶν εὐχῶν πλειστάκις ἐγένοντο θέαι, τοτὲ μὲν ἐκ τῆς συναρχίας τῶν τεσσάρων ἱερέων, τοτὲ δὲ ὑπὸ τῶν ὑπάτων. **2.** καὶ κατ᾽ ἰδίαν δὲ καὶ κατὰ πόλεις σύμπαντες οἱ πολεῖται ὁμοθυμαδὸν συνεχῶς ἔθυσαν ὑπὲρ τῆς ἐμῆς σω[τ]ηρίας.

1. The senate voted to undertake prayers on behalf of my safety through the consuls and priests every fifth year. Along with these prayers there were shows very often, sometimes resulting from collaboration between the four priests, and at other times the consuls. **2.** Furthermore, all citizens with one accord continuously both in private and by cities sacrificed on behalf of my safety.

CHAPTER 10

1. τὸ ὄν[ομ]ά μου συνκλήτου δόγματι ἐνπεριελήφθη εἰς [τοὺ]ς σαλίων ὕμνους. καὶ ἵνα ἱερὸς ὦι διὰ [βίο]υ [τ]ε τὴν δημαρχικὴν ἔχωι ἐξουσίαν, νό[μωι] ἐκυρώθη. **2.** ἀρχιερωσύνην, ἣν ὁ πατήρ [μ]ου [ἐσχ]ήκει, τοῦ δήμου μοι καταφέροντος εἰς τὸν τοῦ ζῶντος τόπον, οὐ προσεδεξάμ[η]ν. [ἣ]ν ἀρχιερατείαν μετά τινας ἐνιαυτούς, ἀποθανόντος τοῦ προκατειλ-ηφότος αὐτὴν ἐν πολειτικαῖς ταραχαῖς, ἀνείληφα, εἰς τὰ ἐμὰ ἀρχαιρέσια ἐξ ὅλης τῆς Ἰταλίας τοσούτου πλήθους συνεληλυθότος, ὅσον οὐδεὶς ἔνπροσθεν ἱστόρησεν ἐπὶ Ῥώμης γεγονέναι Ποπλίωι Σουλπικίωι καὶ Γαΐωι Οὐαλγίωι ὑπάτοις.

1. My name was incorporated into the hymns of the Salii by decree of the senate. And it was ratified by law that I might be sacrosanct throughout my life and have tribunician power. **2.** I did not accept the position of chief priest, which my father had held, when the people were handing it down to me in place of its living incumbent. I recovered this position as chief priest after some years, once the man who had previously seized it in the civil disturbances had died; for my election in the consulship of Publius Sulpicius and Gaius Valgius such a great crowd assembled from the whole of Italy, the like of which no one has recorded as having previously happened at Rome.

CHAPTER 11

aram [Fortunae] Red[ucis a]nte aedes Honoris et Virtutis ad portam
Cap[enam pro] red[itu me]o senatus consacravit, in qua ponti[fices et]
vir[gines Ve]stal[es anni]versarium sacrificium facere [iussit eo] di[e quo,
co]nsul[ibus Q(uinto) Luc]retio et [M(arco) Vi]nic[i]o, in urbem ex [Syria
redieram, et diem Augustali]a ex [c]o[gnomine] nos[t]ro appellavit.

The senate consecrated the altar of Fortune the Home-Bringer in front of
the temple of Honour and Virtue at the Capena Gate in thanks for my
return, and ordered the priests and Vestal Virgins to perform an annual
sacrifice there on the day [12 October] on which, in the consulship of
Quintus Lucretius and Marcus Vinicius [19 BC], I had returned to the city
from Syria, and it named the day *Augustalia* after me.

CHAPTER 12

1. [ex senatus auctoritat]e pars [praetorum e]t tribunorum [plebis cum
consule Q(uinto)] Lu[c]retio et principibus viris [ob]viam mihi mis[s]a
e[st in Campan]iam, qui honos [ad ho]c tempus nemini praeter [m]e
e[st decretus. **2.** cu]m ex H[isp]ania Gal[liaque, rebu]s in iis provincis
prosp[e]re [gest]i[s], R[omam redi], Ti(berio) Nerone P(ublio) Qui[nctilio
c]o(n)s(ulibus), aram [Pacis A]u[g]ust[ae senatus pro] redi[t]u meo
consa[c]randam [censuit] ad campum [Martium, in qua m]agistratus et
sac[er]dotes [vi]rgines[que] V[est]a[les ann]iver[sarium sacrific]ium facer[e
iussit].

1. In accordance with a resolution of the senate, some of the praetors and
tribunes of the people with the consul Quintus Lucretius and leading men
were sent to Campania to meet me; this honour has been decreed for no
one except me up to this time. **2.** When I returned to Rome from Spain and
Gaul, having settled affairs successfully in these provinces, in the consulship
of Tiberius Nero and Publius Quinctilius [13 BC], the senate decreed that
an altar of Augustan Peace should be consecrated in thanks for my return
on the field of Mars, and ordered magistrates and priests and Vestal Virgins
to perform an annual sacrifice there.

CHAPTER 11

βωμὸν Τύχης Σωτηρίου ὑπὲρ τῆς ἐμῆς ἐπανόδου πρὸς τῆι Καπήνηι
πύληι ἡ σύνκλητος ἀφιέρωσεν, πρὸς ὧι τοὺς ἱερεῖς καὶ τὰς ἱερείας
ἐνιαύσιον θυσίαν ποιεῖν ἐκέλευσεν ἐν ἐκείνηι τῆι ἡμέραι ἐν ἧι ὑπάτοις
Κοΐντωι Λουκρητίωι καὶ Μάρκωι Οὐινουκίωι ἐκ Συρίας εἰς Ῥώμην ἐπαν-
εληλύθειν, τήν τε ἡμέραν ἐκ τῆς ἡμετέρας ἐπωνυμίας προσηγόρευσεν
Αὐγουστάλια.

The senate consecrated an altar of Fortune the Saviour near the Capena
Gate on account of my return; at it the senate ordered the priests and
priestesses to carry out an annual sacrifice on that day on which in the
consulship of Quintus Lucretius and Marcus Vinucius I returned to Rome
from Syria, and it called the day *Augustalia* from our name.

CHAPTER 12

1. δόγματι σ[υ]νκλήτου οἱ τὰς μεγίστας ἀρχὰς ἄρξαντες [σ]ὺν
μέρει στρατηγῶν καὶ δημάρχων μετὰ ὑπάτου Κοΐντου Λουκρητίου
ἐπέμφθησάν μοι ὑπαντήσοντες μέχρι Καμπανίας, ἥτις τειμὴ μέχρι τούτου οὐδὲ ἑνὶ εἰ μὴ ἐμοὶ ἐψηφίσθη. **2.** ὅτε ἐξ Ἰσπανίας καὶ Γαλατίας, τῶν
ἐν ταύταις ταῖς ἐπαρχείαις πραγμάτων κατὰ τὰς εὐχὰς τελεσθέντων,
εἰς Ῥώμην ἐπανῆλθον Τιβερίωι [Νέ]ρωνι καὶ Ποπλίωι Κοιντιλίωι ὑπάτοις, βωμὸν Ε[ἰρ]ήνης Σεβαστῆς ὑπὲρ τῆς ἐμῆς ἐπανόδου ἀφιερωθῆναι
ἐψηφίσατο ἡ σύνκλητος ἐν πεδίωι Ἄρεως, πρὸς ὧι τούς τε ἐν ταῖς
ἀρχαῖς καὶ τοὺς ἱερεῖς τάς τε ἱερείας ἐνιαυσίους θυσίας ἐκέλευσε ποιεῖν.

1. By decree of the senate the most important magistrates with some of the
praetors and plebeian tribunes with consul Quintus Lucretius were sent all
the way to Campania to meet me; up to this time, this honour has been
voted to no one except me. **2.** When I returned to Rome from Hispania and
Gaul, once the affairs in these provinces had been auspiciously completed,
in the consulship of Tiberius Nero and Publius Quintilius, the senate
voted that an altar of Augustan Peace be consecrated on the field of Mars
on account of my return; at it the senate ordered those in office and the
priests and the priestesses to carry out annual sacrifices.

CHAPTER 13

[Ianum] Quirin[um, quem cl]aussum ess[e maiores nostri voluer]unt, cum [p]er totum i[mperium po]puli Roma[ni terra marique es]set parta victoriis pax, cum, pr[iusquam] nascerer, [a condita] u[rb]e bis omnino clausum [f]uisse prodatur m[emori]ae, ter me princi[pe senat]us claudendum esse censui[t].

Our ancestors wanted Janus Quirinus to be closed when peace had been achieved by victories on land and sea throughout the whole empire of the Roman people; whereas, before I was born, it is recorded as having been closed twice in all from the foundation of the city, the senate decreed it should be closed three times when I was leader.

CHAPTER 14

1. [fil]ios meos, quos iuv[enes mi]hi eripuit for[tuna], Caium et Lucium Caesares, honoris mei caussa senatus populusque Romanus annum quintum et decimum agentis consules designavit, ut [e]um magistratum inirent post quinquennium, et ex eo die, quo deducti sunt in forum, ut interessent consiliis publicis decrevit sena[t]us. 2. equites [a]utem Romani universi principem iuventutis utrumque eorum parm[is] et hastis argenteis donatum appellaverunt.

1. My sons, whom fortune snatched away from me when young men, Gaius and Lucius Caesars, the senate and people of Rome appointed as consuls when they were fourteen years old, as a way of honouring me, on the understanding that they should enter upon the magistracy five years later; and the senate decreed that from the day on which they were brought into the forum they should take part in the councils of state. 2. Moreover the Roman equestrians all together presented each of them with silver shields and spears and hailed each of them as leader of the youth.

CHAPTER 13

Πύλην Ἐνυάλιον, ἣν κεκλῖσθαι οἱ πατέρες ἡμῶν ἠθέλησαν εἰρηνευομένης τῆς ὑπὸ Ρωμα<ί>οις πάσης γῆς τε καὶ θαλάσσης, πρὸ μὲν ἐμοῦ, ἐξ οὗ ἡ πόλις ἐκτίσθη, τῶι πάντι αἰῶνι δὶς μόνον κεκλεῖσθαι ὁμολογεῖται, ἐπὶ δὲ ἐμοῦ ἡγεμόνος τρὶς ἡ σύνκλητος ἐψηφίσατο κλεισθῆναι.

It is agreed that the gate of War, which our ancestors desired to be closed once all land and sea was at peace under the Romans, has before me, since the foundation of the city, in the whole era been closed twice only, whereas under my leadership the senate voted for it to be closed three times.

CHAPTER 14

1. υἱούς μου Γάϊον καὶ Λεύκιον Καίσ[α]ρας, οὓς νεανίας ἀνήρπασεν ἡ τύχη εἰς τὴν ἐμὴν τειμ[ὴ]ν ἥ τ[ε] σύνκλητος καὶ ὁ δῆμος τῶν Ρωμαίων πεντεκαιδεκαέτεις ὄντας ὑπάτους ἀπέδειξεν, ἵνα μετὰ πέντε ἔτη εἰς τὴν ὕπατον ἀρχὴν εἰσέλθωσιν· καὶ ἀφ᾽ ἧς ἂν ἡμέ[ρα]ς εἰς τὴν ἀγορὰν κατ-αχθ[ῶ]σιν ἵνα μετέχωσιν τῆς συ[ν]κλήτου ἐψηφίσατο. 2. ἱππεῖς δὲ Ρω-μαίων σύν[π]αντες ἡγεμόνα νεότητος ἑκάτερον αὐτῶν προσηγόρευ-σαν, ἀσπίσιν ἀργυρέαις καὶ δόρασιν [ἐτ]είμησαν.

1. My sons Gaius and Lucius Caesars, whom fortune snatched away as young men, as an honour to me, both the senate and the people of Rome appointed as consuls when they were fifteen years old, so that after five years they might enter upon the office of consul. And it voted that they should be members of the senate from the day on which they were led down into the forum. 2. Moreover the Roman equestrians all together hailed each of them as leader of the youth, and honoured them with silver shields and spears.

CHAPTER 15

1. plebei Romanae viritim HS trecenos numeravi ex testamento patris mei, et nomine meo HS quadringenos ex bellorum manibiis consul quintum dedi, iterum autem in consulatu decimo ex [p]atrimonio meo HS quadringenos congiari viritim pernumer[a]vi, et consul undecimum duodecim frumentationes frumento pr[i]vatim coempto emensus sum, et tribunicia potestate duodecimum quadringenos nummos tertium viritim dedi. quae mea congiaria p[e]rvenerunt ad [homi]num millia nunquam minus quinquaginta et ducenta. **2.** tribuniciae potestatis duodevicensimum, consul XII, trecentis et viginti millibus plebis urbanae sexagenos denarios viritim dedi. **3.** et colon[i]s militum meorum consul quintum ex manibiis viritim millia nummum singula dedi; acceperunt id triumphale congiarium in colonis hominum circiter centum et viginti millia. **4.** consul tertium dec[i]mum sexagenos denarios plebei, quae tum frumentum publicum accipieba[t], dedi; ea millia hominum paullo plura quam ducenta fuerunt.

1. To the members of the Roman plebs I paid 300 sesterces each in accordance with my father's will, and in my own name I gave 400 sesterces out of the plunder from warfare when I was consul for the fifth time [29 BC], and also a second time in my tenth consulship [24 BC] out of my personal assets I paid out 400 sesterces each as a handout, and as consul for the eleventh time [23 BC] I bought up grain as a private individual and distributed twelve grain rations, and in my twelfth year of tribunician power [12 BC] I gave 400 sesterces each for a third time. These handouts of mine never reached fewer than 250,000 men. **2.** In my eighteenth year of tribunician power, as consul for the twelfth time [5 BC], I gave 60 *denarii* each to 320,000 of the urban plebs. **3.** And as consul for the fifth time [29 BC] I gave to the colonists who had been my soldiers 1,000 sesterces each out of plunder; about 120,000 men in the colonies received this handout to mark my triumphs. **4.** As consul for the thirteenth time [2 BC] I gave 60 *denarii* each to the commoners who at that time were in receipt of public grain; these were a few more than 200,000 men.

CHAPTER 15

1. δήμωι Ῥωμαίων κατ' ἄνδρα ἑβδομήκοντα π[έντ]ε δηνάρια ἑκάστωι ἠρίθμησα κατὰ διαθήκην τοῦ πατρός μου, καὶ τῶι ἐμῶι ὀνόματι ἐκ λαφύρων [π]ο[λ]έμου ἀνὰ ἑκατὸν δηνάρια πέμπτον ὕπατος ἔδωκα, πάλιν τε δέ[κατο]ν ὑπατεύων ἐκ τ[ῆ]ς ἐμῆς ὑπάρξεως ἀνὰ δηνάρια ἑκατὸν ἠρίθ[μ]ησα καὶ ἑνδέκατον ὕπατος δώδεκα σειτομετρήσεις ἐκ τοῦ ἐμοῦ βίου ἀπεμέτρησα καὶ δημαρχικῆς ἐξουσίας τὸ δωδέκατον ἑκατὸν δηνάρια κατ' ἄνδρα ἔδωκα· αἵτ[ι]νες ἐμαὶ ἐπιδόσεις οὐδέποτε ἧσσον ἧλθ[ο]ν ε[ἰ]ς ἄνδρας μυριάδων εἴκοσι πέντε. **2.** δημα[ρ]χικῆς ἐξουσίας ὀκτωκαιδέκατον ὕπατ[ος] δ[ωδέκατον] τριάκοντα τρισὶ μυριάσιν ὄχλου πολειτικ[οῦ ἑ]ξήκοντα δηνάρια κατ' ἄνδρα ἔδωκ[α. **3.** κα]ὶ ἀποίκοις στρατιωτῶν ἐμῶν πέμπτον ὕπατος ἐ[κ] λαφύρων κατὰ ἄνδρα ἀνὰ διακόσια πεντήκοντα δηνάρια ἔδ[ωκα]· ἔλαβον ταύτην τὴν δωρεὰν ἐν ταῖς ἀποικίαις ἀνθρώπων μυριάδες πλεῖον δώδε[κα. **4.** ὕ]πατος τ[ρι]σκαιδέκατον ἀνὰ ἑξήκοντα δηνάρια τῶι σειτομετρουμένωι δήμωι ἔδωκα· [οὗ]τος ἀριθμὸς πλείων εἴκοσι μυριάδων ὑπῆρχεν.

1. To the people of Rome individually I counted out 75 *denarii* each in accordance with the testament of my father, and in my name from the spoils of war as consul for the fifth time I gave 100 *denarii* each, and again in my tenth consulship I counted out 100 *denarii* each from my own property, and as consul for the eleventh time I measured out twelve corn rations from my own property, and in my twelfth tribunician power I gave 100 *denarii* per person. These free gifts of mine never reached fewer than 250,000 people. **2.** In my eighteenth tribunician power and as consul for the twelfth time I gave to 330,000 of the citizen populace 60 *denarii* per person. **3.** And as consul for the fifth time from the spoils I gave colonists who had been my soldiers each 250 *denarii* per person. More than 120,000 men in the colonies received this gift. **4.** As consul for the thirteenth time I gave to the people who receive the corn dole 60 *denarii* each. This number was more than 200,000.

CHAPTER 16

1. pecuniam [pr]o agris, quos in consulatu meo quarto et postea consulibus M(arco) Cr[a]sso et Cn(aeo) Lentulo Augure adsignavi militibus, solvi municipis; ea [s]u[mma s]estertium circiter sexsiens milliens fuit, quam [p]ro Italicis praedis numeravi, et ci[r]citer bis mill[ie]ns et sescentiens, quod pro agris provincialibus solvi. id primus et [s]olus omnium qui deduxerunt colonias militum in Italia aut in provincis ad memoriam aetatis meae feci. **2.** et postea, Ti(berio) Nerone et Cn(aeo) Pisone consulibus, itemque C(aio) Antistio et D(ecimo) Laelio co(n)s(ulibus) et C(aio) Calvisio et L(ucio) Pas<s>ieno consulibus et L(ucio) Le[nt]ulo et M(arco) Messalla consulibus et L(ucio) Caninio et Q(uinto) Fabricio co(n)s(ulibus), milit[i]bus, quos emeriteis stipendis in sua municipi[a dedux]i, praem[i]a numerato persolvi; quam in rem sestertium q[uater m]illiens cir[cite]r impendi.

1. I paid money to municipalities for the lands which in my fourth consulship [30 BC] and later in the consulship of Marcus Crassus and Gnaeus Lentulus Augur [14 BC] I allotted to soldiers; the total amount which I paid was about 600,000,000 sesterces for Italian estates, and about 260,000,000 for land in the provinces. I was the first and only one to have done this of all those who have settled colonies of soldiers in Italy or in the provinces, as far as people living in my era recall. **2.** And later, in the consulship of Tiberius Nero and Gnaeus Piso [7 BC] and again in the consulship of Gaius Antistius and Decimus Laelius [6 BC] and in the consulship of Gaius Calvisius and Lucius Pasienus [4 BC], and in the consulship of Lucius Lentulus and Marcus Messalla [3 BC], and in the consulship of Lucius Caninius and Quintus Fabricius [2 BC], I paid cash rewards in full to the soldiers whom I settled in their own municipalities once they had completed their terms of service; for this purpose I paid out about 400,000,000 sesterces.

CHAPTER 17

1. quater [pe]cunia mea iuvi aerarium ita ut sestertium milliens et quing[en]tie[n]s ad eos qui prae<e>rant aerario detulerim. **2.** et M(arco) Lepido et L(ucio) Ar[r]unt[i]o co(n)s(ulibus) in aerarium militare, quod ex consilio m[eo] co[ns]titutum est, ex [q]uo praemia darentur militibus qui vicena [aut plu]ra sti[pendi]a emeruissent, H̶S̶ milliens et septing[e]nti[ens ex pa]t[rim]onio [m]eo detuli.

1. Four times I assisted the treasury with my own money, transferring 150,000,000 sesterces to those who were in charge of the treasury. **2.** And in the consulship of Marcus Lepidus and Lucius Arruntius [AD 6], I transferred 170,000,000 sesterces out of my personal assets into the military treasury, which was established on my advice, and from which rewards were given to soldiers who had completed twenty or more years of service.

CHAPTER 16

1. χρήματα {ἃ} ἐν ὑπατείαι τετάρτηι ἐμῆ[ι] κα[ὶ] μετὰ ταῦτα ὑπάτοις Μάρκω[ι] Κράσσω[ι] καὶ Ναΐωι Λέντλω[ι] Αὔγουρι ταῖς πόλεσιν
ἠρίθμησα ὑπὲρ ἀγρῶν, οὓς ἐμέρισα τοῖς στρατ[ιώ]ταις· κεφαλαίου
ἐγένοντο ἐν Ἰτ[α]λία[ι] μὲν μύριαι π[εντακι]σχε[ίλιαι μυ]ριάδες, τ[ῶ]ν
[δὲ ἐ]παρχειτικῶν ἀγρῶν [μ]υ[ριάδες ἑξακισχείλ]ιαι πεν[τακό]σ[ιαι].
τοῦτο πρῶτος καὶ μόνος ἁπάντων ἐπόησα τῶν [κατα]γαγόντων
ἀποικίας στρατιωτῶν ἐν Ἰταλίαι ἢ ἐν ἐπαρχείαις μέχρι τῆς ἐμῆς ἡλικίας.
2. καὶ μετέπειτα Τιβερίωι Νέρωνι καὶ Ναΐωι Πείσωνι ὑπάτοις καὶ πάλιν
Γαΐωι Ἀνθεστίωι καὶ Δέκμωι Λαιλίωι ὑπάτοις καὶ Γαΐωι Καλουισίωι
καὶ Λευκίωι Πασσιήνωι [ὑ]πάτο[ι]ς καὶ Λευκίωι Λέντλωι καὶ Μάρκωι
Μεσσάλ[α]ι ὑπάτοις κ[α]ὶ Λευκίωι Κανινίωι καὶ Κοΐντωι Φαβρικίωι
ὑπάτοις στρατιώταις ἀπολυομένοις, οὓς κατήγαγον εἰς τὰς ἰδίας
πόλ[εις], φιλανθρώπου ὀνόματι ἔδωκα μυριάδας ἐγγὺς [μυρία]ς.

1. In my fourth consulship and after this in the consulship of Marcus
Crassus and Gnaeus Lentulus Augur I paid money to the cities for lands,
which I distributed to soldiers. Of the sum total there were in Italy
150,000,000, whilst for the provincial lands 65,000,000. I was the first
and only one to do this of all those establishing colonies of soldiers in
Italy or in the provinces up until my generation. 2. And afterwards in the
consulship of Tiberius Nero and Gnaeus Piso, and again in the consulship
of Gaius Anthestius and Decimus Laelius, and in the consulship of Gaius
Calvisius and Lucius Passienus, and in the consulship of Lucius Lentulus
and Marcus Messala, and in the consulship of Lucius Caninius and Quintus Fabricius, I gave to soldiers being discharged from service, whom I
settled in their own cities, nearly 100,000,000 in the name of a gratuity.

CHAPTER 17

1. τετρά[κ]ις χρήμασιν ἐμοῖς ὑπέλαβον τὸ αἰράριον, εἰς ὃ κατήνενκα
[<τρισ>χ]ειλίας [ἑπτ]ακοσίας πεντήκοντα μυριάδας. 2. καὶ Μάρκωι
Λε[πίδω]ι καὶ Λευκίωι Ἀρρουντίωι ὑπάτοις εἰς τὸ στρατιωτικὸν
αἰράριον, ὃ τῆι [ἐμῆι] γ[ν]ώ[μηι] κατέστη, ἵνα ἐξ αὐτοῦ αἱ δωρεαὶ
τοῖς ἀπολυομένοις στρατ[ι]ώταις δίδωνται, ο[ἳ εἴκ]οσι ἐνιαυτοὺς ἢ
πλείονας ἐστρατεύσαντο, μυριάδας τετρα[κ]ισχειλίας διακοσίας πεντήκοντα ἐκ τῆς ἐμῆς ὑπάρξεως κατήνενκα.

1. Four times I supported the treasury with my money, until I paid out
37,500,000. 2. Moreover in the consulship of Marcus Lepidus and Lucius
Arruntius I paid out 42,500,000 from my property to the military treasury,
which was set up at my suggestion, so that from it the bounties may be
given to soldiers being discharged from service, who served for twenty years
or more.

CHAPTER 18

[ab illo anno q]uo Cn(aeus) et P(ublius) Lentuli c[ons]ules fuerunt, cum deficerent [ve]ct[i]g[alia, tum] centum millibus h[omi]num tum pluribus multo frume[ntarios et n]umma[rio]s t[ributus ex horr]eo et patr[i]monio m[e]o edidi.

From the year in which Gnaeus and Publius Lentulus were consuls [18 BC], whenever public revenues were lacking, I gave out distributions of grain and money from my own granary and assets, sometimes to 100,000 men, sometimes to many more.

CHAPTER 19

1. curiam et continens ei chalcidicum templumque Apollinis in Palatio cum porticibus, aedem divi Iuli, lupercal, porticum ad circum Flaminium, quam sum appellari passus ex nomine eius qui priorem eodem in solo fecerat, Octaviam, pulvinar ad circum maximum, **2** aedes in Capitolio Iovis Feretri et Iovis Tonantis, aedem Quirini, aedes Minervae et Iunonis Reginae et Iovis Libertatis in Aventino, aedem Larum in summa sacra via, aedem deum Penatium in Velia, aedem Iuventatis, aedem Matris Magnae in Palatio feci.

1. I built the senate house and the *chalcidicum* adjacent to it, and the temple of Apollo on the Palatine with its porticoes, the temple of deified Julius, the *lupercal,* the portico near the Flaminian Circus, which I allowed to be called Octavian after the name of the man who had built an earlier one on the same foundation, the *pulvinar* at the *Circus Maximus,* **2.** the temples on the Capitol of Jupiter Feretrius and of Jupiter the Thunderer, the temple of Quirinus, the temples of Minerva and of Queen Juno and of Jupiter Libertas on the Aventine, the temple of the *Lares* at the top of the Sacred Way, the temple of the *Penates* on the Velia, the temple of Youth and the temple of the Great Mother on the Palatine.

CHAPTER 18

[ἀπ᾽ ἐκ]είνου τ[ο]ῦ ἐνιαυτοῦ, ἐξ οὗ Νάϊος καὶ Πόπλιος Λέντλοι ὕπατοι ἐγένοντο, ὅτε ὑπέλειπον αἱ δημόσιαι πρόσοδοι, ἄλλοτε μὲν δέκα
μυριάσιν, ἄλ[λοτε] δὲ πλείοσιν σειτικὰς καὶ ἀργυρικὰς συντάξεις ἐκ τῆς
ἐμῆς ὑπάρξεως ἔδωκα.

From that year, from when Gnaeus and Publius Lentulus were consuls,
when public revenues were falling short, I gave payments in the form of
corn and cash from my property sometimes to 100,000, and at other times
to more.

CHAPTER 19

1. βουλευτήριον καὶ τὸ πλησίον αὐτῶι Χαλκιδικόν, ναόν τε Ἀπόλλωνος ἐν Παλατίωι σὺν στοαῖς, ναὸν θεοῦ Ἰουλίου, Πανὸς ἱερόν,
στοὰν πρὸς ἱπποδρόμωι τῶι προσαγορευομένωι Φλαμινίωι, ἣν
εἴασα προσαγορεύεσθαι ἐξ ὀνόματος ἐκείνου Ὀκταουΐαν, ὃς πρῶτος
αὐτὴν ἀνέστησεν, ναὸν πρὸς τῶι μεγάλωι ἱπποδρόμωι, 2. ναοὺς ἐν
Καπιτωλίωι Διὸς Τροπαιοφόρου καὶ Διὸς Βροντησίου, ναὸν Κυρείνου, ναοὺς Ἀθηνᾶς καὶ Ἥρας Βασιλίδος καὶ Διὸς Ἐλευθερίου ἐν Ἀουεν-
τίνωι, Ἡρώων πρὸς τῆι ἱερᾶι ὁδῶι, Θεῶν Κατοικιδίων ἐν Οὐελίαι, ναὸν
Νεότητος, ναὸν Μητρὸς Θεῶν ἐν Παλατίωι ἐπόησα.

1. I built the senate house and next to it the *chalcidicon*, and the temple
of Apollo on the Palatine with its porticoes, the temple of the god Iulius,
the shrine of Pan, the portico near the racecourse called Flaminian, which
I allowed to be called Octavian after the name of that man who first set it
up, the temple near the great racecourse, 2. temples on the Capitol of Zeus
Trophy-Bearer and of Zeus Thunderer, the temple of Quirinus, temples of
Athena and of Queen Hera and of Zeus Liberator on the Aventine, of the
Heroes next to the Sacred Way, of the household gods on the Velia, the
temple of Youth, temple of the Mother of the gods on the Palatine.

CHAPTER 20

1. Capitolium et Pompeium theatrum utrumque opus impensa grandi refeci sine ulla inscriptione nominis mei. **2.** rivos aquarum compluribus locis vetustate labentes refeci, et aquam quae Marcia appellatur duplicavi fonte novo in rivum eius inmisso. **3.** forum Iulium et basilicam quae fuit inter aedem Castoris et aedem Saturni, coepta profligataque opera a patre meo, perfeci, et eandem basilicam consumptam incendio, ampliato eius solo, sub titulo nominis filiorum m[eorum i]ncohavi, et, si vivus non perfecissem, perfici ab heredibus [meis ius]si. **4.** duo et octoginta templa deum in urbe consul sex[tu]m ex [auctori]tate senatus refeci, nullo praetermisso quod e[o] tempore [refici debeba]t. **5.** consul septimum viam Flaminiam a[b urbe] Ari[minum munivi pontes]que omnes praeter Mulvium et Minucium.

1. I restored the Capitoline temple and theatre of Pompey, incurring great expense for both buildings, without inscribing my name anywhere on them. **2.** I restored aqueduct channels in several places which were collapsing through old age, and I doubled the capacity of the aqueduct which is called Marcian by introducing a new spring into its channel. **3.** I completed the Julian forum and the basilica which was between the temple of Castor and the temple of Saturn, building projects which had been started and almost finished by my father, and I started work on the same basilica under an inscription in the name of my sons, after it had been destroyed by fire, expanded its site, and, if I do not complete it in my lifetime, I have ordered it to be completed by my heirs. **4.** I restored eighty-two temples of the gods in the city as consul for the sixth time [28 BC], in accordance with a resolution of the senate, and I neglected none which needed repair at this time. **5.** In my seventh consulship [27 BC] I paved the Flaminian Way from the city to Ariminum and all the bridges expect the Mulvian and Minucian.

CHAPTER 20

1. Καπιτώλιον καὶ τὸ Πομπηΐου θέατρον ἑκάτερον τὸ ἔργον ἀναλώμασιν μεγίστοις ἐπεσκεύασα ἄνευ ἐπιγραφῆς τοῦ ἐμοῦ ὀνόματος. **2.** ἀγωγοὺς ὑδάτω[ν ἐν πλεί]στοις τόποις τῆι παλαιότητι ὀλισθάνοντας ἐπεσκεύασα καὶ ὕδωρ τὸ καλούμενον Μάρ⌐κ⌐ιον ἐδίπλωσα πηγὴν νέαν εἰς τὸ ῥεῖθρον [αὐτοῦ ἐποχετεύσ]ας. **3.** ἀγορὰν Ἰουλίαν καὶ βασιλικήν, ἥτις ἦν μετα[ξὺ τ]οῦ τε ναοῦ τῶν Διοσκό[ρω]ν καὶ <τοῦ> Κρόνου προκαταβεβλημένα ἔργα ὑπὸ τοῦ [πατρός μου ἐτελείωσα κ]αὶ τὴν αὐτὴν βασιλικὴν [κατακαυθεῖσαν ἐν αὐξηθέντι] ἐδάφει αὐτῆς ἐξ ἐπιγραφῆς ὀνόματος τῶν ἐμῶν υἱῶν ὑπ[ηρξάμη]ν, καὶ εἰ μὴ αὐτὸς τετελειώκ[ο]ι[μι, τ]ελε[ι]ω[θῆναι ὑπὸ] τῶν ἐμῶν κληρονόμων ἐπέταξα. **4.** δ[ύ]ο [καὶ ὀγδο]ήκοντα ναοὺς ἐν τῆι πόλ[ει ἕκτ]ον ὕπ[ατος δόγμα]τι συνκ[λ]ήτου ἐπεσκεύασ[α ο]ὐ]δένα π[ε]ριλ[ιπών, ὃς] ἐκείνωι τῶι χρόνωι ἐπισκευῆς ἐδεῖτο. **5.** [ὕ]πα[τος ἕ]βδ[ο]μον ὁδὸν Φ[λαμινίαν ἀπὸ] Ῥώμης εἰς Ἀρίμινον γ[εφ]ύρας τε τὰς ἐν αὐτῆι πάσας ἔξω δυεῖν τῶν μὴ ἐπ[ι]δεομένων ἐπ[ι]σκευῆς ἐπόησα.

1. I repaired the Capitolium and theatre of Pompey, both buildings at the highest costs, without inscribing my name. **2.** I repaired aqueducts in very many places that were falling down through old age and the water called Marcian I doubled, having conducted a new source into its channel. **3.** I completed the Julian forum and the basilica, which was between the temple of the Dioscori and that of Cronos, buildings whose foundations were laid by my father, and began the same basilica which had been burnt down on an augmented site, with an inscription in the name of my sons, and if I should not myself have completed it, I ordered it to be completed by my heirs. **4.** I repaired eighty-two temples in the city in my sixth consulship by decree of the senate, leaving none that needed repair at that time. **5.** In my seventh consulship I constructed the Flaminian Way from Rome to Ariminum and all the bridges on it except for two that were not in need of repair.

CHAPTER 21

1. in privato solo Martis Ultoris templum [f]orumque Augustum [ex ma]n[i]biis feci. theatrum ad aedem Apollinis in solo magna ex parte a p[r]i[v]atis empto feci, quod sub nomine M(arci) Marcell[i] generi mei esset. **2.** don[a e]x manibiis in Capitolio et in aede divi Iu[l]i et in aede Apollinis et in aede Vestae et in templo Martis Ultoris consacravi, quae mihi constiterunt HS circiter milliens. **3.** auri coronari pondo triginta et quinque millia municipiis et colonis Italiae conferentibus ad triumpho[s] meos quintum consul remisi, et postea, quotienscumque imperator a[ppe]llatus sum, aurum coronarium non accepi, decernentibus municipii[s] et colonis aequ[e] benigne a⌈t⌉que antea decreverant.

1. On private ground I built from plunder the temple of Mars the Avenger and the Augustan forum. I built the theatre which was in the name of my son-in-law Marcus Marcellus near the temple of Apollo on ground mostly bought from private individuals. **2.** I consecrated gifts out of plunder in the Capitoline temple, and in the temple of the deified Julius, and in the temple of Apollo, and in the temple of Vesta, and in the temple of Mars the Avenger, which cost me about 100,000,000 sesterces. **3.** I remitted 35,000 pounds of crown-gold which the municipalities and colonies of Italy contributed for my triumphs in my fifth consulship [29 BC], and later, every time that I was hailed as victorious general, I refused crown-gold even though the municipalities and colonies decreed it just as generously as they had done before.

CHAPTER 21

1. ἐν ἰδιωτικῶι ἐδάφει <ναὸν> Ἄρεως Ἀμύντορος ἀγοράν τε Σεβαστὴν
ἐκ λαφύρων ἐπόησα. θέατρον πρὸς τῶι Ἀπόλλωνος ναῶι ἐπὶ ἐδάφους
ἐκ πλείστου μέρους ἀγορασθέντος ἀνήγειρα ἐπὶ ὀνόματι Μαρκέλλου
τοῦ γαμβροῦ μου. **2.** ἀναθέματα ἐκ λαφύρων ἐν Καπιτωλίωι καὶ
ναῶι Ἰουλίωι καὶ ναῶι Ἀπόλλωνος καὶ Ἑστίας καὶ Ἄ[ρεω]ς ἀφιέρ-
ωσα, ἃ ἐμοὶ κατέστη ἐγγὺς μυριάδω[ν δι]σχε[ι]λίων πεντακ[οσίων].
3. εἰς χρυσοῦν στέφανον λειτρῶν τρισ[μυρίων] πεντακισχειλίων κατα-
φερούσαις ταῖς ἐν Ἰταλίαι πολιτείαις καὶ ἀποικίαις συνεχώρη[σ]α
τὸ [πέμ]πτον ὑπατεύων καὶ ὕστερον, ὁσάκις αὐτοκράτωρ προσηγορεύθην, τὰς εἰς τὸν στέφανον ἐπαγγελίας οὐκ ἔλαβον ψηφιζομένων
τῶν π[ολιτει]ῶν καὶ ἀποικιῶν μετὰ τῆς αὐτῆς προθυμίας ὡς τὸ α[ὐτὸ
πρὶν ἐψηφίσαντο].

1. On private ground I built from spoils of war the temple of Ares the
Avenger and the Augustan forum. I raised a theatre near the temple of
Apollo on ground that had been for the most part bought, in the name
of Marcellus my son-in-law. **2.** I consecrated dedications from spoils in
the Capitol and temple of Julius and temple of Apollo and of Hestia and
of Ares, which cost me nearly 2,500,000. **3.** In my fifth consulship I gave
remission to citizen-towns and colonies in Italy paying 35,000 pounds of
crown-gold, and later, whenever I was hailed as victorious general I did
not take the offers of a crown, even though the citizen-towns and colonies
voted for it with the same eagerness as previously.

CHAPTER 22

1. ter munus gladiatorium dedi meo nomine et quinquiens filiorum meorum aut n[e]potum nomine; quibus muneribus depugnaverunt hominum
ci[rc]iter decem millia. bis athletarum undique accitorum spectaculu[m]
p[o]pulo pra[ebui me]o nomine et tertium nepo[tis] mei nomine. **2.** ludos
feci m[eo no]m[ine] quater, aliorum autem m[agist]ratuum vicem ter et
viciens. [pr]o conlegio XVvirorum magis[ter con]legii collega M(arco)
Agrippa lud[os s]aeclares C(aio) Furnio C(aio) Silano co(n)s(ulibus) [feci.
c]onsul XIII ludos Mar[tia]les pr[imus fec]i, quos p[ost i]d tempus deinceps
ins[equen]ti[bus] annis [s(enatus) c(onsulto) et lege fe]cerunt [co]n[s]ules.
3. [ven]ation[es] best[ia]rum Africanarum meo nomine aut filio[ru]m meorum et nepotum in ci[r]co aut in foro aut in amphitheatris popul[o d]edi
sexiens et viciens, quibus confecta sunt bestiarum circiter tria m[ill]ia et
quingentae.

1. Three times I gave gladiatorial games in my own name and five times
in the name of my sons or grandsons; about 10,000 men fought in the
arena in these shows. Twice in my own name I presented to the people a
spectacle of athletes summoned from every place and three times in the
name of my grandson. **2.** I provided games in my own name four times,
and also on behalf of other magistrates twenty-three times. On behalf of
the college of the Fifteen as master of the college with Marcus Agrippa
as my colleague I provided centennial games in the consulship of Gaius
Furnius and Gaius Silanus [17 BC]. In my thirteenth consulship [2 BC], I
was the first to provide games of Mars, which after this time from then
on in succeeding years the consuls provided in accordance with senatorial
decree and by law. **3.** I gave to the people hunting shows of African wild
beasts in my own name or in the name of my sons and grandsons in the
circus or forum or amphitheatre twenty-six times; in these around 3,500
beasts were killed.

CHAPTER 22

1. τ[ρὶ]ς μονομαχίας ἔδωκα τῶι ἐμῶι ὀνόματι καὶ πεν[τάκις τῶι υἱῶν μου ἢ] υἱ[ἱ]ωνῶν· ἐν αἷς μονομαχίαις ἐπύκτευσαν ὡς μύρι[ο]ι. δὶς ἀθλ-ητῶ[ν] παντ[όθεν] μετακεκλημένων τὴν τοῦ ἀγῶνος θέαν τῶι δήμ[ωι π]αρέσχον τ[ῶι ἐ]μῶι ὀνόματι καὶ τρίτον τοῦ ἐμοῦ υἱωνοῦ. **2.** θέας ἐποίησα δι᾽ ἐμοῦ τετράκ[ις], διὰ δὲ τῶν ἄλλων ἀρχῶν ἐν μέρει τρὶς καὶ εἰκοσάκις. ὑπὲρ τῶν δεκαπέντε ἀνδ[ρ]ῶν, ἔχων συνάρχοντα Μᾶρκον Ἀγρίππαν, θέας τὰς διὰ ἑκατὸν ἐτῶν γεινομένας ὀν[ομαζομένα]ς σαικ-λάρεις ἐπόησα Γαΐωι Φουρνίωι καὶ Γαΐωι Σε[ι]λανῶι ὑπάτοις. ὕπατος τρισκαιδέκατον θέας Ἄρει πρῶτος ἐπόησα, ἃς μετ᾽ ἐκεῖνο[ν χ]ρόνον ἐξῆς [τοῖς μ]ετέπειτα ἐνιαυτοῖς δόγματι συνκλήτου καὶ νόμωι ἐπόη-σαν οἱ ὕπα[τοι. **3.** θηρομαχίας τῶι δήμωι τῶν] ἐκ Λιβύης θηρίων ἐμῶι ὀνόματι ἢ υἱῶν ἢ υἱων[ῶν ἐν τῶι ἱπποδρόμωι ἢ ἐν τῆι ἀγορᾶι ἢ ἐν τοῖς] ἀμφιθεάτροις ἔδωκα ἑξάκις καὶ εἰκοσάκις, ἐν [αἷς κατεσφάγη θηρία ἐνγὺς τρισχείλια] καὶ πεντακόσια.

1. Three times I gave gladiatorial shows in my name and five times in the names of my sons or grandsons. In these gladiatorial shows about 10,000 men fought. Twice I presented to the people in my name the spectacle of a contest of athletes summoned from every side and for a third time in the name of my grandson. **2.** I put on spectacles by myself four times, and by other magistrates in their turn twenty-three times. On behalf of the Fifteen, with Marcus Agrippa as colleague, I put on the spectacles that occur after 100 years called *saeclares*, in the consulship of Gaius Furnius and Gaius Silanus. As consul for the thirteenth time I was the first to put on spectacles for Ares, which after that time thereafter in the years afterwards the consuls put on in accordance with a decree of the senate and a law. **3.** I gave beast hunts to the people of wild animals from Libya in my name or that of my sons and grandsons in the racecourse or in the forum or in the amphitheatre twenty-six times, during which nearly 3,500 animals were slaughtered.

CHAPTER 23

navalis proeli spectaculum populo de[di tr]ans Tiberim, in quo loco nunc
nemus est Caesarum, cavato [s]olo in longitudinem mille et octingentos
pedes, in latitudine[m mille] e[t] ducent⌈os⌉; in quo triginta rostratae naves
triremes a[ut birem]es, plures autem minores inter se conflixerunt; q[uibu]s
in classibus pugnaverunt praeter remiges millia ho[minum tr]ia circiter.

I gave to the people the spectacle of a naval battle, in the place on the other
side of the Tiber which is now the grove of the Caesars, after a site 1,800 feet
in length, 1,200 in width had been excavated; on it thirty warships, with
three or two banks of oars, and even more of smaller size, fought against
each other; in these fleets about 3,000 men fought, besides the rowers.

CHAPTER 24

1. in templis omnium civitatium prov[inci]ae Asiae victor ornamenta reposui quae spoliatis tem[plis is] cum quo bellum gesseram privatim possederat.
2. statuae [mea]e pedestres et equestres et in quadrigeis argenteae steterunt
in urbe XXC circiter, quas ipse sustuli, exque ea pecunia dona aurea in aede
Apollinis meo nomine et illorum qui mihi statuarum honorem habuerunt
posui.

1. As victor, I replaced in the temples of all the cities in the province of
Asia the ornaments which the man against whom I had waged war had
held in his private possession after plundering the temples. **2.** The eighty
or so statues made of silver, depicting me on foot, on horseback, and in a
four-horse chariot, which stood in the city, I myself removed, and from the
money realized I placed golden gifts in the temple of Apollo in my name
and in the name of those who had honoured me with the statues.

CHAPTER 23

ναυμαχίας θέαν τῶι δήμ[ωι ἔδω]κα π[έρ]αν τοῦ Τι[βέριδος, ἐν ὧι
τό]πω[ι] νῦν ἐστιν ἄλσος Καισάρων, ἐκκεχωσμ[ένης τῆς γῆς] ε[ἰ]ς
μῆκ[ο]ς χειλίων ὀκτακοσίων ποδῶν, ἐπὶ πλάτος χιλίων διακο[σ]ίων· ἐν
ἧι τριάκο[ν]τα ναῦς ἔμβολα ἔχουσαι τριήρεις ἢ δίκροτοι, αἱ δέ ἥσσονες
πλείους ἐναυμάχησαν. ἐν τ[ούτω]ι τῶι στόλωι ἠγωνίσαντο ἔξω τῶν
ἐρετῶν πρόσπου ἄνδρες τρ[ι]σχ[ε]ί[λ]ιοι.

I gave to the people a spectacle of a sea battle on the other side of the
Tiber, in the place where the Caesars' grove now is, once land had been
removed, 1,800 feet in length, 1,200 in breadth. On it thirty ships with
rams – triremes or two-banked ships – and many smaller boats did battle.
In this fleet fought about 3,000 men, discounting the rowers.

CHAPTER 24

1. [εἰς ν]αοὺς πασῶν πόλεων τῆς Ἀσίας νεικήσας τὰ ἀναθέ[ματα
ἀπ]οκατέστησα, [ἃ] κατεσχήκει ἱεροσυλήσας ὁ ὑπ' ἐμοῦ καταγωνισθεὶς
πολέ[μιος]. 2. ἀνδριάντες πεζοὶ καὶ ἐφιππποί μου καὶ ἐφ' ἅρμασιν ἀργυροῖ
εἱστήκεισαν ἐν τῆι πόλει ἐγγὺς ὀγδοήκοντα, οὓς αὐτὸς ἦρα, ἐκ τούτου τε τοῦ χρήματος ἀναθέματα χρυσᾶ ἐν τῶι ναῶ[ι] τοῦ Ἀπόλλωνος
τῶι τε ἐμῶι ὀνόματι καὶ ἐκείνων, οἵτινές με [τ]ούτοις τοῖς ἀνδριᾶσιν
ἐτείμησαν, ἀνέθηκα.

1. After my victory I reinstated into temples of all cities in Asia the dedications which the enemy against whom I had prevailed had plundered
and was holding in his possession. 2. Nearly eighty silver pedestrian and
equestrian statues of me and statues in chariots had been set up in the city,
which I myself removed, and from this money I set up golden dedications
in the temple of Apollo both in my name and in the name of those who
honoured me with these statues.

CHAPTER 25

1. mare pacavi a praedonibus. eo bello servorum qui fugerant a dominis suis et arma contra rem publicam ceperant triginta fere millia capta dominis ad supplicium sumendum tradidi. **2.** iuravit in mea verba tota Italia sponte sua et me bel[li] quo vici ad Actium ducem depoposcit. iuraverunt in eadem ver[ba provi]nciae Galliae, Hispaniae, Africa, Sicilia, Sardinia. **3.** qui sub [signis meis tum] militaverint, fuerunt senatores plures quam ~~DCC~~, in ii[s qui vel antea vel pos]tea consules facti sunt ad eum diem quo scripta su[nt haec LXXXIII, sacerdo]tes cir[c]iter CLXX.

1. I brought the sea under control from pirates. In this war I handed back to their masters for punishment almost 30,000 captured slaves who had run away from their masters and taken up arms against the state. **2.** The whole of Italy of its own accord swore an oath of allegiance to me and demanded me as its commander for the war in which I conquered at Actium. The Gallic and Spanish provinces, Africa, Sicily, and Sardinia swore the same oath of allegiance. **3.** There were more than 700 senators who served under my standards at that time, among whom there were 83 who either before or afterwards up until the day on which these words were written were made consuls, and about 170 priests.

CHAPTER 25

1. θάλασσα[ν] πειρατευομένην ὑπὸ ἀποστατῶν δούλων [εἰ]ρήνευσα· ἐξ ὧν τρεῖς που μυριάδας τοῖς δε[σπόται]ς εἰς κόλασιν παρέδωκα. **2.** ὤμοσεν εἰς τοὺς ἐμοὺς λόγους ἅπασα ἡ Ἰταλία ἑκοῦσα κἀ[μὲ πολέμου], ὧι ἐπ᾽ Ἀκτίωι ἐνείκησα, ἡγεμόνα ἐξη[τήσατο· ὤ]μοσαν εἰς τοὺς [αὐτοὺ]ς λόγους ἐπαρχεῖαι Γαλατία Ἰσπανία Λιβύη Σι[κελία Σαρ]δώ. **3.** οἱ ὑπ᾽ ἐμ[αῖς σημέαις] τότε στρατευ[σάμε]νοι ἦσαν συνκλητικοὶ πλε[ίους ἑπτ]α[κοσί]ων· ἐν [αὐτοῖς οἳ ἢ πρότερον ἢ μετέπει]τα ἐγένοντο ὕπατοι ἄχρι ἐ[κ]ε[ί]ν[ης τῆς ἡ]μέ[ρας ἐν ἧι ταῦτα γέγραπτα]ι ὀ[γδοή]κοντα τρεῖς, ἱερεῖς πρόσπου ἑκατὸν ἑβδομή[κ]οντα.

1. I brought peace to a sea that was being subjected to piracy by runaway slaves; out of these I handed over about 30,000 to their owners for punishment. **2.** The whole of Italy swore allegiance to my words willingly and demanded me as its leader for the war in which I was victorious at Actium; the provinces of Gaul, Hispania, Libya, Sicily, and Sardinia swore allegiance to the same words. **3.** The senators who served in the army under my standards at that time were more than 700; of these, those who previously or afterwards were made consuls, up until the day on which this was written – 83; priests about 170.

CHAPTER 26

1. omnium provinc[iarum populi Romani,] quibus finitimae fuerunt gentes quae non p[arerent imperio nos]tro, fines auxi. **2.** Gallias et Hispanias provincias, i[tem Germaniam, qua inclu]dit Oceanus a Gadibus ad ostium Albis flumin[is, pacavi. **3.** Alpes a re]gione ea quae proxima est Hadri-ano mari [ad Tuscum pacari fec]i nulli genti bello per iniuriam inlato. **4.** cla[ssis m]ea p[er Oceanum] ab ostio Rheni ad solis orientis regionem usque ad fi[nes Cimbroru]m navigavit, quo neque terra neque mari quisquam Romanus ante id tempus adit, Cimbrique et Charydes et Sem-nones et eiusdem tractus alii Germanorum popu[l]i per legatos amicitiam meam et populi Romani petierunt. **5.** meo iussu et auspicio ducti sunt [duo] exercitus eodem fere tempore in Aethiopiam et in Ar[a]biam quae appel[latur] Eudaemon, [magn]aeque hos[t]ium gentis utr[iu]sque cop[iae] caesae sunt in acie et [c]om[plur]a oppida capta. in Aethiopiam usque ad oppidum Nabata pervent[um] est, cui proxima est Meroe. in Arabiam usque in fines Sabaeorum pro[cess]it exercitus ad oppidum Mariba.

1. I extended the territory of all those provinces of the Roman people which had neighbouring peoples who were not subject to our authority. **2.** I brought under control the Gallic and Spanish provinces, and similarly Germany, where Ocean forms a boundary from Cadiz to the mouth of the River Elbe. **3.** I brought the Alps under control from the region which is nearest to the Adriatic Sea as far as the Tyrrhenian Sea, but attacked no people unjustly. **4.** My fleet navigated through Ocean from the mouth of the Rhine to the region of the rising sun as far as the territory of the Cimbri; no Roman before this time has ever approached this area by either land or sea, and the Cimbri and Charydes and Semnones and other German peoples of the same region sent envoys to request my friendship and that of the Roman people. **5.** Under my command and auspices two armies were led at almost the same time into Aethiopia and the Arabia which is called Fortunate, and substantial enemy forces of both peoples were slaughtered in battle and many towns captured. The army reached into Aethiopia as far as the town of Nabata, to which Meroe is nearest. The army advanced into Arabia as far as the territory of the Sabaei to the town of Mariba.

CHAPTER 26

1. πασῶν ἐπαρχειῶν δήμο[υ Ῥω]μαίων, αἷς ὅμορα ἦν ἔθνη τὰ μὴ ὑποτασσ[όμ]ενα τῆι ἡμετέραι ἡγεμονία<ι> τοὺς ὅρους ἐπεύξ[ησ]α. 2. Γαλατίας καὶ Ἰσπανίας ὁμοίως δὲ καὶ Γερμανίαν καθὼς Ὠκεανὸς περικλείει ἀπ[ὸ] Γαδε[ίρ]ων μέχρι στόματος Ἄλβιος ποταμο[ῦ ἐν] εἰρήνη<ι> κατέστησα. 3. Ἄλπης ἀπὸ κλίματος τοῦ πλησίον Εἰονίου κόλπου μέχρι Τυρρηνικῆς θαλάσσης εἰρηνεύεσθαι πεπόηκα οὐδενὶ ἔθνει ἀδίκως ἐπενεχθέντος πολέμου. 4. στόλος ἐμὸς διὰ Ὠκεανοῦ ἀπὸ στόματος Ῥήνου ὡς πρὸς ἀνατολὰς μέχρι ἔθνους Κίμβρων διέπλευσεν, οὗ οὔτε κατὰ γῆν οὔτε κατὰ θάλασσαν Ῥωμαίων τις πρὸ τούτου τοῦ χρόνου προσῆλθεν· καὶ Κίμβροι καὶ Χά⌈ρ⌉υ⌈δ⌉ες καὶ Σέμνονες ἄλλα τε πολλὰ ἔθνη Γερμανῶν διὰ πρεσβειῶν τὴν ἐμὴν φιλίαν καὶ τὴν δήμου Ῥωμαίων ἠ<ι>τήσαντο. 5. ἐμῆι ἐπιταγῆι καὶ οἰωνοῖς αἰσίοις δύο στρατεύματα ἐπέβη Αἰθιοπίαι καὶ Ἀραβίαι τῆι εὐδαίμονι καλουμένηι μεγάλας τε τῶν πολεμίων δυνάμεις κατέκοψεν ἐν παρατάξει καὶ πλείστας πόλεις δοριαλώτους ἔλαβεν καὶ προέβη ἐν Αἰθιοπίαι μέχρι πόλεως Ναβάτης ἥτις ἐστὶν ἔγγιστα Μερόη<ι>, ἐν Ἀραβίαι δὲ μέχρι πόλεως Μαρίβας.

1. I enlarged the boundaries of all provinces of the Roman people, which had as neighbours peoples that were not subject to our rule. 2. I settled peacefully Gauls and Spains, and likewise also Germania, an area enclosed by Ocean from Cadiz up to the mouth of the river Elbe. 3. I made peaceful the Alps from the region near the Ionian bay as far as the Tyrrhenian sea, but made war on no tribe unjustly. 4. My fleet sailed through Ocean from the mouth of the Rhine eastwards as far as the tribes of Cimbri, where neither by land nor by sea has any Roman before this time gone; and Cimbri and Charydes and Semnones and many other tribes of Germans sought through embassies my friendship and that of the Roman people. 5. Under my command and with auspicious omens two armies attacked Aethiopia and Arabia called Fortunate, and they cut in pieces great forces of the enemies in pitched battle and they captured very many cities and advanced in Aethiopia as far as the city of Nabata which is very near to Meroe, and in Arabia as far as the city Mariba.

CHAPTER 27

1. Aegyptum imperio populi [Ro]mani adieci. **2.** Armeniam maiorem interfecto rege eius Artaxe, c[u]m possem facere provinciam, malui maiorum nostrorum exemplo regn[u]m id Tigrani, regis Artavasdis filio, nepoti autem Tigranis regis, per T[i(berium) Ne]ronem trade[r]e, qui tum mihi privignus erat. et eandem gentem postea d[e]sciscentem et rebellantem domit[a]m per Gaium filium meum regi Ariobarzani, regis Medorum Artaba[zi] filio, regendam tradidi, et post eius mortem filio eius, Artavasdi; quo [i]nterfecto Ti[gra]ne<m>, qui erat ex regio genere Armeniorum oriundus, in id regnum misi. **3.** provincias omnis, quae trans Hadrianum mare vergunt ad orien[te]m Cyrenasque, iam ex parte magna regibus eas possidentibus, et antea Siciliam et Sardiniam occupatas bello servili reciperavi.

1. I added Egypt to the empire of the Roman people. **2.** Although I could have made Greater Armenia a province, on the assassination of Artaxes its king, I preferred, in accordance with the example set by our ancestors, to hand this kingdom over to Tigranes, son of King Artavasdes, and also grandson of King Tigranes, through the agency of Tiberius Nero, who at the time was my stepson. And when the same people later revolted and rebelled, they were subdued through the agency of Gaius, my son, and I handed them over to King Ariobarzanes, son of Artabazus King of the Medes, for him to rule, and after his death to his son, Artavasdes; on his assassination, I sent into this kingdom Tigranes, who was descended from the Armenian royal family. **3.** I regained all the provinces across the Adriatic Sea which slope down towards the east and Cyrene, which were at that stage mostly in the hands of kings, and previously Sicily and Sardinia which had been occupied at the time of the slave war.

CHAPTER 28

1. colonias in Africa, Sicilia, [M]acedonia, utraque Hispania, Achai[a], Asia, S[y]ria, Gallia Narbonensi, Pi[si]dia militum deduxi. **2.** Italia autem XXVIII colonias, quae vivo me celeberrimae et frequentissimae fuerunt, me[a auctoritate] deductas habet.

1. I settled colonies of soldiers in Africa, Sicily, Macedonia, both Spains, Achaea, Asia, Syria, Gallia Narbonensis, Pisidia. **2.** Moreover Italy has twenty-eight colonies settled under my authority, which have been in my lifetime very busy and densely populated.

CHAPTER 27

1. Αἴγυπτον δήμου Ῥωμαίων ἡγεμονίαι προσέθηκα. **2.** Ἀρμενίαν τὴν μ[εί]ζονα ἀναιρεθέντος τοῦ βασιλέως δυνάμενος ἐπαρχείαν ποῆσαι μᾶλλον ἐβουλήθην κατὰ τὰ πάτρια ἡμῶν ἔθη βασιλείαν Τιγράνηι Ἀρταουάσδου υἱῶι, υἱωνῶι δὲ Τιγράνου βασιλέως δ[οῦ]ν[α]ι διὰ Τιβερίου Νέρωνος, ὃς τότε μου πρόγονος ἦν· καὶ τὸ αὐτὸ ἔθνος ἀφιστάμενον καὶ ἀναπολεμοῦν δαμασθὲν ὑπὸ Γαΐου τοῦ υἱοῦ μου βασιλεῖ Ἀριοβαρζάνει, βασιλέως Μήδων Ἀρταβάζου υἱῶι, παρέδ-ωκα, καὶ μετὰ τὸν ἐκείνου θάνατον τῶι υἱῶι αὐτοῦ Ἀρταουάσδη<ι>· οὗ ἀναιρεθέντος Τιγράνην, ὃς ἦν ἐκ γένους Ἀρμενίου βασιλικοῦ, εἰς τὴν βασιλείαν ἔπεμψα. **3.** ἐπαρχείας ἁπάσας, ὅσαι πέραν τοῦ Εἰονίου κόλπου διατείνουσι πρὸς ἀνατολάς, καὶ Κυρήνην ἐκ μείσζονος μέρους ὑπὸ βασιλέων κατεσχημένας καὶ ἔμπροσθεν Σικελίαν καὶ Σαρδὼ{ι} προκατειλημ<μ>ένας πολέμωι δουλικῶι ἀνέλαβον.

1. I handed Egypt over to the rule of the Roman people. **2.** After the king had been killed, even though I could have made Greater Armenia a province, I preferred according to our ancestral customs to give a kingdom to Tigranes, son of Artavasdes, and grandson of King Tigranes, through Tiberius Nero, who at that time was my stepson; and when the same people were revolting and renewing war, but were subdued by Gaius my son, I handed it over to King Ariobarzanes, son of Artabazes King of the Medes, and after his death to his son Artavasdes. After he was killed I sent Tigranes, who was descended from an Armenian royal family, to the kingdom. **3.** I recovered all provinces, which extend eastwards beyond the Ionian bay, and Cyrene, which had been occupied for the greater part by kings, and Sicily and Sardinia which had previously been seized in the slave war.

CHAPTER 28

1. ἀποικίας ἐν Λιβύηι, Σικελίαι, Μακεδονίαι, ἐν ἑκατέρα<ι> τ⌐ῆι⌐ Ἰσπανίαι, Ἀχαίαι, Ἀσίαι, Συρία<ι> Γαλατίαι τῆι περὶ Νάρβωνα, Πισιδίαι στρατιωτῶν κατήγαγον. **2.** Ἰταλία δὲ εἴκοσι ὀκτὼ ἀποικίας ἔχει ὑπ᾿ ἐμοῦ καταχθείσας, αἳ ἐμοῦ περιόντος πληθύουσαι ἐτύγχανον.

1. I established colonies of soldiers in Libya, Sicily, Macedonia, in both Spains, Achaea, Asia, Syria, Gaul around Narbo, and Pisidia. **2.** Moreover, Italy has twenty-eight colonies established by me, which succeeded in being populous in my lifetime.

CHAPTER 29

1. signa militaria complur[a per] alios d[u]ces ami[ssa] devicti[s hostibu]s re[cipe]ravi ex Hispania et [Gallia et a Dalm]ateis. **2.** Parthos trium exercitu<u>m Romanorum spolia et signa re[ddere] mihi supplicesque amicitiam populi Romani petere coegi. ea autem si[gn]a in penetrali, quod e[s]t in templo Martis Ultoris, reposui.

1. I subdued the enemy and recovered from Spain and Gaul and from the Dalmatians several military standards which had been lost by other generals. **2.** I compelled the Parthians to give back to me spoils and standards of three Roman armies and humbly to request the friendship of the Roman people. These standards moreover I deposited in the innermost sanctum which is in the temple of Mars the Avenger.

CHAPTER 30

1. Pannoniorum gentes, qua[s a]nte me principem populi Romani exercitus nunquam adit, devictas per Ti(berium) [Ne]ronem, qui tum erat privignus et legatus meus, imperio populi Romani s[ubie]ci, protulique fines Illyrici ad ripam fluminis Dan[u<v>]i. **2.** citr[a] quod [D]a[cor]u[m tr]an[s]gressus exercitus meis a[u]sp[iciis vict]us profligatusque [es]t, et pos[tea tran]s Danu<v>ium ductus ex[ercitus me]u[s] Da[cor]um gentes im[peri]a p(opuli) R[omani perferre] coe[git].

1. The Pannonian peoples had never had an army of the Roman people come near them before I became leader. I made them subject to the rule of the Roman people, once they were subdued through the agency of Tiberius Nero, who at that time was my stepson and deputy, and I advanced the boundary of Illyricum to the bank of the river Danube. **2.** An army of Dacians which crossed over onto this side of that river was conquered and overwhelmed under my auspices, and afterwards my army was led across the Danube and compelled the Dacian peoples to endure the commands of the Roman people.

CHAPTER 29

1. σημέας στρατιωτικὰς [πλείστας ὑ]πὸ ἄλλων ἡγεμόνων ἀποβεβλη-
μένας [νικῶν τοὺ]ς πολεμίους ἀπέλαβον ἐξ Ἰσπανίας καὶ Γαλατίας καὶ
παρὰ Δαλματῶν. **2.** Πάρθους τριῶν στρατευμάτων Ῥωμαίων σκῦλα
καὶ σημέας ἀποδοῦναι ἐμοὶ ἱκέτας τε φιλίαν δήμου Ῥωμαίων ἀξιῶσαι
ἠνάνκασα. ταύτας δὲ τὰς σημέας ἐν τῶι Ἄρεως τοῦ Ἀμύντορος ναοῦ
ἀδύτωι ἀπεθέμην.

1. I recovered from Spain and Gaul and from the Dalmatians very many
military standards which had been lost by other leaders, defeating the
enemies. **2.** I compelled Parthians to give back to me spoils and standards
of three Roman armies and as suppliants to ask for friendship with the
Roman people. I put these standards away in the innermost sanctuary of
the temple of Ares the Avenger.

CHAPTER 30

1. Παννονίων ἔθνη, οἷς πρὸ ἐμοῦ ἡγεμόνος στράτευμα Ῥωμαίων οὐκ
ἤνγισεν, ἡσσηθέντα ὑπὸ Τιβερίου Νέρωνος, ὃς τότε μου ἦν πρόγονος καὶ πρεσβευτής, ἡγεμονίαι δήμου Ῥωμαίων ὑπέταξα τά τε
Ἰλλυρικοῦ ὅρια μέχρι Ἴστρου ποταμοῦ προήγαγον. **2.** οὗ ἐπειτάδε
Δάκων διαβᾶσα πολλὴ δύναμις ἐμοῖς αἰσίοις οἰωνοῖς κατεκόπη καὶ
ὕστερον μεταχθὲν τὸ ἐμὸν στράτευμα πέραν Ἴστρου τὰ Δάκων ἔθνη
προστάγματα δήμου Ῥωμαίων ὑπομένειν ἠνάγκασεν.

1. After the tribes of Pannonians, whom no army of Romans approached
before I was leader, were defeated by Tiberius Nero, who was at that time
my stepson and deputy, I made them subject to the rule of the Roman
people and I advanced the boundaries of Illyricum as far as the river Ister.
2. A great force of Dacians crossed over from there onto this side and was
cut in pieces under my favourable omens and later my army was transferred
across the Ister and forced the tribes of Dacians to submit to the commands
of the Roman people.

CHAPTER 31

1. ad me ex In[dia regum legationes saepe] m[issae sunt non visae ante id t]em[pus] apud qu[em]q[uam] R[omanorum du]cem. **2.** nostram amic[itiam appetive]run[t] per legat[os] B[a]starn[ae Scythae]que et Sarmatarum qui su[nt citra fl]umen Tanaim [et] ultra reg[es, Alba]norumque rex et Hiberorum e[t Medorum].

1. Embassies of kings from India were often sent to me, such as have not ever been seen before this time in the presence of any Roman general. **2.** The Bastarnae sought our friendship through envoys, and the Scythians, and kings of the Sarmatians who are on both sides of the river Don, and the king of the Albanians and of the Hiberians and of the Medes.

CHAPTER 32

1. ad me supplices confugerunt [r]eges Parthorum Tirida[te]s et post[ea] Phrat[es,] regis Phratis filiu[s], Medorum Ar[tavasdes, Adiabenorum A]rtaxares, Britann[o]rum Dumnobellaunus et Tin[comarus, Sugambr]orum Maelo, Mar[c]omanorum Sueborum [. . . rus]. **2.** ad [me re]x Parthorum Phrates, Orod[i]s filius, filios suos nepot[esque omnes] misit in Italiam non bello superatu[s], sed amicitiam nostram per [libe]ror[um] suorum pignora petens. **3.** plurimaeque aliae gentes exper[tae sunt p(opuli) Ro]m(ani) fidem me principe, quibus antea cum populo Roman[o nullum extitera]t legationum et amicitiae [c]ommercium.

1. Kings of the Parthians, namely Tiridates and later Phraates, son of King Phraates, Artavasdes King of the Medes, Artaxares of the Adiabenians, Dumnobellaunus and Tincomarus of the Britons, Maelo of the Sugambri, ?-rus of the Suebic Marcomanni fled for refuge to me as suppliants. **2.** Phraates, son of Orodes, King of the Parthians, sent all his sons and grandsons into Italy to me, even though he had not been conquered in war, but asking for our friendship through pledging his children. **3.** And while I have been leader very many other peoples have experienced the good faith of the Roman people; between them and the Roman people previously no embassies or exchange of friendship had existed.

CHAPTER 31

1. πρὸς ἐμὲ ἐξ Ἰνδίας βασιλέων πρεσβεῖαι πολλάκις ἀπεστάλησαν, οὐδέποτε πρὸ τούτου χρόνου ὀφθεῖσαι παρὰ Ῥωμαίων ἡγεμόνι. **2.** τὴν ἡμετέραν φιλίαν ἠξίωσαν διὰ πρέσβεων Βαστάρνοι καὶ Σκύθαι καὶ Σαρματῶν οἱ ἐπιτάδε ὄντες τοῦ Τανάιδος ποταμοῦ καὶ οἱ πέραν δὲ βασιλεῖς, καὶ Ἀλβανῶν δὲ καὶ Ἰβήρων καὶ Μήδων βασιλέες.

1. Embassies of kings were dispatched to me from India many times; these had never before this time been seen in the presence of a Roman leader. **2.** Bastarnae and Scythians asked for our friendship through embassies, and the Sarmatians who are on this side of the river Don and the kings beyond, and furthermore kings of the Albanians and Iberians and Medes.

CHAPTER 32

1. πρὸς ἐμὲ ἱκέται κατέφυγον βασιλεῖς Πάρθων μὲν Τειριδάτης καὶ μετέπειτα Φραάτης, βασιλέως Φράτου [υἱός, Μ]ήδ[ων] δὲ Ἀρταο[υάσδ]ης, Ἀδιαβ[η]νῶν [Ἀ]ρτα[ξάρης, Βρετα]ννῶν Δομνοελλαῦνος καὶ Τ[ινκόμαρος, Σουγ]άμβρων [Μ]αίλων, Μαρκομάνων [Σουήβων —]ρος. **2.** [πρό]ς ἐμὲ βασιλε⌈ὺ⌉ς Πάρθων Φρα[άτης, Ὠρώδο]υ υἱὸ[ς, υ]ἱοὺς [αὐτοῦ] υἱωνούς τε πάντας ἔπεμψεν εἰς Ἰταλίαν, οὐ πολέμωι λειφθείς, ἀλλὰ τὴν ἡμ[ε]τέραν φιλίαν ἀξιῶν ἐπὶ τέκνων ἐνεχύροις. **3.** πλεῖστά τε ἄλλα ἔθνη πεῖραν ἔλ[α]βεν δήμου Ῥωμαίων πίστεως ἐπ' ἐμοῦ ἡγεμόνος, οἷς τὸ πρὶν οὐδεμία ἦν πρὸς δῆμον Ῥωμαίων π[ρε]σβειῶν καὶ φιλίας κοινωνία.

1. Kings fled to me for protection as suppliants – of the Parthians Tiridates and afterwards Phraates, son of King Phraates, and of the Medes Artavasdes, of the Adiabeni Artaxares, of the Britons Domnovellaunus and Tincomarus, of the Sugambri Maelo, of the Suebic Marcomanni ?-ros. **2.** King of the Parthians Phraates, son of Orodes, sent his sons and all his grandsons to Italy to me, not because he had been captured in war, but requesting our friendship on pledging the children. **3.** Very many other tribes besides gained experience of the good faith of the Roman people under my leadership, with whom previously the Roman people had no exchange of embassies and friendship.

CHAPTER 33

a me gentes Parthorum et Medoru[m per legatos] principes earum gentium reges pet[i]tos acceperunt: Par[thi Vononem, regis Phr]atis filium,
regis Orodis nepotem, Medi Arioba[rzanem], regis Artavazdis filium, regis
Ariobarzanis nepotem.

From me the Parthian and Median peoples received kings, whom they had
requested through envoys drawn from their leaders: the Parthians received
Vonones, son of King Phraates, grandson of King Orodes, the Medes
Ariobarzanes, son of King Artavazdes, grandson of King Ariobarzanes.

CHAPTER 34

1. in consulatu sexto et septimo, postqua[m b]el[la civil]ia exstinxeram,
per consensum universorum [po]tens re[ru]m om[n]ium, rem publicam
ex mea potestate in senat[us populi]que R[om]ani [a]rbitrium transtuli.
2. quo pro merito meo senat[us consulto Au]gust[us appe]llatus sum et
laureis postes aedium mearum v[estiti] publ[ice coronaq]ue civica super
ianuam meam fixa est, [et clu]peus [aureu]s in [c]uria Iulia positus, quem
mihi senatum pop[ulumq]ue Rom[anu]m dare virtutis clement[iaequ]e
iustitiae et pieta[tis caus]sa testatu[m] est pe[r e]ius clupei [inscription]em.
3. post id tem[pus a]uctoritate [omnibus praestiti, potest]atis au[tem n]ihilo
ampliu[s habu]i quam cet[eri, qui m]ihi quoque in ma[gis]tra[t]u conlegae
f[uerunt].

1. In my sixth and seventh consulships [28–27 BC], after I had put an end to
civil wars, although by everyone's agreement I had power over everything,
I transferred the state from my power into the control of the Roman senate
and people. **2.** For this service, I was named Augustus by senatorial decree,
and the doorposts of my house were publicly clothed with laurels, and
a civic crown was fastened above my doorway, and a golden shield was
set up in the Julian senate house; through an inscription on this shield
the fact was declared that the Roman senate and people were giving it to
me because of my valour, clemency, justice, and piety. **3.** After this time I
excelled everyone in influence, but I had no more power than the others
who were my colleagues in each magistracy.

CHAPTER 33

παρ᾽ ἐμοῦ ἔθνη Πάρθων καὶ Μήδων διὰ πρέσβεων τῶν παρ᾽ αὐτοῖς πρώτων βασιλεῖς αἰτησάμενοι ἔλαβ[ον]. Πάρθοι Οὐονώνην, βασιλέως Φράτου υ[ἱ]όν, βασιλ[έω]ς Ὡρώδου υἱωνόν, Μῆδοι Ἀριοβαρζάνην, βα[σ]ιλέως Ἀρταβάζου υἱὸν, βασιλέως Ἀριοβαρζάν[ου υἱω]νόν.

Kings received Parthian and Mede peoples from me, having requested them through embassies of their leading men: Parthians received Vonones, son of King Phraates, grandson of King Orodes, Medes Ariobarzanes, son of King Artabazes, grandson of King Ariobarzanes.

CHAPTER 34

1. ἐν ὑπατείαι ἕκτηι καὶ ἑβδόμηι μετὰ τὸ τοὺς ἐνφυλίους ζβέσαι με πολέμους [κ]ατὰ τὰς εὐχὰς τῶν ἐμῶν πολε[ι]τῶν ἐνκρατὴς γενόμενος πάντων τῶν πραγμάτων, ἐκ τῆς ἐμῆς ἐξουσίας εἰς τὴν τῆς συνκλήτου καὶ τοῦ δήμου τῶν Ῥωμαίων μετήνεγκα κυρίαν. **2.** ἐξ ἧς αἰτίας δόγματι συνκλήτου Σεβαστὸς προσ[ηγορε]ύθην καὶ δάφναις δημοσίαι τὰ πρόπυλά [μου ἐστέφθ]η, ὅ τε δρύινος στέφανος ὁ διδόμενος ἐπὶ σωτηρίαι τῶν πολειτῶν ὑπερά[ν]ω τοῦ πυλῶνος τῆς ἐμῆς οἰκίας ἀνετέθη ὅπ[λ]ον τε χρυσοῦν ἐν τῶι βο[υ]λευτηρίωι ἀνατεθ[ὲ]ν ὑπό τε τῆς συνκλήτου καὶ τοῦ δήμου τῶν Ῥω[μα]ίων διὰ τῆς ἐπιγραφῆς ἀρετὴν καὶ ἐπείκειαν κα[ὶ δ]ικαιοσύνην καὶ εὐσέβειαν ἐμοὶ μαρτυρεῖ. **3.** ἀξιώμ[α]τι πάντων διήνεγκα, ἐξουσίας δὲ οὐδέν τι πλεῖον ἔσχον τῶν συναρξάντων μοι.

1. In my sixth and seventh consulships, after I had extinguished the civil wars, although I was in control of all affairs in accordance with the prayers of my fellow citizens, I transferred rights of ownership from my power to that of the senate and people of Rome. **2.** From this cause by senatorial decree I was called Sebastos and my entranceway was publicly crowned with laurels, and the oak wreath which is given for saving fellow citizens was set up above the gateway of my house, and a golden shield, set up in the council chamber by the senate and people of Rome, bore witness through its inscription to my valour and clemency and justice and piety. **3.** I excelled all in rank, but I had no more power than those who shared office with me.

CHAPTER 35

1. tertium dec[i]mum consulatu[m cum gereba]m, sena[tus et e]quester ordo populusq[ue] Romanus universus [appell]av[it me p]atr[em p]atriae, idque in vestibu[lo a]edium mearum inscribendum et in c[u]ria [Iulia e]t in foro Aug(usto) sub quadrig[i]s, quae mihi ex s(enatus) c(onsulto) pos[it]ae [sunt, censuit. **2.** cum scri]psi haec, annum agebam septuagensu[mum sextum].

1. When I was holding my thirteenth consulship [2 BC], the senate and equestrian order and people of Rome all together hailed me as father of the fatherland, and decreed that this title should be inscribed in the forecourt of my house and in the Julian senate house and in the Augustan forum under the chariot, which was set up in my honour by senatorial decree. **2.** When I wrote this I was in my seventy-sixth year [AD 13/14].

APPENDIX

1. summa pecun[i]ae, quam ded[it vel in aera]rium [vel plebei Romanae vel di]missis militibus: denarium sexien[s milliens]. **2.** opera fecit nova: aedem Martis, [Iovis] Ton[antis et Feretri, Apollinis,] divi Iuli, Quirini, Minervae, [Iunonis Reginae, Iovis Libertatis,] Larum, deum Penatium, Iuv[entatis, Matris Magnae; lupercal, pulvina]r ad circum, curiam cum Ch[alcidico, forum Augustum, basilica]m Iuliam, theatrum Marcelli, [p]or[ticum Octaviam, nemus trans T]iberim Caesarum. **3.** refecit Capito[lium sacra]sque aedes [nu]m[ero octoginta] duas, thea[t]rum Pompei, aqu[arum r]iv[os, vi]am Flamin[iam]. **4.** impensa p[raestita in spec]tacul[a] sca[enica et munera] gladiatorum at[que athletas et venationes et] naumachi[am] et donata pe[c]unia [colonis, municipiis, opp]i[dis] terrae motu incendioque consumpt[is] a[ut viritim] a[micis senat]oribusque, quorum census explevit, in[n]umera[bili]s.

1. The total amount of money which he gave either to the treasury or to the commoners of Rome or to discharged soldiers: 600,000,000 *denarii*. **2.** He built new works: the temples of Mars, Jupiter the Thunderer and Feretrius, Apollo, the deified Julius, Quirinus, Minerva, Queen Juno, Jupiter Libertas, the *Lares*, the *Penates*, Youth, the Great Mother; the *lupercal, pulvinar* at the Circus, senate house with the *chalcidicum*, Augustan forum, Julian basilica, theatre of Marcellus, Octavian portico, grove of the Caesars across the Tiber. **3.** He restored the Capitoline temple and eighty-two sacred shrines, the theatre of Pompey, aqueducts, Flaminian Way. **4.** Expenses supplied for theatrical shows and gladiatorial games and for athletes and hunting shows and the mock sea fight, and money given to colonies, municipalities, and towns destroyed by earthquake or by fire, or individually to friends and senators, whose census qualification he topped up: too many to count.

CHAPTER 35

1. τρισκαιδεκάτην ὑπατείαν ἄγοντός μου ἥ τε σύνκλητος καὶ τὸ
ἱππικὸν τάγμα ὅ τε σύνπας δῆμος τῶν Ῥωμαίων προσηγόρευσέ με
πατέρα πατρίδος καὶ τοῦτο ἐπὶ τοῦ προπύλου τῆς οἰκίας μου καὶ ἐν
τῶι βουλευτηρίωι καὶ ἐν τῆι ἀγορᾶι τῆι Σεβαστῆι ὑπὸ τῶι ἅρματι,
ὅ μοι δόγματι συνκλήτου ἀνετέθη, ἐπιγραφῆναι ἐψηφίσατο. 2. ὅτε
ἔγραφον ταῦτα, ἦγον ἔτος ἑβδομηκοστὸν ἕκτον.

1. While I was holding my thirteenth consulship, both the senate and the
equestrian order and the people of Rome all together hailed me as father
of the fatherland, and voted that this was inscribed on the entranceway of
my house and in the council chamber and in the Augustan forum beneath
the chariot, which was set up for me by senatorial decree. 2. When I was
writing these things, I was in my seventy-sixth year.

APPENDIX

1. συγκεφαλαίωσις ἠριθμημένου χρήματος εἰς τὸ αἰράριον ἢ εἰς τὸν
δῆμον τὸν Ῥω[μαί]ων ἢ εἰς τοὺς ἀπολελυμένους στρατιώτας ἒξ
μυριάδες μυριάδων. 2. ἔργα καινὰ ἐγένετο ὑπ' αὐτοῦ ναοὶ μὲν Ἄρεως,
Διὸς Βροντησίου καὶ Τροπαιοφόρου, Πανός, Ἀπόλλωνος, θεοῦ Ἰουλίου,
Κυρείνου, Ἀ[θη]νᾶς, Ἥρας Βασιλίδος, Διὸς Ἐλευθερίου, Ἡρώ[ων, Θεῶν
Π]ατρίων, Νεότητος, Μητρὸς Θεῶν, β[ουλευτήριον] σὺν Χαλκιδικῶι,
ἀγορᾶ{ι} Σεβαστή{ι}, θέατρον Μαρκέλλου, β[α]σιλικὴ Ἰουλία, ἄλσος
Καισάρων, στοαὶ ἐ[ν] Παλατ[ί]ωι, στοὰ ἐν ἱπποδρόμωι Φλαμινίωι.
3. ἐπεσκευάσθ[η τὸ Κα]πιτώλιον, ναοὶ ὀγδοήκοντα δύο, θέ[ατ]ρον
Π[ομ]πηΐου, ὁδὸς Φλαμινία, ἀγωγοὶ ὑδάτων. 4. [δαπ]άναι δὲ εἰς θέας
καὶ μονομάχους καὶ ἀθλητὰς καὶ ναυμαχίαν καὶ θηρομαχίαν δωρεαί
[τε] ἀποικίαις πόλεσιν ἐν Ἰταλίαι, πόλεσιν ἐν ἐπαρχείαις σεισμῶι κα[ὶ]
ἐνπυρισμοῖς πεπονηκυίαις, ἢ κατ' ἄνδρα φίλοις καὶ συνκλητικοῖς, ὧν
τὰς τειμήσεις προσεξεπλήρωσεν, ἄπειρον πλῆθος.

1. Summary of money paid to the treasury or to the people of Rome or
to soldiers who had been discharged: 600,000,000. 2. New works were
built by him: temples of Ares, Zeus Thunderer and Trophy-Bearer, Pan,
Apollo, god Julius, Quirinus, Athene, Queen Hera, Zeus Liberator, Heroes,
ancestral gods, Youth, Mother of Gods; council chamber with *Chalcidicon*, Augustan forum, theatre of Marcellus, basilica Julia, grove of Caesars,
porticoes on the Palatine, portico in the Flaminian racecourse. 3. Repaired
were the Capitolium, eighty-two temples, theatre of Pompey, Flaminian
Way, aqueducts. 4. In addition, expenditure for spectacles, namely gladiatorial and athletes and sea battle and wild-beast hunt, and gifts to colonies
and cities in Italy, to cities in the provinces that had suffered as a result of
earthquake and fires, or individually to friends and senators, whose census
valuation he made up to the full amount, countless quantity.

Commentary

HEADING

With this Latin heading, we perhaps start with an implicit statement that Augustus' deeds are worthy both of being recorded in history and of being celebrated in the highest form of poetry, epic. This might be indicated if the way in which the words *rerum gestarum divi Augusti quibus orbem* form a solemn spondaic hexameter verse is not purely coincidental (Koster (1978) 242; Hoeing (1908) 90; see 1.1n. ***exercitum privato consilio***; 27.1n. ***Aegyptum***).

The heading at Ancyra is in much larger lettering (8–4 cm) than the rest of the inscription (2 cm), and extends over the first three columns of the text. At Antioch, the heading extends above the first two columns. The original inscription at Rome must also have had a similar heading (perhaps, taking our cue from Suetonius, *index rerum gestarum divi Augusti quibus orbem terrarum imperio populi Romani subiecit et impensarum quas in rem publicam populumque Romanum fecit*, 'summary of the achievements of the deified Augustus, by which he made the world subject to the rule of the Roman people, and of the expenses which he incurred for the state and people of Rome'), since otherwise the start of the inscription, *annos undeviginti natus* ('Aged nineteen years old'), is too abrupt (Koster (1978) 246). The grandeur of the language suggests that the heading was composed at Rome, even though not by Augustus himself.

The Greek title at Ancyra is also in much larger lettering (9 cm) than the rest of the text (3 cm). The tone of the Latin and Greek versions is markedly different. Whereas the Latin emphasizes Augustus' world conquest and his benefactions to the people of Rome, the Greek makes no mention of his conquests and leaves open the possibility that his gifts may have been to the provinces as much as to Rome (Vanotti (1975) 314; Botteri (2003a) 244; see introduction p. 28).

rerum gestarum/of the achievements   Significant differences between the Latin and Greek headings suggest that each was adapted to its audience, appealing respectively to the people of Rome and to provincials (see

102

introduction pp. 26–30). The phrase *res gestae* refers primarily to achievements in warfare (as illustrated by the relative clause here), and was thought to provide the proper subject for historical writings (Sall. *Cat.* 3.2, 4.2; Livy *praef.* 3 = LACTOR D1; Petron. *Sat.* 118). Referring to Augustus' deeds as *res gestae* implies that they are worthy of a place in a history. In addition, the way in which the opening words form a complete hexameter verse perhaps evokes the world of epic poetry and raises Augustus' deeds even higher above history into the realm of heroic endeavour. Perhaps the common *recusatio* motif found in Augustan poets (for example, Virg. *G.* 3.46–8 = LACTOR G11; Prop. 2.10.19–20 = LACTOR G17; Hor. *Carm.* 4.15 = LACTOR G45), postponing the daunting task of celebrating Augustus in an epic poem, was responding to a real sentiment on the emperor's part that his deeds should be celebrated in such a work.

divi Augusti/of the deified Augustus   This reference to Augustus, deified by decree of the senate on 17 September (*Fasti Amit., Ant. Min., Viae dei Serpenti* = EJ p. 52 = *Inscr. Ital.* XIII.ii 193, 209, 215, 510), just under a month after his death on 19 August in AD 14, shows that this heading did not purport to be written by Augustus himself.

orbem terrarum imperio populi Romani subiecit/he made the world subject to the rule of the Roman people   Claims to world conquest achieved a new prominence early on during Octavian's rise to power and became a recurrent theme of the Augustan era (see introduction pp. 36–7; 3, 13, 25–33; Nicolet (1991b) 29–30). Shortly after Actium, Virgil celebrated Rome's domination of West and East alike, blurring together Octavian's recent conquest over Egypt with exaggerated claims of the submission of Britons, Indians, and Parthians (Virg. *G.* 3.16–33 = LACTOR G11), and later he was to attribute a prediction of Rome's world domination in the *Aeneid* to none other than Jupiter himself (Virg. *Aen.* 1.278–9 = LACTOR G36). Coins minted in *c.* 32–29 BC presented this claim in symbolic terms, depicting on their reverse an image of Victory standing on a globe, holding a wreath and palm (*RIC* I² 59 no. 255; *BM Coins, Rom. Emp.* I 99 no. 604; Simon (1993) 91 no. 49; cf. *RIC* I² 59 no. 254, 60 no. 268; *BM Coins, Rom. Emp.* I 42 no. 217, 99 nos. 602–3, 101 nos. 622–3; Simon (1993) 91 nos. 50–1; Nicolet (1991b) 41). The perception arose during this period that Rome's power really had become universal in scope, as expressed neatly by Ovid: 'The expanse of the city of Rome and of the world is the same' (*Romanae spatium est urbis et orbis idem, Fast.* 2.684). Monuments set up in the city of Rome itself implicitly supported the contention that Rome now controlled the known world. Agrippa's Map – whether a graphic depiction or a written description – displayed Roman knowledge, and, by extension, control of the world (Nicolet (1991b) 98–114). Provinces and peoples now appeared in public art, with the later Sebasteion at Aphrodisias perhaps imitating a prototype in the capital (Smith (1988) 50, 71–5; Nicolet (1991b) 45–7). The most likely candidate is Augustus' *porticus ad nationes*, which displayed statues of all the peoples of the world (Serv. *Aen.* 8.721), surpassing the mere fourteen displayed by Pompey (Plin. *HN* 36.4.41). The significant figure of Hercules – synonymous with exploring the ends of the world – appeared at its entrance (Plin. *HN* 36.4.39). This perception of Rome's power having become universal made an impact on the types of historical works produced during this period by provincial writers like Strabo and Diodorus Siculus. Their ambitious universal histories, which claimed to be no less than the history of everything at every time, encompassed a similar world view to that espoused in the *RGDA* (Clarke (1999b) espec. 276–8). The same point can be made for Strabo's universal geography (Clarke (1999a) 312). Augustus' claims to world conquest reached their final summation in the *RGDA* and his funeral procession, which included images and inscriptions of his conquests (Dio Cass. 56.34.3; Tac. *Ann.* 1.8.3–4).

inpensarum/of the expenses A summary of these expenses was also added to the end of the *RGDA* in what is known as the 'appendix'. This was not part of the original document, but was probably composed for a provincial audience in the Greek east (see introduction p. 19).

incisarum in duabus aheneis pilis/inscribed upon two bronze columns The *RGDA* at Rome was displayed outside Augustus' Mausoleum on the field of Mars (*Campus Martius*), on either side of the entrance to the building (see introduction pp. 3–6, with Map 1, City of Rome; Eck (2003) 131; Scheid (2007) ix–x). This detail allows us to form a more accurate picture of the text's display outside the Mausoleum. Whereas Suetonius (*Aug.* 101.4) refers to *aeneis tabulis* ('bronze tablets'), the word *pilis* implies that the bronze plaques bearing the inscription were fixed to freestanding columns, rather than to a wall of the Mausoleum (von Premerstein (1932): 205–17; Scheid (2007) viii–ix). We also learn here that the inscription was displayed on two columns.

THE AFTERMATH OF THE IDES OF MARCH (1–2)

The *RGDA* begins with the tumultuous events of 44/43 BC following the assassination of Julius Caesar, which heralded the emergence of young Caesar, as Octavian was known at the time. The *RGDA* is carefully constructed, with the opening two chapters, which deal with his swift ascent into the limelight as a nineteen-year-old, being balanced by the final two chapters (34–5), which provide a retrospective upon the highest accolades given to him by the senate and people of Rome from the point of view of the elderly *princeps* now at the end of his life, aged seventy-six (Ramage (1987) 19–20).

Through his use of literary allusions, Augustus puts a positive gloss on his illegal early career by inviting comparison between his own interventions as a *privatus* on behalf of the state with those of earlier champions of Rome, such as L. Brutus, P. Scipio Nasica, and Pompey (see 1.1n. **exercitum privato consilio**). His opening sentences also put forward an implicit claim on his part to have fulfilled Cicero's ideal of what a *princeps* should be (Wagenvoort (1936) 341, Schäfer (1957) 317, 334; 13n. **me principe**). The opening sentence may even reproduce the text of the inscription beneath the gilded equestrian statue decreed in his honour by the senate on 2 January 43 BC, and set up on the *rostra*, the first of many monuments to be set up in his honour at Rome, and still to be seen during Tiberius' reign (Vell. Pat. 2.61.3; App. *B Civ.* 3.8.51; Mannsperger (1982) 333, 336–7; Alföldy (1991) 307; Simon (1993) 37).

Chapter 2 illustrates Augustus' *pietas* and *iustitia* in taking vengeance for Caesar's death at the hands of the 'liberators', two of the virtues celebrated later on the golden shield voted to him by senate and people (34.2). The triumph over Brutus and Cassius was not quite the personal victory claimed here, however (see 2n. **vici bis acie**).

1.1 annos undeviginti natus/aged nineteen years old   The opening sentence plunges straight into the crisis following the assassination of Julius Caesar by the conspirators, or 'liberators', led by Brutus and Cassius. It ignores the first few months subsequent to the Ides of March, during which Octavian hurried back to Italy from Apollonia in Macedonia, where he had been helping to prepare troops for Caesar's planned attack on Parthia. During those months, Octavian, who up to that point had played little role in public life, faced considerable difficulties in claiming his inheritance from his great-uncle Caesar, who had nominated him in his will as his heir on condition that he assume his name (*condicio nominis ferendi*; Suet. *Iul.* 83.2; Linderski (1996b) 148–53; Konrad (1996) 124–5; Schmitthenner (1973) 104–15). Instead of the normal procedure for accepting such an inheritance, inserting the testator's name alongside his own, the new Caesar actually changed his whole name and patronymic (App. *B Civ.* 3.2.11); 'the nature of Octavian's interpretation of what his posthumous adoption meant was anyway rather irregular' (Williams (2001) 190). He thus assumed the name C. Iulius Caesar, preferring not to be called 'Octavianus', although 'Octavian' has become the standard way of referring to him in modern scholarship, though 'dubious and misleading' (Syme (1939) 113). At the same time, he distributed largesse to the people of Rome (see 15.1n. **ex testamento patris mei**). He met with opposition from Antony, who was the current consul and fancied himself as the new leader of the Caesarians (Syme (1939) 106–7), but was supported by senators like Cicero, who hoped to use Octavian to destroy Antony, and then to remove Octavian himself (Cic. *Fam.* 11.20.1; Syme (1939) 122, 141–3). (For this period, see Syme (1939) ch. 8).

By starting with an explicit reference to his age, Augustus takes us to the period after his nineteenth birthday on 23 September 44 BC. By the end of October he had successfully ventured into Campania in order to raise troops by rallying his father's veterans to his cause, and securing their support with sizeable sums of money (Cic. *Att.* 16.8; Syme (1939) 125). The opening of the *RGDA* was imitated by Velleius Paterculus in his account of the same events (2.61.1: *C. Caesar XVIIII annum egressus, mira ausus ac summa consecutus privato consilio . . . veteranos excivit paternos*; Woodman (1983) 127–8). By emphasizing his age, Augustus calls to mind other youthful champions of Rome whom he had surpassed, notably Scipio Africanus, who had been granted consular *imperium* aged only twenty-four, without having previously served as consul or praetor (Livy 28.43.11), and Pompey, who had raised a private army in support of Sulla at the age of twenty-three (Cic. *Leg. Man.* 21.61; Skard (1955) 120 n. 3; Syme (1939) 316).

These opening words display the stylistic mannerism of including all five vowels at the beginning of a text, elevating its literary tone. Augustus shares this technique with a number of authors who wished to start significant works with an impressive gesture. In epic poetry we find *arma virumque cano* (Virg. *Aen.* 1.1), and in historical prose *urbem Romam a principio* (Tac. *Ann.* 1.1). The feature also occurs in hymns, such as *Phoebe silvarumque* (Hor. *Carm. Saec.* 1), and *enos lases iuvate* (*Carmen Arvale*) (Lauffer (1982)). Like the use of hexameter rhythm in the heading, it sends a message that this text and the achievements recorded in it are of weighty significance.

exercitum privato consilio/an army at my personal decision This refers to Octavian's assembling of an army of Caesarian veterans in Campania, from mid-October 44 BC, during which he cultivated their sense of loyalty to him as Julius Caesar's heir with generous bribes (Cic. *Att.* 16.8). The crucial point is that Octavian had no authority to do so; by translating *privato* simply as 'mine', the Greek version fails to take account of the technical meaning of *privatus*, that is, pertaining to someone who is not a magistrate, acting without *imperium*. He omits to mention that after a failed attempt at Rome in November to consolidate his position and to persuade the veterans to fight against Antony, he persuaded two of Antony's legions to join him, and shifted his army north into Etruria (App. *B Civ.* 3.40–2; Syme (1939) 125, 143–4). Although suborning the troops of Antony, the consul in office, was illegal, his actions received retrospective sanction as soon as Antony ceased to be consul in January 43 BC, when Cicero intervened in the senate to ensure that Octavian was granted *imperium* (Cic. *Phil.* 5.45–6; see 1.2). Cicero had prepared the way for this in speeches delivered earlier on 20 December 44 BC to the senate and people in turn

(Cic. *Phil.* 3–4: 20 December; *Phil.* 5: 1 January; Syme (1939) 162–3, 167), in which he portrayed Octavian's raising of a private army as a brave and honourable deed forestalling Antony's intention to inflict a massacre upon Rome (Cic. *Phil.* 3.3–4; 4.2–4). Close echoes of the *Philippics* may be found in the *RGDA*, such as *privato consilio rem publicam . . . Caesar liberavit* (Cic. *Phil.* 3.5).

Augustus' words echo Cicero's account of how the first hero of the Republic, L. Brutus, expelled the Tarquinii from Rome (Cic. *Rep.* 2.46, *vir ingenio et virtute praestans L. Brutus depulit a civibus suis iniustum illud durae servitutis iugum. qui **cum privatus esset**, totam rem publicam sustinuit, primusque in hac civitate docuit in conservanda civium libertate esse privatum neminem. **quo auctore et principe** concitata civitas . . . exulem et regem ipsum et liberos eius et gentem Tarquiniorum esse iussit*; Ramage (1987) 67). Cicero describes how Brutus rescued the Roman state even though he was only a *privatus*, becoming its *princeps*, the title Augustus likes to use of himself in the *RGDA* (e.g. 13). The phrasing of the *RGDA* also recalls Cicero's praise for P. Cornelius Scipio Nasica Serapio, who, he claimed, rescued the state from the tyranny of Ti. Sempronius Gracchus in 133 BC though only a *privatus* (Cic. *Brut.* 212, *ex dominatu Ti. Gracchi **privatus in libertatem rem publicam vindicavit***; cf. Cic. *Cat.* 1.3; Schäfer (1957) 232). Such praise for the actions of private individuals who intervened in state affairs was in accordance with Stoic and Peripatetic ideals that non-magistrates could, and should, intervene in public affairs for the benefit of the state (see Cic. *Tusc.* 4.23.51 for an enunciation of this ideal by Scipio Nasica in the Gracchus affair; Béranger (1973) 257). In short, Augustus is aligning himself with both the abstract ideal and the actual examples of indivuals prepared to protect the state even in a private capacity, which recur in Cicero's philosophical works (Schäfer (1957) 324). Such individuals, it seems, were deserving of the title of *princeps*, and this is also the title with which Cicero elevated the young Caesar (Cic. *Phil.* 5.28; Wagenvoort (1936) 332–3).

Literary allusion, however, can be a double-edged tool. As well as evoking positive parallels from Cicero, these words also recall the fact that it was the raising of a private army by Aemilius Lepidus in 77 BC, in defiance of the senate's authority, which prompted the senate to decree a state of emergency (*quoniam <M.> Lepidus **exercitum privato consilio paratum** . . . contra huius ordinis auctoritatem ad urbem ducit, uti Ap. Claudius interrex cum Q. Catulo pro consule . . . urbi praesidio sint operamque dent ne quid res publica detrimenti capiat*, Sall. *Hist.* 1.77.22M). This parallel, by contrast, points up the stark alternative, that it was Octavian, not Antony, who was the real enemy of the state (cf. Braunert (1974) 344–9, 355).

These opening words have a metrical flavour, containing a spondaic hexameter, which strikes an epic posture: *exerci/tum privato consilio et privata impensa* (Hoeing (1908) 90; heading; 27.1n. **Aegyptum**).

a dominatione factionis oppressam/oppressed by a despotic faction
The word *factio* has both a collective meaning, referring to a 'group, clique, faction', and a verbal force, referring both to an actual 'way of doing things', and a potential 'capacity to get things done'. The precise connotations of the word can be difficult to pin down, and sometimes more than one meaning may be active. In his use of the word *factio* here, Augustus is primarily using it as a collective noun, to refer to his enemies (Seager (1972)). Velleius' account of the same events is apparently derived from this official version (Vell. Pat. 2.61.1, *torpebat oppressa **dominatione Antonii** civitas*, 'the state was in paralysis oppressed by the tyranny of Antony', with Woodman (1983) 126; 1.1n. ***annos undeviginti natus***), and demonstrates how Augustus chooses to use a negative periphrasis to avoid naming Antony. The latter's status as consul in 44 BC was repeatedly undermined by Cicero's specious claim that, in abandoning him, his legions had in effect declared him to be a public enemy (Cic. *Phil.* 3.6, 3.14, 4.1–2, 4.4–8, 5.3–4). The *RGDA* echoes Cicero's extreme language in attributing tyrannical designs to Antony, the usual complaint made against overweening individuals at Rome (Cic. *Phil.* 3.29, *huius impuri latronis feremus taeterrimum crudelissimumque dominatum?*; cf. 3.34, 5.44, 12.14–15, *rem publicam oppressisset Antonius*; Wirszubski (1960) 104–5).

The topsy-turvy political situation alluded to here resulted in the Caesarian supporters Octavian, Hirtius, and Pansa fighting against another Caesarian, Antony, in order to free one of Caesar's assassins, D. Iunius Brutus Albinus, from being besieged at Mutina in Cisalpine Gaul (spring, 43 BC) (Vell. Pat. 2.61.4). Antony was laying claim to the province of Cisalpine Gaul, which occupied a crucial strategic position for control of Italy and the West, in place of his allotted province of Macedonia, in virtue of the *lex de permutatione provinciarum*, which had been passed on 1 June 44 BC (Livy *Per.* 117; Syme (1939) 115). The wording of the Greek translation (ἐκ τῆς τῶν συνομοσαμένων δουλήας, 'from the slavery imposed by the conspirators'), however, brings to mind the conspiracy of Brutus and Cassius rather than Antony (cf. Plut. *Vit. Brut.* 12), possibly because this would have been of more interest to an audience in the Greek east, given the location of the battles there and the exactions suffered by the communities in that region at the hands of the 'liberators', and also perhaps because this was more obviously a legitimate struggle endorsed by the *lex Pedia* (see 2; Vanotti (1975) 306–7; Scheid (2007) 28).

in libertatem vindicavi/I liberated Since this first sentence refers only to events during the autumn and winter of 44 BC, with the next section (1.2) moving on to the senate's meeting of January 43 BC, Augustus' claim to have rescued the state perhaps relates to having forced Antony to leave Rome, but probably should not be pressed for a very specific significance, being rather a conventional way of claiming to have acted in defence of the public good (Wirszubski (1960) 100–4). Once again, Augustus' choice of words echoes the *Philippics*, where Cicero repeatedly returned to the theme of the young Caesar's deliverance of the state (Cic. *Phil.* 3.3, 3.5, 4.2, 4.4; Skard (1955) 119–20; Schäfer (1957) 322; Walser (1955) 354–5; Ehrhardt (1986)). The phrase also recalls the technical term, *vindicatio in libertatem*, used of the juridical act of freeing slaves. In this way, the expression implies that Antony was a *dominus*, enslaving Rome (Walser (1955) 354).

Claims to be protecting the people's *libertas* were a common motif in political discourse, a 'convenient term of political fraud' (Syme (1939) 154–6; cf. Wirszubski (1960) 103–4). The slogan had been used to justify the actions of both Pompey and Caesar, the former in raising a private army from his father's veterans at his own expense in support of Sulla, the latter in taking up arms against the state (Pompey: Caes. *B Afr.* 22.2, *urbemque Romanam in libertatem vindicavit*; cf. 1.1n. **annos undeviginti natus**; Fugmann (1991) 307; Lehmann (2004); Caesar, *B Civ.* 1.22.5, *ut se et populum Romanum factione paucorum oppressum in liberatem vindicaret*). The close parallel between Octavian and Pompey had been noted by Cicero in the *Philippics*, to the former's advantage (Cic. *Phil.* 5.44). Indeed, the words relating to Pompey cited briefly above belong to a more extensive passage, full of resonance for Augustus' claims in the *RGDA*. These occur in a speech delivered by Cato to Cn. Pompeius, the son of Pompey the Great, in which he urges him to emulate his father (Caes. *B Afr.* 22.2, *'tuus' inquit 'pater istuc aetatis cum esset et animadvertisset rem publicam ab nefariis sceleratisque civibus oppressam bonosque aut interfectos aut exsilio multatos patria civitateque carere, gloria et animi magnitudine elatus privatus et adulescentulus paterni exercitus reliquiis collectis paene oppressam funditus et deletam Italiam urbemque Romanam in libertatem vindicavit* – ' "Your father," he said, "when he was of the same age as you and had observed that the state was overwhelmed by criminal and wicked citizens, and that good men had either been killed or punished with exile from their fatherland and were being kept away from the state, carried away by glory and by great-spiritedness, though a private individual and young man, mustered the remants of his father's army and freed Italy and the city of Rome when it had been almost completely overwhelmed and destroyed" '; Skard (1955) 120–1; Ehrhardt (1986) 133). It is perhaps to be understood that Octavian has succeeded in being a real heir to Pompey the Great in rivalling his actions, where his actual son failed. At any rate, by the end of this first sentence, it is clear that the *RGDA* is concerned with setting Augustus into the context of great Romans of the past, and showing how he has surpassed them (Fugmann (1991) 307; Schäfer (1957) 322–3). (For a hostile version of the same events, cf. Tac. *Ann.* 1.10.1; see introduction pp. 48–50).

Octavian repeated his claim to have rescued the state after Actium, when the foreign threat of Cleopatra was added to that posed by Antony. Coins issued by a mint in the Greek east in 28 BC depict on their obverse Octavian

Fig. 9 Octavian, defender of liberty; *Cistophorus* of Ephesus, 28 BC (coin: obverse and
reverse, *RIC* I² 79 no. 476 = LACTOR N6).

wreathed in laurel and proclaim him to be LIBERTATIS P(opuli) R(omani)
VINDEX (see Figure 9). On their reverse, a female figure enclosed within
a laurel wreath is identified as PAX ('peace'). She is represented holding a
caduceus, and to her right a snake emerges from a *cista mystica*, a basket
used in the cult of Dionysus (*RIC* I² 79 no. 476 = *BM Coins, Rom. Emp.* I
112 nos. 691–3 = Simon (1993) 40–3 no. 3 = EJ no. 18 = LACTOR N6;
Wirszubski (1960) 105–6). These coins appear to be a deliberate response
to coins issued earlier in the east by Antony in *c.* 39 BC (*BM Coins, Rom.
Rep.* II 502 nos. 133–4; Mannsperger (1973) 383–5, 400–1, cf. Rich and
Williams (1999) 174), which depict on their obverse Antony's head bound

Fig. 10 Antony's head bound with a wreath of ivy; bust of Octavia upon a *cista mystica* (coin: obverse and reverse, *BM Coins, Rom. Rep.* II 502 nos. 133–4). © The Trustees of the British Museum.

with a wreath of ivy and on their reverse a bust of Octavia upon a *cista mystica* (Figure 10). Both sets of coins depict a female figure with a *cista mystica*, and Octavian's wreath of Apollo's laurel may be taken as trumping Antony's wreath of Dionysus' ivy (cf. Zanker (1988) 46–53 and Beacham (2005) 154–8 for representation of the conflict between the two triumvirs as Apollo v. Dionysus). A large monumental inscription from the Roman forum, perhaps to be associated with the arch set up to commemorate Augustus' triple triumph in 29 BC, similarly celebrated his preservation of the state (*ILS* 81 = EJ no. 17 = LACTOR H17).

1.2 senatus decretis honorificis/the senate passed honorific decrees
The senate granted retrospective approval to Octavian, sanctioning his
illegal acts (see 1.1n. ***exercitum privato consilio***), and granted him further
powers and honours during an extended meeting beginning on 1 January
43 BC. On Cicero's proposal, Octavian was adlected to the senate. He
was also given extraordinary *imperium pro praetore* and a privileged *locus
sententiae* (see 1.2n. ***consularem locum sententiae***) despite his youth (Cic.
Phil. 5.45–8, 11.20; Livy *Per.* 118; Dio Cass. 46.29.2). On the proposal of his
stepfather Philippus, he was voted a gilded equestrian statue to be set up on
the rostra in the Roman forum. Finally, he was entrusted with conducting
the war against Antony alongside the consuls Hirtius and Pansa in virtue of
an emergency decree, or *senatus consultum ultimum* (see 1.3; Cic. *Ad Brut.*
1.15.7; Vell. Pat. 2.61.3; Suet. *Aug.* 10.3; App. *B Civ.* 3.51; Dio Cass. 46.29.5;
Syme (1939) 167; Mannsperger (1982) 333). The *RGDA* does not mention
that he was also to be allowed to stand for the consulship ten years early
(i.e. aged thirty-two), perhaps in order not to draw attention to the fact
that he did not actually end up having to wait those further thirteen years
(see 1.4).

**C. Pansa et A. Hirtio consulibus/in the consulship of Gaius Pansa
and Aulus Hirtius**   Both new men (*novi homines*), Gaius Vibius Pansa
Caetronianus and Aulus Hirtius had been designated consuls for 43 BC by
Caesar before his assassination, having been close allies of the dictator since
the mid-50s BC. Octavian sought their support on his arrival in Italy after
the Ides (Cic. *Att.* 14.11.2). Described as 'mere municipal aristocrats, [who]
lacked experience of affairs, vigour of personality and family influence'
(Syme (1939) 133), Cicero lauded them in public, but painted quite a
different picture of them in his private letters, which reveal them to have
possessed a tendency to self-indulgence and lethargy (Cic. *Att.* 16.1.4, *Fam.*
9.20.2; cf. the opinion of his brother, *Fam.* 16.27.1). Despite their efforts
to achieve peace by reconciling the opposing Caesarians, they both died
during the conflict with Antony at Mutina (see 1.4).

The Greek translation of the consular date here and elsewhere in the
RGDA (e.g. 6.1, 12.2, 16.1) reflects Latin linguistic usage, using a dative
construction as an equivalent of the Latin ablative absolute, instead of a
genitive one, which would be the expected idiom (Wigtil (1982a) 628–9;
Adams (2003) 504).

**consularem locum sententiae/consular precedence in stating my
opinion**   At meetings of the senate, after the matter for discussion had
been outlined, senators were invited to give their opinions in strict hierar-
chical order. In general, the presiding magistrate would first ask ex-consuls
(*consulares*) for their opinion, starting with the *princeps senatus* (see 7.2n.

princeps senatus), and then proceeding to ex-praetors, praetors, and other senators in descending order of rank (Lintott (1999) 78).

imperium mihi dedit/it gave me supreme command *Imperium* is the supreme power granted to high-ranking magistrates, who were entitled to be accompanied by lictors carrying rods and axes in bundles (*fasces*), to sit upon a folding chair (*sella curulis*), and to wear the purple-bordered *toga praetexta* (Lintott (1999) 95–6). This grant to Octavian is dated to 7 January, according to the *Fasti Praenestini* (*Inscr. Ital.* XIII.ii 113, 392; EJ p. 44 = LACTOR C2). By AD 12/13, this day was one of the imperial anniversaries celebrated at the altar to the *numen* of Augustus at Narbo, and this *imperium* was thought to have had universal application (*VII quoq. Idus Ianuar. qua die primum imperium orbis terrarum auspicatus est* = EJ no. 100 A23–5 = *ILS* 112 = LACTOR L17). Formally, the grant made Octavian subordinate to the consuls. The Greek version makes explicit the specific meaning of *imperium* here, as the authority of a magistrate symbolized by *fasces*.

1.3 res publica ne quid detrimenti caperet/To prevent the state from suffering harm This is the usual formula referring to the 'last decree of the senate' (*senatus consultum ultimum*), deployed in the late Republic in times of extreme political crisis, when the senate considered the state to be in grave danger from Roman citizens. The decree declared a state of emergency by requesting magistrates, usually the consuls, to take any necessary measures to ensure that the state came to no harm. It did not bestow any particular powers upon them, but 'these vague and reassuring phrases were understood by the senators who endorsed them to be an encouragement to the magistrates to use force against fellow-citizens without concerning themselves with the strict legality of what they did' (Drummond (1995) 88–95; Lintott (1999) 89–93, quotation from 89). It was passed on 1 January 43 BC.

1.4 populus autem eodem anno me consulem . . . creavit/In this same year, moreover, the people appointed me consul After the deaths of both consuls in April (see 1.4), Rome remained without a consul for several months. Augustus emphasizes popular support for his election as consul, passing over the fact that he met with strong opposition from the senate, which rejected an embassy of soldiers who had requested rewards for themselves and the consulship for Octavian (Suet. *Aug.* 26.1; App. *B Civ.* 3.88; Dio Cass. 46.43). Consequently, Octavian marched back to Rome at the head of his army, and secured his election as consul with his distant relative Q. Pedius on 19 August 43 BC (Livy *Per.* 119; Dio Cass. 46.45–6.1; Syme (1939) 185–6).

cos. uterque in bello cecidisset/both consuls had fallen in war Hirtius was killed in action against Antony on 21 April 43 BC at the battle of Mutina, which nonetheless successfully raised the seige on D. Brutus and caused Antony to flee westwards, whilst Pansa died two days later of a wound inflicted upon him at the battle of Forum Gallorum on 14 April (cf. Cic. *Fam.* 10.30, an eye-witness account of the battle by Servius Sulpicius Galba; Syme (1939) 173–4). There were rumours that Octavian had brought about their convenient demise, which allowed him to take control of their armies, by killing Hirtius himself in the confusion of battle, and by arranging for poison to be added to Pansa's wound (Suet. *Aug.* 11; Tac. *Ann.* 1.10.2). The doctor who had attended to him, Glyco, was subsequently imprisoned, although his guilt was not believed by all (Cic. *Ad Brut.* 1.6.2). Both consuls were granted the honour of a public funeral and being buried on the *Campus Martius* (Coarelli (1999b); Macciocca (1999)), and Cicero even proposed the unprecedented measure of setting up a war memorial to honour the fallen (Cic. *Phil.* 14.31–5; Dio Cass. 46.38.2; Cooley 'Commemorating the war dead of the Roman world', in *Cultures of Commemoration. War Memorials, Ancient and Modern*, eds. P. Low, G. J. Oliver, and P. J. Rhodes (Oxford University Press, forthcoming)).

triumvirum rei publicae constituendae/triumvir for settling the state After having extorted the consulship with threats of violence, Octavian promptly resigned from the post in order to join ranks with Antony and Lepidus as triumvir. Antony had fled into Gaul following his defeat at Mutina, where he joined forces with Lepidus, then governor of Gallia Narbonensis. After bringing their combined armies back into Italy, they joined Octavian (at first very much the junior partner) in the triumvirate, in order to track down the 'liberators'. By not mentioning Antony by name in 1.1, Augustus obscures the fact that by the end of the same chapter Antony has been transformed from enemy of the state into triumviral colleague. This phrase echoes the official title given to the triumvirate of Octavian, Antony, and Lepidus, as illustrated on *denarii* minted in Africa *c.* 40–37 BC, which depict on their obverse the head of Lepidus, labelled LEPIDVS PONT(ifex) MAX(imus) III V(ir) R(ei) P(ublicae) C(onstituendae), and Octavian on their reverse, with the words CAESAR IMP(erator) III VIR R(ei) P(ublicae) C(onstituendae) (*BM Coins, Rom. Rep.* II 579 nos. 29–31). (See 7.1nn. for further discussion of the triumvirate.)

2 qui parentem meum interfecerunt/Those who killed my father Whilst Antony equivocated after Caesar's assassination, leaving open the possibility of a conciliation with the 'liberators', Octavian early on championed the cause of avenging Caesar's death (Syme (1939) 97–8, 105–6, 116–19). Here he avoids naming Brutus and Cassius, leaders of the plot against Julius Caesar. They portrayed their actions as freeing the state from a tyrant, and issued coins on the theme of liberty, most famously depicting a cap of liberty framed by two daggers with the caption 'Ides of March' (*RRC* 518 no. 508.3; cf. *RRC* 513–15 nos. 498–503). Many editions print the verb *trucidaverunt*, a strongly emotive word meaning 'slaughtered', but this reading is uncertain, given that the Latin text is incomplete here, and that the verb in the Greek version is not preserved, either. Octavian cannily transformed his nomination by Julius Caesar in his will as his chief heir into a claim to have been adopted by him, and made his alleged adoption by Julius Caesar into the cornerstone of his rise to power, since it provided him with financial resources, loyal veterans, and the kudos of becoming *divi filius* (see 1.1n. **annos undeviginti natus**). He took pains to advertise his status as Caesar's heir (15.1), organizing the *ludi victoriae Caesaris* in 44 BC in honour of Venus Genetrix, ancestress of the Julian family (Plin. *HN* 2.23.93 = LACTOR K44). Antony scathingly claimed that Octavian owed everything to his name (Cic. *Phil.* 13.24; Syme (1939) 112–13).

in exilium expuli iudiciis legitimis/I drove into exile by way of the courts of law The 'liberators' were exiled in their absence according to the judgement of a special tribunal established by the *lex Pedia de interfectoribus Caesaris*, proposed on 19 August 43 BC immediately after his election as consul (with Octavian as his colleague) by Q. Pedius, a nephew and close ally of Julius Caesar (Vell. Pat. 2.69.5; Suet. *Aug.* 10.1). Both Appian (*B Civ.* 3.95) and Dio Cassius (46.48–9) give a negative picture of the tribunal, representing it as a tool with which Octavian could rid himself of personal opponents, regardless of whether or not they had actually been involved in the assassination or had even been in Rome at the time (Ridley (2003) 166–7).

ultus eorum facinus/exacting retribution for their crime The idea of vengeance was emphasized by vowing the temple of Mars Ultor ('the Avenger') (see 21.1) at Philippi.

bellum inferentis rei publicae/while they were making war upon the state Augustus is careful to claim that Brutus and Cassius started hostilities. The Latin phrase *res publica* is here alone translated by the Greek word *patris*, lending a more emotive tone to Augustus' defeat of Brutus and Cassius (Vanotti (1975) 308–9).

vici bis acie/I defeated them twice in battle There were two battles at Philippi (Macedonia) on 3 and 23 October 42 BC, but Octavian was not himself victorious, despite this claim (cf. *Fasti Praen.*, *Inscr. Ital.* XIII.ii 135, 524 = EJ p. 54 = LACTOR C37; Scheid (2007) 30 condones this claim, however, stating that Augustus can claim these as his victories since the battles must have been fought under his auspices, as well as under Antony's).

Rather, he was impeded from fighting through illness, being hardly able to stand (App. *B Civ.* 4.108; Suet. *Aug.* 13.1; Dio Cass. 47.37.3, 41.4; cf. Plut. *Vit. Brut.* 38.2, 41). In the first battle, both sides were partially victorious. Antony defeated Cassius, who committed suicide in the mistaken belief that Brutus had also been defeated, but Brutus' soldiers attacked Octavian's men, and captured the camp of Antony and Octavian (Livy *Per.* 124; Vell. Pat. 70.1–4; App. *B Civ.* 4.110–13; Dio Cass. 47.45.2–46.5). This claim in the *RGDA* contrasts with what Augustus wrote in his autobiography, where he stated that he had arisen from his sickbed in order to absent himself from the camp on that day in response to a warning received by one of his friends in a dream (App. *B Civ.* 4.110; Suet. *Aug.* 91.1; Plut. *Vit. Brut.* 41.4, *Vit. Ant.* 22). On another reckoning, Octavian avoided the engagement by lurking for three days in a marsh (Plin. *HN* 7.45.148). The second battle, which again appears to have been fought chiefly by Antony, resulted in the suicide of Brutus (Livy *Per.* 124; Dio Cass. 47.48.4–49.1; Plut. *Vit. Ant.* 22).

AUGUSTUS' SUCCESSES IN WARFARE AND TRIUMPHAL CELEBRATIONS (3–4)

These chapters abandon the chronological structure used so far, to relate Augustus' achievements in warfare. After recording his military victories (3), Augustus relates the ceremonies celebrating them (4). Complementing the previous chapter, they illustrate the other two virtues (*virtus* and *clementia*) celebrated by the golden shield voted in his honour by the senate and people (34.2).

3.1 bella . . . civilia externaque/wars . . . civil and foreign   Suetonius lists five civil wars (*Aug.* 9). In addition to those already alluded to in the opening chapters of the *RGDA* – at Mutina against Antony in 43 BC (see 1), and at Philippi against Brutus and Cassius in 42 BC (see 2) – Augustus fought at Perusia against Lucius Antonius (Antony's brother) in 41–40 BC, in the seas around Sicily against Sextus Pompey (son of Pompey the Great) in 36 BC (see 25.1), and finally against Antony, culminating in the battle of Actium in 31 BC and capture of Alexandria in 30 BC (although this war was depicted by Augustus at the time as being waged against a foreign foe, Cleopatra) (cf. 25.2–3, 27.1, 34.1). Augustus' achievement in ending the long years of civil war caused great relief among his contemporaries (e.g. Hor. *Epod.* 9 = LACTOR G5; '*laudatio Turiae*' *ILS* 8393 col. II 25 = EJ no. 357 = LACTOR T37f; cf. Vell. Pat. 2.89.2–3 = LACTOR E89.2–3; Tac. *Ann.* 1.2.1 = LACTOR F2.1), and was still remembered under Tiberius, when in AD 20 Cn. Calpurnius Piso was accused of trying to foment civil war: 'He also tried to stir up civil war, though all the evils of civil war had long been buried by the divine nature of deified Augustus and by the virtues of Ti. Caesar Augustus' (*bellum etiam civile excitare conatus sit, iam* *pridem numine divi Aug(usti) virtutibusq(ue) Ti. Caesaris Aug(usti) omnibus civilis belli sepultis malis, SCPP* 45–7, Eck *et al.* (1996) 42).

The only foreign wars conducted by Augustus in person were campaigns in Dalmatia (Balkans) in 35–33 BC and in Cantabria (north-west Spain) in 26–25 BC (Suet. *Aug.* 20.1). Wars were conducted elsewhere under his auspices by his legates (see 4.2) in Aquitania (south-west France), Pannonia and Illyricum (Balkans), the Alpine regions, Germany (all these listed in Suet. *Aug.* 21.1), Aethiopia and Arabia (see 26–7; Eutr. 7.9–10 = LACTOR N1).

terra et mari/by land and sea   The celebration of an individual's rule over land and sea follows in Hellenistic footsteps, and first emerges at Rome with Pompey (Cic. *Balb.* 6.16, *cuius res gestae omnis gentis cum clarissima victoria terra marique peragrassent*; Momigliano (1942) 63; for Augustus' rivalry with Pompey, see introduction pp. 32–3, heading, 1.1, 3.1, 5.2, 20.1, 25.1, 27.2, 31.2). A statue in Octavian's honour was set atop a column in the forum at Rome following his victory at Naulochus in 36 BC, with an inscription commemorating his long awaited re-imposition of peace by land and sea (App. *B Civ.* 5.130; Zanker (1988) 41–2). Peace by land and sea was the necessary prerequisite for closing the gates of Janus (13), and appears to have been a new twist given to the traditional theme by the Romans, perhaps during the Augustan era itself (Momigliano (1942) 63–4). The *Pax* panel on the altar of Augustan Peace (*ara Pacis Augustae*), depicting a mother nursing two infants flanked by personifications of breezes above land and sea, shows the incorporation of the idea into public art at Rome (see 12.2n. **aram Pacis Augustae**).

toto in orbe terrarum saepe gessi/I have often conducted . . . across the whole world   Augustus' claims to world conquest were in implicit rivalry with Alexander and Pompey (see introduction pp. 36–7, 32–3 and heading **orbem terrarum imperio populi Romani subiecit**).

victorque omnibus veniam petentibus civibus peperci/and as victor I was merciful to all citizens who asked for pardon   Augustus here lays claim to *clementia* (a particular characteristic of Julius Caesar), specifically in the context of civil strife, an official version of events found also in Velleius Paterculus (2.86.2). His actions after Actium arguably demonstrated a degree of clemency: even a hostile account admits that he did spare some Antonians (Dio Cass. 51.2.4), and he appears to have spared some of the children of Antony and Cleopatra, whilst executing others (Suet. *Aug.* 17.5). His early career, however, was not noted for displays of mercy (cf. Ridley (2003) 169–71). On the contrary, he was fully involved in the notorious proscriptions, and reputedly displayed immoderate cruelty after his victories at Philippi and Perusia, including towards citizens who

begged for pardon (Suet. *Aug.* 13, 15; Dio Cass. 48.14.3–5). Even Velleius has
to acknowledge that he had not always shown mercy, but implies that his
earlier cruelty after Philippi and as triumvir was out of character (Vell. Pat.
2.86.2). The contrast between the cruelty of Octavian and the clemency of
Augustus was often repeated, but finds no echo here (cf. Sen. *Clem.* 1.9.1,
11.1 = LACTOR H7, H8).

3.2 externas gentes/As for foreign peoples   This ideal is reminiscent of
Anchises' mission statement for Rome in Virgil's underworld, 'to spare the
conquered and to subdue the proud' (Virg. *Aen.* 6.853, *parcere subiectis
et debellare superbos*), which was also proclaimed in Horace's Centennial
Hymn, where Romans are described as 'superior to those that wage war,
mild to the prostrate enemy' (*Carm. Saec.* 51–2, *bellante prior, iacentem
lenis in hostem*). (See 26–33.)

**3.3 millia civium Romanorum sub sacramento meo fuerunt circiter
quingenta/There have been roughly 500,000 Roman citizens under
oath of allegiance to me**   This total (i.e. 500,000) includes legionaries
and praetorians who served under Augustus from the triumviral period
until his death. Augustus states that he settled over 300,000 veterans in
colonies or municipalities (including the roughly 120,000 soldiers settled
in colonies by 29 BC (15.3)). Tacitus' survey of troop dispositions around the
empire in AD 14 allows us to calculate that about 150,000 were then in service
(Tac. *Ann.* 4.5: twenty-five legions plus three urban and nine praetorian
cohorts). This would leave under 50,000 who died while enlisted under
Augustus. Given that of these some 15,000 were killed in the three legions
of Varus, such a low mortality rate for the army as a whole prompted P.
A. Brunt to argue that Augustus excluded from his total of 500,000 those
150,000 soldiers currently in service in AD 14, and that in reality about two-
fifths of Augustus' soldiers did not live long enough to reach retirement
(Brunt (1971) 339).

Augustus refers here to the standard oath of loyalty taken by troops
individually to a military commander (Campbell (1984) 19–23; Linderski
(1984) 76, 79). The Greek emphasizes its military character by adding the
word στρατεύσασαι (Wigtil (1982a) 633–4). Octavian secured an oath of
a different character from his soldiers in Italy and the western provinces in
32 BC (see 25.2n. *iuravit in mea verba*).

deduxi in colonias/I have settled in colonies   Augustus settled veterans in colonies over a wide geographical area, initially in Italy, but after the
triumviral period all other colonies were founded outside Italy (15.3, 16.1,
28). Colonies were towns of high status, with all of their inhabitants being
entitled to Roman citizenship. They had a useful role to play in introducing
Roman ways into non-Roman areas, of taking control of valuable natural

Fig. 11 Octavian, veiled and laureate, driving a plough drawn by oxen. *Denarius* issued in the east, *c.* 29–27 BC (coin: *BM Coins, Rom. Emp.* I 104 no. 638). © The Trustees of the British Museum.

resources, and of keeping the peace. Augusta Praetoria (modern Aosta) is a prime example (Strabo *Geography* 4.6.7 = LACTOR N12; Dio Cass. 53.25.3–5), as is Pisidian Antioch (see introduction pp. 13–14). His establishment of colonies was commemorated by *denarii* issued in the east, *c.* 29–27 BC, depicting Octavian, veiled and laureate, driving a plough drawn by oxen, symbolic of founding a new town (*BM Coins, Rom. Emp.* I 104 no. 638) (see Figure 11).

remisi in municipia sua/I sent back to their towns   See 16.2.

stipendis emeritis/after they had completed their terms of service In a significant departure from practice during the Republic, Augustus established a professional core to the army out of volunteers who made the army their career, with fixed terms of service, salary, and retirement packages (Keppie (1984) 146–8). In 13 BC, the standard period in service was fixed at twelve years for praetorians and sixteen for legionaries, followed by four years in reserve (Dio Cass. 54.25.6; Suet. *Aug.* 49.2). These were extended in AD 5 to sixteen and twenty years respectively, with a further five years in reserve (Dio Cass. 55.23.1; see 17.2). The mutinies that broke out on the Rhine and Danube at Augustus' death were, however, partly the result of these periods of service not being respected, with some soldiers supposedly having served for thirty or forty years (Tac. *Ann.* 1.17.2). Alongside this core of professional volunteers, conscription continued to be used whenever necessary, notably, but not exclusively, in times of crisis such as AD 6 and AD 9 (Brunt (1990) 193–5).

pro praemiis militiae/as the rewards for their service   On their discharge from service, veterans could now expect a reward for military service, with a cash payment sometimes replacing land grants from 13 BC (Dio Cass. 54.25.5, with cautious comments by Brunt (1962) 83; see 16.1). In AD 5, this sum was fixed at 12,000 sesterces, the equivalent of over thirteen years' gross pay (Dio Cass. 55.23.1; see 17.2). Augustus established a new treasury specifically to meet this demand for funds (see 17.2). In an edict of 31 BC, Octavian assigned further significant privileges to veterans, including exemptions from taxation and requisitioning (*FIRA*² I no. 56; Campbell (1984) 282).

3.4 naves cepi sescentas/I have captured 600 ships   Sextus Pompey lost more than 300 ships in 36 BC, including 30 at Mylae and 283 at Naulochus (App. *B Civ.* 5.108, 118, 121); Antony lost 300 ships at Actium, according to Augustus' autobiography (Plut. *Vit. Ant.* 68.2). A tithe of the different types of ships captured at Actium was dedicated to Neptune and Mars at the campsite memorial of Nicopolis (Strabo *Geography* 7.7.6 = LACTOR H9; Dio Cass. 51.2), where the prows of captured ships featured along a massive podium (Murray and Petsas (1989); Gurval (1995) 65–7; Zachos (2003), (2007: non vidi)); prows were also displayed on the temple of the deified Julius in the Roman forum (see 19.1n. *aedem divi Iuli*).

4.1 bis ovans triumphavi/Twice I have celebrated triumphal ovations An ovation was a lesser celebration than a triumph, usually for a victory over a foreign enemy, in cases where the victorious general did not qualify for a triumph. The commander entered Rome on foot or horseback, dressed in a *toga praetexta* (purple-bordered toga), and wearing a wreath of myrtle (Gell. *NA* 5.6.20–1, 27; Versnel (1970) 166–8). Augustus' choice of phrasing here attempts to raise the status of his ovations almost to that of a triumph (Ridley (2003) 97–8). By contrast, the Greek version seems to retain the distinction between the two forms of celebration. Augustus was awarded an ovation with Antony in November 40 BC after sealing the Treaty of Brundisium. According to the *fasti*, it was awarded because they had made peace with each other, an award without precedent, which, like Virgil's fourth *Eclogue*, reflects the mistaken optimism of the time (*Fasti Triumphales Capitolini: Inscr. Ital.* XIII.i 87 = EJ p. 33). Suetonius gives the misleading impression that the ovation was awarded for Philippi, although he otherwise echoes Augustus' words quite closely (*Aug.* 22.1, *bis ovans ingressus est urbem, post Philippense et rursus post Siculum bellum. curulis triumphos tris egit* – 'Twice he entered the city for an ovation, after Philippi and again after the Sicilian war. He drove triumphal chariots three times').

The other *ovatio*, on 13 November 36 BC, celebrated his defeat of Sextus Pompey; because this was a victory in civil war, it did not qualify for a triumph (*Fasti Triumphales Capitolini: Inscr. Ital.* XIII.i 87 = EJ p. 34).

tris egi curulis triumphos/three times I have driven triumphal chariots   To earn a triumph, a victorious general was required to have killed at least five thousand of the enemy and to have brought his army back home safely. In a full triumph, the victor rode in a golden chariot drawn by four white horses, accompanied by his sons and officers. He was dressed in a purple *tunica palmata* embroidered with palm branches and a *toga picta* of purple wool with gold thread, wore a garland of laurel upon his head, and carried a laurel branch in his right hand and the ivory eagle sceptre of Jupiter in his left. His face and hands were painted red, in imitation of the cult statue of Jupiter in the *Capitolium*. The procession through Rome to the *Capitolium* displayed booty, prisoners (4.3), and placards depicting memorable scenes from the war and identifying the conquered peoples. At the *Capitolium* white oxen were sacrificed to Jupiter and the commander dedicated his laurel wreath to his cult statue. In front of the chariot walked magistrates and senators, and behind it the Romans rescued from the enemy, and the victorious soldiers, singing ribald songs about their commander (Campbell (1984) 133–4, 139; Versnel (1970) 56–7, 95–6; for Augustus' procession, cf. Virg. *Aen.* 8.714–28 = LACTOR G38).

Augustus is referring to his triple triumph in 29 BC, with celebrations on three consecutive days (itself unprecedented), 13–15 August, for his victories in Dalmatia (36–34 BC; see 29.1), at Actium (31 BC; see 25.2), and Egypt (30 BC; see 27.1) (Dio Cass. 51.21.5–7; Livy *Per.* 133 = LACTOR H16; Gurval (1995) ch. 1). Augustus also made a cash distribution to the people of Rome on this occasion (15.1). Cleopatra, rather than Antony, was the official enemy since a triumph could not be granted for a civil war. The *fasti* omit Actium (*Fasti Triumphales Barberiniani* = *Inscr. Ital.* XIII.i 345 = EJ p. 35 = LACTOR N2a; cf. Gurval (1995) 31–3). Both triumph and ovation would be alien to a provincial readership, so the translator provides a version here which tries to explain the difference between the two ceremonies (Marrone (1977) 325). The triumphs were commemorated on *denarii* issued in 29–27 BC. On their reverse they depicted Octavian standing in a decorated *quadriga*, and on their obverse appears Victory standing on a ship's prow, holding a wreath and palm (*RIC* I² 60 nos. 263–4 = *BM Coins, Rom. Emp.* I 101 nos. 616–21 = Simon (1993) 47–9 no. 9). In this way Octavian equalled Pompey's three triumphs, but not Julius Caesar's celebration of four triumphs in 46 BC (Gurval (1995) 20–5).

appellatus sum viciens et semel imperator/I have been hailed twenty-one times as victorious general   A victorious general could be hailed *imperator* by his troops following a resounding victory. He would then

Table 1 *Augustus' acclamations as* imperator

Acclamation	Date	Victory/Victor	Sources
imp. i	43 BC	Forum Gallorum/Hirtius (Octavian left at camp)	Dio Cass. 46.38.1; Ov. *Fast.* 4.673–6
imp. ii	41 BC	Perusia/Octavian	App. *B Civ.* 5.46
imp. iii	by 40 BC	Brundisium treaty/ostensibly, Antony + Octavian	*Ovatio* must be preceded by acclamation
imp. iv	36 BC	Naulochus/Agrippa + Octavian	*Ovatio* must be preceded by acclamation
imp. v	34/33 BC	Illyria/Agrippa + Octavian	*CIL* V 526; preceding triumph of 29 BC
imp. vi	31 BC	Actium/Agrippa + Octavian	Oros. 6.19.14
imp. vii	29 BC	Macedonia/M. Licinius Crassus	Dio Cass. 51.25.2
imp. viii	25 BC	Spain + Germany/ Augustus/ M. Vinicius	Dio Cass. 53.26.4, with Barnes (1974) 21
imp. ix	20 BC	Parthia/Armenia diplomatic victory/Augustus + Tiberius	Dio Cass. 54.8.1, with Barnes (1974) 21–2
imp. x	15 BC	Raetia/Drusus + Tiberius	Barnes (1974) 22
imp. xi	12 BC	Pannonia/Tiberius	Dio Cass. 54.31.4, 33.5
imp. xii	11 BC	Germany/Drusus	Dio Cass. 54.33.5
imp. xiii	10 BC	Pannonia/Tiberius	Syme (1979b) 315
imp. xiv	8 BC	Germany/Tiberius	Dio Cass. 55.6.4
imp. xv	AD 1	Arabia/Gaius	Barnes (1974) 22–3
imp. xvi	AD 3	Artagira (Armenia)/Gaius	Dio Cass. 55.10a.7, with Barnes (1974) 23, Swan (2004) 132
imp. xvii	AD 6	Germany/Tiberius	Dio Cass. 55.28.5–6
imp. xviii	AD 8	Pannonia/Tiberius	Barnes (1974) 24, Woodman (1977) 178
imp. xix	AD 9	Dalmatia/Germanicus + Tiberius	Dio Cass. 56.16.4–17.1, with Barnes (1974) 24
imp. xx	AD 11	Germany/Tiberius	Vell. Pat. 2.120.1–2, with Barnes (1974) 24–5
imp. xxi	AD 13	Germany/Germanicus + Tiberius	Barnes (1974) 25–6; Syme (1979b) 319–20

send despatches wreathed in laurels to the senate reporting his victory, and his *fasces* would be decorated with laurel, which would later be deposited in the temple of Jupiter Capitolinus (see 4.1n. **laurum de fascibus deposui in Capitolio**). Augustus was hailed as *imperator* usually for victories won by himself and by members of his family, but in the sole case of Licinius Crassus in 29 BC also by a commander fighting under his auspices as his legate (Mommsen (1883) 11–17; Barnes (1974); Syme (1979b); Swan (2004) Appendix 3). In Table 1, I suggest on the basis of Appian that Octavian was hailed as *imperator* for the second time after Perusia, but otherwise have collated the most plausible conjectures of other scholars.

In a separate development, from 38, or perhaps 40 BC, Octavian assumed the title *imperator* as his *praenomen*, and this name was made official in 29 BC (Syme (1939) 112–13, (1958) 172–88). By doing so, he began his monopoly on claims of military success, which he later consolidated, and the pattern whereby he became the supreme military commander of the Roman army.

decernente pluris triumphos mihi senatu/although the senate voted me more triumphs   Having celebrated his spectacular triple triumph in 29 BC (see 4.1n. ***tris egi curulis triumphos***), Augustus turned down all future offers of a triumph, in order to keep within traditional limits (and perhaps too because it would have been hard to surpass the celebrations of 29 BC). Only dictators had celebrated more than three triumphs: M. Furius Camillus and M. Valerius Corvinus won four apiece, Julius Caesar five (Simon (1993) 48 n. 73). Augustus also recalled Romulus in this way, since he too had held three triumphs (Dion. Hal. *Ant. Rom.* 2.34.2–4, 54.2, 55.5). Augustus declined triumphs in 25 BC, for his own victories over the Cantabrians and those of M. Vinicius over the Germans (Flor. 2.33; Dio Cass. 53.26.5); possibly in 20 BC, on recovering military standards from the Parthians (Dio Cass. 54.8.3, with Rich (1998) 77–8, 108, 119; see 29.2); in 8 BC for Tiberius' victory over the Germans (Dio Cass. 55.6.6); and in AD 9 for campaigns by Tiberius and Germanicus in Dalmatia (Dio Cass. 56.17.1). Between 27 and 19 BC, five proconsuls commanding troops under their own auspices won triumphs (*Fasti Triumphales Capitolini = Inscr. Ital.* XIII.i 87 = LACTOR N2c–f), but after Agrippa turned down triumphs in 19 and 14 BC (Dio Cass. 54.11.6, 54.24.7), it would have been difficult for others to claim a triumph. Subsequently, only members of the imperial family were granted triumphs, whilst *ornamenta triumphalia* (triumphal ornaments and dress, but no grand parade) were bestowed on others, with Tiberius paving the way as the first to receive them, perhaps in a gesture to make them seem more acceptable because a member of Augustus' own family had been satisfied with them (Campbell (1984) 358–9; Raaflaub (1987) 270–1).

laurum de fascibus deposui in Capitolio/I deposited the laurel from my *fasces* in the Capitoline temple   The laying of a laurel wreath in the lap of Capitoline Jupiter was also the culmination of the ceremony of a triumph (see 4.1n. ***tris egi curulis triumphos***). Augustus is recorded as having done this in 13 BC (Dio Cass. 54.25.4), and in 9 BC he placed laurel in the temple of Jupiter Feretrius (Dio Cass. 55.5.1), both being occasions when he received imperatorial acclamations (see 4.1n. ***appellatus sum viciens et semel imperator***), but did not celebrate a triumph.

votis . . . solutis/in fulfilment of the vows   Augustus is referring to vows made to Capitoline Jupiter before embarking on campaign (cf. Livy 45.39.11).

4.2 per legatos meos auspicis meis/through my deputies under my auspices   As well as their *imperium*, the highest magistrates at Rome also enjoyed the right to take the auspices (*auspicium*), observing the flight of birds in order to check for the gods' approval of a course of action. Before embarking on a military campaign, a commander would take the auspices at Rome, and would then proceed to take the auspices when on campaign before significant actions, such as engaging in battle (Liebeschuetz (1979) 7–29; Scheid (2003) 112–20). By continually holding repeated consulships from 31 to 23 BC, Augustus in effect took control of the taking of auspices at Rome, and then from 27 BC, when he was given control over almost all the legions in the provinces, he took on a new role as commander-in-chief of the Roman army (see Giovannini (1983) 151 for the fundamental transformation of *imperium consulare* implicit in this process). In effect, this meant that others could no longer be awarded triumphs, 'for, to be able to celebrate a triumph, it was necessary to have possessed the auspices throughout the war in question. From now on, wars were under the leadership (*ductu*) of a general, but under the auspices of the emperor' (Scheid (2003) 119). Even proconsuls, usually thought of as more independent than Augustus' legates, could be represented as conducting military activity under the auspices of Augustus (*AE* 1940.68 = EJ no. 43 = LACTOR M4). The cameo known as the 'Gemma Augustea' (see Figure 12) provides a visual representation of this idea (von Hesberg (1978) 982–3 fig. 45).

decrevit senatus supplicandum esse/the senate . . . decreed that thanksgiving should be offered   *Supplicationes* were days of ceremonial thanksgiving and sacrifices to the gods for success, decreed by the senate. Traditionally they were voted when the senate received a despatch from a commander announcing a victory, and asking for a thanksgiving to be performed in his name (Versnel (1970) 172). Originally lasting only a single day, both Pompey and Julius Caesar had been celebrated with *supplicationes* lasting many days. Octavian shared his first *supplicatio*, which lasted for an unprecedented 50 days, with Hirtius and Pansa, after their success at Mutina (Cic. *Phil.* 14.11.29; App. *B Civ.* 3.74). Augustus accepted *supplicationes* for victories won by his legates, such as in 20 BC to celebrate the recovery of the standards from the Parthians and Tiberius' success in Armenia (Dio Cass. 54.8.3, 9.5), and in 11 BC for the campaign of L. Calpurnius Piso

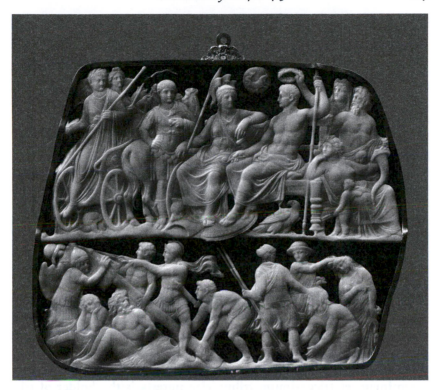

Fig. 12 *Gemma Augustea.*

Pontifex in Thrace (Dio Cass. 54.34.7; cf. *ILS* 918 = *CIL* XIV 3613 = EJ no. 199 = LACTOR M50, with Syme (1973)). The duration of 890 days for Augustus' fifty-five *supplicationes* indicates an average of 16 days for each celebration. In addition, other occasions might also be celebrated by a *supplicatio*, such as the suppression of a conspiracy in 22 BC (Dio Cass. 54.3.8). This expression is simplified in the Greek version (Reichmann (1943) 22).

4.3 reges aut regum liberi novem/nine kings or kings' children Prisoners-of-war were led in procession in front of the triumphal chariot and the most important of them were usually executed before the sacrifice to Jupiter (Versnel (1970) 95). Six out of the nine paraded during the triple triumph of 29 BC can be identified (Gurval (1995) 28–9). Cleopatra was said to have committed suicide precisely to avoid this humiliation (Hor. *Carm.* 1.37.25–32); instead, an effigy of her was paraded on a couch, along with her children Alexander Helios and Cleopatra Selene (Dio Cass. 51.21.8). Two foreign kings from the east who had supported Antony with troops for Actium were paraded and then executed, Alexander of Emesa (Dio Cass. 51.2.2), and Adiatorix, tetrarch of Galatia, whose wife and two sons were also displayed, the younger of whom was also executed (Strabo *Geography* 12.3.35).

4.4 consul fueram terdeciens/I had been consul thirteen times Augustus was appointed consul in 43 (1.4) and 33 BC, and then each year from 31–23 BC. At this time, the consulship was the cornerstone of his power, and between 28 and 24 BC he stayed in office for the whole twelve months. In June 23 BC he resigned and declined to resume office even when popular pressure mounted in 21 and 19 BC (see 5.3n. *consulatum*, 12.1n. *cum consule Q. Lucretio*). Instead, he received tribunician power in 23 BC (see 4.4n. *septimum et tricensimum tribuniciae potestatis*), and consular power in 19 BC (see 5.3n. *consulatum*, 8.3–4). He subsequently assumed the consulship only twice, in 5 and 2 BC, when he introduced his adopted sons Gaius and Lucius into public life (see 14.1n. *quo deducti sunt in forum*, 15.2, 15.4; Suet. *Aug.* 26). (For a chart tracking Augustus' consulships (date, place of assumption, date of abdication, months held), see Carter (1982) 121; for discussion of the so-called 'constitutional settlements', see Crook (1996) and Gruen (2005).)

cum scribebam haec/at the time of writing This indicates a date of composition after 1 July AD 14 (see 35.2; introduction pp. 42–3).

septimum et tricensimum tribuniciae potestatis/the holder of tribunician power thirty-seven times Augustus was granted tribunician power for the thirty-seventh time on 1 July AD 14. He had been granted tribunician sacrosanctity in 36 BC (Dio Cass. 49.15.6; see 10.1), but tribunician power was arguably first granted to him in 23 BC (cf. Carter (1982) 124–5; Brunt and Moore (1967) 10–11), when he resigned from the consulship, to last for the rest of his life (Dio Cass. 53.32.5; Ferrary (2001) 115–21). The granting of the powers of a tribune separately from the office marked a radical departure from traditional practice (although it was perhaps prefigured by the grant of censorial powers to Augustus and Agrippa in 28 BC, see 8.2n. *in consulatu sexto censum populi . . . egi*), as did Augustus' possession of it initially without a colleague, and without its having to be renewed annually (Gruen (2005) 40). Later, Agrippa (18–12 BC) and Tiberius (6–1 BC, AD 4–14) were nominated in turn as his colleague in tribunician power (6.2).

Tribunician power gave Augustus wide-ranging powers in Rome, and came to be viewed as the 'title of the highest rank' (cf. Tac. *Ann.* 3.56, *summi fastigii vocabulum*). He could summon the senate whenever he wanted and submit a motion to it, summon the popular assembly and propose legislation, impose a veto on the actions of other magistrates, intervene on behalf of citizens who were being unfairly treated by other magistrates, and force citizens to obey his orders. Referring to an emperor's year of tribunician power became an alternative standard system for dating, alongside the traditional naming of consuls: 'It represents an implicit, indeed an explicit, acknowledgement that Augustus' powers did not rest on magisterial offices that were subject to annual review and election, or on specific provinces with territorial boundaries and time limits requiring renewal . . . the tribunician years rolled on, uninterrupted, symbolic of stability and a continuum' (Gruen (2005) 41–2). Augustus is perhaps highlighting his tribunician power here in a bid to be seen as the people's champion, the traditional role of the plebeian tribunes (cf. Bosworth (1999) 17; contra, Gruen (2005) 40). This whole sentence provides a smooth transition to the subject matter of the following chapters, which deal with Augustus' position within the state, the powers which he rejected and the offices which he accepted.

POWERS REJECTED AND OFFICES ACCEPTED (5–7)

Augustus first emphasizes his reluctance to accept extraordinary powers, and his insistence on behaving with constitutional propriety (5–6). He finishes by listing those offices and priesthoods which he held for a considerable number of years (7).

5.1 dictaturam . . . non recepi/the post of dictator . . . I did not accept it
The dictatorship gave supreme civil and military powers to an individual in an emergency for a limited duration (Tac. *Ann.* 1.1 = LACTOR F1). There were two main forms of the post, one appointing an office-holder to command the army for a fixed term (originally for a maximum of six months), the other for performing a specific task, such as organizing the festival of the *feriae Latinae* (Lintott (1999) 109–13). Julius Caesar's appointment as perpetual dictator (*dictator perpetuus*) undermined the principle that the post was a short-term emergency measure, and led to the dictatorship being abolished on Antony's proposal after his assassination (Cic. *Phil.* 1.13.32, 2.36.91, 5.4.10; Syme (1939) 107). Specific circumstances in 22 BC of the type that would earlier have resulted in the appointment of a dictator prompted the people to demand Augustus as dictator, threatening the senate with violence should it not agree; floods and thunderstorms at Rome accompanied by bad omens and plague in Italy had resulted in the continuation from the previous year of famine at Rome (Dio Cass. 54.1.1–3; Alföldy (1972)). The *plebs* was perhaps concerned that Augustus would not otherwise regard it as his responsibility to alleviate the food shortage, given that this was the first year since 31 BC that Augustus had not assumed office as consul (Garnsey (1988) 240; Rich (1990) 172; for Augustus' solution to these problems, see 5.2).

Velleius repeats the claim that the people offered the post to Augustus on several occasions (Vell. Pat. 2.89.5), and Suetonius records how

Augustus rejected the post with dramatic gestures, getting down onto bended knee and pulling his toga from his shoulders (Suet. *Aug.* 52; cf. Dio Cass. 54.1.4; Flor. 2.34.65 mistakenly states that Augustus was called *dictator perpetuus*). The reason for this is the implication that, had he accepted the post, Augustus would in effect have been acknowledging his assumption of a monarchical role at Rome (cf. Euseb. *Chron.* 1994 = 24 BC, 'When the monarchy is granted to him, Augustus refuses it', *Augustus, cum ei monarchia deferetur, rennuit*). Augustus may have intended to recall Scipio Africanus, who also refused a perpetual dictatorship (Val. Max. 4.1.6; see 5.3n. **consulatum**). The juxtaposition of this refusal at the start of this chapter with the mention of Augustus' tribunician power at the end of the previous one may also invite comparison with Scipio's attitude to tribunician power. Whereas Africanus later attacked tribunes trying to arrest his brother, and consequently was accused by Tiberius Gracchus of dissolving tribunician power (Livy 38.56.9–10), Augustus accepted tribunician power and put it to good use (see 6.2; Bosworth (1999) 17).

et apsenti et praesenti/both when I was absent and when I was present   Augustus was absent from Rome at the time in Campania, but he returned to Rome to sort out the crisis. In his refusal of the dictatorship, Augustus may have wanted to emphasize the differences between himself and Caesar. He is perhaps alluding to the fact that Caesar undertook his second dictatorship in 48 BC when absent from Italy, contrary to traditional practice (Alföldy (1972) 9).

a populo et a senatu/by both people and senate   This provides an over-simplified, positive account of events, if the narrative in Dio Cassius (54.1.3) is accurate, where the people shut the senate up in its council chamber, threatening to burn the building down if the senate did not accede to its request to appoint Augustus as dictator (Garnsey (1988) 220). (For the word order see 8.1n. *iussu populi et senatus*.)

M. Marcello et L. Arruntio consulibus/in the consulship of Marcus Marcellus and Lucius Arruntius   This pair held office in 22 BC. M. Claudius Marcellus Aeserninus belonged to a noble family, but had not enjoyed a distinguished career, having tried to back both Pompey and Caesar whilst serving as *quaestor* in Spain in 48 BC (Dio Cass. 42.15.1–16.2). His consulship ended a long hiatus in the progression of his career, but by this time he was an old man (*PIR²* C926; Syme (1986) 41, 43). The 'new man' (*novus homo*) L. Arruntius (*PIR²* A1129; Syme (1986) 41, 43, 264) had been a supporter of Pompey proscribed by the triumvirs in 43 BC, but he returned to Italy in 39 BC after the treaty of Misenum, and ended up commanding ships at Actium (Vell. Pat. 2.77.3, 85.2).

5.2 curationem annonae/manage the corn supply   Provisioning Rome
was the responsibility of the *aediles ceriales*, but in the previous year,
23 BC, Augustus had provided the people with a year's supply of corn
at his own expense, in addition to the usual distributions (see 15.1), which
explains why they turned to him to solve the crisis in 22 BC. We might
wonder whether his ability to solve a food shortage so rapidly does not
suggest that he had been stockpiling stores in anticipation of such a crisis, perhaps even worsening the shortage, but, on a more charitable view,
he may instead simply have bought up stocks hoarded by others (Carter
(1982) 175; Rich (1990) 172). Once again, we find Augustus both emulating
and surpassing Pompey, who had been given command over Rome's corn
supply throughout the world for a five-year period, after supplies reached
a crisis point in 57 BC (Dio Cass. 54.1.3; Cic. *Att.* 4.1.7; Pavis D'Escurac
(1976) 11–14; Rickman (1980) 53–8; Garnsey (1988) 201, 216–17, 240; for
emulation of Pompey see introduction pp. 32–3, heading, 1.1, 3.1, 5.2, 20.1,
25.1, 27.2, 31.2). Augustus' phrasing, and the context of his rejection of the
dictatorship, implies that he accepted responsibility for the grain supply as
a temporary measure at a time of crisis, but this is perhaps a misleading
impression (Pavis D'Escurac (1976) 17–19).

From 18 BC, Augustus made further subventions of grain and money
when necessary (18) and also reorganized the system of distributing the
corn dole, but further crises in AD 6–7 prompted him to set up a formal
system to control the supply, and not just the distribution, of grain at Rome
(Dio Cass. 55.26.2, 55.31.4; Brunt and Moore (1967) 44). He appointed two
senior senators as officials in charge of securing the capital's grain supply;
their duties were transferred some time before AD 14 to a prefect of the
grain supply (*praefectus annonae*) of equestrian rank, answerable to the
emperor himself (Pavis D'Escurac (1976) 22–32; Rickman (1980) 63–4;
Garnsey (1988) 232–3). Ensuring a regular and reliable supply of grain to
the vast population of Rome was one of the surest ways of preventing
popular unrest, as later emperors also understood (cf. Tac. *Ann.* 1.2.1). In
addition to his administrative changes, Augustus' conquest of Egypt and
military advances elsewhere in North Africa also helped in the long term
by creating new, significant sources of grain (Garnsey (1988) 231).

5.3 consulatum/consulship   This offer of a perpetual consulship was
presumably made as an alternative to the dictatorship, which he had refused
(5.1). Popular pressure on Augustus to resume office as consul continued
into 21 and 19 BC (Dio Cass. 54.6.1–3; see 12.1n. ***cum consule Q. Lucretio***).
Scipio Africanus had also rejected the chance to become perpetual dictator
and consul (Val. Max. 4.1.6). On one view, Augustus did, however, accept
consular power (*imperium consulare*) for life in 19 BC (Dio Cass. 54.10.5;
Rich (1990) 187, following Jones (1951) 117; cf. 8.3–4; contra, Crook (1996)
91–2; Cotton and Yakobson (2002) 196–203), but this was perhaps simply

an acknowledgement of the implication of the senate's decision in 23 BC that Augustus should not have to lay down his *imperium* on crossing the city's sacred boundary, or *pomerium* (Dio Cass. 53.23.5; Ferrary (2001) 120–1).

6.1 consulibus M. Vinicio et Q. Lucretio/In the consulship of Marcus Vinicius and Quintus Lucretius   A 'new man' (*novus homo*) from Cales in Campania, M. Vinicius became suffect consul in 19 BC (in place of C. Sentius Saturninus), and went on to pursue a distinguished military career in Illyricum and on the Rhine, where he won triumphal decorations (*ornamenta triumphalia*), and became a close friend of Augustus (Dio Cass. 53.26.4–5; Vell. Pat. 2.104.2; Suet. *Aug.* 71.2; *PIR* V444; Syme (1986) 44, 332, 393, 426). His fellow consul Q. Lucretius Vespillo was an elderly 'new man' (*novus homo*), who had commanded troops for Pompey in 49 BC and survived being proscribed (Val. Max 6.7.2; App. *B Civ.* 4.6.44; *PIR*² L412). For the circumstances of his appointment, see 12.1n. **cum consule Q. Lucretio**. Their partnership occurred in the second half of the year.

P. Lentulo et Cn. Lentulo/Publius Lentulus and Gnaeus Lentulus   Despite coming from a noble family, this pair of Cornelii Lentuli (P. Cornelius Lentulus Marcellinus and Cn. Cornelius Lentulus), who shared the consulship in 18 BC, was otherwise undistinguished, and even their precise identity is unclear (*PIR*² C1396, 1378; Syme (1986) 50, 287).

Paullo Fabio Maximo et Q. Tuberone/Paullus Fabius Maximus and Quintus Tubero   Paullus Fabius Maximus was a close friend of Augustus, married to his cousin Marcia. He became consul almost as soon as was feasible, in 11 BC (having been born in 46 BC). He was then appointed by Augustus to one of the top jobs in the state the very next year (Syme (1986) ch. 28; *PIR*² F47). As proconsul of Asia 10/9 BC, he effusively introduced into the province a calendar in Augustus' honour, which celebrated New Year's Day on his birthday, 23 September (EJ no. 98/*SEG* 4.490/*RDGE* no. 65 = LACTOR H34; see 13n. **priusquam nascerer**). Apart from the fact that he was a *quindecimvir*, nothing further is known about the career of Q. Aelius Tubero (*PIR*² A274; Syme (1986) 306–7).

curator legum et morum/guardian of laws and customs   Augustus' claim to have turned down this post fits into his practice of rejecting any office that seemed unconstitutional (see 5.1, 5.3; Gruen (2005) 35). He is not, therefore, simply alluding to the traditional task of censors to judge their peers' behaviour, invidious though this task may have been. His objections must also have been founded precisely upon the fact that he alone was being offered a post with supreme power (*summa potestate solus*; Ridley (2003) 105–6). The fact that Augustus had to turn down the offer on three occasions suggests that there was a great deal of unrest during these years (Ridley (2003) 102). By contrast, Suetonius states that he did accept the post for life (*Aug.* 27.5, *recepit et morum legumque regimen aeque perpetuum*) and Dio Cassius records two occasions, in 19 BC and 12 BC, on which he undertook to supervise morals for a period of five years (54.10.5, 30.1), but both of these authors are confused about this matter in different ways (Carter (1982) 125–6; Rich (1990) 187; Crook (1996) 91, with n. 110). This discrepancy may have arisen from the fact that although Augustus states that he rejected the office, he did in fact accomplish what was required of him by virtue of his tribunician power instead. As a result, the later writers may have assumed that he had accepted the post, given that he exercised its functions (Ridley (2003) 106). Certainly, contemporary poets writing after the events related here give the impression that Augustus had effectively taken steps to regulate morals at Rome through his legislation (see 6.2; Hor. *Epist.* 2.1.1–3 = LACTOR G46, *c.* 12 BC; Ov. *Met.* 15.832–4 = LACTOR G55, *Tr.* 2.233–4, AD *c.* 9 = LACTOR G56, *urbs quoque te et legum lassat tutela tuarum / et morum, similes quos cupis esse tuis* – 'The city also wearies you, and the guardianship of your laws and morals, which you desire to be similar to your own'). (For detailed discussion of the problems posed by this paragraph, see Ridley (2003) 101–8.) Augustus' care for the grain supply, laws, and customs mentioned here and in the previous chapter is similar to a claim made of Zeus in Euhemerus: 'he prepared laws, customs, and grain' (*leges mores frumentaque paravit*, Lactant. *Div. Inst.* 1.11.45 = *FGrH* 63 F23; Bosworth (1999) 16. For the significance of this parallel, see introduction p. 41).

contra morem maiorem/contravened ancestral custom Augustus was keen to appear as the defender of Rome's ancestral customs (see introduction pp. 39–40).

6.2 quae tum per me geri senatus voluit, per tribuniciam potestatem perfeci/The things which the senate wanted to be accomplished by me at that time, I executed by virtue of my tribunician power This statement has been fairly criticized for its opaqueness, since it leaves entirely open what the senate did actually want Augustus to do. His listing of three separate consular years (6.1) implies that he has in mind legislation passed in different years, but he perhaps intended to recall primarily, but not exclusively, what has come to be termed his 'moral legislation' of 18 BC. Morality at Rome had traditionally been a public matter; two censors periodically assessed the moral conduct of all citizens when drawing up their census lists; censured citizens could be removed from their voting tribe, and senators and equestrians could be demoted (Lintott (1999) 117–19). This was, however, the first occasion when legislation was passed on the subject (Williams (1962) 28–9. For a different interpretation that Augustus was primarily aiming to protect property inheritance and transferral of social status between generations, see Wallace-Hadrill (1981b)). Augustan writers give the impression of dissatisfaction with morals at Rome (Livy *praef.* 9 = LACTOR D1, Hor. *Carm.* 3.6 = LACTOR G28, 3.24), but this was nothing new: Romans often envied the apparent morality of past generations (cf. Sall. *Cat.* 10).

Augustus intervened in the moral behaviour of Roman society chiefly through his legislation of 18 BC, which he introduced by right of his tribunician power. His laws encouraging marriage and penalizing adultery (*leges Iuliae de maritandis ordinibus, de adulteriis coercendis*, see LACTOR pp. 354–67) were highlighted during the hymn sung at the Centennial Games the following year (see 22.2) and received favourable press from Horace elsewhere too (Hor. *Carm. Saec.* 17–20 = LACTOR L28; cf. *Carm.* 4.5.21–4 = LACTOR G43). Nevertheless, the law on marriage was unpopular and had to be modified by the *lex Papia Poppaea* in AD 9. We may doubt, therefore, whether the senate had really commissioned Augustus to pass this particular law in the form he chose (Brunt and Moore (1967) 47; cf. 8.5). His other laws of 18 BC took action to prevent electoral corruption (*lex Iulia de ambitu*) and to restrain spending on luxuries (*lex sumptuaria*; Dio Cass. 54.16.1; Suet. *Aug.* 34.1).

conlegam/colleague   By disassociating tribunician power from the office of plebeian tribune (see 4.4n. ***septimum et tricensimum tribuniciae potestatis***), Augustus was able to acquire hand-picked colleagues to share his power. Although under his successors such grants came to be a way of signalling an heir, this was not immediately the case under Augustus for either Tiberius or Agrippa. They were both granted tribunician power only once they had earned the honour (Gruen (2005) 44, 45–6, 48; Tac. *Ann.* 3.56.2 comments with the benefit of hindsight). Augustus' first colleague was his close collaborator and son-in-law M. Agrippa (see 8.2n. ***conlega M. Agrippa***), who received a grant of tribunician power covering the five-year period 18–13 BC via a senatorial decree which was then ratified as a *lex* by the people (Ameling (1994) 5). This was then renewed for a further five-year period in 13 BC, but was curtailed by his death in 12 BC (see Augustus' funerary eulogy of Agrippa, *P. Köln* 10 = EJ no. 366 = LACTOR T14, + updated version in Ameling (1994) 1–2; Dio Cass. 54.12.4). The ostensibly equal status of Augustus and Agrippa that resulted from these grants was visually represented on a *denarius*-type issued at Rome in 13 BC (see Figure 13). On its reverse it depicted the togate figures of Augustus and Agrippa seated on the rostra next to each other, sharing an honorific double seat (*bisellium*) (*RIC* I² 73 nos. 406–7 = *BM Coins, Rom. Emp.* I 23–4 nos. 115–17 = Simon (1993) 53, 56–7 no. 12 = LACTOR H27). After Agrippa's death, Tiberius did not immediately receive tribunician power, not even when he became Augustus' son-in-law in 11 BC. He had to wait until

Fig. 13 Augustus and Agrippa as colleagues. *Denarius*, 13 BC (coin: reverse, *RIC* I² 73 nos. 406–7 = LACTOR H27).

6 BC, when he was granted tribunician power for a five-year period (Suet. *Tib.* 9.3; Dio Cass. 55.9.4). His second grant in AD 4 (coinciding with his adoption by Augustus) was for a ten-year period, and it was duly reconfirmed a final time in AD 13 (Dio Cass. 55.13.2, 56.28.1 with Swan (2004) 142–3; Suet. *Tib.* 16.1, five-year term).

7.1 triumvirum rei publicae constituendae/one of the triumvirs for settling the state   The triumvirate of M. Aemilius Lepidus, M. Antonius (Antony), and C. Iulius Caesar (Octavian) – in that order of seniority – was negotiated in secrecy between the three men at Bononia (App. *B Civ.* 4.1.2, Dio Cass. 46.55.3–56.1), and officially approved by the *lex Titia de triumviris rei publicae constituendae* of 27 November 43 BC (*Fasti Colotiani = Inscr. Ital.* XIII.i 274 = EJ p. 32; see 1.4). This plebiscite was proposed by a tribune and voted into effect immediately, without the statutory wait for three days (*trinundinum*) between proposal and vote to allow for scrutiny of the measure (App. *B Civ.* 4.2.7; cf. Dio Cass. 47.2.1; Lintott (1999) 44). In theory, the triumvirs received consular powers, but they took upon themselves the tasks of appointing straight away magistrates for each of their five years in office and of sharing out the provinces between themselves (App. *B Civ.* 4.1.2). In addition, they allocated priesthoods as they chose (Dio Cass. 47.15.1, 48.36.4), and had the right to consult the senate (Gell. *NA* 14.7.5). Between them, they controlled a formidable array of soldiers. Their execution of personal political enemies through the proscriptions was the most notorious aspect of their rule at Rome (App. *B Civ.* 4.1.3, 4.2.5–4.5.30, 6.36–51; Dio Cass. 47.3–13), but they also made irregular and over-abundant magisterial appointments. At the same time, however, the senate and people still exercised some of their traditional functions (Millar (1973) 50–4).

per continuos annos decem/for ten consecutive years   The *lex Titia* established the triumvirate for a fixed term of five years. Their powers therefore initially elapsed on 31 December 38 BC, when they informally assumed a second five-year period in office down to the end of 33 BC, which Octavian and Antony agreed upon together at Tarentum in the summer of 37 BC. It perhaps received retrospective authorization later in the year (contra, App. *B Civ.* 5.95). Both Augustus and Suetonius (*Aug.* 27.1) state that the triumvirate lasted for ten years, and Augustus draws attention to his length of service by postponing the time clause until after the main verb (7.2); the *Fasti Consulares Capitolini* (*Inscr. Ital.* XIII.i 59, with Brunt and Moore (1967) 48) mention the triumvirate for 37 BC, apparently marking the start of its second term (cf. *CIL* V 525 = *ILS* 77: a building inscription set up by Octavian as *cos. design. tert. iiivir r.p.c.iter*). Appian (*Ill.* 28) made an error in stating that the triumvirate ceased at the end of 32 BC (Pelling (1996) 67–8). Augustus had not conveniently 'forgotten' about a year-long period before the renewal of the triumvirate at the end of 37 BC, when his position in the state was questionable, nor did he need to camouflage the gap in official powers occurring in the year before his third consulship, which commenced on 1 January 31 BC. Instead, the oath of loyalty sworn in 32 BC (25.2) was represented as justifying his position at Rome (Girardet (1995); cf. Ridley (2003) 172–7).

7.2 princeps senatus/the highest ranking member of the senate   This was traditionally the title given to the most senior member of the senate, who had the privilege of speaking first in debates (Lintott (1999) 78). Octavian would not have qualified for this position under normal circumstances, but he assumed this title in 28 BC, at the time of his first revision of the senate's membership (Dio Cass. 53.1.3; see 8.2). He then held it until his death (see 13 for Augustus' adoption of the title *princeps* in a more general sense). The Greek periphrasis explains what the significance of this title is (Vanotti (1975) 309).

usque ad eum diem/right until the very day   On the date of composition of the *RGDA*, see introduction pp. 42–3; 4.4, 8.4, 25.3, 35.2.

7.3 pontifex maximus/chief priest   Augustus reports his membership of all four major priestly colleges, listed in hierarchial order. He starts with his post as head of the most prestigious college of *pontifices*, who were in charge of overseeing state cult. He had become a *pontifex* in 47 BC, through the influence of Julius Caesar, replacing Domitius Ahenobarbus who had been killed at Pharsalos (Nic. Dam. 4 = *FGrH* 90 F127.4.9; Vell. Pat. 2.59.3; Lewis (1955) 28 no. 3) – co-option was the standard procedure for nominating new *pontifices* (Lintott (1999) 183–4) – and then *pontifex maximus* in 12 BC at the death of Lepidus (10.2). Traditionally, an individual held only one priesthood for life, but Julius Caesar had become both *augur* and *quindecimvir* in 47 BC, despite his appointment already in 63 BC as *pontifex maximus*. In compensation, it seems, one member was added to each of these three colleges, and possibly three more to the *septemviri* (Gordon (1990) 182). Augustus' accumulation of priesthoods underpinned his various religious revivals (see 7.3, 10.2, 13, 19.1, 19.2, 20.4, 22.2; cf. Suet. *Aug.* 30.2–31.4), and, in effect, made him appear as a new Numa (second king of Rome, notable for his religious activities) as well as a Romulus (Gordon (1990) 183–4).

Only with Augustus did the *pontifex maximus* come to act as chief priest, with overall religious authority at Rome extending beyond the college of the *pontifices*, and after his death it became standard practice for each successive *princeps* to assume the post, which became incorporated into imperial titulature. Augustus' priestly functions in Roman society were an important part of his self-representation, with images of him *capite velato* (with his head veiled as required for making a sacrifice) making up 20 out of his 230 surviving portaits. They conveyed the message that Augustus was a crucial intermediary with the gods in securing their support for Rome. At Rome, the relief on the altar of Augustan Peace (see 12.2n. **aram Pacis Augustae**) and the lifesize 'via Labicana' statue are the most famous of such images (Gordon (1990) 211–13; Zanker (1988) 126–8, with figs. 100a, 104; Beard, North, and Price (1998) 186–92) (see Figure 14).

augur, XVvirum sacris faciundis, VIIvirum epulonum/*augur*, one of the Fifteen for conducting sacred rites, one of the Seven in charge of feasts   Augustus was nominated as an *augur* between 42 and 40 BC (Lewis (1955) 40 no. 14), as *xvvir* by 37–35 BC (Lewis (1955) 48 no. 4), and as *viivir* some time before 16 BC (Lewis (1955) 57 no. 7). Augurs were responsible for taking auspices, in order to ascertain divine will, by observing the flight and song of birds. In 29 BC Augustus revived the *augurium salutis*, the 'augury for safety', a ceremony determining whether the consuls could offer a prayer for the state's safety, which could only be performed in peacetime (Suet. *Aug.* 31.4; Dio Cass. 51.20.4; *ILS* 9337). The Fifteen were in charge of the Sibylline books and oversaw foreign cults in Rome (see 22.2). The Seven supervised public religious feasts at festivals and games. Translating the title of this priesthood into Greek presented a challenge, because it would involve also explaining the nature of *epulae*; the translator therefore simplifies here (Marrone (1977) 326). Augustus' unprecedented accumulation of all four priesthoods was commemorated on *denarii* issued at Rome in 16 BC, depicting a *simpulum* (ladle), *lituus*

Fig. 14 Statue of Augustus, from the via Labicana, Rome.

(augurs' ceremonial staff), *patera* (sacrificial bowl), and tripod, i.e. symbols of the four priesthoods (*RIC* I² 69 no. 367 = *BM Coins, Rom. Emp.* I 20 nos. 98–9 = Simon (1993) 58 no. 15 = LACTOR L1; cf. *RIC* I² 73 no. 410 = Simon (1993) 58 no. 16, 13 BC = *BM Coins, Rom. Emp.* I 24 nos. 119–20). (For Augustus' accumulation of priesthoods, see Figure 15.)

Fig. 15 Augustus' accumulation of priesthoods. *Denarius*, 16 BC (coin: reverse, *RIC* I² 69 no. 367 = LACTOR L1).

frater arvalis/Arval brother There were twelve Arvals, all of the highest social status, in the priestly college, which was restructured by Augustus in about 29 BC (Scheid (2005) 181; for the list of members in AD 14, see *CIL* VI 2023a = LACTOR L7, with Scheid (1998) no. 2). Their headquarters for the cult of the Dea Dia were located in a sacred grove in the suburbs of Rome (modern Magliana). Originally given oversight for the purification of fields, the priesthood increasingly became devoted to religious rites in honour of the imperial family.

sodalis Titius/member of the fraternity of Titus There are different explanations for the origins of this ancient priesthood, founded either by Romulus in honour of Titus Tatius, king of the Sabines and Romulus' co-ruler (Tac. *Hist.* 2.95.1), or founded by Titus Tatius himself to uphold Sabine rites (Tac. *Ann.* 1.54.1). A completely separate tradition, deriving the priesthood's name instead from the twittering of birds, suggests some connection with augury (Varro *Ling.* 5.15, *ab avibus titiantibus*). It was revived by Augustus at roughly the same time as the Arvals, *c.* 29 BC. The *sodales Titii* provided a model for the *sodales Augustales*, who were created for the task of upholding cult of Augustus in AD 14 (Tac. *Ann.* 1.54.1; Scheid (2005) 181).

fetialis/fetial priest The *fetiales* belonged to another obscure priesthood revived by Augustus, with oversight for making treaties and declaring war (for the possible involvement of *fetiales* in concluding a treaty with Lycia in 46 BC, see Mitchell (2005) 238–9; cf. the *SC de Aphrodisiensibus* of 39 BC, which alludes to officials – τοὺς θεμιστῆρας – in what is perhaps a translation of the Latin word *fetiales* – Reynolds (1982) no. 8, ll. 83–5, with commentary on pp. 89–90). They were depicted as having an ancient rite for declaring war on a foreign foe by casting a spear onto its territory (Livy 1.32.12–14). Octavian supposedly revived this rite in 32 BC (or, according to Wiedemann (1986) 482–3, invented it), when declaring war on (Antony and) Cleopatra, designating land in Rome by the temple of Bellona as foreign soil, precisely in order to present it as a foreign, not civil, conflict (Dio Cass. 50.4.4–5).

RE-ORDERING SOCIETY (8)

Augustus here substantiates his claim to have restored the Roman citizen body in terms of numbers and behaviour.

8.1 patriciorum numerum auxi/I increased the number of patricians Patricians formed an élite within the aristocracy, supposedly created by Romulus; their status was initially hereditary only. The patricians were thought to have dominated politics in early Rome, but they lost their dominance following the 'conflict of the orders' (Lintott (1999) 164–5), and by Augustus' time the distinction between patricians and plebeians had little significance, although the tribunes of the plebs could only be plebeians, whilst some priesthoods were still reserved for patricians, including the post of *flamen dialis*, which remained vacant during the period 87–11 BC (Suet. *Aug.* 31.4). Augustus created new patricians in 29 BC in virtue of the *lex Saenia de plebeis in patricios adlegendis* passed at the end of 30 BC (Dio Cass. 52.42.5; for a list of new patrician families, cf. Scheid (2007) 39). He was following the lead given by Julius Caesar, who had raised some plebeian families into the patriciate through the *lex Cassia* in 45 BC, including the Octavii (Tac. *Ann.* 11.25 = LACTOR T1; Suet. *Aug.* 2.1). The need for these interventions arose partly from the immediate effects of the proscriptions and civil wars, and partly from a long-term erosion of patrician numbers. Only fourteen of around fifty patrician clans known from the fifth century still survived by the time of the late Republic (*OCD* 3rd edn. s.v. 'patricians' 1123–4). The practice of partible inheritance, by which all sons shared equally in inheriting their father's wealth, led to families facing a difficult balancing act if they wished to ensure male heirs without fragmenting the family's wealth.

iussu populi et senatus/by command of the people and senate This unexpected word order, in place of the usual phrase *senatus populusque*, stresses the role of the people (cf. 5.1).

8.2 senatum ter legi/I revised the membership of the senate three times Augustus' claim to have revised the membership of the senate three times does not concur with Dio Cassius, who mentions five *lectiones*, in 29 BC (52.42.1), 18 BC (54.13.1), 13 BC (54.26.3), 11 BC (54.35.1), and AD 4 (55.13.3), but this discrepancy can be explained. Dio's implausible separate listing of two revisions so close together, in 13 and 11 BC (Jones (1968) 22), may in reality represent the start and finish of a single revision (Astin (1963) 229) or be mistaken in identifying the process in 13 BC as a *lectio* (Rich (1990) 205). The last revision in AD 4 can also be discounted, because Dio records that Augustus set up a commission to carry out the revision; he did not actually execute it himself (Jones (1968) 22; Brunt and Moore (1967) 50; contra, Rich (1990) 215, who prefers AD 4 as the third *lectio*; cf. Swan (2004) 144). Augustus' three revisions, therefore, fell in the years 29 BC, 18 BC, and 11 BC. The first revision was accomplished through the ad hoc grant of censorial power made to him for carrying out his first census of the citizen body as a whole (see 8.2n. *in consulatu sexto censum populi . . . egi*), and roughly coincided with his creation of new patricians too (8.1).

The senate had reached a peak of 1,000 members under Julius Caesar, who had co-opted many of his supporters, and membership of the body had been brought into disrepute (Suet. *Aug.* 35.1; Dio Cass. 43.47.3, 52.42.1). The senate had allegedly included even freedmen (Dio Cass. 40.63). Augustus took a number of measures to increase the dignity both of the senate as a body and of senators as individuals. He more than doubled the minimum property requirement for potential senators from 400,000 to 1 million sesterces (Dio Cass. 54.17.3; see Appendix 4n. *senatoribusque, quorum census explevit*); there had previously been no separate requirement for senators, who simply had to meet the minimum also required for equestrians. He also introduced the notion of senatorial status as a hereditary rank. These two measures served to differentiate senators from equestrians more clearly (Nicolet (1984) 91–3). As a result of the first revision, 190 senators were pruned from the list (Dio Cass. 52.42.1–3). By 18 BC Augustus had further drastically reduced the number of senators to 600 (Dio Cass. 54.13.4–14.1). His revisions were not uncontroversial, however: Dio makes a connection between the revision in 18 BC and subsequent plots against Augustus (54.15.1), and the hostility in the senate which caused Augustus to wear a breastplate beneath his toga (Dio Cass. 54.12.3) may partly also be attributable to his purges of its membership (Suet. *Aug.* 35.1–2; cf. Jones (1968) 26).

in consulatu sexto censum populi . . . egi/in my sixth consulship I conducted a census of the population Augustus' reference to his consulship here gives the impression that he performed the census through his consular power, but his consulship really serves only as a means of dating the census. The *Fasti Venusini* record that Octavian and Agrippa were granted censorial power with which to carry out the census (*Inscr. Ital.* XIII.i 254 = EJ p. 35 + no. 323, *idem censoria potest. lustrum fecer.*

= LACTOR p. 38). They did not, however, assume the office of censor (Suet. *Aug.* 27.5; Parsi-Magdelain (1964) 401; Jones (1968) 24; contra Dio Cass. 52.42.1). As with tribunician power later (see 4.4n. **septimum et tricensimum tribuniciae potestatis**), we see the new phenomenon of a magisterial power being bestowed separately from the office itself. There was no formal need for them to be granted censorial powers, since they could have acted through their consular powers, but this would have been a departure from the traditional functions of the consuls (Brunt and Moore (1967) 46). Augustus appears, therefore, deliberately to be concealing his censorial power, perhaps because he felt uncomfortable with being seen too openly as censor to Rome's upper classes (Ridley (2003) 103 n. 10; Astin (1963) 232; Jones (1968) 26; Carter (1982) 126). Augustus' fruitless appointment of two censors in 22 BC further illustrates the problems inherent in performing the functions of censor (Vell. Pat. 2.95.3; Dio Cass. 54.2.1–3), which contributed to the de facto devolution of censorial functions to the *princeps*. The word order in 8.3, *iterum consulari cum imperio lustrum solus feci*, juxtaposing *iterum* with mention of his consular power, rather than with his performance of the census, also adds to the impression that the first census, like the second, was carried out through consular power.

conlega M. Agrippa/with Marcus Agrippa as my colleague M. Agrippa was one of Augustus' chief props in securing and retaining power. He stands out in the *RGDA* as the only Roman to be represented as Augustus' peer (see introduction p. 37). He was roughly the same age as Augustus, and worked alongside him from the earliest days in Apollonia (Vell. Pat. 2.59.5), perhaps even having been his schoolfellow (Nic. Dam. 7 = *FGrH* 90 F127.7.16). His family was of no distinction, and he glossed over his humble background by choosing not to refer to his *gentilicium*, Vipsanius, a practice followed by Augustus in the *RGDA* (Sen. *Controv.* 2.4.12–13 = LACTOR T2; Syme (1939) 129). He played a crucial role in the various military operations following Caesar's assassination which gradually eliminated Octavian's opponents, culminating in his naval victories at Mylae and Naulochus in 36 BC over Sextus Pompey and at Actium in 31 BC over Antony. As aedile in 33 BC he performed a number of unglamorous tasks in order to win over the people of Rome to his friend's cause (see 20.2n. **rivos aquarum**). He was singled out as Augustus' close collaborator and colleague on several key occasions. Consul in 37 BC, he later shared the office with Augustus in the crucial years 28 and 27 BC. He was also the first man other than Augustus to be granted tribunician power in 18 BC (see 6.2n. **conlegam**). They jointly organised the *ludi saeculares* (22.2), and took the census, as mentioned here. When Augustus was seriously ill in 23 BC, he handed over his signet ring to Agrippa (Dio Cass. 53.30.2). Agrippa married Augustus' daughter Julia, and their sons Gaius and Lucius became Augustus' heirs presumptive (see 14). On his death in 12 BC, Augustus pronounced his eulogy at his public funeral (EJ no. 366 = LACTOR T14 + Ameling (1994) 1–2), and had him buried in the Mausoleum (see introduction pp. 5–6).

lustrum post annum alterum et quadragensimum feci/I performed the ceremony of purification forty-two years after the last one The *lustrum* is the religious ceremony of purification marking the close of the census; by extension, the word can also refer to the five-year period intervening between each census period, or *lustratio*. The census begun in 29 BC was brought to a formal close in 28 BC (Dio Cass. 52.42.1, 53.1.3). The last census had been performed in 70/69 BC, registering 910,000 male adult citizens (Livy *Per.* 98; Brunt and Moore (1967) 51), even though the census was supposed to be taken regularly at five-yearly intervals.

civium Romanorum censa sunt capita quadragiens centum millia et sexaginta tria millia/in this census 4,063,000 individual Roman citizens were registered This figure initially gives the impression that the citizen population had more than quadrupled since the last census of 70/69 BC, when around 900,000 citizens were registered (Liv. *Per.* 98). It is unlikely that such an increase can be explained purely as the result of population growth, and of the granting of citizenship to provincials in colonies (see 28) and municipalities, to soldiers, and to freedmen and freedwomen. P. A. Brunt supported the contention that the huge increase was the result of a change in the criteria for counting citizens, arguing that under Augustus women and children as well as adult male citizens were included in the census (Brunt (1971) ch. 7). More recently, Elio Lo Cascio has persuasively advanced an alternative hypothesis, that the huge increase betrays a high level of under-registration during the Republic. He observes that the census of 28 BC is depicted in the *RGDA* as a resumption of an old tradition, and so it is unlikely that the way in which the census was carried out was radically different from the previous counts of adult male citizens. In particular, Lo Cascio throws doubt on Brunt's contention by examining comparative data from model life tables (Lo Cascio (1994) espec. 29–32, 36–40). It still remains the case that, given the practical difficulties of administering a census and the likelihood of people trying to evade it because of its connection with taxation, these figures are likely to have under-recorded the real citizen population by something in the order of 20–25 per cent (Brunt (1971) 116).

Augustus documents a steady increase in the numbers of Roman citizens in each of his three censuses, implicitly demonstrating the benefits brought by his rule. He includes a sequence of three consular dates in order to emphasize the growth in citizen numbers during his period of leadership (Ridley (1988) 271). The Greek spoils this by mistakenly reporting the first figure as 4,603,000 rather than 4,063,000 (a palaeographic error explained by Nicolet (1991a) 124–5; see introduction p. 29). It is likely that this increase reflects changes to the composition of the citizen body rather than any dramatic rise in the population.

8.3 iterum consulari cum imperio lustrum solus feci/for a second time I conducted a census on my own with consular power The powers through which Augustus conducted his last two censuses are even more obscure than is the case for his first census (see 8.2n. *in consulatu sexto censum populi . . . egi*; Ferrary (2001) 125–7). This statement raises the possibility that Augustus was granted consular powers on an ad hoc basis, specifically for carrying out the census. This, however, would have been unnecessarily heavy-handed since he only needed censorial, not consular, powers in order to perform this task. It is more likely, therefore, that Augustus' consular power was derived from a grant of lifelong consular power made to him in 19 BC (Dio Cass. 54.10.5; Jones (1951) 118; see 5.3n. *consulatum*). In any case, Augustus' execution of a census on his own with consular power marks a new departure from traditional practice (contra, Jones (1968) 25, who argues that Augustus accepted censorial powers in 29, 19, and 12 BC), but was the result of the failure of his attempt to appoint censors in 22 BC (see 8.2n. *in consulatu sexto censum populi . . . egi*): in the late Republic, consuls would take on the financial functions of censors if the latter could not perform them (Lintott (1999) 115; Ferrary (2001) 126). The suggestion that the senate passed a decree authorizing Augustus to carry out the census in virtue of his consular power on each of the three occasions further illustrates the difficulties faced by modern scholars in analysing Augustus' powers (Brunt and Moore (1967) 46). For the Greek translation of *consulari cum imperio*, see introduction p. 27.

Dio does not mention a census in 8 BC, but he does for 11 BC (54.35.1). It is possible that Dio has recorded the start of a census in 11 BC, which was completed only in 8 BC. This is plausible given that Augustus was undertaking the census alone, and was much absent from Rome during these years (Astin (1963) 230–1).

C. Censorino et C. Asinio cos./in the consulship of Gaius Censorinus and Gaius Asinius The consuls for 8 BC, both of noble families, were alleged to have bribed their way into office, with the tacit complicity of Augustus (Dio Cass. 55.5.3; Syme (1986) 79). This evidently did not hinder their future careers. Both C. Marcius Censorinus (*PIR*[2] M222) and C. Asinius Gallus (*PIR*[2] A1229) went on to be proconsul of Asia, perhaps in AD 2 and 6/5 BC respectively (Syme (1986) 62). Gallus, however, fell into disfavour under Tiberius for his outspokenness (and probably because he married Tiberius' former wife Vipsania in 11 BC, shortly after Tiberius had been forced to divorce her in order to marry Julia) and starved to death in

AD 33 after three years in jail (Tac. *Ann.* 1.12.2, 6.23.1; Dio Cass. 58.3.1–6; Syme (1986) 137–8).

8.4 conlega Tib. Caesare filio meo/with Tiberius Caesar my son as colleague   A law proposed by the consuls was passed in order to allow Tiberius to act as Augustus' colleague in taking the census (Suet. *Tib.* 21).

Sex. Pompeio et Sex. Appuleio cos./in the consulship of Sextus Pompeius and Sextus Appuleius   Both of the consuls for AD 14 were distantly related to Augustus (Dio Cass. 56.29.5). The former (*PIR²* P584; Syme (1986) 414) was the addressee of Ovid's fourth book of letters from Pontus, and a friend of Germanicus. He progressed to become proconsul of Asia, possibly in AD 24/25. By contrast, no more is heard of his colleague, who perhaps died shortly thereafter (*PIR²* A962; Syme (1986) 317).

civium Romanorum capitum quadragiens centum millia et non-genta triginta et septem millia/in this census were registered 4,937,000 individual Roman citizens   The *Fasti Ostienses* (EJ p. 40 = *AE* 1946.169) give an alternative figure of 4,100,900 (or possibly, since the stone is broken, 4,100,937), perhaps 'a premature and incomplete count' (Brunt (1971) 113, 119–20), or, more likely, just an error of transcription, a result of confusion arising from the Roman system of abbreviating numerals (Nicolet (1991a) 123–6). In addition to the three censuses mentioned here by Augustus, Dio records two other partial censuses (assessing only the wealthier citizens in Italy) in 11 BC (54.35.1) and AD 4 (55.13.4).

8.5 legibus novis me auctore latis/By means of new laws brought in under my sponsorship   Augustus is probably referring primarily to the legislation which he introduced through his tribunician power in 18 BC (see 6.2). By juxtaposing his new laws with the steadily increasing numbers of citizens, Augustus is perhaps implying the success of his laws in encouraging population growth (Nicolet (1991a) 127).

exempla maiorum exolescentia iam ex nostro saeculo reduxi/I revived many exemplary ancestral practices which were by then dying out in our generation   To judge from the context of this statement, one example of such a practice may be his revival of the taking of the census, itself concerned not just with a statistical count of citizens, but with assessing the moral worthiness of those citizens (Lo Cascio (1994) 31; Lintott (1999) 115–16). Augustus promoted the ideal of restoring traditional Roman morality and religious practices (see 6.2, 13, 19.1, 19.2, 20.4, 22.2). In doing so, he drew upon the long-held view that Rome's pre-eminence in the world was the result of the Romans' superiority to others, founded upon a traditional code of behaviour, an ideal expressed by the poet Ennius, 'Roman affairs and strength rely upon traditional morality' (*moribus antiquis res stat Romana virisque*, Enn. *Ann.* 5.1 = Skutsch (1985) fr. 156). In trying to win over the senate to his unpopular marriage legislation, he read out to the senate the speech originally delivered in 131 BC by the censor Q. Caecilius Metellus Macedonicus, 'on the necessity of increasing offspring', *de prole augenda*, in which he had encouraged senators to marry and produce children (Livy *Per.* 59; Suet. *Aug.* 89.2; cf. speech to the people delivered by Q. Caecilius Metellus Numidicus, as censor in 102 BC, 'on the necessity of marrying', *ad uxores ducendas*: Gell. *NA* 1.6).

ipse multarum rerum exempla imitanda posteris tradidi/I myself handed down to later generations exemplary practices for them to imitate   This is a key phrase for understanding Augustus' conception of his place in society, and is echoed in the description of Augustus attributed to Jupiter, 'he shall regulate morality by his own example' (*exemploque suo mores reget*, Ov. *Met.* 15.834). It continues a line of thinking about the characteristics of an ideal monarch chosen because of his virtue, as explored through words ascribed to Scipio Africanus in Cicero's *On the Republic*, where he is described as one who does not impose laws upon people which he himself does not obey, but offers his own way of living as a law (Cic. *Rep.* 1.52, *nec leges inponit populo quibus ipse non pareat, sed suam vitam ut legem praefert suis civibus*; Schäfer (1957) 326). This, in turn, was derived from Greek philosophical writers (see Woodman (1977) 245, with references). Imperial ideology quickly espoused this ideal of the *princeps* leading by example, with this description in Velleius Paterculus of the chief characteristics of the best *princeps*, Tiberius, 'the best *princeps* teaches his citizens to act correctly by what he does, and although he is the greatest in power, he is greater in his example' (2.126.4, *nam facere recte civis suos princeps optimus faciendo docet, cumque sit imperio maximus, exemplo maior est*). Alongside Augustus, the whole *domus Augusta* was held up as an example (see introduction pp. 40–1). When the equestrians protested vociferously in the theatre against his marriage legislation, Augustus displayed his own great-grandchildren as examples to them (Suet. *Aug.* 34.2). This must have made the allegations of adultery against the two Julias particularly embarassing. The Greek version (*I transmitted myself to posterity as a model*) appears to echo closely Euhemerus' account of Zeus's intention to serve as a role model, *exemplum ceteris ad imitandum dedit* (see introduction p. 41; Bosworth (1999) 11 n. 74).

RELIGIOUS HONOURS FOR AUGUSTUS (9–12)

Augustus first describes how all members of Roman society expressed their concern for his well-being through religious prayers and offerings (9). The next chapter turns to formal religious honours decreed by the senate and people (10). He then turns to the setting up of two altars to celebrate his homecoming from extended trips to the east and west on two momentous occasions (11–12).

9.1 vota pro salute mea/vows for my good health   Several kinds of prayers for Augustus' welfare were undertaken at Rome: annual vows on 1 January (cf. Suet. *Aug.* 57.1; EJ no. 41 = *ILS* 99 = LACTOR L6; Dio Cass. 51.19.7; Weinstock (1971) 217–18), four-yearly vows, and vows in times of crisis. Dio Cassius (54.19.7) records vows made in 16 BC on behalf of his safe return, subsequently fulfilled with sacrifices and prayers on his return in 13 BC (Dio Cass. 54.27.1). Inscribed bases were set up to record the votive games organized for this occasion by the two consuls, Tiberius and Varus (12.2). The vows are commemorated by coins issued in 16 BC, whose obverse legend reads 'To Jupiter Greatest and Best, the senate and people of Rome took vows for the safety of Imperator Caesar because through him the state is in a more expansive and peaceful condition' (I O M / SPQR V S / PR S IMP CAE/ QVOD PER EV/ R P IN AMP / ATQ TRAN / S E: *RIC* I² 68 no. 358 = *BM Coins, Rom. Emp.* 92 = LACTOR L10). It was traditional for vows to be made by the consuls each year on 1 January 'for the welfare of the state', *pro salute rei publicae* (see Livy 21.63.7–8; Simon (1993) 66), but the sheer number of prayers and vows offered on behalf of a single individual was unprecedented. Not even Julius Caesar, for whom public prayers every four years were decreed in 45 BC, had rivalled the scale of vows offered and fulfilled for Augustus' well-being (App. *B Civ.* 2.16.106).

The vows mentioned here were associated with games, or *ludi*, organized in turn by consuls and different colleges of priests every four years. These were the first games at Rome to be held on a regular cycle, like famous games in Greece, and the content of their performances had both a Greek and a Roman flavour, including a gymnastic competition and horse racing as well as gladiators (Polverini (1978) 326–30; Caldelli (1993) 21–4; Newby (2005) 27). The senate decreed the festival in Octavian's honour in 30 BC, to celebrate his victory over Cleopatra (Dio Cass. 51.19.2), and the games were first celebrated by Octavian and Agrippa as consuls in 28 BC (Dio Cass. 53.1.4–6; Simon (1993) 67; but Gurval (1995) 120–3 questions the link with Actium). Later games organized by the *xvviri* in 16 BC are known (Dio Cass. 54.19.8). The games in AD 9 featured an actress who was over 100 years old, who had performed many years earlier at the dedication of Pompey's Theatre (Plin. *HN* 7.48.158). The *ludi pontificales* referred to by Suetonius (*Aug.* 44.3) may well also have been part of this cycle. Expenditure on these games was used as a model for the *ludi saeculares* in 17 BC (*AE* 1988.20 = LACTOR L27a; see also 22.2). The vows were commemorated on coins issued at Rome in *c.* 16 BC, showing Victory on their obverse (alluding to Actium), and on their reverse the image of a

priest making a libation at an altar with an attendant opposite him leading
a sacrificial bull, with the legend PRO VALETVDINE CAESARIS (*RIC*
I² 69 no. 369 = Simon (1993) 64–5 nos. 20–1 = *BM Coins, Rom. Emp.*
I 19†). The Greek translation of *vota suscipere* is closely modelled on the
Latin expression, using an unusual verb, εὐχὰς ἀναλαμβάνειν, instead of
ποιεῖσθαι (Adams (2003) 469). Other votive games celebrating Augustus'
safe return (*pro reditu*) were celebrated by the consuls in 13 BC, 8 BC, and
7 BC (EJ nos. 36, 38–9 = *ILS* 88, 8894, 95 = *CIL* VI 386, 36789, 385; see
also 12.2).

vivo me/in my lifetime   This phrase is omitted in the Greek since
having games performed in one's lifetime in the Greek world was not the
exceptional honour it was at Rome (Scott (1932); Vanotti (1975) 311). In the
Greek east, other individual Romans, such as T. Flamininus, had already
received this sort of honour, but it was a novelty at Rome (Gurval (1995)
122; Weinstock (1971) 315, listing further examples). Although a similar
festival at Rome had been voted in honour of Julius Caesar in 44 BC, it
was probably never actually celebrated (Dio Cass. 44.6.2; Weinstock (1971)
310–17).

**sacerdotum quattuor amplissima collegia/the four most eminent
colleges of priests**   This refers to the four major colleges of priests at
Rome, the *pontifices*, *augures*, *quindecimviri*, and *septemviri* (see 7.3). The
Greek version appears mistakenly to assume that Augustus is referring to a
college of four priests rather than to the four colleges of priests, translating
quattuor with *sacerdotum* instead of with *amplissima collegia*. This betrays a
lack of familiarity with Rome's institutions. A less likely alternative is that
the Greek is the result of a stonecutter's error (Reichmann (1943) 23), with
ἱερέων for ἱερειῶν, but the Greek word ἱέρεια usually translates *sacerdos*
rather than *sacerdotium* ('priesthood') elsewhere in the *RGDA* (Marrone
(1977) 317 n. 2, Wigtil (1982b) 191).

**9.2 privatim etiam et municipatim ... apud omnia pulvinaria pro vale-
tudine mea supplicaverunt/moreover ... in private and as a municipality have, with one accord, repeatedly offered prayers for my good
health at all public feasts**   In 30 BC, in response to his victory over
Cleopatra, the senate decreed that prayers should be made publicly for
Octavian as well as for the people and senate by the priests and Vestals
(see 9.1), and that at all feasts, both public and private, libations should
be poured to him (Dio Cass. 51.19.7). *Pulvinaria* refer to public feasts
given on religious occasions. This phrase is omitted in the Greek version,
since no equivalent could be found in a Greek cultural context (Vanotti
(1975) 311–12; Marrone (1977) 316). In the private context, libations seem to
have been made in connection with rituals honouring the household *Lares*

(Ov. *Fast.* 2.636–8; Hor. *Carm.* 4.5.29–36; see Petron. *Sat.* 60 for the continuation of this ritual under Nero; Gradel (2002) 207–9). These prayers for Augustus were foreshadowed by vows made by municipalities on behalf of Julius Caesar and Pompey (50 BC), which Cicero characterized as really for a god in the former's case, and only feigned for the latter when ill (Cic. *Att.* 8.16.1, 9.5.4).

universi cives unanimiter continenter/all citizens with one accord, repeatedly   This expression belies the often repeated assertion that Augustus' style is peculiarly terse in the *RGDA* (cf. Ridley (2003) 45). Augustus betrays through this repetition how keen he is to claim universal support (cf. 25.2, 34.1, 35).

10.1 in saliare carmen/into the hymn of the *Salii*   The twelve *Salii* belonged to an ancient patrician priesthood of Mars Gradivus, established by king Numa in order to guard a sacred shield said to have fallen from the sky as a gift to Numa from Jupiter as a pledge of empire (Ov. *Fast.* 3.345–92). It was camouflaged by the manufacturing of a further eleven identical shields, which were carried by the priests in their twice yearly procession through the streets of Rome (perhaps marking the start and end of the campaigning season in March and October respectively), when they danced (whence their name, from *salire*) dressed as archaic foot soldiers, and sang their hymn to safeguard Rome in war (Dion. Hal. *Ant. Rom.* 2.70.1–5; Beard, North, and Price (1998) 43). By this time the archaic Latin verse of the hymn had become incomprehensible (Hor. *Epist.* 2.1.86–9; Quint. *Inst.* 1.6.40–1), but it invoked both the gods in general and individual gods by name (Festus *Gloss. Lat.* p. 3L); the addition of Augustus' name to it, perhaps in 29 BC (see Dio Cass. 51.20.1), may have produced one of few words readily recognizable to its listeners, and perhaps even to its performers. This inclusion of Augustus in the Salian hymn may have brought to mind Hercules, whose deeds were celebrated in their hymn by Virgil's *Salii* (Verg. *Aen.* 8.285–305; Huttner (1997) 375; see Hor. *Carm.* 3.14.1–4 for further comparison of the two). It created a precedent for the inclusion of the names of other members of the imperial family, including Gaius and Lucius Caesars, and Germanicus and Drusus (EJ no. 94a lines 4–5 = LACTOR J65; Tac. *Ann.* 2.83.1, 4.9). In contrast to Augustus, however, they were given this honour only after their death. A *denarius* issued in 17 BC linked Augustus (depicted on the obverse) with the *Salii*, whose priestly hat (*apex*) appears flanked by two sacred shields on its reverse (*RIC* I² 66 no. 343 = *BM Coins, Rom. Emp.* I 14 no. 74 = LACTOR L2).

sacrosanctus in perpetuum/permanently sacrosanct   Octavian was granted the sacrosanctity of a tribune for life in 36 BC (Dio Cass. 49.15.5–6). This created confusion in later sources (Oros. 6.18.34; App. *B Civ.*

5.13.132) about the date at which he assumed tribunician power (Pelling
(1996) 68–9; see 4.4, 10.1n. *tribunicia potestas mihi esset*). Sacrosanctity
protected his person from physical or verbal violence. Augustus does not
mention that Octavia and Livia also received sacrosanctity in 35 BC (Dio
Cass. 49.38.1).

tribunicia potestas mihi esset/I should hold tribunician power
Augustus makes a clear distinction between the grant of sacrosanctity
in 36 BC and of lifelong tribunician power in 23 BC (Jones (1951) 115;
Pelling (1996) 68–9). Dio Cassius records the offer of tribunician power in
30 BC (51.19.6), but Augustus perhaps did not accept it at that time, since
Dio later records the conferment of the power in 23 BC (53.32.5–6), and
Augustus dated his tribunician power from that year.

10.2 pontifex maximus/chief priest Augustus assumed office on
6 March 12 BC (*Fasti Maff., Praen., Fer. Cum.* = *Inscr. Ital.* XIII.ii 74,
121, 279, 420 = EJ p. 47 = LACTOR C15, C40; Ov. *Fast.* 3.415–28 =
LACTOR H30; misdated to 13 BC by Dio Cass. 54.27.2), following the
death of his erstwhile triumviral partner M. Aemilius Lepidus the previous year, transforming it into a post of supreme religious authority at
Rome (see 7.3n. *pontifex maximus*; 10.2nn. *in vivi conlegae mei locum*
and *eo mortuo demum qui civilis tumultus occasione occupaverat*). He
marked the occasion with a donative to the people (see 15.1n. *tribunicia
potestate duodecimum*; *Fasti Cuprenses* = *Inscr. Ital.* XIII.i.245 = EJ p. 37
= LACTOR H28). According to Glen Bowersock, the procession carved
in relief on the altar of Augustan Peace commemorates a real procession
that took place to mark Augustus' election (Bowersock (1990) 390–3; see
also 12.2n. *aram Pacis Augustae*). Following his election, Augustus did
not go to live in the *domus publica*, the official residence of the *pontifex
maximus* in the Roman forum, next to the temple of Vesta. Instead, on
28 April he consecrated part of his house on the Palatine as public property
so as to fulfil the requirement for the residence of the *pontifex maximus*,
gave the *domus publica* to the Vestals, and set up a statue and altar of
Vesta in his own home (Dio Cass. 54.27.3, with Rich (1990) ad loc.; Iacopi
(1995)). In this way, he linked Vesta with the *Penates* of his own household,
making his own house a focal point for the state cult (*Fasti Praen.* = *Inscr.
Ital.* XIII.ii 133, 451–2 = EJ p. 48 = LACTOR C17; Ov. *Fast.* 4.949–54
= LACTOR H31, *Met.* 15.864–5 = LACTOR G55; cf. Beard, North, and
Price (1998) 188–92). The Greek translator here uses a neologism (ἀρχιερατείαν), a *hapax legomenon* in place of the more usual ἀρχιερωσύνη,
which is, however, also used in this section (Marrone (1977) 326). The
office of *pontifex maximus* was held by all successive emperors until Gra-
tian (who acceded in AD 367), and became an integral part of imperial
titulature.

in vivi conlegae mei locum/as a replacement for my colleague during his lifetime The unnamed colleague is M. Aemilius Lepidus, his erstwhile triumviral partner (see 1.4n. *triumvirum rei publicae constituendae*), who in 44 BC had succeeded Julius Caesar as *pontifex maximus* in dubious circumstances (see note below, *eo mortuo demum qui civilis tumultus occasione occupaverat*). Augustus may have shown ostensible respect for tradition by not forcing the exiled Lepidus out of office, but in fact he did not need to do so since instead he succeeded in gradually isolating him within the priestly college. He appears to have controlled the election of *pontifices* from 40 BC, consistently filling it with his own supporters; candidates for the pontificate who were of suspect loyalty were elected instead to less important priesthoods (Scheid (2005) 180). Augustus also intervened in many aspects of public religious life before 12 BC (including taking the *augurium salutis*, rebuilding several temples in accordance with a senatorial decree (20.4), reviving priesthoods, closing the gates of Janus), but only those for which he could do so without having to consult Lepidus as *pontifex maximus*. A striking instance of this is the celebration of the *ludi saeculares*, conducted by the *quindecimviri*, whose college was headed by none other than Augustus (see 22.2). He was careful to build only new temples that had been vowed before Lepidus' exile in 36 BC, with the exception of the temple of Jupiter Tonans, which was, however, reputedly founded in order to fulfil Augustus' personal obligation to the god, rather than established as a new public cult (see 19.2n. *Iovis Tonantis*). Otherwise, he waited until Lepidus died before raising matters in the remit of the *pontifex maximus*, such as the re-appointment of a *flamen Dialis* (for a different view, see Bowersock (1990) 392–3), recruitment of Vestals, and regulating the calendar (Scheid (2005) 188–92, (2000) 60–2, (1999) 7–19). Nevertheless, Augustus' claim to have behaved with propriety is later echoed by Seneca (*Clem.* 1.10.1 = LACTOR H29). The Greek version omits to translate *conlegae*, perhaps because a Greek reader would be unaware that the *pontifex maximus* was regarded as a colleague of the other *pontifices* (Vanotti (1975) 312).

populo id sacerdotium deferente/even though the people were offering me this priesthood This occurred in 36 BC, on his return to Rome following his defeat of Sextus Pompey (App. *B Civ.* 5.131; Dio Cass. 49.15.3), and perhaps on other occasions too (Dio Cass. 54.15.8). The Greek version is strongly influenced by the Latin original, in translating the verb *deferre* with καταφέρειν (Adams (2003) 470).

quod pater meus habuerat/which my father had held Julius Caesar had been elected as *pontifex maximus* in 63 BC, and in 44 BC the senate took the unprecedented step of decreeing that any son of his – natural or adopted – should in turn inherit the post (Dio Cass. 44.5.3).

eo mortuo demum qui civilis tumultus occasione occupaverat/on the eventual death of the man who had taken the opportunity of civil unrest to appropriate it This is both a typically roundabout and a typically negative way for Augustus to refer to one of his opponents. After Julius Caesar's assassination, M. Aemilius Lepidus had acquired the post in dubious circumstances (Liv. *Per.* 117; Vell. Pat. 2.63.1). His appointment was fixed by Antony, who profited from the confusion of the times to transfer the election from the people's assembly to the *pontifices*, in the hope that he would thereby secure the support of Lepidus and his soldiers (Dio Cass. 44.53.6–7; Scheid (1999) 3–4). In 36 BC, on finding himself in command of twenty-two legions in Sicily on the defeat of Sextus Pompey, Lepidus had attempted to challenge Octavian's ascendancy, but was defeated by him, and subsequently exiled from Rome, to live out his days at Circeii in southern Latium (Suet. *Aug.* 16.4). He died in 13 BC. Augustus is clearly implying here that, in his guise as Julius Caesar's adopted son, he was the one who should have been appointed in 44 BC, not Lepidus (see 10.2n. *quod pater meus habuerat*). A cautionary note should be proffered, however: the idea that Lepidus' appointment was irregular occurs only in non-contemporary sources, of the Augustan period or later (Ridley (2003) 177–80).

cuncta ex Italia ad comitia mea confluente multitudine/from the whole of Italy a crowd flooded together for my election Augustus several times draws attention to the loyal support which he enjoyed from the whole of Italy (see introduction p. 39; 9.2, 16.1, 21.3, 25.2). A *denarius* issued in Rome by L. Caninius Gallus in 12 BC depicts an abbreviated inscription which commemorates Augustus' election as *pontifex maximus*, if it is correctly expanded as C(omitia) C(aesaris) / AVG / VS / TI, 'election of Caesar Augustus' (*RIC* I² 74 no. 418 = Hill (1989) 61; Simon (1993) 58 no. 18 = *BM Coins, Rom. Emp.* I 27 no. 132). The *Fasti Praenestini* record local festivities by the chief magistrates and people in the town to celebrate his election (*Inscr. Ital.* XIII.ii 121, 420–1). Augustus emphasizes his return to traditional practice, with a popular assembly electing the *pontifex maximus*, in contrast to the irregular procedure followed by Antony in 44 BC (see note above, **eo mortuo demum qui civilis tumultus occasione occupaverat**). Later emperors during the first century AD followed this practice of offering themselves as the only candidate for the people to elect (Taylor 1942).

P. Sulpicio C. Valgio consulibus/in the consulship of Publius Sulpicius and Gaius Valgius A *novus homo* from Lanuvium, Publius Sulpicius Quirinius was consul in 12 BC, and became governor of Galatia–Pamphylia where he campaigned against the Homanadenses (see introduction p. 13), and then of Syria. On his death in AD 21, he received a public funeral at Tiberius' request (Tac. *Ann.* 3.48). C. Valgius Rufus, a *novus homo* with a reputation for literary compositions in prose and verse, was one of three suffect consuls during this year. He replaced M. Valerius Messalla Appianus, who must have died shortly after assuming office in January, since Augustus' election as *pontifex maximus* took place on 6 March.

11 aram Fortunae Reducis/the altar of Fortune the Home-Bringer The senate voted this altar (Coarelli (1995)) on Augustus' return to Rome, bringing back the standards from Parthia in 19 BC, after his absence in the East since 22 BC. It was decreed on 12 October 19 BC, and dedicated on 15 December (*Fasti Amit. – Aug(ustalia), np. Ludi in Circo. Fer(iae) ex s(enatus) c(onsulto), q(uod) e(o) d(ie) Imp. Caes(ar) Aug(ustus) ex transmarin(is) provinc(iis) Urbem intravit araq(ue) Fort(unae) Reduci constit(uta)*; *Fer. Cum. = Inscr. Ital.* XIII.ii 195, 279, 519–20, 538 = EJ pp. 53, 55 = LACTOR C35, C39). It was probably dedicated in the form of a simple small altar in the same year as it was decreed (Torelli (1982) 28). The goddess is translated by a Greek equivalent, as 'Saving Fortune' (Reichmann (1943) 22). Fortuna Redux was associated with the *porta triumphalis* at Rome (Torelli (1982) 29), and so in some ways this honour is to be interpreted as a substitute for a triumph, an honour which Augustus steadfastly refused after 29 BC (4.1). The altar is commemorated on coins issued at Rome in 19 BC, depicting on their obverse Fortuna Victrix and Fortuna Felix, and on their reverse a decorated altar inscribed FOR RE on a plain podium, together with the words 'To Caesar Augustus by senatorial decree' / CAESARI AVGVSTO EX S C (*RIC* I² 65 no. 322 = *BM Coins, Rom. Emp.* I 1–2 nos. 2–4 = Simon (1993) 70 nos. 26–7). Other coins issued in 19/18 BC depict on their obverse Augustus adorned with a laurel wreath (the traditional decoration for a triumphal general), and on their reverse an altar with the legend 'Fortune the Home-Bringer, to Caesar Augustus, the Senate and People of Rome'/ FORT[VN] RED CAES AVG SPQR or FORTVN REDV / CAESARI AVG / SPQR (*RIC* I² 45 nos. 53–6 = *BM Coins, Rom. Emp.* I 63–4 nos. 358–60, 64 no. 361 = LACTOR L9). Dio Cassius (54.10.3) records that other honours were voted on the same occasion, which Augustus rejected. For the rather different emphasis in Dio's account of this episode and the likelihood that Augustus is here presenting a distorted version of events, see 12.1n. **cum consule Q. Lucretio.**

aedes Honoris et Virtutis ad portam Capenam/the temple of Honour and Virtue at the Capena gate Although, in adapting the text for an audience ignorant of Rome's topography, the Greek version omits the altar's precise location (Reichmann (1943) 22; Marrone (1977) 318–19), it was very significant for its associations with triumphs. Indeed, the very coupling of *Honos* and *Virtus* evokes the victories of successful generals, who win glory (*honos*) through their courage in battle (*virtus*) (Richardson (1978) 245). The altar would have been situated on the route by which

Augustus entered Rome along the *via Appia*, having disembarked from
the east at Brundisium. It was the place where the people usually sent off
proconsuls to their provinces and welcomed them back. These two temples
were strongly associated with triumphs, and were just one of four pairs of
temples to these deities set up in Rome to celebrate triumphal returns from
different directions to Rome. In choosing to dedicate this particular altar
in this location the senate was underlining the triumphal associations of
Augustus' return (Torelli (1982) 29).

pontifices et virgines Vestales/the priests and Vestal Virgins   The
presence of the Vestals is significant, since they appeared only at the most
important occasions (Lacey (1996) 46 n. 118). The priestly titles are translated in only very general terms into Greek (see also 12.2; Reichmann (1943)
23; Vanotti (1975) 313; Marrone (1977) 326).

**consulibus Q. Lucretio et M. Vinicio/in the consulship of Quintus
Lucretius and Marcus Vinicius**   For this consular pair, see 6.1n. *consulibus M. Vinicio et Q. Lucretio* and 12.1n. *cum consule Q. Lucretio*.

in urbem/to the city   Although *urbs* is a common usage for referring
to Rome ('the city' par excellence), the Greek translator prefers to avoid
any ambiguity here.

Augustalia/*Augustalia*   After Augustus' death, the celebration of the
Augustalia became more elaborate, with games being celebrated over 5–12,
and then 3–12 October annually (*Inscr. Ital.* XIII.ii 373; Tac. *Ann.* 1.15.2,
54.2). To name the games after Augustus rather than after the goddess was
an unprecedented step (Scheid (2005) 190), recalling practice in the Greek
east rather than at Rome, where festivals had been named after Roman
honorands, such as the *Moukieia* for Q. Mucius Scaevola in 94 BC, or
the *Verria* for Verres (Volkmann (1954/5) 84). Dio's suggestion that these
ludi were celebrated first in 11 BC may be the result of his confusion with
games in honour of Augustus' birthday (Dio Cass. 54.34.2; Rich (1990) 213).
Alternatively, it may reveal that the introduction of a major new festival
to Rome's religious calendar was postponed until Augustus himself had
become *pontifex maximus*, which would have enabled Augustus to avoid
having to consult his political enemy Lepidus on the matter (Scheid (1999)
9–13; see 10.2).

ex cognomine nostro/after me   For the *cognomen* Augustus, see 34.2.

**12.1 pars praetorum et tribunorum plebis/some of the praetors and
tribunes of the people**   At this time there were probably ten praetors,
aged thirty or more, who were second in the hierarchy of the senate

to the consuls (Crook (1996) 125). The ten tribunes were regarded as representatives and champions of the people.

cum consule Q. Lucretio/with the consul Quintus Lucretius There is some debate about whether or not Augustus is deliberately disguising the circumstances surrounding the appointment of Q. Lucretius Vespillo to the consulship in 19 BC, as represented in Dio Cassius (54.10.1–2). In this year, C. Sentius Saturninus had been elected as one of the consuls, whilst the other consulship was held in reserve for the absent Augustus. On his refusing to take up the post, unrest and violence broke out at Rome. This was attributed to the rabble-rousing activities of Egnatius Rufus. He was a senator who had gained so much popular support when, as aedile in 22 BC, he had used his own slaves as a public fire brigade (Dio Cass. 53.24.4–6, mistakenly under 26 BC) that he had been elected to the praetorship the very next year (21 BC). It seems that by 19 BC he fancied his chances as consul, but his candidature was opposed by the sole elected consul Sentius Saturninus (Vell. Pat. 2.92.4). Once his supporters had rioted, he was apprehended and put to death for 'conspiracy' (Vell. Pat. 2.91.3–4). The senate sent a delegation to Augustus asking him to settle the matter. He promptly appointed one of the delegation, Lucretius Vespillo, as consul (see Birley (2000) 746–7 for the intriguing possibility that his nomination was a 'symbolic burial of the ultra-*popularis* position that seemed to have been adopted in 23'). His nomination as Augustus' preferred candidate for the consulship would then have been approved as a matter of course by the electoral assembly, the *comitia centuriata*. Dio asserts that the altar to Fortune was voted to Augustus as a consequence of this episode, and for other achievements (Dio Cass. 54.10.3). Either Dio is mistaken, or Augustus has reversed the chronological relationship of the altar (11) and the deputation (12).

One view of this passage, therefore, is that, by naming Lucretius Vespillo as already being consul, Augustus is hiding the fact that Lucretius Vespillo was in effect simply appointed by him, and is avoiding having to allude to unrest in the capital. The fact that Augustus mentions only the one consul strongly suggests that Sentius Saturninus felt that he had to stay at Rome during the time of unrest, and that Lucretius Vespillo was not yet consul at the time when he embarked upon the delegation recorded here. The fact that he is mentioned only after praetors and tribunes, even though he would have taken precedence as a consul, hints at the fact that he had not actually been made consul yet. The translator of the *RGDA* realised that this was odd, and altered his Greek version, in order to maintain the usual hierarchy. The whole character of the delegation is also changed by being placed after the vote of the altar to Fortuna Redux (11), which becomes purely an honour in return for Augustus' achievements in Syria, with no connection to unrest at Rome (Ridley (2003) 180–2; Parsi-Magdelain (1964)

394–8; for another view exculpating Augustus, cf. Rich (1990) 186–7, (1998) 73–4; Lacey (1996) 149; cf. Birley (2000) 719–20). The unrest at Rome led to the people calling upon Augustus to take up the *cura legum et morum* (see 6.1). In chapters 11–12, therefore, Augustus transforms desperate remedies in a time of crisis into unprecedented honours.

principibus viris/leading men   By this Augustus perhaps refers to men who were senior senators of consular rank, or 'leading citizens' (Lacey (1996) 149; see 13n. *me principe*).

obviam mihi missa est in Campaniam/were sent to Campania to meet me   Augustus was in Campania on his way home from the east, via Greece.

honos ad hoc tempus nemini praeter me est decretus/this honour has been decreed for no one except me up to this time   A similar embassy had gone all the way to Brundisium to meet him in 30 BC (Dio Cass. 51.4.4–5).

12.2 ex Hispania Galliaque/from Spain and Gaul   Augustus was absent in the west from 16 to 13 BC (see 26.2n. *Gallias et Hispanias provincias*).

Ti. Nerone P. Quinctilio consulibus/in the consulship of Tiberius Nero and Publius Quinctilius   The pairing of Tiberius (consul for the first time) and P. Quinctilius Varus is a curious one, since at that time they were both sons-in-law of Agrippa (EJ no. 366 = LACTOR T14). Having governed Africa and Syria, Varus notoriously met his end in AD 9 at the hands of Arminius' Germans in the Teutoburg Wood, along with his three legions (Vell. Pat. 2.117.2–119; Suet. *Aug.* 23.1–2; Tac. *Ann.* 1.61–2; Dio Cass. 56.18–22.1; cf. Syme (1986) ch. 23; *PIR*² Q30). These consuls jointly organized votive games to celebrate Augustus' return (*CIL* VI 386 = EJ no. 36 = *ILS* 88 = LACTOR L11; see also 9.1n. *vota pro valetudine mea*).

aram Pacis Augustae/an altar of Augustan Peace   The altar (Torelli (1999)) was vowed on the day of Augustus' return from the west on 4 July 13 BC (*Fasti Amit., Ant. Min.* = *Inscr. Ital.* XIII.ii 189, 208, 476; EJ p. 49 = LACTOR C20), and dedicated on 30 January (Livia's birthday) in 9 BC (*Fasti Praen., Verul.* = *Inscr. Ital.* XIII.ii 117, 161, 404–5 = EJ p. 46 = LACTOR C12; Ov. *Fast.* 1.709–22 = LACTOR K13). Originally, the senate decreed that an altar should be set up in the senate house (Dio Cass. 54.25.3). Augustus evidently refused that altar, but did accept the construction of the altar of Augustan Peace, just as he had previously accepted the altar to Fortuna Redux (11). Both of these altars were in effect substitutes for triumphs, which Augustus refused after 29 BC (see 4.1). The altar itself

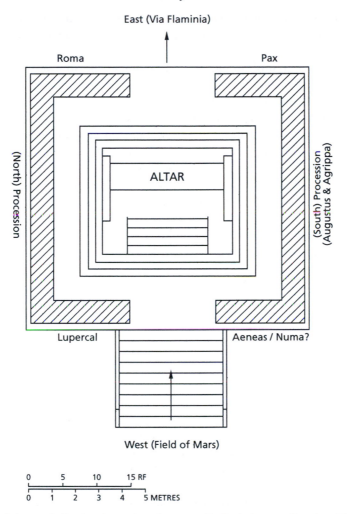

East (Via Flaminia)

Roma | Pax

ALTAR

(North) Procession | (South) Procession (Augustus & Agrippa)

Lupercal | Aeneas / Numa?

West (Field of Mars)

0   5   10   15 RF

0   1   2   3   4   5 METRES

Fig. 16 Diagram indicating decorative scheme on *Ara Pacis Augustae* (based on Claridge (1998) 185 fig. 81).

is situated within an impressive enclosure imitating the shrine of Janus Quirinus (Torelli (1982) 31–3), and is famous for its complex decorative scheme, reflective of Augustan ideology (see Figure 16). It has four panels at its short ends. These depict *Roma* seated upon a pile of weapons; a female figure nursing two infants, whose identity is disputed, but who is possibly *Pax* (or perhaps *Tellus* or *Italia* – see discussion in Zanker (1988) 172–7); Aeneas sacrificing to the *Penates*, or perhaps Numa sealing a peace treaty through a sacrifice (Rehak (2001) 196–200); the *lupercal* with Mars, Faustulus, the twins and the she-wolf. Along its long sides are processional scenes depicting Augustus *capite velato* preceded by lictors and followed by other priests, members of the imperial family (including women and

children), and other Romans as they prepare for a sacrifice (Simon (1967);
Torelli (1982); Zanker (1988) 120–3, 172–5, 203–4; Kleiner (1992) 90–9,
(2005) 221–5).

It is easy, but misleading, to underestimate the innovation involved
in introducing the cult of *Pax Augusta* to Rome. Such deities did become
commonplace under later emperors, but this was the first known instance of
an 'august(an)' deity: not only did the new deity's title encapsulate the idea
that Rome could now enjoy a special relationship with the gods specifically
through the mediation of Augustus, but it also facilitated the dissemination
of such cult beyond Rome, contributing to cultural unification of the
empire (Cooley (2006) 246–52; cf. Panciera (2003)). Furthermore, this was
the first monument in Rome for the cult of any kind of *Pax*.

ad campum Martium/on the field of Mars   The altar was originally
located one mile from the *pomerium*, where the character of magistrates'
power changed, from *imperium militiae* to *imperium domi*, as they entered
Rome from abroad, and from where Augustus' *intercessio tribunicia* would
have taken effect (Dio Cass. 51.19.6). Its location at the point where military
power was put aside suited its dedication to Peace (Torelli (1982) 29–30).
The attractive theory of a meaningful relationship between the altar of
Augustan Peace and the '*horologium Augusti*', with a shadow being cast
upon the altar on Augustus' birthday, 23 September, signifying that his
birth had heralded a new era of peace, has been quashed (Buchner (1976),
accepted by Zanker (1988) 144 and Bowersock (1990) 383–8, but disproved
by Schütz (1990) 444–52; cf. Barton (1995) 44–6. Further, the so-called
horologium was not a sundial, but a meridian instrument, being designed
not to record all the hours of daylight, but to chart the changing length
of the shadow cast at midday: Schütz (1990) 433, 454). The altar was
excavated from beneath the Palazzo Fiano-Almagià in the fascist era (1937–
8), and reconstructed by the Mausoleum, to celebrate the bimillenary of
Augustus' birth on 23 September 1938 (see introduction pp. 51–2). It would
have been visible to travellers entering the city from the north along the
via Flaminia, the route taken by Augustus returning from the western
provinces, just as the *ara Fortunae Reducis* was located on his route back to
Rome from the eastern provinces (see 11n. **aedes Honoris et Virtutis ad
portam Capenam**).

virginesque Vestales/and Vestal Virgins   See 11n. **pontifices et virgines Vestales**.

anniversarium sacrificium/an annual sacrifice   Like the *ara Fortunae Reducis*, an anniversary sacrifice was ordained for the altar of Augustan
Peace, with the additional involvement of magistrates alongside the *pontifices* and Vestals. This sacrifice is depicted on a frieze inside the enclosure, on

Fig. 17 *Ara Pacis Augustae*, Rome: interior scene of sacrifice.

the altar proper (see Figure 17). It shows Vestals, *apparitores* (attendants), and a *lictor Vestalium*, together with three sacrificial victims escorted by *victimarii* (the slave officials who actually struck the death blow upon the sacrificial animals) bearing the necessary equipment, a *camillus* (a priests' boy-attendant), and a priest or magistrate followed by two *apparitores* (Torelli (1982) 36, with pl. II.10). The *Feriale Cumanum* appears to record a *supplicatio imperio Caesaris Augusti custo[dis i(mperi) R(omani)]* (perhaps 'supplication for the authority of Caesar Augustus, guardian of the Roman empire') on the day of the altar's dedication (30 January). This foreshadows the idea of peace throughout the empire in the next chapter of the *RGDA* (EJ p. 46 = *Inscr. Ital.* XIII.ii 279, 404; see Ramage (1987) 61).

THE CLOSURE OF THE GATES OF JANUS (13)

Since the gates of the shrine of Janus (more properly, simply a passageway consisting of two gates with double doors joined by lateral walls to form a rectangle) in the north-eastern corner of the Roman forum near the senate house remained closed in times of peace, this section follows on logically from the dedication of the altar of Augustan Peace (see 12.2. For the relationship between the two monuments, see Torelli (1982) 31–5). It is possible that this 'tradition' was another example of spurious religious revivalism on Augustus' part (Syme (1979a) 188; for other examples, see 20.4n. *duo et octoginta templa deum*), and perhaps accounts for the elaborate explanation of the tradition given by Augustus here (Herbert-Brown (1994) 185–96, espec. 188–9, 196).

13 Ianum Quirinum/Janus Quirinus According to one version of its origins current in the Augustan era, Rome's second king, Numa, was thought to have built the shrine, and to have instituted the practice of closing its gates in times when Rome was at peace with its neighbours (Livy 1.19.2; see also 13n. *bis omnino clausum fuisse*). The Greek version glosses the gates' associations with war (Reichmann (1943) 22).

maiores nostri/Our ancestors Augustus often claimed to be revitalizing ancestral customs (see introduction p. 38, 6.1, 27.2).

per totum imperium populi Romani/throughout the whole empire of the Roman people The use of the word *imperium* to mean a geographical area, the Roman empire, is new under Augustus (Richardson (2003) 141–2; see 12.2n. *anniversarium sacrificium*; introduction pp. 27–8).

terra marique/on land and sea See 3.1n. **terra et mari**.

esset parta victoriis pax/peace had been achieved by victories Augustus' explanation of the ceremonial closing of the gates of Janus reflects the ideology of *Pax Augusta* being 'pacification after military victory' rather than simply 'peace' (Rich (2003)). The word *pax* is emphasized by being postponed until the end of its clause. The victory monument at La Turbie (see 26.3n. *Alpes*) and the altar of Augustan Peace (see 12.2n. *aram Pacis Augustae*) also embody this ideal. The Greek version omits the explicitly militaristic phrase *parta victoriis pax* (Reichmann (1943) 22; Vanotti (1975) 313).

priusquam nascerer/before I was born Augustus is making an implicit claim that his birth marked a new age for Rome. This implication is captured exactly by use of the word αἰών in the Greek version, rather than χρόνος. Trenchant criticisms have been raised against the attractive idea that the dedication of the altar of Augustan Peace in conjunction with the '*horologium*' was designed to express on a monumental scale the idea that Augustus' birth marked a new era (see 12.2n. *ad campum Martium*). Nevertheless, Augustus promoted in other ways the idea that the time of his birth was exceptionally favourable for its astrological connections, and others also presented the theme of his birth heralding a new era. So confident was he in its exceptional nature, that Augustus even published details of his horoscope in an edict, apparently in AD 11 (Dio Cass. 56.25.5).

Images of the zodiacal sign of capricorn appeared on coins issued in Rome and in the provinces, on glass-pastes and cameos, including the *Gemma Augustea* (see Figure 12) (Suet. *Aug.* 94.12; *RIC* I² 49–50 nos. 124–30, 53 no. 174, 80 no. 477, 81 nos. 488–9, 85 nos. 541–2, 85–6 nos. 544–8; *BM Coins, Rom. Emp.* I 56 nos. 305–8, 62 nos. 344–9, 80 nos. 465–6, 106 nos. 653–5, 107 no. 664; von Hesberg (1978) 982–3 no. 45), and incorporated into architecture (see introduction p. 15 for the capricorn at Antioch; Barton (1995) 48–51). It had no single meaning, but could refer to the moment both of Augustus' birth and conception, and to his good fortune, as well as invoking the advent of a new year (Barton (1995)). In poetry, we find Augustus' birth associated with the closing of the gates of Janus in Jupiter's prophecy to Venus (Virg. *Aen.* 1.286–96; Ensslin (1932) 362–5). In *c.* 9 BC, the *Koinon* of Asia decreed that henceforth Augustus' birthday would mark the beginning of each new year, since divine providence had arranged for Augustus to be born as a saviour who has brought an end to warfare. This step was based on a proposal made by the province's proconsul and close ally of Augustus, Paullus Fabius Maximus (see 6.1n. **Paullo Fabio Maximo**), whose edict declared that Augustus' birthday had inaugurated a new beginning of everything, bringing about a 'new look to the whole world' (EJ no. 98b ll. 33–6, 98a ll. 4–9 = *RDGE* no. 65 = *SEG* 4.490 = LACTOR H34a–b).

bis omnino clausum fuisse/having been closed twice   The practice of keeping the gates of Janus open unless Rome was not involved in warfare anywhere was thought to have been established by the second king of Rome, Numa Pompilius (see 13n. **Ianum Quirinum**). He was also the first to close the gates for a period of forty-three years. The second occasion when the gates were closed was after the end of the First Punic War against Carthage in 235 BC, in the consulship of C. Atilius and T. Manlius, but they were then re-opened in the same year (Varro *Ling.* 5.165; Livy 1.19.3–4; Plut. *Vit. Num.* 20, *De Fort. Rom.* 9 = *Mor.* 322B).

ter . . . senatus claudendum esse censuit/the senate decreed it should be closed three times   There is considerable debate about Augustus' choice of words here, and whether they betray the fact that the Senate voted for the closure three times, but that the gates were actually closed only twice (Ridley (2003) 114–15; Syme (1979a) 188–204). On 11 January 29 BC, while Octavian was still absent from Rome in the east, the gates were closed to mark the end of the war against Antony and Cleopatra (*Fasti Praen.* = *Inscr. Ital.* XIII.ii.113, 395 = EJ p. 45 = LACTOR C4). In this way, Actium was represented as Octavian's decisive victory (Livy 1.19.3; Plut. *De Fort. Rom.* 9 = *Mor.* 322B, *Vit. Numa* 20; Dio Cass. 51.20.4). They were subsequently re-opened before Augustus set off to Spain in 27 BC (Oros. 6.21.1), even though there had been campaigns in the Balkans in the intervening period, and were closed for a second time at the end of the Cantabrian War in 25 BC, when Augustus was again still abroad (Dio Cass. 53.26.5). The gates probably then remained shut until Augustus set out for Gaul in 16 BC (Rich (1990) 163). A closure decreed in 11/10 BC to celebrate the victories of Drusus in Germany and of Tiberius in Dalmatia and Pannonia, was actually pre-empted by a Dacian attack across the Danube into Pannonia, and the revolt of Dalmatia (Dio Cass. 54.36.2; see 30.2n. **Dacorum transgressus exercitus**). A third closure of the gates is mentioned by Suetonius (Suet. *Aug.* 22.1), but there is no firm evidence as to when this occurred. It is possible that Suetonius' account is simply a misreading of Augustus' ambiguous statement in the *RGDA*. The claim in Orosius (6.22.1, 22.5), that the gates of Janus were closed for the third time in 2 BC, the year of Christ's birth, is implausible given the evidence for military activity in the Rhine and Danube regions at this time, and simply reflects his desire to link the Saviour's birth with the outbreak of ecumenical peace. More problematic, however, is another passage in Orosius (7.3.7 = LACTOR K49), where he claims to cite Tacitus' *Histories*, for a statement that the gates of Janus were opened when Augustus was a *senex*. According to Mommsen ((1883) 51), this is all part of a pious interpolation, but, in contrast to the passage of Orosius cited earlier, there is no obvious explanation why this should be the case, and we should probably instead consider the statement as authentic. Various dates have been proposed for a third closure of the gates. One possibility is that the gates were closed between the end of the German war in 8/7 BC and 1 BC, when Gaius set out for Armenia (Mommsen (1883) 50; Syme (1979a) 202). This would fit the description of Augustus as *senex*, assuming the authenticity of Orosius' quotation, and it would not be surprising that we do not have mention of such a closure in the summary narrative of Dio Cassius, given the lacunose survival of his work covering this period. An alternative hypothesis links a third closure of Janus with the dedication of the altar of Augustan Peace in 9 BC (Hanell (1960) 98–102), but this would involve ignoring the continuation of warfare in the north for the next couple of years (Syme (1979a) 202).

me principe/when I was leader   Augustus chooses to describe himself as *princeps* in the *RGDA* (see 30.1, 32.3; Reinhold (2002) 63). This was not an official title (although it recalls the traditional position of the *princeps senatus*, 'leader of the house' – see 7.2n. **princeps senatus**), nor did it bestow particular powers, but was adopted by Augustus to indicate his leading role in the state, and finds an echo in Horace, who hailed him as 'greatest of the *principes*' (*maxime principum, Carm.* 4.14.6). The title expresses the same principle voiced by Augustus at the close of the *RGDA*, that his position in the state was based upon *auctoritas* (34.3). He could equally well allude to others as *principes* too, both among his contemporaries and later generations (12.1; Suet. *Aug.* 31.5, with Carter (1982) ad loc.), and even uses the word to describe non-Roman eastern envoys (33). The Greek translation, however, reflects the reality of a clear distinction in status between Augustus and other *principes*. It carefully differentiates between Augustus the *princeps*, for which it uses the word ἡγεμών (cf. EJ no. 311 V.86, senatorial decree from Cyrene, 4 BC = *SEG* 9.8 = LACTOR M78), Augustus the *princeps senatus*, for which it provides an explanatory gloss (see 7.2), and other Roman *principes*, which it translates as the 'foremost office-holders' (Wagenvoort (1936) 344). This differentiation, however, may not be quite so clear-cut since the significance of the Greek word ἡγεμών is difficult to pin down: it could equally well evoke the world of Roman magistrates, a moderate monarch, and a Ciceronian-style *princeps* (Vanotti (1997) 366–9). Above all, however, the word *princeps* evoked the idea that he wielded influence as a private citizen rather than as a magistrate, and had been used of individual Romans during the Republic, notably L. Brutus, founder of the Republic (Cic. *Rep.* 2.46, cited above 1.1n. **exercitum privato consilio**), and Pompey (Wagenvoort (1936) 325–7). The idea of a *princeps* being of benefit to the Roman state was championed theoretically in the philosophical writings of Cicero, who outlined how a *princeps* had to be nourished by glory, maintaining that government could only exist so long as all citizens showed honour to the *princeps* (*Rep.* 5.9; cf. Wagenvoort (1936) 206–21, 323–38; Schäfer (1957)). The emphasis in much of the *RGDA* on honours given to Augustus should be viewed in this context (Ramage (1987) 86). Indeed, in the aftermath of Julius Caesar's assassination, Cicero proposed himself to the senate and people as a *princeps*, as a means of protecting everyone's liberty (*Fam.* 12.24.2, January 43 BC; Wagenvoort (1936) 209–11). Augustus was perhaps drawing upon Greek philosophical theory via Cicero's *De Republica* in devising his conception of how to be a *princeps* (Schäfer (1957) 310–20; see introductory note to **The aftermath of the Ides of March (1–2)**), but not in terms of inserting himself into a constitution. The idea that Augustus was self-consciously fashioning a new system of government is over-influenced by the hindsight of later authors such as Tacitus (*Ann.* 1.9.5, *non regno neque dictatura, sed principis nomine*) and Dio Cassius.

HONOURS FOR AUGUSTUS VIA HIS SONS (14)

Augustus laments the early demise of his adopted sons, who had received signal honours from senate and people, and equestrians, which in effect designated them as his successors, but which Augustus interprets as really honouring him. It is unclear whether he intended to set up a dual system of government through them, or whether he was adopting a 'belt and braces' approach, which, even so, did not in the event suffice to secure the succession. The account here fits closely with inscribed fragments from his Mausoleum (see introduction pp. 5–6; Hurlet (1997) 113–25 offers detailed discussion of chronological problems).

14.1 filios meos/My sons   His grandsons Gaius (*PIR*² C. Iulius Caesar 216) and Lucius (*PIR*² L. Iulius Caesar 222), sons of his daughter Julia and Agrippa, were born in 20 BC (Dio Cass. 54.8.5) and 17 BC (Dio Cass. 54.18.1) respectively. A fragmentary calendar from Hispellum suggests that Gaius was born between 14 August and 13 September, and that Lucius was born between 14 June and 15 July (*AE* 1981.316; Vassileiou (1984b) 46–52; Hurlet (1997) 113). They were both adopted by Augustus in 17 BC (Dio Cass. 54.18.1; Vell. Pat. 2.96.1; Suet. *Aug.* 64.1), perhaps on 26 June (Hurlet (1997) 428–9 n. 55). Their dynastic significance was advertised on *denarii* minted at Rome in 13 BC, which depicted Augustus on their obverse, and Julia in between Gaius and Lucius on their reverse (Simon (1993) 72, 74 no. 28a = *BM Coins, Rom. Emp.* I 21 no. 106 = *RIC* I² 72 no. 404; Zanker (1988) 216 fig. 167b). The same image appears on an intaglio which was converted into a mediaeval signet ring (King (1885) 222, pl. XXXV.2; Vollenweider (1964) 76) (see Figure 18). In the same year, Gaius made a first public appearance by taking part in the Trojan Games (Dio Cass. 54.26.1), and both brothers appeared on the altar of Augustan Peace (Zanker (1988) 215–18, Hurlet (1997) 114–15; see also 12.2n. **aram Pacis Augustae**). As they grew older, their stylized portraits made them appear as miniature versions of Augustus, distinguishable from each other only by decoding the arrangement of locks in their hairstyles. This underlined their privileged place in society, offering a visual explanation of what it meant to be *principes iuventutis* (Zanker (1988) 219–20, with figs. 174–5; see also 14.2n. **principem iuventutis**).

quos iuvenes mihi eripuit fortuna/whom fortune snatched away from me when young men   Lucius died suddenly aged eighteen of an illness on 20 August AD 2 at Massilia (Marseilles) (*Fasti Ant. Min.* = *Inscr. Ital.* XIII.ii 208 = EJ p. 51 = LACTOR C28). Gaius died aged twenty-two 21 February AD 4 in Lycia on his way back to Italy after having been wounded in Armenia (*Fasti Cuprenses* = *Inscr. Ital.* XIII.i 245 = EJ p. 39 = LACTOR J60; *Fasti Verul.* = *Inscr. Ital.* XIII.ii 165, 413 = EJ p. 47 = LACTOR C14; cf. Flor. 2.32.42–4 = LACTOR J59, Dio Cass. 55.10a.8–9; see also 27.2n. **eandem gentem postea desciscentem et rebellantem domitam per Gaium filium meum**). Their unexpected deaths within an eighteen-month period caused Augustus great grief (Sen. *Controv.* 4 praef. 5 = LACTOR J62), although Suetonius (*Aug.* 65.1) asserts that he was more affected by Julia's misconduct than by her sons' deaths.

The *RGDA* here reflects the dissemination of an official way of speaking of these deaths. The language of the *RGDA* is echoed at the start of Augustus' will, in which he explained that Tiberius was his chief heir,

Fig. 18 Comparison of coin and intaglio. *Denarius* minted at Rome in 13 BC: obverse, Augustus; reverse, Julia between Gaius and Lucius ((a) coin: *RIC* I² 72 no. 404 and (b) intaglio: King (1885) 222 pl. XXXV.2). © The Trustees of the British Museum.

'since cruel fortune has snatched away from me my sons Gaius and Lucius' (*quoniam atrox fortuna Gaium et Lucium filios mihi eripuit*, Suet. *Tib.* 23, on which see Levick (1972); cf. Vell. Pat. 2.103.1). Roman society as a whole expressed its sense of loss at their deaths. The colony of Pisa, of which Lucius had been patron, passed elaborate decrees regarding annual ceremonies lamenting their deaths, echoing the language of the *RGDA* (*ILS* 139 = EJ no. 68 = LACTOR J64; *ILS* 140 = EJ no. 69 = LACTOR J61). Augustus does not mention the posthumous honours which are revealed by the *Tabula Hebana* (EJ no. 94a lines 4–12 = LACTOR J65), namely that their names were added to the hymn of the *Salii* (see 10.1n. ***in saliare carmen***), and that ten centuries involved in the election of praetors and consuls were to be named after them. Tacitus records the hostile tradition that made Livia in some way responsible for both deaths, in stereotypical 'wicked stepmother' mode (Tac. *Ann.* 1.3.3 = LACTOR F3.3; see also Dio Cass. 55.10a.10).

consules designavit/appointed as consuls The unprecedentedly early appointment of the two brothers as consuls was celebrated in honorific inscriptions set up in the Roman forum. Gaius was proclaimed to be the first Roman ever to be appointed to the consulship when only fourteen years old (*[hi]c pr[i]mus om[nium annos] / [natus] XIIII c[o(n)s(ul) creatus est]*: *CIL* VI 3748 = 31271 = 36893, a marble base found near the basilica Julia); the same precocity in Lucius was commemorated on prominent public monuments in the forum (*ILS* 136 = *CIL* VI 900 + 31197 + 31272 + 36880; *CIL* VI 36908 = EJ no. 65 = LACTOR K15; Hurlet (1997) 118–19). The Greek version mistranslates their age, as fifteen years old, not in their fifteenth year. They were exempted from having to complete the usual career progression, serving as quaestor and then as praetor. Dio Cassius (55.9.2) asserts that the Roman people had elected Gaius as consul in 6 BC, against Augustus' wishes (cf. Tac. *Ann.* 1.3.2), but that he conceded the following year, 5 BC, that his son should be designated for the consulship after a five-year period (cf. Swan (2004) 83–4). Gaius duly took up office on 1 January AD 1, with his brother-in-law L. Aemilius Paullus as colleague, but was absent in Syria for the whole tenure of his consulship. Lucius was designated as consul in the first half of 2 BC, with the intention that he take up office after a five-year period, but he died before he did so. By becoming consul aged nineteen, Gaius followed the precedent set by his adoptive father (see 1.4n. ***populus autem eodem anno me consulem . . . creavit***).

quo deducti sunt in forum/on which they were brought into the forum This refers to the coming-of-age ceremony, usually at the festival of *Liberalia* (17 March: cf. Ov. *Fast.* 3.771–2), when Roman boys aged between fourteen and sixteen changed from wearing the *toga praetexta* (with a purple border) and *bulla* to the plain *toga virilis*. The boy was led into the forum by his father and was registered as a full citizen ready for military service in the *tabularium* on the Capitol. Having not held the consulship since his resignation in 23 BC, Augustus resumed office as consul in 5 BC (for the twelfth time) and 2 BC (for the last and thirteenth time) for a few months (resigning at the end of March or April), precisely for the purpose of introducing his sons officially into public life (Suet. *Aug.* 26.2). According to Dio Cassius (55.9.9), Gaius was admitted to the senate at the same time (see 14.1n. ***ut interessent consiliis publicis***), took the title *princeps iuventutis* (see 14.2n. **principem iuventutis**), and became a cavalry commander. Augustus also marked the occasions with donatives to the people of Rome (15.2, 15.4). The council of Sardis sent a message of congratulation to Augustus to mark Gaius' coming-of-age (*IGRom* IV 1756 lines 1–21 = EJ no. 99 = LACTOR J56). The fact that this inscription does not mention the title of *princeps iuventutis* appears to support the idea that the equestrians may have acclaimed Gaius some time later. The chronological relationship between the various honours is not entirely clear (Hurlet (1997) 117–18, 121–5). It is likely that the coming-of-age ceremonies took place first, before other honours were enacted, but this may have been on 1 January or 17 March, or some other date. Possibly Lucius was the first to perform his ceremonial coming-of-age in the new Augustan forum, to where such ceremonies were transferred in 2 BC (Dio Cass. 55.10.2).

ut interessent consiliis publicis/they should take part in the councils of state The Greek version of the *RGDA* makes clear that what is in question here is their attendance at meetings of the senate (Reichmann (1943) 22). Both Gaius and Lucius were given permission to attend meetings of the senate once they had come of age. If Dio Cassius is correct (55.9.4), this is one of the honours granted to Gaius in 6 BC, but postponed until after his coming-of-age in the following year (Dio Cass. 55.9.9; Hurlet (1997) 118). This honour was alluded to in the *elogia* for the dead princes in Augustus' Mausoleum (*CIL* VI 894 + 40367, 895 + 31195 + 40360, *[— decrevit senatus, ut interesset] / consiliis publicis*), which echo the language of the *RGDA*. They were also permitted to sit among the senatorial class at games and feasts (Hurlet (1997) 118). This treatment of Gaius and Lucius was indicative of Augustus' broader policy of attempting to create a hereditary senatorial class by formalizing the practice for sons of senators to wear the tunic with a broad purple stripe (*latus clavus*) beneath the toga, and allowing them to attend meetings of the senate (Suet. *Aug.* 38.2; Nicolet (1984) 93). Gaius was present for the first time as part of Augustus' own *consilium* in 4 BC (Joseph. *BJ* 20.22.25 = LACTOR M42).

14.2 equites autem Romani universi/Moreover the Roman equestrians all together The theme of the consensus of Roman society in supporting Augustus, which becomes such a prominent feature of Augustus' account of his position in society at the end of the *RGDA* (see 34.1), is foreshadowed here. The equestrian order attained a new importance under Augustus, playing a prominent part in public life and developing a corporate identity (see 35.1n. **senatus et equester ordo populusque Romanus universus**; Rowe (2002) ch. 2). Augustus laid a fresh emphasis upon membership of the *ordo* by carrying out a *recognitio equitum* in 13 BC and probably at five-yearly intervals thereafter, equivalent to his *lectio senatus*, and by reviving the *ordo*'s annual parade on horseback, each year on 15 July, the *transvectio* (Suet. *Aug.* 38–9; Ov. *Tr.* 2.89–91 = LACTOR G56; Ov. *Tr.* 2.541–2; Nicolet (1984) 96–8). The equestrians were allocated a section of fourteen rows of seats in the theatre, which may have been named after Gaius and Lucius, as part of the package of honours voted to them after their deaths (Demougin (1988) 794–812, espec. 808–9 on Mart. 5.14.1–5). It is an attractive idea that the equestrians staged acclamations in honour of Gaius and Lucius precisely from their area of reserved seating in the theatre (Rowe (2002) 69–71, 77–81). Finally, their new prominence was reflected in the part played by the equestrians at the ceremonies for Augustus' funeral (Dio Cass. 56.42.2; Suet. *Aug.* 100.2).

principem iuventutis/ leader of the youth   This new title encapsulates the emergent monarchical and dynastic nature of Augustus' rule at Rome. The *iuventus* may be defined as including equestrians up to the age of thirty-five (known as the *iuniores*) and youths from senatorial families before they entered the senate in their mid-twenties (Swan (2004) 90). The choice of the novel title '*princeps* of the youth' for Gaius clearly implied that he would in time succeed Augustus as *princeps* (see 13n. **me principe**). The most striking enunciation of this principle can be found in Ovid, who describes Gaius as 'now leader of the youth, later to be leader of the elders' (*nunc iuvenum princeps, deinde future senum, Ars Am.* 1.194). Augustus closely supervised the upbringing and education of his adopted sons, even ensuring that they copied his handwriting (Suet. *Aug.* 64.3) and expressed the desire in a letter to Gaius that they should 'take over my post' (διαδεχομένων *stationem meam*, Gell. *NA* 15.7.3 = LACTOR J57). The dynastic expectation was also present in many inscriptions: most notably, the deceased Gaius is described at Pisa as 'already designated a leader who was most just and most like his father in his virtues' (*iam designatum iustissimum ac simillumum parentis suis virtutibus principem, ILS* 140, lines 12–13 = EJ no. 69 = LACTOR J61). The concept was also translated into Greek (*IG* XII 2, 164b, 165c Mytilene). A fragmentary inscription found in the theatre of Marcellus set up in honour of Gaius or Lucius – *[C(aio)* or *L(ucio) Caesari Augusti filio, Divi I]ulii nepoti, / [— principi] iuventutis a se / [appellato post deposita p]ueritiae insignia. / [equester ordo pe]rmissu senatus, CIL* VI 40326. Cf. Vassileiou (1984a), Hurlet (1997) 120–1) – appears to allude to him being acclaimed as *princeps iuventutis* by the equestrian order (see 14.2n. **equites autem Romani universi**) after his coming-of-age (see 14.1n. **quo deducti sunt in forum**).

parmis et hastis argenteis/with silver shields and spears   These round shields and spears appear on *aurei* and *denarii* minted in Lugdunum, 2 BC–AD 11 (*BM Coins, Rom. Emp.* I 88–91 nos. 513–43; *RIC* I² 55–6 nos. 205–12; Simon (1993) 72–3, 75; LACTOR J58) (see Figure 19). On their obverse Augustus appears wreathed in laurel as *pater patriae* (see 35.1).

Fig. 19 Gaius and Lucius as *principes iuventutis. Aureus*, 2 BC/AD 11 (coin: reverse, *RIC* I²
55–6 nos. 205–12 = LACTOR J58).

On their reverse stand the togate figures of Gaius and Lucius, with veiled
heads (*capite velato*), holding spears and round shields. The legend reads C
L CAESARES AVGVSTI F COS DESIG PRINC IVVENT ('Gaius and
Lucius Caesars, sons of Augustus, consuls designate, leaders of the youth').
In addition are depicted symbols of their priesthoods, the *simpulum* for
Gaius, who was *pontifex* from 6/5 BC (Dio Cass. 55.9.4; Lewis (1955) 31 no.
19), and the *lituus* for Lucius, who was *augur* from 3/2 BC (Lewis (1955)
43 no. 32). An engraved cornelian gem now in Florence Archaeological
Museum provides a close parallel for the imagery on this coin, with the
difference that the brothers are not *capite velato* (Vollenweider (1964) 78,
79 fig. 6). Augustus does not mention their priesthoods. These shields and
spears were set up in the *curia* in their honour after their deaths (Dio Cass.
55.12.1, mistakenly describing them as 'golden').

AUGUSTUS' DONATIONS TO THE PEOPLE OF ROME AND TO HIS VETERAN SOLDIERS (15–18)

Traditionally, chapters 15–24 are regarded as the *RGDA*'s second section,
dealing with Augustus' expenditure (*impensae*) on behalf of the Roman
people (see introduction p. 34), as mentioned in the inscription's heading.
All of the expenditure mentioned in the *RGDA* is attributable to Augustus
personally in some way; it does not represent expenditure made from
regular income received by the Roman state (Millar (1992) 191). Augustus
turns first to distributions of cash and grain made to the citizenry of Rome
and veteran colonists (ch. 15): he insistently records the sources of money

spent (inheritance from Julius Caesar, war plunder, own property) in order to make clear that the expenditure came out of his private pocket. He then outlines the rewards paid to his veteran soldiers (ch. 16). This chapter adds more details to Augustus' earlier brief mention of his programme of veteran colonization (3.3), and alludes to the shift in policy after 14 BC, when veteran soldiers might receive cash gratuities rather than allotments of land (Brunt (1962) 83 points out that the policy of replacing land allotments by cash bounties was not always implemented: 'Augustus had then not given up the practice of settling veterans on the land but only that of disturbing Italian property-rights. At all times in the Principate veterans received lands'). He next records his interventions to bolster the state treasury and his establishment of a new military treasury (ch. 17), as well as how he had intervened in making distributions of grain and cash whenever the state treasury experienced a shortfall in revenues (ch. 18). Securing the goodwill of the citizenry of Rome and maintaining that of his veteran soldiers were crucial for his regime; the sigificance of the former is revealed by Augustus' remark, cited by Suetonius (*Aug.* 41.3), that he had decided to continue making distributions of grain instead of abolishing them only in order to prevent someone else in the future from gaining popular support by reviving them (cf. Nicolet (1980) 204). Indeed, he ensured that he alone monopolized the practice of distributing gifts to the populace of Rome (van Berchem (1939) 123).

Augustus includes a consular date for each handout so as to reveal why each one was made (Ridley (1988) 271). This allows us to trace the remarkable intensity with which largesse was distributed by Augustus during the crucial years 30–27 BC, when he was consolidating his victory over Antony, when he handed out well in excess of 800 million sesterces, amounting to as much as a third of the total sum which he is said to have spent in the course of his lifetime (Appendix 1n. ***denarium sexiens milliens***; Brunt and Moore (1967) 57). This would have been enough to provide the minimum property valuation for 800 senators. Augustus rejoiced in a wide variety of sources of wealth right from the start of his political career. In the early days, he inherited vast sums from Julius Caesar, both directly as his heir and indirectly via Caesar's friends and freedmen, and through his control of the funds which Caesar had amassed for military purposes and of the annual tribute from eastern provinces (Syme (1939) 130–1). As triumvir he shared responsibility for spending state funds, and for supplementing them through proscriptions, confiscations, and new taxes (Syme (1939) 187, 193–6). After the culmination of his struggle against Antony, he took control of Egypt, which was outstandingly wealthy in terms of its production of grain and for the fortune left behind by Cleopatra, last of the Ptolemies (see 15.1n. ***nomine meo HS quadringenos ex bellorum manibiis consul quintum dedi***). Throughout his career, Augustus received substantial bequests from wealthy individuals (Rogers (1947) 141–3), such as King Herod (4 BC,

Joseph. *AJ* 17.190 = LACTOR T36) although he allegedly then returned
the gift to Herod's children (Joseph. *AJ* 17.323), and Vedius Pollio (15 BC,
Dio Cass. 54.23.1–6), as well as from members of his own family (such as
Agrippa in 12 BC, Dio Cass. 54.29.5) and freedmen; indeed, he declared in
his will that he had acquired 1,400 million sesterces from legacies in his
last twenty years alone, but had spent almost all of it for the benefit of the
state (Suet. *Aug.* 101, cf. 66.4). This was a huge sum: it has been calculated
that even two such rich provinces as Gaul and Egypt combined would
only have produced an annual revenue amounting to just over half of this
total (Millar (1992) 154–5). Augustus also basically controlled the revenues
of the state treasury, or *aerarium* (Dio Cass. 53.22.3–4, with Rich (1990)
ad loc.), as well as his huge private wealth (see Millar (1963), Rathbone
(1996) 320–2 on the vexed question of the relationship between state and
imperial finances; Speidel (2000) on the theme of Augustus' finances as a
whole; see also 17.1n. **eos qui praeerant aerario**).

**15.1 plebei Romanae viritim HS trecenos numeravi/To the mem-
bers of the Roman plebs I paid 300 sesterces each**   Handouts of wine
and oil (*congiaria*) had been made to freeborn citizens living in Rome by
individual magistrates during the Republic. The earliest known historical
example was that of P. Cornelius Scipio and M. Cornelius Cethegus after
their election as aediles in 213 BC (Livy 25.2). Julius Caesar was the first
to promise a distribution of cash (300 sesterces) in 49 BC, in a cynical bid
to secure popular support for his seizure of money from the state treasury
to pay his soldiers in the lead-up to Pharsalus (Dio Cass. 41.16–17). After
a three-year wait, the people did actually receive the promised handout
after Caesar's quadruple triumph in 46 BC, with an additional 100 sesterces
in compensation for the delay, together with distributions of corn and oil
(Dio Cass. 43.21.3; Suet. *Iul.* 38.1; van Berchem (1939) 119–21). In assessing
the actual worth of all the cash handouts recorded in this chapter, it is
worth noting that a legionary's annual pay amounted to 900 sesterces, and
so Augustus' handouts represented significant sums to the individual recipients. Following the precedent set by Caesar and Augustus, all subsequent
emperors continued the practice of making substantial handouts to the
people of Rome.

ex testamento patris mei/in accordance with my father's will   As
well as nominating his great-nephew as his chief heir in his will (see 1.1n.
annos undeviginti natus), Julius Caesar bequeathed 300 sesterces each
to the people of Rome, and left his *horti* on the other side of the Tiber
(Trastevere) for public enjoyment (Suet. *Iul.* 83.2; Dio Cass. 44.35.2–3;
App. *B Civ.* 2.143; Plut. *Vit. Brut.* 20.2). In the face of Antony's attempts to
hinder him from assuming the guise of Caesar's heir (Plut. *Vit. Brut.* 22, *Vit.
Ant.* 16, with Pelling (1988) 157; Syme (1939) 115), Octavian sold property in

order to fund the distribution (App. *B Civ.* 3.21, 23), and probably increased the number of beneficiaries beyond what had been envisaged by Caesar. It is likely that Caesar had intended the legacy to be paid out to 150,000 citizens, the number fixed by him as eligible for receipt of grain dole in 46 BC (Suet. *Iul.* 41.3; Dio Cass. 43.21.4). Octavian distributed the legacy (perhaps in late May/June 44 BC) to at least 250,000 citizens (cf. *quae mea congiaria pervenerunt ad hominum millia numquam minus quinquaginta et ducenta*), perhaps even to as many as 300,000 individuals (App. *B Civ.* 3.17). By presenting himself as Caesar's heir, and by distributing such largesse in accordance with the terms of his will in 44 BC, the young Caesar, Octavian, took a huge step forwards into the limelight of Roman political life, and began the process of supplanting Antony as Caesar's political heir (see 2n. *qui parentem meum trucidaverunt*). He quickly consolidated his position by celebrating games, the *ludi victoriae Caesaris* (20–30 July), during the course of which a comet appeared, just in time to be interpreted as a sign of Caesar's apotheosis (Plin. *HN* 2.23.93–4 = LACTOR K44, H3; Dio Cass. 45.7.1; App. *B Civ.* 3.28; Syme (1939) 117). This first handout organized by Octavian set the trend for expenditure on a massive scale, amounting as it did to at least 75 million sesterces.

nomine meo HS quadringenos ex bellorum manibiis consul quintum dedi/in my own name I gave 400 sesterces out of the plunder from warfare when I was consul for the fifth time   Augustus made a cash handout in 29 BC following the celebration of his triple triumph (see 4.1n. *tris egi curulis triumphos*). It was traditional practice for a victorious general to spend money raised from war booty on some public project, such as building a temple or giving games. The influx of wealth in 29 BC was so significant as to lead to a large cut in interest rates (Suet. *Aug.* 41.1; from 12 per cent to 4 per cent: Dio Cass. 51.21.5). Cleopatra's wealth included not only ancestral Ptolemaic possessions in Egypt (see Dio Cass. 51.8.6, 11.3, 17.6), but also assets in other lands given to her by Antony, such as balsam plantations near Jericho and copper mines in Cyprus (Millar (1963) 30).

iterum autem in consulatu decimo/and also a second time in my tenth consulship   Augustus made this distribution in 24 BC on his return from the Cantabrian wars (see 26.2n. *Gallias et Hispanias provincias*), even though he did not celebrate a triumph (Dio Cass. 53.28.1; 4.1n. *decernente pluris triumphos mihi senatu*).

HS quadringenos congiari viritim pernumeravi/I paid out 400 sesterces each as a handout   Only those registered among the *plebs frumentaria* (see 15.1n. *consul undecimum duodecim frumentationes*; 15.4n. *quae tum frumentum publicum accipiebat*) were eligible for *congiaria* (see 15.1n. *plebei Romanae viritim HS trecenos numeravi*). Fronto makes a

sharp distinction between the limited recipients of *congiaria* and the universal audience for games (Fronto *Principia Historiae* 20/A259 p. 213, ed. van
den Hout (Leipzig: Teubner, 1988), *congiarieis frumentariam modo plebem
singillatim placari ac nominatim, spectaculis universum interdum esse . . .*).
The Greek version translates *congiarium* in two different ways within the
same chapter (15.1 ἐπιδόσεις, 15.3 δωρεὰν), perhaps because of the difficulty
of explaining a concept alien to the Greek east (Vanotti (1975) 314).

**consul undecimum duodecim frumentationes . . . emensus sum/as
consul for the eleventh time I distributed twelve grain rations**   A limited, but substantial, number of adult male citizens (below equestrian rank)
resident in Rome was eligible for the grain dole (see 15.4n. *quae tum frumentum publicum accipiebat*). The free distribution of five *modii* of grain
per month (a sizeable ration, which would have been more than enough for
a single individual, but which was insufficient to meet a family's need for
bread: Brunt (1971) 382; Rickman (1980) 10, 173) had been introduced by a
law promulgated by the tribune P. Clodius in 58 BC, replacing the previous
system of a monthly ration of grain sold at a subsidized rate (Dio Cass.
38.13.1; Rickman (1980) 172; Nicolet (1980) 194; Robinson (1992) 151–2). In
23 BC (*consul undecimum*), at the time of a severe grain shortage, Augustus
supplied an additional monthly grain dole for a whole year, which would
have amounted to some 15 million *modii* of grain, presumably because it
had become too expensive for individuals to buy the extra grain necessary
to them (see 5.2n. *curationem annonae*). The shortage resulted at least
partly from stored grain being destroyed by flooding at Rome (Dio Cass.
53.33.5). This crisis also marked the start of Tiberius' political career: as
quaestor, he helped to alleviate the crisis by bringing in emergency supplies
(Vell. Pat. 2.94.3, with Woodman (1977) ad loc.; cf. Suet. *Tib.* 8; Garnsey
(1988) 219). Dio Cassius (55.26.3) claims that Augustus also supplemented
the grain dole in AD 6, at another time of crisis, but this is not mentioned
by Augustus (and according to Brunt and Moore (1967) 59–60 its omission indicates the incomplete revision of the *RGDA* by Augustus in his
later years: see introduction, section 6 for discussion of the work's date of
composition).

**tribunicia potestate duodecimum/in my twelfth year of tribunician
power**   This is the only place in the *RGDA* where an event is dated by
means of Augustus' tribunician power alone (Lacey (1996) 166–7). The
exact dating of tribunician years is debated, but probably corresponds
to a twelve-month period starting in late June/July, resulting in a period
that does not coincide with a calendar year (Rich (1990) 169; Lacey (1996)
chs. 4, 7). In the *RGDA*, other events occurring in the period after Augustus
had ceased to hold an annual consulship are usually dated by the year's
consuls. Augustus' choice of dating formula here appears to be influenced

by his theme: reference to his tribunician power is appropriate to the context of benefiting the *plebs* (Ridley (1988) 283). This distribution of 400 sesterces in 12/11 BC is described by Dio Cassius (54.29.4) as being the result of a legacy made by the recently deceased Agrippa, but in the *Fasti Cuprenses* (*Inscr. Ital.* XIII.i.245 = EJ p. 37 = LACTOR H28) it is associated with Augustus' election as *pontifex maximus* (see 10.2), which, however, actually occurred when Augustus was in his eleventh year of tribunician power (6 March 12 BC). Agrippa, however, died towards the end of March in 12 BC (Dio Cass. 54.28.3, with Rich (1990) ad loc.). In either case, therefore, a couple of months elapsed before the handout was made (at the earliest in late June/July 12 BC), which may go some way to explaining why two different reasons are found for it.

15.2 tribuniciae potestatis duodevicensimum, consul XII/In my eighteenth year of tribunician power, as consul for the twelfth time Augustus made this *congiarium* in early 5 BC, to celebrate Gaius' entry into public life (see 14.1n. ***quo deducti sunt in forum***).

trecentis et viginti millibus/to 320,000   The Greek version makes a mistake in translating this number as τριάκοντα τρισὶ μυριάσιν (330,000). This statistic for the number of the *plebs frumentaria* in 5 BC provides us with the best basis for calculating the total free population of Rome at the time as between three-quarters of a million and a million. In addition, there may have been somewhere in the region of 200,000 slaves in the city. It is generally agreed that the population of Rome under Augustus must have been about one million, making it by far the largest city in antiquity (Rickman (1980) 8–10).

sexagenos denarios/60 *denarii* each   So far, Augustus has used sesterces as the unit for currency values, but he switches here to *denarii* (4 sesterces = 1 *denarius*). This can be explained by the fact that this cash handout was being presented as an equivalent to a handout of grain. The annual distribution of grain consisted of 60 *modii* over 12 months, with each *modius* being worth 4 sesterces/1 *denarius*. Describing the handout as 60 *denarii* rather than 240 sesterces makes clear its equivalence to a year's worth of public grain distributions, and this is repeated at 15.4 (see Duncan-Jones (1982) 146, 345). Suetonius (*Aug.* 41.2) mistakenly records handouts of 250 sesterces.

15.3 colonis militum meorum consul quintum/as consul for the fifth time to the colonists who had been my soldiers   This sentence disturbs the chronological sequence of the chapter, by inserting the distribution to veteran colonists in 29 BC between the handouts of 5 and 2 BC (Ridley (1988) 271; Gagé (1935) 100). The handout of 29 BC more naturally belongs in the context of 15.1, complementing his distribution to the *plebs* (*nomine meo HS quadringenos ex bellorum manibiis consul quintum dedi*). The fact that Augustus chooses to postpone mentioning his generosity to the veteran colonists until after he has continued the theme of handouts to the citizenry of Rome is understandable thematically, but it is puzzling why he does not first mention the handout of 2 BC to the urban *plebs*, before ending with the veterans. What the structure of this chapter implies, therefore, is a distinction between the *plebs Romana/urbana* (15.1–2), the veteran colonists (15.3), and the *plebs frumentaria* (15.4) as newly defined in 2 BC (see 15.4n. **quae tum frumentum publicum accipiebat**).

acceperunt id triumphale congiarium in colonis hominum circiter centum et viginti millia/about 120,000 men in the colonies received this handout to mark my triumphs   The implication that around 120,000 veterans were settled as colonists in the aftermath of Actium has been questioned, since Octavian's legions can only have included around 40,000–50,000 soldiers ready for retirement at the time. We should probably assume that the handout was distributed not only to Octavian's troops who were entering retirement at this time, but was also made to Antony's veterans, and to discharged soldiers already settled earlier as colonists after the battles of Philippi and Naulochus. This would have been unusual for a triumphal handout, which would normally have benefited only the soldiers who had fought to achieve the triumph, but perhaps reflects a canny move by Octavian to secure more widespread support in the colonies (Keppie (1983) 74–5).

15.4 consul tertium decimum/As consul for the thirteenth time   This handout in 2 BC marked the entry into public life (*deductio in forum*) of Lucius Caesar (see 14.1). Augustus does not mention a *congiarium* of 300 sesterces distributed in AD 13 on the occasion of Tiberius' triumph (Suet. *Tib.* 20; van Berchem (1939) 143). Presumably Augustus chose not to mention it because it was primarily regarded as Tiberius', and so this omission cannot be interpreted as a sign that an earlier draft of the *RGDA* had not been updated.

sexagenos denarios/60 *denarii* each   See 15.2n. *sexagenos denarios*.

quae tum frumentum publicum accipiebat . . . ea millia hominum paullo plura quam ducenta fuerunt/who at that time were in receipt of public grain; these were a few more than 200,000 men   The way in which Augustus describes recipients of his handouts changes in the course of this chapter, from *plebs Romana* to *plebs urbana*, and finally to the *plebs quae tum frumentum publicum accipiebat*. This last description reflects an important shift in the practice of distributing grain at Rome in

2 BC, when the *plebs frumentaria* could no longer be regarded as simply the same as the *plebs urbana* or *plebs Romana*. A similar linguistic shift can be observed in Dio Cassius: he uses the word δῆμος to describe the beneficiaries of Augustus' earlier handouts (51.21.3, 29 BC; 53.28.1, 24 BC; 54.29.4, 12 BC), but uses a much more precise phrase to refer to the recipients in 2 BC, τὸ τοῦ δήμου τοῦ σιτοδοτουμένου πλῆθος (Dio Cass. 55.10.1, with Swan (2004) ad loc.; Virlouvet (1995) 186–9; cf. Yavetz (1969) 143–6). When Clodius introduced free handouts of grain, the number of recipients was not subject to a quota, but the handout was available to all who could demonstrate their citizenship and domicile in Rome. Julius Caesar had made an attempt in 46 BC to restrict the number of recipients to 150,000 (Suet. *Iul.* 41.3; Dio Cass. 43.21.4), but this was not observed in the aftermath of his assassination. Instead, the number of recipients evidently rose once more, with as many as 320,000 qualifying for handouts in 5 BC. By 2 BC, however, Augustus had reduced the number to 200,000, according to Dio Cassius (55.10.1), by carrying out a review of those registered as eligible, district by district (Suet. *Aug.* 40.2). This chapter of the *RGDA* ends, however, with a curiously imprecise statement, that stands out in a text that is otherwise strikingly precise in its numerical reckonings, that the *plebs frumentaria* amounted to 'a few more than 200,000 men' (*millia hominum paullo plura quam ducenta*). It is likely that Augustus did not intend to impose a quota of 200,000 on the register of the *plebs frumentaria*, and that Dio was mistaken in believing 200,000 to be his target, and that he subsequently reduced the number eligible even further down to 150,000. The word *tum* implies that this number was later modified (Rickman (1980) 175–85; Virlouvet (1995) 192–6, 370). His introduction of a quota represented a radical change from previous practice.

As a result of Augustus' new system, not all freeborn citizens domiciled in Rome were eligible for the handouts, so that registration as part of the *plebs frumentaria* was a source of pride for some, which they recorded on their epitaphs (Virlouvet (1995) 198–9; Rickman (1980) 183–4; van Berchem (1939) 36–43). Once a space became free on the register when an individual had died, there appear to have been three ways of becoming registered: by lot, by pursuing a profession in the public interest, or by purchasing the right (Veyne (1990) 244–5).

16.1 pecuniam pro agris/money . . . for the lands   Augustus' practice of paying for land replaced the triumviral one of simply appropriating territory from various wealthy Italian towns for assignation to veteran colonists, which had caused serious discontent (App. *B Civ.* 4.1.3, 5.2.12–13; Syme (1939) 196; cf. Virg. *Ecl.* 1 = LACTOR G1, *Ecl.* 9). Naturally, he avoids mentioning these earlier phases of veteran settlement in 41/40 and 36 BC (Ramage (1987) 35; Brunt and Moore (1967) 42). Initially, the land was in Italy and in the provinces, but after 14 BC no more land in Italy was assigned to veterans (Keppie (1983) 208; see 28 for further details of colonization).

in consulatu meo quarto/in my fourth consulship   In 30 BC, after his victory at Actium but before the final showdown at Alexandria, Octavian faced an emergency created by vast numbers of mutinous veteran soldiers. He was forced to make a swift journey over wintry seas from Samos to Brundisium in order to pacify them, making land distributions not only to those who had fought for him, but also to those who had fought for Antony and Lepidus (Suet. *Aug.* 17.3; Hyginus (2) (Gromaticus) *Constitutio <Limitum>* p. 140 line 34 + p. 142 lines 1–4 in Campbell (2000); Aigner (1979) 174–5). To his own veterans, he gave territory belonging to Italian towns which had supported Antony. These erstwhile Antonians were compensated with lands in Macedonia, northern Italy, and perhaps Carthage, or with cash (Dio Cass. 51.4.6, with Reinhold (1988) ad loc.). For example, a colony of Octavian's veterans was established at Augusta Bagiennorum (Reg. IX, Liguria). Soldiers from that town, who had fought for Antony, were punished by being sent as colonists to settlements beyond Italy, rather than being permitted to return home, whilst their town and territory were restructured for the benefit of Octavian's veterans. Although one of the displaced veterans of Antony's fourth legion succeeded in returning home, where he died, many veterans must have died far from their original homes (*AE* 1996.679 = *Suppl. It.* n.s. 19 (2002) 222–3 no. 2, with analysis by G. Mennella and E. Bernardini, 196–7).

consulibus M. Crasso et Cn. Lentulo Augure/in the consulship of Marcus Crassus and Gnaeus Lentulus Augur   Both consuls of 14 BC were representatives of the old aristocracy at Rome, by adoption and by birth. M. Licinius Crassus Frugi (*PIR²* L189), born a Piso, was adopted into another distinguished family by the consul of 30 BC, and after his consulship became proconsul of Africa in 9/8 BC. Cn. Cornelius Lentulus Augur became proconsul of Asia only in 3/2 BC, delayed perhaps by his involvement in military activities in the Balkans (see Syme (1986) ch. 21; *PIR²* C1379; see also 30.2n. *Dacorum gentes imperia populi Romani perferre coegit*). He reputedly owed his advancement to Augustus (Sen. *Ben.* 2.27.1).

summa sestertium circiter sexsiens milliens/the total amount . . . about 600,000,000 sesterces   Six hundred million sesterces may have provided land for some 24,000 veterans, assuming the cost of land to be about 500 sesterces per *iugerum*, and with each veteran receiving 50 *iugera*, but these figures are far from certain (Keppie (1983) 76, with n. 122).

id primus et solus omnium/I was the first and only one . . . of all
The novelty of Augustus' actions lay not in the fact that the lands were
being paid for, given that public revenues had been used for this purpose
already during the Republic, but in the fact that he was using his own
funds to do so (Gagé (1935) 102; Brunt and Moore (1967) 59; Ridley (2003)
149–50).

**deduxerunt colonias militum in Italia aut in provincis/have settled
colonies of soldiers in Italy or in the provinces** On the colonies in
Italy, see 16.1n. *in consulatu meo quarto*. The soldiers who retired in
14 BC would presumably have been those recruited for service during the
civil war against Antony. They were settled in already existing colonies in
Gallia Narbonensis (possibly Arelate, Narbo, Arausio, Baeterrae, Novio-
dunum, Lugdunum, Forum Iulii, and Raurica) and in new colonies in
Spain (perhaps Ilici, Tucci, Astigi) (Dio Cass. 54.23.7; Keppie (1983) 83;
3.3n. *deduxi in colonias*). Augustus does not mention colonies established
on lands seized from conquered peoples, such as Aosta, since they did not
represent expenditure on his part (Brunt and Moore (1967) 42). The Greek
translation gives a literal rendering of the Latin expression, using κατάγειν
ἀποικίας, instead of the more usual Greek idiom of ἀποικίας ἐκπέμπειν
or ἀποστέλλειν ἀποίκους (Adams (2003) 470).

ad memoriam aetatis meae/as far as people living in my era recall
An alternative interpretation sees this phrase as meaning 'as a record of my
age' (Ridley (2003) 149).

**16.2 Ti. Nerone et Cn. Pisone consulibus/in the consulship of Tiberius
Nero and Gnaeus Piso** The year 7 BC heralded Tiberius' second consulship (following his first in 13 BC), punctuating a period of promotion
for Augustus' stepson; except for Augustus, iterated consulships were also
held only by Agrippa (37, 28, 27 BC) and T. Statilius Taurus (37, 26 BC). In
the period between his two consulships, Tiberius had enjoyed significant
military success in Pannonia (see 30.1n. *devictas per Ti. Neronem*) and
Germany, and had married Augustus' daughter Julia (11 BC), after the death
of her second husband Agrippa (Dio Cass. 54.35.4). Cn. Calpurnius Piso
belonged to a distinguished family (*PIR*² C287; Syme (1986) 369–75), and
owned land in Illyricum which Augustus had given to him (*SCPP* 85–6;
Eck *et al.* (1996) 44, 202–7); his father, who had a reputation for possessing
a fiercely independent character, had been Augustus' fellow consul in the
crisis year of 23 BC (Tac. *Ann.* 2.43.2 = LACTOR H42; Dio Cass. 53.30.1–2;
*PIR*² C286). Piso, consul in 7 BC, later became governor of Africa, and then
Syria, but ended up committing suicide in AD 20 having been accused of
maiestas and the murder of Germanicus. Before then, Tiberius and Piso
had been close friends and collaborators: just before his death, Piso recalled

that their friendship had lasted for over forty-five years (Tac. *Ann.* 3.16.4), and Piso had been entrusted by Tiberius with the task of keeping a check on Germanicus in Syria in AD 19 (Tac. *Ann.* 2.43.2). His wife Plancina (probably the granddaughter of Munatius Plancus, consul in 42 BC) was a close friend of Livia (Tac. *Ann.* 2.43.4, 2.82.1, 3.15.1; *SCPP* 109–20: Eck *et al.* (1996) 46, with comments on 87–8; *PIR*² M737).

C. Antistio et D. Laelio cos./in the consulship of Gaius Antistius and Decimus Laelius   The father of C. Antistius Vetus had been consul in 30 BC; his two sons also became consuls in AD 23 and 28. Having served as consul in 6 BC, he himself later became proconsul of Asia (*PIR*² A771). The *novus homo* D. Laelius Balbus was also a *quindecimvir* (*PIR*² L47).

C. Calvisio et L. Pasieno consulibus/in the consulship of Gaius Calvisius and Lucius Pasienus   These are the consuls for 4 BC. C. Calvisius Sabinus (*PIR*² C353) was son of the consul of 39 BC (*PIR*² C352) who was a loyal supporter of both Julius Caesar and his heir, and who had earned a triumph for campaigning successfully in Spain in 28 BC, from the proceeds of which he rebuilt the *via Latina* (see 20.5n. **viam Flaminiam ab urbe Ariminum**). The *novus homo* L. Passienus Rufus later earned triumphal decorations in Africa as proconsul (Vell. Pat. 2.116.2 = LACTOR E 2.116.2; *PIR*² P148).

L. Lentulo et M. Messalla consulibus/in the consulship of Lucius Lentulus and Marcus Messalla   Both of the consuls for 3 BC belonged to distinguished families. Their period in office lasted for the whole year, breaking the pattern of suffect consulships which had been a notable feature of 5 and 4 BC. L. Cornelius Lentulus was also a *flamen Martialis*, and later became proconsul of Africa (*PIR*² C1384). M. Valerius Messalla Messallinus was also a *quindecimvir*. He later governed Illyricum, and received triumphal decorations in AD 12 (Ov. *Pont.* 2.2.89–92; *PIR* V93). He was celebrated for his 'loyalty towards the whole Julian name' (*pietas in totum nomen Iuli*) by Ovid (*Pont.* 2.2.21), whose appeals to him from exile to intercede on his behalf yielded no fruit, however, and is depicted by Tacitus as consistently sycophantic towards Tiberius (*Ann.* 1.8.4, 3.18.2–3).

L. Caninio et Q. Fabricio cos./in the consulship of Lucius Caninius and Quintus Fabricius   This consular pair held office towards the end of 2 BC (Ridley (1988) 286). L. Caninius Gallus (*PIR*² C390) was an Arval and *quindecimvir*; he held office as suffect consul from 1 August, initially with Augustus, then with Fufius Geminus by 18 September, and finally, by 1 December, with Q. Fabricius (*PIR*² F86), about whom almost nothing further is known (Degrassi (1952) 5).

emeriteis stipendis in sua municipia deduxi/I settled in their own municipalities once they had completed their terms of service   During this period, legionary soldiers were mostly recruited from within Italy and sixteen years was the standard length of service. (For Augustus' changes to the length of service and to their rewards on discharge, see 3.3n. *stipendis emeritis*; 3.3n. *pro praemiis militiae*; 17.2n. *qui vicena aut plura stipendia emeruissent.*)

praemia/cash rewards   Before the *aerarium militare* was established (see 17.2), Augustus funded the payment of cash gratuities to retiring soldiers himself. The Greek version emphasizes the payments as being the personal generosity of Augustus, φιλανθρώπου ὀνόματι ἔδωκα ('I gave . . . in the name of a gratuity').

sestertium quater milliens circiter impendi/I paid out about 400,000,000 sesterces   This total perhaps represents payments in the region of 12,000 sesterces to 30,000 veterans (Keppie (1983) 208).

17.1 quater/Four times   Three out of these four occasions can be identified (Speidel (2000) 146–7): for the *ludi Actiaci* in 28 BC (see Dio Cass. 53.2.1; 9.1n. *vota pro valetudine mea*); for road building in 16 BC (see 20.5n. *viam Flaminiam ab urbe Ariminum*); and in 12 BC, Augustus paid the tribute owing to the treasury from the province of Asia following damaging earth tremors, which prevented it from meeting its obligations (Dio Cass. 54.30.3).

aerarium/treasury   Under the Republic, the state treasury was housed in the temple of Saturn at the south-west corner of the Roman forum beneath the Capitol, in the safe-keeping of the temple's podium. A number of small rooms adjacent to the temple served as the treasury's administrative offices (Corbier (1974) 631–2).

eos qui praeerant aerario/those who were in charge of the treasury   During the Republic, the officials in charge were two annual quaestors, the *quaestores urbani*, relatively junior magistrates, who were answerable to the consuls (Corbier (1974) 633). Julius Caesar replaced them with two *praefecti* in 45 BC, in the absence of regularly elected quaestors (Dio Cass. 43.48.1–3; Corbier (1974) 634–7). This temporary innovation, which lapsed after the dictator's assassination, foreshadowed Augustus' innovation in 28 BC, when he charged the senate with choosing two *praefecti aerarii* from among the ex-praetors (Dio Cass. 53.2.1; Suet. *Aug.* 36; Tac. *Ann.* 13.29; Corbier (1974) 637–9). Finally, from 23 BC, the number of praetors elected annually was increased from eight to ten, in order to allow for two of them to be selected by lot to supervise the treasury (Dio Cass. 53.32.2;

Corbier (1974) 639). In this way, Augustus shifted the administration onto
relatively senior magistrates, and this change in administrative structure
allowed Augustus rather than the senate to influence which individuals
were appointed to supervise the treasury (Speidel (2000) 127). In addition,
the treasury's regular staff consisted of imperial freedmen and slaves, with
the result that Augustus effectively had control over the issuing of accounts
and over access to detailed financial information (Suet. *Aug.* 101.4; Brunt
(1966) 89–90). Augustus' vague periphrasis avoids getting tangled up in
the niceties of his administrative reforms. This expression is simplified in
the Greek version, which simply refers to the institution, not its officials
(Reichmann (1943) 22; Vanotti (1975) 314).

detulerim/transferring   The use of this verb indicates that this financial transaction, unlike others listed so far, was not regarded simply as a
gift, but as a transfer or deposit of monies (Aigner (1979) 178; cf. Gagé
(1935) 104). The expression is closely paralleled in Livy's account of Scipio's
transfer of funds into the treasury, which he had raised by his campaigning
in Spain in 205 BC (*ex ea pecunia quam ipse in aerarium detulisset*, 28.38).
The verb is also used on the coins commemorating Augustus' funding of
the construction of the *via Flaminia* (see 20.5n. **viam Flaminiam ab urbe
Ariminum**).

**17.2 M. Lepido et L. Arruntio cos./in the consulship of Marcus Lepidus
and Lucius Arruntius**   M. Aemilius Lepidus (*PIR*² A369) came from a
patrician family, and, following his consulship, won *ornamenta triumphalia*
for military successes in the Balkans in AD 8/9 (Vell. Pat. 2.115.2–3; cf. Dio
Cass. 56.17.2). His achievements matched his ancestry in splendour to such
an extent that he could be dubbed 'a man nearest to the Caesars for his
name and fortune' (*vir nomini ac fortunae Caesarum proximus*, Vell. Pat.
2.114.5), and one of those believed to be *capax imperii*, a possible successor
to Augustus, but not desirous of it (Tac. *Ann.* 1.13.2; Syme (1986) ch. 10).
In addition, he was related to Augustus' family by various ties of kinship:
his maternal grandmother was Augustus' first wife, Scribonia; he was a
cousin of Augustus' grandchildren, and his brother was married to Julia
the Younger, Augustus' granddaughter. Later, both his son and daughter
contracted marriages with children of Germanicus (Woodman (1977) 180;
Syme (1939) table IV). His colleague during the first half of the year,
L. Arruntius (*PIR*² A1130), was son of a *novus homo* (see 5.1n. **M. Marcello
et L. Arruntio consulibus**), with connections to descendants of Sulla and
Pompey (Syme (1986) 143, 261–3); he is also one of those named by Tacitus
as *capax imperii*, and perhaps worthy of it.

aerarium militare/military treasury   One of the most significant
changes introduced by Augustus was his establishment of an army that

was both professional and permanent (see 3.3n. **stipendis emeritis**), but
this created new financial demands on the state (Suet. *Aug.* 49.2). Augustus
therefore set up a new, separate military treasury, initially out of his own
funds, to meet the cost of rewards on retirement for veterans. Some confusion is evident in both Suetonius (*Aug.* 49.2) and Dio Cassius (55.24.9),
who give the impression that the treasury was designed to pay the salaries
of serving soldiers as well as the retirement bonuses. This perhaps 'goes
back to Augustus' speech in the senate and a platitude about supporting
soldiers from enlistment to retirement' (Swan (2004) 173). The treasury was
located on the Capitol (*AE* 1978.658/*AE* 1989.626 = Roxan (1985) no. 79,
a military diploma of AD 65; Corbier (2006) 142–6), and was administered
by three *praefecti aerarii militaris* who served a three-year term in office.
They were relatively senior senators chosen by lot from former praetors,
answerable to the emperor himself (Corbier (1974) 664–6). The decision
to set up the treasury in AD 6 (Corbier (1974) 347; Campbell (1984) 158;
contra Aigner (1979) 179–83) may have been prompted by a surge in the
number of soldiers retiring at that time. These were soldiers who had been
recruited to replace the veterans of the civil wars who retired in 14 BC
(see 16.1n. **deduxerunt colonias militum in Italia aut in provincis**; Rich
(1990) 204).

ex consilio meo/on my advice   The treasury must have been set up
formally by the senate, in accordance with a proposal made by Augustus.
By contrast, Suetonius (*Aug.* 49.2) asserts simply that Augustus established
the new treasury, and Dio Cassius (55.25.2) that Augustus gave orders
for it to be administered by three ex-praetors (Brunt (1984) 437). Dio
Cassius (55.25.1–6) also gives a more negative picture of opposition towards
Augustus' initiative, suggesting that he had to back the senate into a corner
before it would concede to his plans to raise new taxes.

**qui vicena aut plura stipendia emeruissent/who had completed
twenty or more years of service**   In AD 5, changes to the length of
service for military personnel were introduced (see 3.3n. **stipendis emeritis** for length of service fixed in 13 BC). Praetorians were to serve for
sixteen years, receiving 20,000 sesterces on discharge at the end of this
term; legionaries for twenty years, receiving 12,000 sesterces (Dio Cass.
55.23.1). The Greek translation explains more directly that the soldiers
concerned are those being discharged at the end of their terms of service
(Vanotti (1975) 314).

**HS milliens et septingentiens ex patrimonio meo detuli/I transferred
170,000,000 sesterces out of my personal assets**   One hundred and
seventy million sesterces would have been sufficient to pay the sum of
12,000 sesterces each to just over 14,000 legionaries. In addition to his

initial deposit of 170 million sesterces (made on behalf of Tiberius as well, if Dio Cass. 55.25.2 is correct), Augustus undertook to make an annual contribution to the treasury (although we do not know whether he actually did so – Dio Cass. 55.25.3, with Swan (2004) 175), which was otherwise funded by taxation: the 1 per cent auction tax (*centesima rerum venalium*) was diverted to the new treasury (Tac. *Ann.* 1.78.2), supplemented by a new 5 per cent inheritance tax on the estates of Roman citizens (*vicesima hereditatium et legatorum*) (Dio Cass. 55.25.5). The introduction of this tax was a radical and unpopular innovation, which remained a source of discontent (Dio Cass. 56.28.4–6: AD 13). Funds were later boosted by the confiscated property of Agrippa Postumus when he was exiled in AD 7 (Dio Cass. 55.32.2) and also by gifts from various client kings and cities (Dio Cass. 55.25.3; Campbell (1984) 172; Corbier (1974) 701–2).

18 Cn. et P. Lentuli/Gnaeus and Publius Lentulus   See 6.1n. *P. Lentulo et Cn. Lentulo*.

vectigalia/public revenues   This refers to the receipt in Rome of taxes in the form of grain rather than money (Garnsey (1988) 219–20).

tum centum millibus hominum tum pluribus multo/sometimes to 100,000 men, sometimes to many more   It is unclear how the 100,000 beneficiaries were chosen: they are fewer in number than the regular recipients of grain dole at the time (see 15.4n. *quae tum frumentum publicum accipiebat . . . ea millia hominum paullo plura quam ducenta fuerunt*), but given the thematic emphasis of the *RGDA*, they are unlikely to be provincials (Gagé (1935) ad loc.; Brunt (1971) 382 n. 1). Augustus is referring to supplementary distributions to only part of the *plebs frumentaria*, making good a shortfall in the regular monthly public distributions.

frumentarios et nummarios tributus/distributions of grain and money   These distributions are listed separately from those recorded in ch. 15, because they result directly from a shortfall in public revenue, which Augustus makes good, perhaps in virtue of his position as *curator annonae* (see 5.2). Suetonius also refers to Augustus providing free or cheap grain in times of shortage (Suet. *Aug.* 41.2). This separate listing of distributions here provides the best indication that his distributions of grain in 23 BC were supplementary to, and not in place of, the standard ones made by the state (see 15.1n. *consul undecimum duodecim frumentationes*; contra Garnsey (1988) 219). Unlike the ones made earlier, the distributions in question here were not made in Augustus' name, but on behalf of the state. The suggestion that the beneficiaries in this chapter were non-citizen residents of Rome, on the grounds that they are referred to as *homines* rather than *cives* is disproved by the fact that the *plebs frumentaria* is also referred to as *homines* at 15.4 (Virlouvet (1995) 191 n. 86; contra van Berchem (1939) 70–1).

ex horreo et patrimonio meo/from my own granary and assets   The Greek version simplifies Augustus' language here, by referring only to ἐκ τῆς ἐμῆς ὑπάρξεως ('from my property') (Vanotti (1975) 315).

AUGUSTUS AND THE CITY OF ROME: BUILDINGS, TRIUMPHAL COMMEMORATIONS, SPECTACLES (19–23)

Chapter 19 starts the second half of the Latin text at Ancyra. It is prominent at Apollonia too, occurring in the fourth column of text, which coincides with the centre of the statue base beneath the statue of Augustus himself. It seems a reasonable assumption, therefore, that this reflects the original layout at Rome, and that the second of the two pillars outside the Mausoleum also began with this chapter. We may suspect that it is not accidental that Augustus' impact upon the physical fabric of the city of Rome is highlighted in this way. (For analysis of the topography of Augustan Rome, together with detailed new maps, see Haselberger *et al.* (2002); see also Map 1, City of Rome, and Map 2, Roman forum).

At the start of this second section, Augustus turns to his building projects in Rome. His pride in his transformation of the city is reflected in his often cited boast, that he was leaving a city of marble in place of the city of brick which had previously existed (Suet. *Aug.* 28.3; cf. Dio Cass. 56.30.4 for a metaphorical interpretation). He omits to mention the many significant building projects carried out by others, whether members of his family or triumphal commanders. Instead of listing the buildings chronologically or topographically, he divides his projects into three sections, starting with *feci*/'I built' (19.2) for new public buildings built upon public land; then using *refeci*/'I restored' or *perfeci*/'I completed' (20.1–4) for his restorations of existing public buildings and his completion of buildings planned by Julius Caesar but left incomplete by him; and ending the list with *in privato solo . . . feci*/'On private ground I built' (21.1), for buildings constructed upon private land previously owned by himself or bought from others. This categorization, however gives a false impression of exactitude. The very first building named, the Julian senate house, falls more accurately into the category mentioned in 20.3 (*coepta profligataque opera a patre meo*). Strictly speaking, the first group of buildings should be those built from scratch by Augustus, but although some fall under this heading (such as the temple of Palatine Apollo), a greater number of those listed here were in fact restorations. This reflects Augustus' desire to represent himself as founder of some of the most important of Rome's ancient cults (see 19.2n. **Iovis Feretri**; cf. Sablayrolles (1981); Ridley (2003) 120–4).

Chapters 22–3 present a third category of *impensae*/'expenses' made by Augustus for the people of Rome. They list shows provided by Augustus in both a private and a public capacity, reflecting the perceived importance of providing entertainment as well as sustenance to the inhabitants of the city of Rome, the 'bread and circuses' made famous by Juvenal. A whole chapter (23) is devoted to the most unusual spectacle displayed by Augustus, the mock naval battle which marked the inauguration of the Augustan forum.

19.1 curiam/senate house　The *curia Julia* (Tortorici (1993)) replaced the *curia Hostilia*, which had been destroyed by fire during a riot at the funeral of the rabble-rousing tribune Clodius in 52 BC (Cic. *Mil.* 33.90; Dio Cass. 40.49.2). It was started by Julius Caesar in 44 BC (Dio Cass. 44.5.1–2), who slightly shifted and realigned the senate house from its previous location. It was dedicated on 28 August 29 BC, thirteen days after Octavian's triple triumph (Dio Cass. 51.22.1). One of the main meeting places of the senate, it housed an altar and statue of Victory, which Octavian probably set up at the time of the building's inauguration (Dio Cass. 51.22.1; 28 Aug. *Fasti Maff., Fasti Vat.* = EJ p. 51 = *Inscr. Ital.* XIII.ii 79, 175, 503–4 = LACTOR C29), the *clupeus virtutis* (34.2), and an inscription hailing Augustus as *pater patriae* from 2 BC (35.1). A *denarius* issued some time during 34–28 BC of Octavian as *Imp. Caesar* appears to depict the *curia*, with a statue of Victory standing at the apex of the building (*RIC* I² 60 no. 266 = *BM Coins, Rom. Emp.* I 103 no. 631 = LACTOR K33 = Simon (1993) 76 no. 31). By starting his list of buildings with the senate's meeting place, Augustus makes an implicit claim that Rome has returned to normal governance. This implicit claim, however, is counter-balanced by the building's situation, squeezed in between the Roman forum and Julian forum, where it appears as a mere annexe to the latter (Sablayrolles (1981) 62). Augustus also carried out a number of other measures to confirm the senate's dignity (see 8.2n. **senatum ter legi**).

chalcidicum/*chalcidicum*　The identification and character of this building has been the subject of some debate, but it is probably to be identified with the southern portico of the Julian forum (Tortorici (1993) 332).

templumque Apollinis in Palatio cum porticibus/temple of Apollo on the Palatine with its porticoes　The temple of Apollo on the Palatine (Gros (1993); Gurval (1995) 123–36) was vowed in 36 BC after Agrippa's naval victory at Naulochus over Sextus Pompey (Dio Cass. 49.15.5), and was dedicated on 9 October 28 BC (*Fasti Ant. Min.* = EJ p. 53 = *Inscr. Ital.* XIII.ii 209, 518–19 = LACTOR C34). By this time the naval battle at Actium rather than Naulochus took centre stage (Dio Cass. 53.1.3).

Augustan poets depicted Apollo as playing a decisive role in the battle itself, in his guise as Actian Apollo (a link which Gurval (1995) 127–36 argues, however, emerged only some ten years later; Virg. *Aen.* 8.704–6 = LACTOR G38; Prop. 4.6, especially 27–68 = LACTOR G39). A *denarius* minted at Rome in 16 BC depicts on its reverse Apollo as a lyre player, standing on a platform decorated with three *foruli* (cases for preserving the Sibylline books) between two anchors, and bearing the inscription APOLLINI ACTIO, 'to Actian Apollo' (*RIC* I² 69 no. 365 = Simon (1993) 91 no. 52; cf. *RIC* I² 52 nos. 170–1, 54 nos. 190a-91; *BM Coins, Rom. Emp.* I 79 nos. 459–62, 82–3 nos. 478–86, 18 no. 95; Simon (1993) 92 no. 54). Octavian also dedicated a victory monument at Apollo's temple at Nicopolis, near the site of the battle (Strabo *Geography* 7.7.6 = LACTOR H9; *AE* 1977.778 = LACTOR H10; see 3.4n. ***naves cepi sescentas***). Apollo's role at Actium fitted in with the way in which Octavian had long claimed a special relationship with the god (Zanker (1988) 48–53; more cautiously Gurval (1995) 87–111). Actian games were held at Nicopolis every four years (Strabo *Geography* 7.7.6 = LACTOR H11).

Although Augustus followed tradition in dedicating a temple to commemorate a military victory, he did not locate it on the field of Mars (*Campus Martius*) outside the city's religious boundary, or *pomerium*, as was customary. Instead, he built it on land which he had purchased on the Palatine (Vell. Pat. 2.81.3 = LACTOR K37), adjacent to his own house, which he presumably intended initially for an extension to his house, but which he decided to declare as public property after it was struck by lightning (Dio Cass. 49.15.5; Suet. *Aug.* 29.3). Shortly before celebrating the *ludi saeculares* in 17 BC, Augustus transferred the Sibylline oracles to the temple of Apollo (Beard, North, and Price (1998) 205). Consequently, the temple and its cult were accorded equal importance as the Capitoline triad during the *ludi saeculares* (see 22.2). Sacrifices to Apollo and Diana took place on the Palatine on the last day of the games, on 3 June (*CIL* VI 32323.139–46 = LACTOR L27q), mirroring earlier sacrifices on the Capitol (*CIL* VI 32323.103–7, 119–32 = LACTOR L27l, L27o). Horace's hymn was even sung on the Palatine before the chorus of children performed it on the Capitol, reflecting the prominence of Apollo and Diana at both the start and the end of the hymn (Zos. 2.5.5 = LACTOR L24; *CIL* VI 32323.147–9 = LACTOR L27r; Hor. *Carm. Saec.* = LACTOR L28). On becoming *pontifex maximus*, Augustus dedicated part of his house as a shrine to Vesta, instead of occupying the official home of the *pontifex maximus* in the Roman forum, next to the shrine of Vesta (Dio Cass. 54.27.3; Beard, North, and Price (1998) 189–91; 10.2n. ***pontifex maximus***). Consequently, Ovid could speak of a single house holding three gods: Apollo, Vesta, and Augustus (Ov. *Fast.* 4.949–54 = LACTOR H31). This action completed the process of inserting Augustus' house into a meaningful historical landscape associated with the origins of Rome, alongside the temple of the

Great Mother, temple of Victory, Romulus' hut, the *lupercal*, and the steps of Cacus (Wiseman (1994) 104).

The temple of Palatine Apollo was noted for its splendour, being the first temple at Rome to be built of Luna marble (Virg. *Aen.* 8.720 alludes to its snowy-white threshold), with intricate ivory doors carved with reliefs (Prop. 2.31.12–14 = LACTOR G19). Augustus melted down silver statues of himself in order to dedicate golden tripods in the temple (24.2), and also dedicated gifts from war spoils there (21.2). The temple was surrounded by a portico, with statues of the mythical Danaids standing in between the columns (Prop. 2.31.1–5 = LACTOR G19). The portico included two libraries, one each for Greek and Latin literature (Suet. *Aug.* 29.3), and it also became a regular meeting place for the senate (Suet. *Aug.* 29.3; *Tabula Hebana*, EJ no. 94a line 1 = Sherk (1988) no. 36B). Augustus sometimes received embassies in the Roman library there (*POxy.* 2435 recto = EJ no. 379 ll. 30–4 = LACTOR M14).

Although it was normal practice to distinguish between an *aedes*, a sacred building built on already consecrated ground, and a *templum*, a temple which is consecrated together with its site (Gagé (1935) 107), Augustus does not stick rigidly to this, for example referring to the temple of Apollo as both *templum* (19.1) and *aedes* (21.2) (Ridley (2003) 123).

aedem divi Iuli/temple of deified Julius   This temple (Gros (1996)) was decreed by the senate in 42 BC at the triumvirs' instigation, in acknowledgement of Caesar's apotheosis, and was built next to the *regia* at the east end of the Roman forum, where his body had been cremated (Dio Cass. 47.18.4). The temple appears before its completion on coins issued at Rome in 36 BC, depicting on their obverse the head of Octavian with a beard of mourning for Caesar, and on their reverse a temple labelled DIVO IVL, with the comet, *sidus Iulium*, in its pediment (on which, Plin. *HN* 2.23.93–4 = LACTOR K44 + H3; *RRC* 537–8 nos. 540/1–2 = *BM Coins, Rom. Rep.* II 580 no. 32 = Simon (1993) 77 no. 32 = LACTOR K45) (see Figure 20). It was dedicated on 18 August 29 BC, three days after Octavian's triple triumph (*Fasti Ant. Min.* = EJ p. 50 = *Inscr. Ital.* XIII.ii 208 = LACTOR C26; for the inauguratory games, see 22.1n. **meo nomine**). In front of the temple was a platform, the *rostra aedis divi Iuli*, on the sides and front of which were displayed the prows of ships captured at Actium (Dio Cass. 51.19.2; see 3.4n. **naves cepi sescentas**), and Egyptian booty was placed inside the temple (Dio Cass. 51.22.2–3; see 21.2). In this way, it mirrored and rivalled the display on the Republican *rostra* opposite of the prows of ships captured by Duilius from the Carthaginians (Sablayrolles (1981) 64–5; see introduction p. 32). This parallel was brought into focus after Augustus' death by the delivery of two eulogies in his honour, one by Tiberius at the temple of the deified Julius, the other by Drusus at the old *rostra* (Suet. *Aug.* 100.3).

Fig. 20 Temple of deified Julius. *Aureus*, 36 BC (coin: obverse and reverse, *RRC* 537–8 no. 540/1–2 = LACTOR K45).

lupercal/*lupercal*   This was a large cave at the base of the Palatine, which was located in a grove with a natural spring, where Romulus and Remus were reputedly suckled by the she-wolf (Coarelli (1996c); Ov. *Fast.* 2.413–22). Its location on the south side of the hill associated it with the temple of Victory, the hut of Romulus, and the house of Augustus. The assimilation of Lupercus to Pan in the Greek translation here accords with the account given by Dionysius of Halicarnassus of the Arcadian origins of the cult (Dion. Hal. *Ant. Rom.* 1.32.3; Reichmann (1943) 22). The ancient festival of the *Lupercalia* began here each year on 15 February (Ov. *Fast.*

2.267–8). Statues of the imperial family were also dedicated in the shrine (*CIL* VI 31200, Drusus). Augustus was keen to associate himself with Romulus, so as to appear as Rome's second founder, even to the extent that he supposedly considered adopting 'Romulus' as a part of his name (Dio Cass. 53.16.7; see also Alföldi (1971) 36–9; 34.2n. ***Augustus appellatus sum***).

The juxtaposition of the *lupercal* and the temple of deified Julius in this chapter calls to mind the links between Julius Caesar and the cult. Traditionally, the cult's priests – the *luperci* – had consisted of two groups, the *Quinctiales/Quinctilii* and the *Fabiani/Fabii*. In 44 BC, Caesar added a third group to their number, the *Iulii*, and also provided financial support to them, which was later withdrawn (Dio Cass. 44.6.2; Suet. *Iul.* 76.1; Cic. *Phil.* 13.31). Suetonius lists the *lupercal* rites as among obsolete cults revived by Augustus (Suet. *Aug.* 31.4), but this is a pretty specious claim: the festival was certainly celebrated in 44 BC, just a month before Caesar's assassination, when Antony attempted to crown him (Plut. *Vit. Ant.* 12; App. *B Civ.* 2.16.109). It does, however, illustrate a (perhaps surprising) desire on Augustus' part to align himself with this aspect of his Caesarian inheritance.

porticum . . . Octaviam/Octavian portico The *porticus Octavia* (Viscogliosi (1999)) was built near the *Circus Flaminius* some time between 167 and 163 BC by the praetor Cn. Octavius to commemorate his naval victory and triumph over King Perseus of Macedonia (Plin. *HN* 34.7.13). It was destroyed by fire and rebuilt in 33 BC with booty from the Dalmatian war (Dio Cass. 49.43.8, although confused with the *porticus Octaviae*; Festus, *Gloss. Lat.* 188L). The military standards won back from Dalmatia were displayed here (see 29.1; App. *Ill.* 5.28). It was not much of a concession on Augustus' part to allow the portico to be known by the name of its original founder (20.1), despite being praised for this modesty in the funeral eulogy for Augustus attributed to Tiberius (Dio Cass. 56.40.5, cf. Dio Cass. 53.2.5), given that this name also recalled Augustus' own family name before his nomination as heir by Julius Caesar. His family probably fostered the idea that it was somehow linked with the distinguished Republican family of Octavii (Suet. *Aug.* 2; Sablayrolles (1981) 66).

pulvinar ad circum maximum/*pulvinar* at the Circus Maximus A *pulvinar* is some sort of elevated structure built into the seating at the Circus, perhaps originally a wooden platform covered with a curtain, for displaying the statues of the gods and the ritual objects (*exuviae*) brought in procession into the Circus before the games began, and providing a place from which the gods could 'watch' the games. It was probably rebuilt following fire damage in 31 BC (Dio Cass. 50.10.3) when Augustus gave it a monumental form, perhaps akin to a shrine, given the way the word is translated into Greek (Humphrey (1986) 78–9; Ciancio Rossetto (1999a); contra the interpretation that sees the Greek as a mistranslation: Reichmann (1943) 22; Vanotti (1975) 311–12; Marrone (1977) 327). This must have provided a visual counterpoint to its religious function. It then also served, however, as an imperial box from which Augustus and his family could watch the games, whilst retaining its religious significance (Suet. *Aug.* 45.1, *Claud.* 4.6). If this interpretation is correct, it raises the intriguing possibility that gods and Augustus and his family sat side by side when watching the chariot races. The juxtaposition of Augustus and the gods was also re-enacted on one occasion during a bout of sickness, when he was carried in at the head of the procession (Suet. *Aug.* 43.5). Augustus' decision to monumentalize the *pulvinar* early on appears to build upon Julius Caesar's interest in the Circus procession and *pulvinar* (Humphrey (1986) 79). Agrippa also contributed to the development of the Circus in 33 BC, adding a new set of eggs and dolphins along the *spina* for lap-counting (Dio Cass. 49.43.2), probably as a means of alluding to his recent naval victories over Sextus Pompey (Humphrey (1986) 262).

19.2 in Capitolio/on the Capitol The Capitoline Hill was central to Roman identity. It was the city's stronghold and religious centre, and believed to be one of the earliest areas to be inhabited under Romulus. The name of the hill was supposed to have been derived from the human head, or *caput*, found when digging the foundations of the first Capitoline temple. This was thought to be an omen promising imperial rule to the city, a symbol that Rome would become the *caput* of the world (Varro *Ling.* 5.7.41; Livy 1.55.5–6, 5.54.7; Edwards (1996) 69–95; Cooley (2000)). As well as accommodating the temple of the Capitoline triad, the hill was home to several other temples and shrines.

Iovis Feretri/of Jupiter Feretrius Founded by Romulus to celebrate his victory over Acron, King of the Caeninenses whom he had killed in single combat, this was considered the oldest temple in Rome (Livy 1.10.4–7; *ILS* 64 = *CIL* X 809 = LACTOR K21, *elogium* for Romulus from Pompeii's forum). Although it is here listed among the new buildings constructed by Augustus, he did in fact merely rebuild it in 31 BC, following advice from Pomponius Atticus (Nep. *Att.* 20.3 = LACTOR P3). Augustus' depiction of himself as builder of the temple was perhaps almost warranted, since it had been without a roof and virtually falling down, but it assimilated his role to that of its original founder, Romulus (Thomas and Witschel (1992) 150; cf. Livy 4.20.7, who describes Augustus as *ipsius templi auctor*). (On Augustus and Romulus, see 19.1n. **lupercal**).

There were diverse explanations for the god's epithet Feretrius, deriving it variously from *ferre* (bringer of peace, or bearer of spoils) or *ferio* (striking an enemy, or striking a flint in treaty making) (Livy 1.10.6, Prop. 4.10.45–8;

Festus *Gloss. Lat.* 81L). The choice in the Greek to offer the translation 'Zeus Trophy-Bearer' reflects the upsurge of interest in the temple and the role of Jupiter Feretrius in receiving the *spolia opima* under Augustus. These were the highly prestigious spoils stripped from an enemy leader killed in single combat. Only two dedications of *spolia opima* are known before Augustus. Then in 29 BC, M. Licinius Crassus, grandson of Julius Caesar's rival, erstwhile supporter of Sextus Pompey and then of Antony, as proconsul of Macedonia, personally killed the king of the Bastarnae in battle, but did not dedicate *spolia opima* in the temple of Jupiter Feretrius. It seems that Octavian blocked his right to dedicate the *spolia opima* on an alleged technicality, namely that Crassus had not fought under his own auspices (see 4.2n. **per legatos meos auspicis meis**). Livy, describing a previous dedication of *spolia opima* by A. Cornelius Cossus in 437 BC makes it clear that all other evidence showed that he was not consul at the time, but that Octavian himself found an inscription on the 400-year-old linen corselet which read 'Aulus Cornelius Cossus, consul'. According to Varro (whose work predated the controversy), any soldier could qualify for the award, provided he had engaged with the enemy leader (Festus *Gloss. Lat.* 202L, 204L), but Octavian evidently did not want his triple triumph to be overshadowed within a year by exceptional military glory accruing to someone other than himself (Livy 4.20.5–8, 11 = LACTOR P4; Dio Cass. 51.24.4; Dessau (1906); Syme (1939) 308–9; Syme (1959) 43–6; Harrison (1989); contra Rich (1996)). Crassus did celebrate a triumph in 27 BC (a sure sign that he *had* fought under his own auspices) (*Fasti Triumphales Capitolini* = *Inscr. Ital.* XIII.i 87 = LACTOR N2c), and Augustus never earned *spolia opima* himself. The temple also housed the sceptre and flintstone used in the ceremonies performed by the *fetiales* (see 7.3n. **fetialis**).

Iovis Tonantis/of Jupiter the Thunderer This was a new temple on the Capitol near to the Capitoline temple, vowed by Augustus after he had narrowly escaped being struck by lightning whilst on campaign in Cantabria in 26–25 BC (Suet. *Aug.* 29.3), and dedicated on 1 September 22 BC (*Fasti Arv., Amit.* = EJ p. 51 = *Inscr. Ital.* XIII.ii 33, 193, 504 = LACTOR C30). Its importance is reflected in its being chosen by Suetonius as one of three temples for special mention (with Mars the Avenger and Palatine Apollo) (Suet. *Aug.* 29.3), and by a dream which Augustus was alleged to have had, in which Capitoline Jupiter was angry at being usurped by the newcomer's cult (Dio Cass. 54.4.2–4; Suet. *Aug.* 91.2). The Elder Pliny notes that its walls were built of solid marble (Plin. *HN* 36.8.50) rather than simply bearing a marble veneer, and it featured on coins issued in 19/18 BC (*RIC* I² 46 no. 63a = *BM Coins, Rom. Emp.* I 64 no. 362 = LACTOR K50 = Simon (1993) 77 no. 33; cf. *RIC* I² 46 nos. 59, 63b-67; *BM Coins, Rom. Emp.* I 64–5 nos. 363–5). During the *ludi saeculares*, some of the preliminary ceremonies were performed in front of this temple, as well as in front of the temples of *Iuppiter Optimus Maximus* and Apollo Palatinus (*CIL* VI 32323.29–34 = LACTOR L27e; see 22.2n. **ludos saeclares**). The juxtaposition of the oldest and the newest cults of Jupiter at Rome serves to legitimate Augustus' innovation in introducing the latter (Sablayrolles (1981) 68).

aedem Quirini/temple of Quirinus   The temple of Quirinus (= the deified Romulus) (Coarelli (1999a)) was vowed by L. Papirius Cursor after his victory over the Samnites, and was built on the Quirinal, on the site of a more ancient shrine to Quirinus, by his son L. Papirius Cursor during his consulship in 293 BC (Livy 10.46.7). It was damaged by fire in 49 BC (Dio Cass. 41.14.3), rebuilt by 45 BC when a statue in Caesar's honour was set up in it (Dio Cass. 43.45.3), and rededicated by Augustus on 29 June 16 BC (Ov. *Fast.* 6.795–6; *Fasti Ven.* = *Inscr. Ital.* XIII.ii 59, 475; Dio Cass. 54.19.4). Like the temple of Jupiter Feretrius, therefore, this was one of the oldest temples in Rome (Plin. *HN* 15.36.120), strongly associated with Romulus. (On Augustus and Romulus, see 19.1n. **lupercal**).

aedes Minervae et Iunonis Reginae et Iovis Libertatis in Aventino/temples of Minerva and of Queen Juno and of Jupiter Libertas on the Aventine   These three temples, whose deities mirrored those of the Capitoline temple, were situated outside the *pomerium* (Rome's sacred boundary) on the Aventine hill, which was considered to have strong links with the commoners (*plebs*) of Rome. The temple of Minerva was built some time before the Hannibalic war, and restored in 16 BC. Minerva was worshipped here in her guise as patron goddess of craftsmen, and her temple served as the headquarters of the association of poets and actors (Vendittelli (1996)).

Juno Regina was originally the patron goddess of Rome's rival Veii, but was persuaded by the Romans to transfer her allegiance, in the process known as *evocatio*, when her cult statue was brought in procession from Veii to Rome. The temple was vowed during the siege of Veii by M. Furius Camillus, and dedicated in 392 BC (Livy 5.21.3 (Camillus' speech), 22.3–7 (*evocatio*), 31.3 (temple dedication); cf. Dion. Hal. *Ant. Rom.* 13.3; Andreussi (1996a)).

Little else is known about the temple of Jupiter Libertas; it may correspond to a temple of Jupiter Liber, rededicated on 1 September (*Fast. Arv.* = *Inscr. Ital.* XIII.ii 33, 504), and whose cult title is close to the Greek translation here of Ζεύς Ἐλευθέριος (Andreussi (1996b)).

aedem Larum in summa sacra via/temple of the *Lares* at the top of the Sacred Way   The shrine of the *Lares* (Coarelli (1996b)) stood at the top of the Sacred Way, leading from the Roman forum to the Palatine, reputedly next to the house of Ancus Martius, fourth king of Rome (Solin. 1.23). An inscription from 4 BC, stating that Augustus was making a dedication to the public *Lares* with money offered to him in his absence by the people, shows that he had restored the shrine by this time (*CIL* VI 456 = *ILS* 99 = EJ no. 41 = LACTOR L6). The *Lares* had a dual role at Rome: domestic gods protecting individual households, and, as in this context, state gods protecting Rome's territory. The Greek version describes them as 'heroes', rather oddly, but explicably in the absence of any equivalent deities in the Greek world (Reichmann (1943) 22). Under Augustus, the *Lares* who were worshipped in every district of the city underwent a transformation, becoming the *Lares Augusti*. The *genius Augusti* was also introduced into each district's crossroads shrine (Beard, North, and Price (1998) 184–6), but this innovation is not mentioned here.

aedem deum Penatium in Velia/temple of the *Penates* on the Velia The cult of the *Penates* was housed not far away from the shrine of the *Lares*, on one of the prominences of the Palatine hill, the Velia (Dion. Hal. *Ant. Rom.* 1.68.1–2). The *Penates* had the same dual role as the *Lares*, protecting both the state and households. They were thought to have been brought from Troy by Aeneas. Their role is explained by the Greek translation (Reichmann (1943) 22).

aedem Iuventatis/temple of Youth This temple (Coarelli (1996a)) was vowed by M. Livius Salinator during the battle of Metaurus against Hasdrubal in 207 BC, but was dedicated on the Aventine near the Circus Maximus over a decade later by C. Licinius Lucullus (Livy 36.36.5–6). It was rebuilt after having been destroyed in fire 16 BC (Dio Cass. 54.19.7).

aedem Matris Magnae in Palatio/temple of the Great Mother on the Palatine The black stone, which was the aniconic cult symbol of Cybele, Great Mother of the Gods, was brought to Rome from Pessinus (Asia Minor) in 204 BC at the suggestion of the Sibylline books, in response to the crisis brought about by Hannibal's invasion of Italy, and the temple was dedicated in 191 BC (Livy 29.10.4–11.8, 14.5). It was restored after a fire in AD 3, not built for the first time (Ov. *Fast.* 4.247–348). Its location on the south-west slope of the Palatine set it into the context of the archaic Rome of Romulus (see 19.1n. **lupercal**), perhaps because Cybele was supposed to have protected Aeneas after the fall of Troy (Pensabene (1996)). This also placed it in proximity to Augustus' house.

20.1 Capitolium/Capitoline temple The cult of the Capitoline triad (*Iuppiter Optimus Maximus* = Jupiter Best and Greatest, Juno, and Minerva) was central to Rome's identity. Although vowed and built by the Tarquinian dynasty, the temple was reputedly dedicated in the first year of the Republic, 509 BC, and came to symbolize the new political order at Rome (Livy 7.3.8; Tagliamonte (1993) 229; see 19.2n. *in Capitolio*). It was restored by Augustus, possibly following the storm damage in 9 BC that was supposedly an omen of the ill fortune about to befall Drusus in that year (Dio Cass. 55.1).

Pompeium theatrum/theatre of Pompey   The first stone theatre in Rome (Gros (1999)) was dedicated as a victory monument on the southern field of Mars (*Campus Martius*) by Pompey the Great, during his second consulship in 55 BC, following his triple triumph of 61 BC, and was inaugurated with spectacular shows displaying animals never before seen in the capital (Cic. *Fam.* 7.1; Plin. *HN* 8.7.20–1). The temple of Venus Victrix at its summit, however, was completed only in 52 BC (Gell. *NA* 10.1.7). Despite Pompey's role as Julius Caesar's chief rival, Augustus took pains to emulate him, perhaps because Pompey was widely thought of as a world conqueror (see introduction pp. 32–3; 1.1, 3.1, 25.1, 27.2, 31.2). Not only did Augustus restore the theatre in 32 BC, but he also transferred Pompey's statue (at whose feet Caesar had been assassinated) from Pompey's *curia* to a prominent place in the theatre (Suet. *Aug.* 31.5). Along with the theatre of Marcellus and a wooden theatre beside the Tiber, the theatre of Pompey hosted Greek musical shows added on as a bonus to the end of the *ludi saeculares* in 17 BC (*CIL* VI 32323.157 = LACTOR L27s–t).

sine ulla inscriptione nominis mei/without inscribing my name anywhere on them   This phrase is emphasized by its position following the main verb, *refeci*. For Augustus' respect for previous builders, see 19.1. In the case of the Capitoline temple, this entailed preserving the name of Q. Lutatius Catulus, to whom the senate had entrusted the task of restoring the temple after it had burnt down in 83 BC (Cic. *Verr.* 4.69). Despite Augustus' disclaimer here, the theatre of Pompey still became known as the *theatrum Augustum Pompeianum* (*CIL* VI 9404).

20.2 rivos aquarum/aqueduct channels   Although Augustus did make a major contribution to improving Rome's water supply, he does not mention the even greater contribution made by Agrippa to transforming Rome's water supply (Sablayrolles (1981) 72). In 33 BC Agrippa built the *aqua Iulia* onto the *aqua Tepula* and repaired the *aquae Appia, Marcia*, and *Anio Vetus*. He did this in his capacity as aedile, a junior office which he undertook despite having already served as consul, and thereby won crucial support for Octavian, who was absent from Rome, at a critical stage in the struggle against Antony. Later, in 19 BC, Agrippa also built the *aqua Virgo*, which supplied his baths, the first major set of public baths at Rome (Frontin. *Aq.* 1.9–10 = LACTOR K54). His two new aqueducts increased Rome's water supply by 70 per cent according to Frontinus' figures (Frontin. *Aq.* 2.65–73). He also established a new administrative system to care for the upkeep of the capital's water supply (Frontin. *Aq.* 2.98 = LACTOR K58).

After Agrippa's death in 12 BC, Augustus inherited from him responsibility for the water supply; he repaired the aqueduct system as a whole and established the office of *curatores aquarum*, water commissioners, to oversee the system (Frontin. *Aq.* 2.99–100 = LACTOR K58; Ashby (1935) 11–13; Robinson (1992) 98–100). The *senatus consultum de rivis, specibus, fornicibus aquae Iuliae Marciae Appiae Tepulae Anienis reficiendis* of 11 BC ('senatorial decree concerning the repair of the conduits, channels, and arches of those aqueducts known as the Julian, Marcian, Appian, Tepulan, and Anio') shows that Augustus made a promise to the senate that he would carry out any necessary repairs at his own expense to conduits, channels, and arches (Frontin. *Aq.* 2.125 = LACTOR K62). The execution of such repairs is recorded in a series of inscriptions (*CIL* VI 1243, *aqua Anio Vetus*; *CIL* VI 1249, *aquae Iulia, Tepula, Marcia*; *CIL* VI 1250 *aqua Marcia*). He increased the supply of the *aqua Appia*, repaired the *aqua Iulia*, built a new branch onto the *aqua Anio Vetus*, and built the *aqua Alsietina* (also known as the *aqua Augusta*) to supply his *naumachia* in 2 BC (see 23; Frontin. *Aq.* 1.11; Ashby (1935) 12–13. (For the *aqua Marcia*, see 20.2n. **aquam quae Marcia appellatur**.)

aquam quae Marcia appellatur/aqueduct which is called Marcian The *aqua Marcia* bringing water into Rome from the Anio valley near Tibur (modern Tivoli) was built in 144 BC by the praetor Q. Marcius Rex (Frontin. *Aq.* 1.7). In response to the growth in Rome's population, Augustus increased the supply of the *aqua Marcia* by linking it to a new underground channel called the *aqua Augusta* some time during 11–4 BC (Frontin. *Aq.* 1.12 = LACTOR K56). An inscription dating to 5/4 BC on an arch of the *aqua Marcia*, which was reused in the later Aurelianic walls, commemorates Augustus' repair of the channels of all the aqueducts (*CIL* VI 1244 = *ILS* 98 = EJ no. 281 = LACTOR K57). Other inscriptions record repairs to the *aqua Marcia* (*CIL* VI 1250–1). Postponing the ablative absolute *fonte novo in rivum eius inmisso* until the end of the sentence brings into focus the scale of Augustus' intervention.

20.3 forum Iulium/Julian forum Julius Caesar had dedicated his new forum and basilica on the last day of his triple triumph on 26 September 46 BC, before they were completed (Dio Cass. 43.22.1–2; *Fasti Arv., Pinc., Praen., Vall.* = *Inscr. Ital.* XIII.ii 35, 48, 135, 151, 514). Even the cult statue of Venus Genetrix was hastily set up before the artist had the chance to finish it (Plin. *HN* 35.45.156). His forum was a new type of public space devoted to political and judicial affairs rather than the usual kind of business centre (App. *B Civ.* 2.15.102). It comprised a rectangular piazza dominated by the

temple of Venus Genetrix, in her guise as ancestress of the Iulii. In front
of the temple was a statue of Julius Caesar's horse, remarkable for its front
hoofs resembling human feet, which had reputedly provided an omen of
his master's world rule (Suet. *Iul.* 61; Plin. *HN* 8.64.155). The temple was
completed after Caesar's assassination in 44 BC (Dio Cass. 45.6.4).

**basilicam quae fuit inter aedem Castoris et aedem Saturni/basilica
which was between the temple of Castor and the temple of Saturn**
The basilica Julia, on the south side of the Roman forum between the
temples of Castor and of Saturn, was also inaugurated whilst still incomplete in 46 BC (Jer. *Chron.* 1971). It was completed by Augustus, but was
soon afterwards damaged in a fire, perhaps in 12 BC. It was rededicated in
AD 12 in honour of Gaius and Lucius (Dio Cass. 56.27.5; Suet. *Aug.* 29.4),
and was subsequently known as the *basilica Gai et Luci* for a short period,
before reverting to its original name, basilica Julia (Giuliani and Verduchi
(1993); see also 20.3n. *si vivus non perfecissem*).

profligata/almost finished   This word, meaning 'almost completed'
(Gell. *NA* 15.5.2), is mistranslated in the Greek version, with its literal
meaning 'cast down', προκαταβεβλημένα (Gordon (1983) 110).

si vivus non perfecissem/if I do not complete it in my lifetime
This clause appears to imply that at the time Augustus was writing these
words, the basilica had still not been completed (but see Scheid (2007) 59
for debate about the phrase's meaning). One possibility is that Augustus
wrote this before AD 12, in which year Dio Cassius records the building's
dedication (Dio Cass. 56.27.5). This would appear to support the idea
that the *RGDA* was not composed in a single draft in AD 14, and that
Augustus failed to update this statement when revising the *RGDA* into its
final form shortly before his death (see introduction pp. 42–3). Another
possibility, however, is that the basilica was dedicated in AD 12 before it
had been completed (Swan (2004) 292). In support of this is the argument
that the basilica never actually received its finishing touches (Lauter (1982)
447–9).

20.4 duo et octoginta templa deum/eighty-two temples of the gods
It was commonly believed that the prosperity of Rome depended upon
its maintaining a good relationship with the gods, and that neglect of the
gods resulted in disaster, notably the civil wars that ripped Roman society
apart in the first century BC (Hor. *Carm.* 3.6.1–8; Beard, North, and Price
(1998) 118, 181–2). It was, therefore, an integral part of Augustus' claim to be
setting Roman society to rights that he should depict himself as upholder
of traditional Roman religious practices. His 'restoration' of Roman religion involved repairing and maintaining cult buildings, mentioned here

(see 19.1–2, 20.1; Ov. *Fast.* 2.59–66 = LACTOR L4; Dio Cass. 53.2.4), and also reviving obsolete cults, ceremonies, and priesthoods, including the *Arvales, Salii, fetiales* (7.3), *flamen Dialis, Lupercalia* (19.1), *compitalia, augurium salutis*, closure of the gates of Janus (13) and *ludi saeculares* (22.2; Suet. *Aug.* 30.2, 31.4; Beard, North, and Price (1998) 192–206). He also completed Caesar's calendar reforms (Suet. *Aug.* 31.2). In Livy, Augustus is referred to as 'founder and restorer of all our temples' (*templorum omnium conditorem ac restitutorem*, Livy 4.20.7), and he is depicted as a new founder of Rome, successor to a series of 'founders', and following on from Romulus and Camillus in particular (Edwards (1996) 44–52; Miles (1988) 194–5, 199–200; see also 35.1). The neglect of temples was probably the result of private failure to maintain them: given that most temples had been founded by victorious generals from the spoils of war (*ex manubiis*), the temples remained the responsibility of them and their descendants (Wallace-Hadrill (2005) 78). Although Augustus here alludes to his activities in 28 BC, he had started the process of 'restoration' much earlier (see 19.2n. **Iovis Feretri**, 31 BC). In reality, however, his 'revivals' were often bogus archaisms, innovations to help secure his leadership at Rome (cf. Cooley (2006) on the *ludi saeculares*; Wiedemann (1986) 482–3 on the spear-throwing rite of the *fetiales*).

consul sextum ex auctoritate senatus/as consul for the sixth time, in accordance with a resolution of the senate Augustus' reference to his consulship here is not simply serving as a dating formula, but it demonstrates that he was enacting the senate's wishes in carrying out his work on the capital's temples, not least since he was not yet *pontifex maximus* at this date (Sablayrolles (1981) 73).

20.5 viam Flaminiam ab urbe Ariminum/Flaminian Way from the city to Ariminum The road was built (most probably) in 220 BC by the censor C. Flaminius (Livy *Per.* 20). It was the main northern highway from Rome, crossing the Apennines and reaching the Adriatic Sea at Fanum Fortunae before following the coastline to Ariminum (Rimini). The area flanking the *via Flaminia* as it led out of Rome was dominated by Augustan monuments, such as the Mausoleum, the altar of Augustan Peace, and the so-called *horologium* (Patterson (1999)). Augustus restored the road in 27 BC, as commemorated by arches erected at the start and the end of the road, on the Mulvian bridge in Rome and at Ariminum (Dio Cass. 53.22.1–2; De Maria (1988) 269 no. 58, 260–2 no. 48). The inscription on the latter also celebrates his repairs to the other major roads in Italy, carried out at his expense (*CIL* XI 365 = *ILS* 84 = EJ no. 286 = LACTOR K68). In the same year, Augustus encouraged other senators to use funds raised from their triumphal booty to repair other major roads of Italy (Suet. *Aug.* 30.1). C. Calvisius Sabinus and M. Valerius Messalla Corvinus each refurbished

Fig. 21 Inscribed column, SPQR / IMP CAE / QVOD V(iae) / M(unitae) S(unt) EX / EA P(ecunia) Q(u)IS / AD A(erarium) DE(dit). Issued at Rome by L. Vinicius, 16 BC (coin: *RIC* I² 68 no. 360–2). © The Trustees of the British Museum.

part of the *via Latina* (*CIL* X 6895, 6897, 6899–901, *AE* 1969/70.89; Tib. 1.7.57–60).

At some time before 20 BC, Augustus introduced the new post of roads' commissioner, *curator viarum*, held by senators of praetorian rank (Suet. *Aug.* 37.1; Dio Cass. 54.8.4; *ILS* 915 = EJ no. 197, P. Paquius Scaeva). This was one of several administrative innovations which he introduced to tackle the logistical problems faced by the now massive capital (along with the *praefecti frumenti dandi*; *curatores aquarum* – see 20.2n. **rivos aquarum**; *praefecti aerarii militaris* – see 17.1n. **eos qui praeerant aerario**; *curatores operum publicorum*; and *curatores frumenti*). Coins issued at Rome by L. Vinicius in 16 BC depicted on their reverse an inscribed column which was set up in Region VII at Rome to commemorate the completion of his programme of road repairs: SPQR / IMP CAE / QVOD V(iae) / M(unitae) S(unt) EX / EA P(ecunia) Q(u)IS / AD A(erarium) DE(dit) ('The senate and people of Rome to Imperator Caesar because the roads have been paved out of the money which he gave to the treasury') (*RIC* I² 68 nos. 360–2; *BM Coins, Rom. Emp.* I 15 nos. 79–81; EJ no. 287; Simon (1993) 80, 82 no. 34a; Hill (1989) 56; cf. *RIC* I² 50 nos. 140–5; *BM Coins, Rom. Emp.* I 75 nos. 432–6, LACTOR K69) (see Figure 21). Augustus' personal involvement in maintaining the road system was also given visual prominence by setting up milestones in his name in great numbers throughout the empire (Alföldy (1991) 299–302).

pontesque omnes praeter Mulvium et Minucium/all the bridges expect the Mulvian and Minucian Around thirty bridges are known and there must originally have been several more. They range from bridges known only from mediaeval and antiquarian sources to those still carrying road traffic today, and from bridges crossing wide valleys to those over tiny, seasonal streams. Several have been lost since the publication of a comprehensive survey of the *via Flaminia* in 1921 (Ashby and Fell (1921)), including those blown up by the retreating Germans in 1944.

The most famous is the bridge now known as the Ponte di Augusto over the River Nar (Nera) at Narnia (Narni). This bridge, 160 m long overall and 8 m wide, crossed a deep river gorge on four arches. The first of these is still standing today, measuring 30 m high and with a span of 19 m. The second and largest arch spanned more than 32 m. Martial (7.93) alluded to the bridge as the pride of the place in his day. Two bridges between Narni and San Gemini carry road traffic today. The Ponte Calamone is 40 m long, with two arches. The Ponte Caldaro is 74 m long and 7.7 m wide. It has five arches of 3.5 m, 5.5 m, 9 m, 5.5 m, 3.5 m. Both of these bridges are named after the rivers they cross. Another almost perfectly preserved bridge is the Ponte Grosso near Pontedazzo, with two arches 7 m in span springing from a central pier of 5.6 m. Two small bridges perhaps indicate the care taken over the project, and one reason for Augustus' pride: the Ponte Fonnaia, about 4 km north of the modern town of Acquasparta in Umbria, crosses the Naia river, which, today at least, is no more than a tiny seasonal stream. Even though the bridge has only a single arch spanning 3.4 m, it is 17–19.5 m wide, crossing the river at an angle and with considerable buttressing. A bridge now known as the Ponte del Diavolo at Cavallara near Bastardo allows a road 14.7 m wide to cross a usually tiny stream, the torrente Puglia. Finally, the five-arch bridge over the river Ariminus in Rimini, still used today, was begun by Augustus and finished by Tiberius in AD 22, forming part of the *via Aemilia* (*CIL* XI 367).

The Mulvian bridge crosses the Tiber two miles to the north of Rome. The Minucian bridge is otherwise unknown, but was perhaps built in 51 BC by the praetor Minucius Thermus, *curator viae Flaminiae* (Cic. *Att.* 1.1.2). The Greek version does not specify the names of the bridges at Rome (Reichmann (1943) 22; Marrone (1977) 319; see introduction pp. 26–7).

21.1 Martis Ultoris templum/temple of Mars the Avenger　　The temple of Mars the Avenger was vowed before the battle of Philippi against the 'Liberators' Brutus and Cassius in 42 BC, in vengeance for the assassination of Caesar (see 2n. **ultus eorum facinus**), but was not completed until 2 BC (Ov. *Fast.* 5.569–78 = LACTOR K18; Suet. *Aug.* 29.2). Its date of dedication was either 12 May, when the *ludi Martiales* took place in the Circus (see 22.2; Ov. *Fast.* 5.597–8 = LACTOR K18; *Fasti Maff.* = *Inscr. Ital.* XIII.ii 76, 456 = LACTOR C18) or, less probably, 1 August (Dio Cass.

60.5.3). (For a summary of this debate, see Simpson (1977); Alföldy (1992) 23–5, favouring 12 May; Swan (2004) 95–6, favouring 1 August; cf. *Inscr. Ital.* XIII.ii 456–7). Its dedication was marked by spectacular games in the Circus Maximus, *Saepta Julia*, and *Circus Flaminius*, and by a mock sea battle (see 22.2n. **ludos Martiales**, 23n. **navalis proeli spectaclum . . . trans Tiberim**; Vell. Pat. 2.100.2 = LACTOR E100.2; Dio Cass. 55.10.6–8). It was the first temple to Mars within Rome's sacred boundary, the *pomerium*. A hypothetical reconstruction of its dedicatory inscription gives a role to Gaius and Lucius alongside Augustus in dedicating the temple (Alföldy (1992) 27–30 + Ganzert and Kockel (1988) 149). Coins of *c.* 18 BC depicting a circular temple of Mars the Avenger probably represent a temple that was proposed for the Capitol (Dio Cass. 54.8.3), but was never actually built (*RIC* I² 43 no. 28 = *BM Coins, Rom. Emp.* I 58 no. 315 = LACTOR K19; see also 29.2n. **in templo Martis Ultoris**). During the period between being vowed and being dedicated, its significance shifted, from vengeance for the murder of Caesar, to celebrating the recapture of legionary standards from the Parthians in 20 BC (Ov. *Ars Am.* 1.179–82; Ov. *Fast.* 5.579–96 = LACTOR K18). A number of ceremonies traditionally carried out at the Capitoline temple were transferred to the new temple of Mars, and signified a new, wider conception of the god's role (Suet. *Aug.* 29.2; Dio Cass. 55.10.2–5). No longer concerned only with protecting soldiers, he became, like Capitoline Jupiter, associated with the welfare of the city as a whole (Bonnefond (1987); Kockel (1995) 289–90).

forumque Augustum/Augustan forum The forum (Kockel (1995)) consists of a long open piazza, dominated at one end by the temple of Mars the Avenger, and flanked by porticoes, with a large hemicycle on each side. It was built to accommodate legal and business activities overflowing from the two existing fora (Suet. *Aug.* 29.1). Although its irregular layout is sometimes said to have been the result of Augustus' refusal to expropriate land from individuals not willing to part with it (cf. *in privato solo*; Suet. *Aug.* 56.2; Galinsky (1996) 198–9), it is more likely to reflect the existing street layout (Kockel (1995) 290). In the north-west hemicycle stood Aeneas, surrounded by kings of Alba Longa, ancestors of the Iulii, down to the recently deceased Marcellus and Elder Drusus. Opposite, in the north-east hemicycle, was Romulus, flanked by military heroes (or *summi viri*) of the Republic responsible for securing Rome's empire (Suet. *Aug.* 31.5; Zanker (1988) 201–3, 210–15; Luce (1990); for a similar 'parade' of Rome's heroes, cf. Virg. *Aen.* 6.756–846). Each statue was accompanied by two inscriptions, a short one recording the honorand's name and summary of his career, and a longer one relating his career, honours, and achievements in more detail (statues: Ganzert and Kockel (1988) 194–9 nos. 80–92; cf. Gell. *NA* 9.11.10 = LACTOR K22; inscriptions: *Inscr. Ital.* XIII.iii; LACTOR

K20–5; *CIL* VI 40931–1021a). Augustus himself was said to have composed these inscriptions (Plin. *HN* 22.6.13). In the centre of the piazza was a statue of Augustus in a triumphal chariot, in his guise as 'father of the fatherland', *pater patriae*, a title granted to him earlier in the same year as the forum was dedicated (35.1). In addition, inscribed bases, which perhaps supported gilded statues of personified provinces, were set up by provinces in his honour (Vell. Pat. 2.39.2; *CIL* VI 31267 = *ILS* 103 = EJ no. 42 = LACTOR K28; Alföldy (1991) 309–10; cf. Alföldy (1992) 67–75, against the view that Velleius is referring to an inscription on the base for the *quadriga*, even perhaps a first draft of the *RGDA* itself; cf. Nicolet (1991b) 42–3. For another view, that names of the provinces may have been set on the architraves of the porticoes, see Luce (1990) 126). Intimations of world conquest were on display in the form of two large paintings of Alexander the Great (Plin. *HN* 35.36.93–4 = LACTOR K27), and were given a physical manifestation in the large variety of polychrome marbles from all around the world used in the forum's architecture (Galinsky (1996) 197–208). With the *basilica Pauli* and the *templum Pacis*, it was shortlisted by the Elder Pliny as one of the most beautiful buildings in Rome, and indeed in the world (Plin. *HN* 36.24.102 = LACTOR K3). The overall effect of the complex was to present Augustus as the central figure in Roman history, linking past and present, gods and mortals, and to exalt the Iulii above all other families at Rome (Ganzert and Kockel (1988) 155–7; Zanker (1988) 211–14; Evans (1992) 109–14; Flower (1996) 224–36; Cooley (2000) 16–17). In a similar way, Augustus also appropriated all the great Romans of the past in his funeral procession (Dio Cass. 56.34.2–3).

ex manibiis/from plunder   Spoils from Philippi financed the project. This phrase may have appeared in the temple's dedicatory inscription (Alföldy (1991) 294–6; cf. Alföldy (1992) 17–32).

theatrum ad aedem Apollinis/theatre near the temple of Apollo The theatre of Marcellus (Ciancio Rossetto (1999b)) was situated on the field of Mars (*Campus Martius*) next to the temple of Apollo Sosianus, which had been restored by C. Sosius in the years following his triumph in 34 BC and consulship in 32 BC (Viscogliosi (1993)). It had been preceded by a *theatrum et proscaenium ad Apollinis* built in 179 BC (Livy 40.51.3). In building this theatre, Augustus completed Caesar's grandiose plans for a theatre to rival Pompey's (Suet. *Iul.* 44.1). It was used for performances of Greek city-games, added on at the end of the *ludi saeculares* in 17 BC (see 22.2n. **ludos saeclares**), even though it was not complete at the time (*CIL* VI 32323.157–8, 161 = LACTOR L27s–t), being dedicated later in 13 or 11 BC (13 BC, Dio Cass. 54.26.1; 11 BC, Plin. *HN* 8.25.65 = LACTOR K53; Ville (1981) 110–11 no. 72).

magna ex parte a privatis empto/mostly bought from private individuals   The Greek version does not translate the idea *a privatis* specifically, and so loses the emphasis in Augustus' own words, which repeat the adjective *in privato solo . . . a privatis.*

quod sub nomine M. Marcelli generi mei esset/which was in the name of my son-in-law Marcus Marcellus   The theatre commemorated M. Claudius Marcellus (*PIR*² C925), husband of Augustus' daughter Julia, and also his nephew, who had appeared as a likely heir (Sen. *Consolatio ad Marciam* 2.3 = LACTOR J29) until he died in 23 BC aged only nineteen, becoming the first occupant of Augustus' Mausoleum (Suet. *Aug.* 29.4; Dio Cass. 53.30.1–2; see introduction p. 5). Virgil's description of him in the 'parade of Roman heroes' in the underworld gives some impression of the profound sense of loss on his death (Virg. *Aen.* 6.860–86 = LACTOR G37; cf. Prop. 3.18 = LACTOR G33).

21.2 dona ex manibiis/gifts out of plunder   The temples chosen by Augustus in which to place dedications paid for from the spoils of war are those in which he had an especial interest: alongside the Capitoline temple (the traditional temple for such dedications), we find the temples of deified Julius, Palatine Apollo, Vesta, and Mars the Avenger.

in Capitolio/in the Capitoline temple   Following his triple triumph in 29 BC, Augustus made dedications in the temple of the deified Julius and in the Capitoline temple (Dio Cass. 51.22.2–3). Suetonius (*Aug.* 30.2) gives an impression of the lavishness of such gifts, mentioning Augustus' dedication of vast quantities of gold, pearls, and gems, although he appears to have exaggerated their real value (cf. Carter (1982) ad loc.; Brunt and Moore (1967) 63).

aede divi Iuli/in the temple of the deified Julius   See 19.1n. *aedem divi Iuli.*

in aede Apollinis/in the temple of Apollo   This is the temple of Palatine Apollo (see 19.1n. *templumque Apollinis in Palatio cum porticibus*).

in aede Vestae/in the temple of Vesta   Rather than the circular temple of Vesta at the eastern end of the Roman forum, this is more likely to be the shrine dedicated in Augustus' house after his assumption of the office of *pontifex maximus* (see 10.2n. *pontifex maximus*).

in templo Martis Ultoris/in the temple of Mars the Avenger   See 21.1n. *Martis Ultoris templum.*

21.3 auri coronari/of crown-gold   The giving of gold by subjects to their rulers was a long-established practice associated with eastern kingship, and had been extended in the Greek east to Roman generals during the second century BC (Cumont (1932/3) 90–3; Brunt and Moore (1967) 63; Millar (1992) 140–1). The giving of crown-gold was an expression of submission and homage on the part of the donor. It became usual for such 'gifts' to be turned into crowns of gold, and by the late Republic the custom of offering crown-gold had become a regular feature of the relationship between provincials and a victorious Roman general, especially on the occasion of his triumph (Gell. *NA* 5.6.5–6). Although the gold was represented as freely given, this did not accurately reflect reality, and the extortion of crown-gold was one charge made against L. Calpurnius Piso by Cicero in 55 BC (Cic. *Pis.* 37.90). The practice had spread into Italy by the time of Julius Caesar at the latest: in 47 BC he acquired crowns in Italy, ostensibly as gifts, to defray his civil war expenses (Dio Cass. 42.50.2, cf. 42.49.3 for gold crowns presented by various kings). By 41 BC, L. Antonius could boast that he had been awarded crowns by Rome's citizen tribes for his victories over Alpine peoples (Dio Cass. 48.4.6; cf. Cn. Domitius Calvinus in 39 BC: Dio Cass. 48.42.4; in general, *RE* II s.v. 'aurum coronarium' (Kubitschek) 2552–3).

pondo triginta et quinque millia municipiis et colonis Italiae conferentibus/35,000 pounds which the municipalities and colonies of Italy contributed   Thirty-five thousand pounds of gold are equivalent to a sum of about 147 million sesterces. Dio Cassius (51.21.4) also mentions that Octavian declined crown-gold offered by Italian towns for his triple triumph in 29 BC. Augustus focuses once again upon his special relationship with Italy (see introduction p. 39; 9.2, 10.2, 25.2). Although Italian towns were excused from contributing crown-gold, provincials were still subject to this 'stealth tax': the city of Rhosos in Syria sent an embassy with a crown to meet Octavian in Ephesos in 31 BC after Actium, as documented in a letter sent by Octavian to Rhosos (*RDGE* no. 58.3, line 79).

ad triumphos meos/for my triumphs   This phrase is omitted in the Greek version, which has a general tendency to tone down the imperialist message of the *RGDA* (see introduction pp. 28–9).

quotienscumque imperator appellatus sum/every time that I was hailed as victorious general   See 4.1n. *appellatus sum viciens et semel imperator*.

aeque benigne atque antea decreverant/just as generously as they had done before   Although the offering of crown-gold retained the illusion of being a voluntary gift, this unnecessary elaboration by Augustus is disingenuous here in ignoring the fact that the 'gift' of crown-gold had really become in effect a form of taxation rather than representing a spontaneous expression of support (Gagé (1935) 117).

22.1 munus gladiatorium/gladiatorial games Originally games were given at Rome by the élite to honour their dead, and this tradition continued into the Augustan period (for games in honour of Agrippa, see 22.1n. *filiorum meorum aut nepotum nomine*), but gladiatorial games had also become a way of winning political favour, with the sponsor aiming to bedazzle the spectators with novelty. Since Augustus realized the potential significance of courting the Roman *plebs* through the presentation of *munera*, restrictions were introduced on the giving of games at Rome (see 22.1n. *depugnaverunt hominum circiter decem millia*), ensuring that Augustus excelled in games giving as in so many other ways (Suet. *Aug.* 43.1; Wiedemann (1992) 5–8).

 meo nomine/in my own name These three occasions can be identified from other sources. At the dedication of the temple of deified Julius in 29 BC (see 19.1n. *aedem divi Iuli*), not only were there gladiatorial combats and fighting between hordes of exotic non-Romans, but also the *lusus Troiae*, chariot races, and wild-beast hunts (Dio Cass. 51.22.4–9; Ville (1981) 99–100 no. 48; see 22.3n. *venationes bestiarum Africanarum*). These shows lasted for several days. In the following year, 28 BC, Octavian and Agrippa celebrated games as consuls to commemorate Actium (Dio Cass. 53.1.4–6; Ville (1981) 100 no. 50; see 9.1n. *vota pro valetudine mea*). Finally, a great variety of shows were presented at the dedication of the temple of Mars the Avenger in 2 BC (see 22.2n. *ludos Martiales*), including the *lusus Troiae*, animal hunts (see 22.3n. *venationes bestiarum Africanarum*), and a mock naval battle (see 23n. *navalis proeli spectaclum . . . trans Tiberim*), as well as gladiatorial fights (Dio Cass. 55.10.6–8; cf. Vell. Pat. 2.100.2. Ville (1981) 104–5 no. 60 argues that these games were given in the name of his sons, and that the third *munus* alluded to here is that given in 12 BC on learning of Agrippa's death – Ville (1981) 102 no. 57, citing Dio Cass. 54.29.6: but see Rich (1990) ad loc.

 filiorum meorum aut nepotum nomine/in the name of my sons or grandsons By presenting games in the names of his potential heirs, Augustus sought to win popular support for the younger members of his family too, and consolidated the expectation of a dynastic handover of power (see introduction pp. 4–5; 14.2n. *principem iuventutis*). He fathered only one child, his daughter Julia, and so adopted her sons Gaius and Lucius as his own in 17 BC (see 14.1n. *filios meos*), and (after both of them had died) also adopted her last son Agrippa Postumus in AD 4, along with his stepson Tiberius (Suet. *Aug.* 65.1). By grandsons he means

Germanicus, who became Augustus' grandson when he was adopted by his uncle Tiberius in AD 4 (Suet. *Tib.* 15.2), and Drusus the Younger, Tiberius' son by birth (although no games are attested in connection with the latter).

Of the five sets of games, we can identify the following:

1. A gladiatorial show presented at the *Quinquatrus* festival (19–23 March) on behalf of Gaius and Lucius, in 12 BC shortly after Augustus' election as *pontifex maximus* (6 March) (Dio Cass. 54.28.3, with Rich (1990) ad loc.; Ville (1981) 102 no. 56).

2. In 7 BC, five years after his death, gladiatorial combats in honour of Agrippa were presented in the *Saepta* presumably in the names of Agrippa's sons (Dio Cass. 55.8.5; Ville (1981) 103–4 no. 59).

3. In AD 6, games were held in memory of Drusus the Elder, who had died in 9 BC, in the names of his sons Germanicus and Claudius (Dio Cass. 55.27.3; Ville (1981) 105–6 no. 61).

4. Augustus is also perhaps alluding to the games given in 16 BC to commemorate his rebuilding of the temple of Quirinus, at which Tiberius and the Elder Drusus represented him in his absence from Rome, even though this was before Tiberius had been adopted as his son (Dio Cass. 54.19.4–5; Ville (1981) 102 no. 55; see 19.2n. **aedem Quirini**).

depugnaverunt hominum circiter decem millia/about 10,000 men fought   On the basis of even a very crude calculation, the participation of about 10,000 gladiators in eight sets of games, this would have made these games utterly unprecedented in scale. Assuming the unlikely situation of an even distribution of gladiators over all eight sets of games, this would result in 1,250 individuals, or 625 pairs per show. Even the unprecedentedly lavish games planned by Julius Caesar on his election as aedile, and which attracted restrictions imposed by the senate, included only 320 pairs of fighters (Plut. *Vit. Caes.* 5; Suet. *Iul.* 10.2; Wiedemann (1992) 6). Such numbers of fighters must have seemed all the more impressive given that Augustus introduced a regulation in 22 BC limiting games-givers to exhibiting only 120 gladiators for their shows, requiring them to obtain permission from the senate for putting on a show, and imposing upon them a maximum of two shows within a single year (Dio Cass. 54.2.4, with Rich (1990) ad loc.).

athletarum undique accitorum spectaculum/a spectacle of athletes summoned from every place   Greek-style athletic contests had first been seen at Rome under the sponsorship of M. Fulvius Nobilior in 186 BC, following his successful campaigning in Greece (Livy 39.22.1–2), and had been incorporated into the varied programme of spectacles at Rome since then (Newby (2005) 21–7). Boxing, wrestling, and running were all popular entertainment. Only one of the occasions mentioned here by Augustus can be identified. The games given by Octavian and Agrippa in 28 BC

inaugurated Rome's first cycle of games in imitation of Greek ones, and
so appropriately enough included Greek-style athletics, alongside shows of
a more Roman flavour. They took place in a temporary wooden stadium
set up on the field of Mars (*Campus Martius*) (Dio Cass. 53.1.5; Suet. *Aug.*
43.1; see 9.1n. ***vota pro valetudine mea***). Running races were sometimes
held in the Circus Maximus (Suet. *Aug.* 43.2). Suetonius also mentions that
Augustus increased the privileges enjoyed by athletes (Suet. *Aug.* 45.3).

nepotis mei nomine/in the name of my grandson   See 22.1n. ***filio-***
rum meorum aut nepotum nomine.

22.2 ludos/games   Whereas the word *munus* is used to refer to gladiatorial
shows, *ludi* were the regular shows organized annually by magistrates during a religious festival in the theatre (*ludi scaenici*) or circus (*ludi circenses*).
Suetonius paraphrases these words of Augustus, but adds an extra explanation of his own, which suggests that he sometimes drew closely upon the
RGDA in composing his biography: 'he says that he gave games in his own
name four times, and on behalf of other magistrates, who were either absent
or incapable, twenty-three times' (*fecisse se ludos ait suo nomine quater, pro*
aliis magistratibus, qui aut abessent aut non sufficerent, ter et vicies – Aug.
43.1; Carter (1982) ad loc.; Gagé (1935) 39–40. See Scheid (2007) lxiii–lxiv
for general discussion of Suetonius' use of the *RGDA*).

meo nomine quater/in my own name four times   Perhaps the *ludi*
victoriae Caesaris in 44 BC (Dio Cass. 45.6.4; Plin. *HN* 2.23.93 = LACTOR
K44) rather than the *ludi saeculares* (contra Carter (1982) 158) should be
added as the fourth set of games to those mentioned earlier (see 22.1n.
meo nomine), given that Augustus co-presented the *ludi saeculares* with
Agrippa on behalf of the college of *quindecimviri* rather than in his own
name (see 22.2). The distinction is unclear in these cases, however, between
ludi presented by Augustus in his own name and those offered on behalf
of others.

pro conlegio XVvirorum magister conlegii/On behalf of the college
of the Fifteen as master of the college   The college of *quindecimviri*
(which actually had twenty-one members at this time, listed in the inscribed
acta of the games: *CIL* VI 32323 lines 150–2 = LACTOR L27r; cf. Schnegg-
Köhler (2002) ch. 10) oversaw the conduct of foreign cults at Rome. This
included being in charge of the Sibylline books, which were proclaimed
to have prompted the celebration of the *ludi saeculares* in 17 BC (see 22.2n.
ludos saeclares), and to have given instructions as to how the rituals were
to be performed (Zos. 2.4.2, 2.5.5–2.6.1 = LACTOR L23, L25). Augustus
had been a *quindecimvir* since 37–35 BC (see 7.3n. ***augur, XVvirum sacris***
faciundis, VIIvirum epulonum), and, as president of the *quindecimviri*

in 17 BC, played a leading role in the organization and execution of the *ludi saeculares*. He took turns with Agrippa in performing sacrifices and leading prayers during the celebrations (*CIL* VI 32323 lines 90–9, 103–7, 115–18, 135–7, 139–46 = LACTOR L27j, L27l, L27n, L27p, L27q; see 22.2n. **collega M. Agrippa**), and personally distributed purificatory incense cakes (*suffimenta*) to Rome's citizens during the few days before the games, as commemorated on *aurei* minted the following year (*BM Coins, Rom. Emp.* I. 16 no. 85 = *RIC* I² 67 no. 350 = Simon (1993) 84 no. 38 = LACTOR L26). One reason for celebrating these games was that they were not in the jurisdiction of Lepidus, the *pontifex maximus*, but could be controlled by Augustus by virtue of his position at the head of the priestly college (see 10.2n. **in vivi conlegae mei locum**). The Greek version does not translate the Latin phrase *magister conlegii*, probably because this was a concept alien to Greek religious organization (Marrone (1977) 317).

collega M. Agrippa/with Marcus Agrippa as my colleague At this time Augustus' partner in tribunician power (see 6.2n. **conlegam**), Agrippa was jointly in charge with him of organizing the games (*CIL* VI 32323 line 53 = LACTOR L27g) and shared a prominent role in the games (see 8.2n. **conlega M. Agrippa**). Agrippa led the sacrifice and prayer to Juno (*CIL* VI 32323 lines 120–2 = LACTOR L27o), and jointly with Augustus performed sacrifices and prayers to Jupiter on 1 June (*CIL* VI 32323 lines 103–7 = LACTOR L27l), and to Apollo and Diana on 3 June (*CIL* VI 32323 lines 139–46 = LACTOR L27q). He also appears to have presided over chariot racing during the additional games added onto the end of the *ludi saeculares* proper (*CIL* VI 32323 line 165 = LACTOR L27t).

ludos saeclares/centennial games The celebration of *ludi saeclares* (or *saeculares*), centennial games, was thought to mark the beginning of a new *saeculum* in Rome's history every 100 years. Augustus had the chronological sequence of the *ludi* recalculated into a 110-year cycle, so as to suit a celebration in 17 BC to mark the dawning of a new Golden Age (Censorinus *DN* 17.7–11 = LACTOR L21–2; Hor. *Carm. Saec.* vv. 21–4; cf. Cooley (2006) 230–6). Ironically, the Greek version provides an explanation of what the games are, as well as transliterating the Latin word *saeculares*, but it makes the mistake of explaining them as happening every 100 years, rather than the new Augustan scheme of every 110 years (Reichmann (1943) 22; Vanotti (1975) 315; Marrone (1977) 321; Wigtil (1982a) 634).

These celebrations bolstered Augustus' regime by glorying in the far-reaching extent of Rome's empire (with especial trumpeting of the 'defeat' of the Parthians: see also 29.2), by rejoicing in the divine support given by the gods to Rome's imperialist mission (Hor. *Carm. Saec.*, espec. vv. 53–76), and by commending to Rome's citizens the controversial legislation passed by Augustus in the previous year, 18 BC (*lex Iulia de maritandis ordinibus, lex Iulia de adulteriis*; see 6.2n. **quae tum per me geri senatus voluit, per tribuniciam potestatem perfeci**), by which he had attempted to reinforce family values (cf. Hor. *Carm. Saec.* vv. 1–36, espec. 17–20). The games included spectacles of various sorts, sacrifices, prayers, and banquets, which took place in different areas of the city of Rome, including the Capitol (*CIL* VI 32323 lines 103–7 = LACTOR L27l: sacrifice to Jupiter; *CIL* VI 32323 lines 119–32 = LACTOR L27o: sacrifice to Juno; *CIL* VI 32323 line 148 = LACTOR L27r: hymn singing), Palatine (*CIL* VI 32323 lines 139–46 = LACTOR L27q: sacrifice to Apollo and Diana; *CIL* VI 32323 lines 147–8 = LACTOR L27r: hymn singing), and the area known as the Tarentum on the field of Mars (*Campus Martius*), where a wooden theatre was set up especially for the duration of the games (*CIL* VI 32323 lines 90–9 = LACTOR L27j: sacrifice to Fates; *CIL* VI 32323 lines 100–2 = LACTOR L27k: nocturnal games, banquet; *CIL* VI 32323 line 108 = LACTOR L27m: Latin games; *CIL* VI 32323 lines 115–18 = LACTOR L27n: sacrifice to goddesses of childbirth; *CIL* VI 32323 lines 134–8 = LACTOR L27p: sacrifice to Mother Earth, banquet). The ceremonies and shows were for the benefit of Roman citizens and their wives, and, in an attempt to popularize the recent controversial *leges Iuliae*, special prominence was given to *matresfamiliae* (senior married women), who enjoyed their own banquets and performed their own prayers to Juno (*CIL* VI 32323 lines 101–2 = LACTOR L27k; *CIL* VI 32323 line 109 = LACTOR L27m; *CIL* VI 32323 lines 123–31 = LACTOR L27o; *CIL* VI 32323 line 138 = LACTOR L27p), and to a chorus of boys and girls who had both parents still living, who sang Horace's hymn (*CIL* VI 32323 lines 147–9 = LACTOR L27r). Events took place by night and day from 31 May to 3 June, preceded by several days on which materials for purificatory fumigation were distributed (*CIL* VI 32323 lines 29–36, lines 64–89 = LACTOR L27e, i), and followed by additional spectacles on 5–12 June (*CIL* VI 32323 lines 155–65 = LACTOR L27s–t).

This brief reference in the *RGDA* is complemented by several other contemporary sources. In particular, a large inscription was set up (cf. re-edition by Schnegg-Köhler (2002)) with a view to memorializing the celebration of the games (*CIL* VI 32323 lines 58–63 = EJ no. 30A–B = LACTOR L27h). It gives information about the planning and preparatory stages before the rites proper, which it covers in great detail, and it also records the performance of additional shows over several days after the end of the main programme of events. Horace's *Carmen Saeculare*, the hymn composed to round off proceedings, illustrates themes such as Rome's world empire, and Augustus' marriage legislation (see above). The whole proceedings must have generated an atmosphere of great excitement, not least since it was believed that the next games would be held only after a further 110 years. Coins issued in both 17 and 16 BC depicted scenes such as the distribution of purificatory materials by Augustus (see 22.2n. **pro** *conlegio XVvirorum magister conlegii*), and the announcement of the games by heralds (17 BC: *BM Coins, Rom. Emp.* I 13 nos. 69–73 = *RIC* I² 66 no. 339 = Simon (1993) 84 no. 36), sometimes alongside a sacrificial scene (*BM Coins, Rom. Emp.* I 74 no. 431 = *RIC* I² 50 no. 138 = Simon (1993) 85 no. 40). Other coins depicted an inscription commemorating Augustus' organization of the games (16 BC, IMP CAES AVG LVD SAEC. XV S F: *BM Coins, Rom. Emp.* I 17 no. 89 = *RIC* I² 68, 354–8 = Simon (1993) 85 no. 39). (On the coins in general, see Schnegg-Köhler (2002) ch. 11; Simon (1993) 84–9 nos. 36–42).

C. Furnio C. Silano cos./in the consulship of Gaius Furnius and Gaius Silanus Before becoming consul in 17 BC, C. Furnius (*PIR*² F591) had been in the Iberian peninsula, being involved in military action during the Cantabrian war (Flor. 2.33.48–53 = LACTOR N48) and serving as governor of Tarraconensis *c.* 22–19 BC (Syme (1986) 44). Despite an unimpeachable aristocratic background, nothing more is known about his colleague, C. Iunius Silanus (Syme (1986) 50; *PIR*² I823).

consul XIII/In my thirteenth consulship For the circumstances of his thirteenth, and last, consulship, see 14.1n. *quo deducti sunt in forum*.

ludos Martiales/games of Mars Augustus established these games for the dedication of the temple of Mars the Avenger in 2 BC (see 21.1n. *Martis Ultoris templum*). They enjoyed the same high status as the *ludi Romani* in honour of Capitoline Jupiter and the *ludi Apollinares* for Palatine Apollo: for these games senators were exempted from the usual prohibition against supplying race horses (Dio Cass. 55.10.5, with Swan (2004) ad loc.). Together, the two new Augustan temples undercut the hitherto dominant prestige of Capitoline Jupiter (Bonnefond (1987) 277).

fecerunt consules/the consuls provided Some detail is known of the *ludi Martiales* in AD 12 presided over by Germanicus as consul: because the Tiber had flooded the Circus Maximus, the games were celebrated in a desultory fashion in the Augustan forum, but were then held a second time in grandiose style when the Circus Maximus became available as a venue again (Dio Cass. 56.27.5; see 22.3n. *meo nomine aut filiorum meorum et nepotum*).

22.3 venationes bestiarum Africanarum/hunting shows of African wild beasts The display of exotic animals at Rome was another medium for competition among the élite of the late Republic (see 22.1n. *munus gladiatorium*; Wiedemann (1992) 59–60). For example, M. Aemilius Scaurus was celebrated as the first to exhibit a hippopotamus, along with five crocodiles, at the games he presented as aedile in 58 BC (Plin. *HN* 8.40.96). M. Caelius

Rufus as aedile in 50 BC was clearly eager that his games should not disappoint, pestering Cicero to supply panthers from his province of Cilicia (Cic. *Fam.* 8.9; Cicero's reply, *Fam.* 2.11). Roman spectators could be courted by some fresh novelty, and Pliny the Elder records how elephants were displayed fighting against different types and numbers of opponents from 99 BC down to Nero's reign (Plin. *HN* 8.7.19–22). In this, as in other ways, however, Augustus surpassed his predecessors in terms both of the rarity of a species and of the sheer quantity of animals put on display – not always perhaps in terms of a single show, given that Pompey had exhibited 600 lions (Plin. *HN* 8.20.53), but cumulatively over time (*circiter tria millia et quingentae*). In a single show he displayed 420 leopards, surpassing the 150 exhibited by Scaurus in 58 BC, and even the 410 by Pompey. At the dedication of the theatre of Marcellus in 13/11 BC, he arranged for the slaughter of 600 African wild beasts, and was also the first to exhibit a tamed tiger in a cage (Dio Cass. 54.26.1; Plin. *HN* 8.24.64–25.65 = LACTOR K53, R25). The logical progression of Augustus' account here emerges clearly from the fact that the first *ludi Martiales* of 2 BC were particularly notable for their beast hunts: 260 lions were hunted in the Circus Maximus, and then 36 crocodiles in the flooded *Circus Flaminius* (Dio Cass. 55.10.8).

meo nomine aut filiorum meorum et nepotum/in my own name or in the name of my sons and grandsons As with gladiatorial shows, Augustus supervised wild-beast hunts in the names of other members of his family, as well as on his own account. One example of this are the 200 lions presented by his grandson Germanicus during the *ludi Martiales* of AD 12 (Dio Cass. 56.27.5; Ville (1981) 113–15 no. 77; see 22.1n. **meo nomine**; 22.1n. **filiorum meorum aut nepotum nomine**).

in circo aut in foro aut in amphitheatris/in the circus or forum or amphitheatre The Circus Maximus was the most prestigious location for beast hunts at this time, especially for large scale hunts rather than one-to-one fights between hunter and hunted (Humphrey (1986) 71). In addition, the *Circus Flaminius* was flooded for the staging of the aquatic hunt featuring thirty-six crocodiles for the inaugural *ludi Martiales* in 2 BC (Dio Cass. 55.10.8). The Roman forum could be adapted for shows: underground galleries ran beneath its surface, from which fighters and animals could emerge, and awnings for the spectators' comfort could be erected (Purcell (1995) 331–2). The amphitheatre of Statilius Taurus was built *ex manubiis* in 30/29 BC, the first permanent monument of its type at Rome (Dio Cass. 51.23.1; Suet. *Aug.* 29.5).

circiter tria millia et quingentae/around 3,500 Table 2 gives a good flavour of the lavishness of *venationes* organized by Augustus (cf. Ville (1981) 108 no. 65, 112 nos. 74–5, 115–16 no. 78). His example made it a necessity for

Table 2 *Animal hunts organized by Augustus*

Event/ Date/Location	Spectacle	Source
Dedication, temple of divus Julius 29 BC	Vast numbers + rhinoceros, hippopotamus	Dio Cass. 51.22.5
Dedication, theatre of Marcellus 13/11 BC	600 African wild beasts	Dio Cass. 54.26.1
Ludi Martiales, 2 BC, Circus Maximus	260 lions	Dio Cass. 55.10.8
Ludi Martiales, 2 BC, *Circus Flaminius*	36 crocodiles	Dio Cass. 55.10.8
Ludi Martiales, AD 12, *Forum Augustum*	Presumably unimpressive animals	Dio Cass. 56.27.4
Ludi Martiales, AD 12 Circus Maximus	200 lions	Dio Cass. 56.27.5
?	420 leopards	Plin. *HN* 8.25.65

emperors to provide ever more lavish spectacles in their desire to make an impact upon their audiences: Trajan, for example, provided victory games over 123 days, with the slaughter of 11,000 animals and combat between 10,000 gladiators (Dio Cass. 68.15.1).

23 navalis proeli spectaclum . . . trans Tiberim/the spectacle of a naval battle . . . on the other side of the Tiber   A large artificial lake (*c.* 540 by 360 m, probably elliptical in shape) containing an island (presumably 'Salamis') was built on the far side of the Tiber, at the foot of the Janiculum Hill in modern Trastevere (Suet. *Aug.* 43.1; Coleman (1993) 51–4, with figs. 1–2). Known as the *naumachia Augusti*, it was supplied with water by the *aqua Alsietina* (Frontin. *Aq.* 1.22; see 20.2n. **rivos aquarum**). The only previous show of this kind to be recorded had been given by Julius Caesar at his triumph in 46 BC (Suet. *Iul.* 39.4; Coleman (1993) 50). The unusually spectacular show exhibited here was a re-enactment of the naval battle at Salamis in 480 BC between Athenians and Persians, which saw off the threat to Greece posed by the massive invasion of Xerxes. It was presented in 2 BC as part of the celebrations to inaugurate the temple of Mars the Avenger in the Augustan forum (21.1; Dio Cass. 55.10.7). For Velleius Paterculus, the splendour of this spectacle only served to emphasize all the more the subsequent disgrace of Julia (Vell. Pat. 2.100.2).

   The decision to recreate this particular battle finds resonances in Augustan art and literature. During the early Augustan period, examples are found of two image-types carved in a classicizing neo-Attic style, which are strikingly similar in their symmetrical layout and overall theme. They all represent a Victory and a warrior on either side of a trophy, but some allude to Salamis and others to Actium (Hölscher (1984), espec. 203). In this way, Salamis was depicted as the forerunner of the naval battle at

Actium (Hölscher (1984) 201), both battles being proclaimed as the victory of west over east. In addition, the modern-day Parthians could be referred to as Persians (*Persi*) in contemporary poetry (Hor. *Carm.* 3.5.4). This had the effect of magnifying the significance of Augustus' diplomatic success in regaining the standards, by implicitly equating the threat from Parthia with the huge expeditions mounted by Darius and Xerxes. Attention was focused upon the Parthians during the celebrations inaugurating the temple of Mars the Avenger since this was where the recovered standards found their permanent home (29.2). There also appears to have been some expectation that Gaius Caesar would set off to the east to mount a new campaign, as he did in the following year (Ov. *Ars Am.* 1.171–228 = LACTOR G47; Dio Cass. 55.10.18; Syme (1974) 15–16; Nicolet (1991b) 43–5). In this way, the mock naval battle evoked three different aspects of the west triumphing over the east under Augustus, namely Actium, recovery of the standards from Parthia, and Gaius' expedition. It might also have held out an implicit promise that Rome regarded itself as protector of the Greek east against Parthia (Syme (1974) 15; Bowersock (1984) 174–5). Augustus uses a Latinate periphrasis here in order to avoid the Greek word *naumachia*, in contrast to the Appendix, section 4 (Gelsomino (1958) 149).

nemus est Caesarum/is the grove of the Caesars   A grove was planted in honour of Gaius and Lucius around the lake (Tac. *Ann.* 14.15; Suet. *Aug.* 43.1). A monument in their memory was set up on the island in the middle of the lake (Dio Cass. 66.25.3–4; Papi (1996). The artificial lake was used later by Nero for an extravagant feast (Dio Cass. 62.20.5) and by Titus for a mock battle (Dio Cass. 66.25.3–4; Suet. *Tit.* 7). Traces of it were still visible when Dio Cassius was writing (Dio Cass. 55.10.7).

AUGUSTUS' GIFTS TO THE GODS (24)

24.1 omnium civitatium provinciae Asiae/of all the cities in the province of Asia   This is the first mention in the *RGDA* of any place beyond Italy. The Greek version does not translate the word *provinciae*, perhaps in a self-conscious attempt to avoid alluding to its status as a mere province. By contrast, the word is translated in referring to western provinces at 25.2 (Vanotti (1975) 316).

victor/As victor   Augustus is referring to the period after Actium.

ornamenta reposui/I replaced the ornaments   It was traditional for Roman generals to seize artworks from conquered towns as the legitimate spoils of war, which they then displayed in their triumphal processions through Rome. M. Claudius Marcellus' sack of Syracuse in 212 BC and subsequent transferral of Greek works of art was said to have been a defining

moment in the introduction of Greek culture into Rome (Livy 25.40.1–3).
In other cases, cult objects were transferred from a captured town to Rome
in the process known as *evocatio*; this was thought to represent the deity
literally abandoning his or her former home in order to take up a new
abode at Rome. The most famous instance of this was the transferral of
Juno Regina from Veii to Rome in 396 BC (Livy 5.21.3, 22.4–7; Val. Max.
1.8.3; Alcock (1993) 178–9; 19.2n. **aedes Minerva et Iunonis Reginae**).

Augustus and Agrippa issued a decree as consuls in 27 BC undertaking
to protect sacred property in Asia Minor (*RDGE* no. 61 = *RGE* no. 95
= *SEG* XVIII no. 555; Pleket (1958) 49–63 no. 57; Dignas (2002) 120–
8); their actions should be seen against the background of the economic
hardship faced by the province following its role as sphere of operations
for a whole sequence of Romans engaged in civil war: Dolabella, Labienus,
Sextus Pompey, Brutus and Cassius, and finally Antony (Bowersock (1965)
85). This was just one of several measures taken by Rome's new leader
in the years immediately following Actium in order to help the region to
recover (see 27.3). Augustus is said to have been prompted by a dream to
return to Ephesos a statue of Apollo by the artist Myron which Antony
had seized (Plin. *HN* 34.19.58). Strabo comments on Augustus' restoration
to Rhoeteium of a statue of Ajax carried off to Egypt by Antony that this
was typical of his general practice of giving back statues to their owners
(Strabo *Geography* 13.1.30 = LACTOR H12). Of a further three colossal
statues by Myron seized by Antony from the sanctuary of Hera at Samos,
Augustus returned two (Athena and Heracles), but placed the one of Zeus
in a shrine on the Capitol at Rome (Strabo *Geography* 14.1.14 = LACTOR
H13). In choosing to mention his restoration of artworks to Asia Minor,
Augustus may also have intended to recall the precedent set by Alexander
the Great, who had returned to Greece the statues of men and gods and
other votive offerings seized by Xerxes (Arr. *Anab.* 7.19.2, 3.16.7; Plin. *HN*
34.19.70; Scheer 1995). This would fit into the wider pattern of Augustus'
imitation of Alexander in the *RGDA* (see introduction pp. 36–7; 26.2, 31.1).
In another case, Augustus gave compensation in the form of remission of
tribute to Cos for taking its painting of Aphrodite Anadyomene so as
to be able to display it in the temple of deified Julius in her role as
divine ancestress of the Iulii (Strabo *Geography* 14.2.19; Plin. *HN* 35.36.91 =
LACTOR K46).

Although this statement focuses upon Augustus' restoration of artworks,
he did also continue the traditional practice of seizing artworks from those
whom he conquered (Bowersock (1965) 86). In particular, he confiscated a
statue of Athena and the tusks of the Calydonian Boar from the sanctuary
of Athena Alea at Tegea in Arcadia because it had supported Antony, and
displayed them at Rome (Paus. 8.46.1–5). Furthermore, Augustus' new
foundations at Patrai and Nicopolis received cult statues from Aetolia
and Acarnania (Paus. 7.18.8–9, 21.1). These transfers provided tangible

illustrations of Roman power, shifting sacred images from their traditional
homes to towns newly founded by Augustus (Alcock (1993) 140–1, 175–7).
In the case of Tegea, removing cult objects from that sanctuary was of
regional significance, because the cult there had provided a focus for the
whole Peloponnese. Even so, there are two fundamental differences between
the treatment of Greek art by Augustus and Antony. Whereas Augustus
was indeed following traditional practice in seizing artworks from defeated
opponents, Antony plundered artwork from towns which were his allies,
acting like a latter-day Verres, treating the Greek east as if it were his private
property. Secondly, on seizing artworks, Augustus displayed them in public
places, whereas Antony treated them as private property, allegedly handing
them over to Cleopatra in Egypt (Strabo *Geography* 13.1.30; Dio Cass.
51.17.6). Romans accepted public magnificence but deplored private luxury
(cf. Agrippa's behaviour as reported by Plin. *HN* 35.9.26 = LACTOR T5).
(For detailed analysis of this chapter, see Scheer (1995).)

is cum quo bellum gesseram/the man against whom I had waged war
This is a roundabout way of referring to Antony, incidentally revealing
that the war was indeed against him, and not Cleopatra (Ridley (2003)
125). The Greek version is expressed more strongly, with Antony referred
to as the defeated enemy (Vanotti (1975) 317).

24.2 statuae meae/statues depicting me   The juxtaposition of this statement with the previous one implies some sort of link between Augustus'
melting down of statues and his relationship with the Greek east after
Actium. It is likely, therefore, that the statues were set up at Rome by
Greek dedicators, in thanks for the return of plunder mentioned in the
previous sentence. The large number of statues and their being made out
of precious metal evoked the types of honour more usually associated with
Hellenistic kings (cf. Plin. *HN* 33.54.151), which explains why Augustus
decided to melt them down so swiftly (Stewart (2003) 172–3; Zanker (1988)
86). Suetonius refers to this action in discussing Augustus' refusal of ruler
cult, adding that all silver statues set up in his honour at Rome were melted
down, and that the proceeds were used for making golden tripods for Palatine Apollo (Suet. *Aug.* 52; see 19.1n. **templumque Apollinis in Palatio
cum porticibus**). Dio Cassius, however, claims that Augustus disingenu-
ously used the money for financing road-building, notably the *via Flaminia*
in 27 BC, whilst claiming to be funding the work from his own purse (Dio
Cass. 53.22.3). Augustus perhaps removed the statues by virtue of being
censor (28 BC; see 8.2), following the precedent set by the censors of 158 BC,
who removed statues set up privately (without the authorization of a senatorial decree or *lex*) from the crowded Roman forum (Plin. *HN* 34.14.30).
There may also be a link with the production of a large issue of silver
denarii in 29/28 BC commemorating Actium and Apollo (Pekáry (1975)).

AUGUSTUS' *RES GESTAE*: SUPPRESSION OF
ROME'S INTERNAL ENEMIES (25)

This chapter is generally considered to mark the start of the final section of the *RGDA* (see introduction p. 34 for a critique of this traditional analytical framework). Here Augustus appears to turn from the expenditure which he has incurred on behalf of the state – his *impensae* – to his *res gestae* proper, those words usually referring to successful military exploits. The fact that chapter 25 actually deals with two episodes of civil war, against Sextus Pompey and against Antony, is obscured. The first conflict is represented as a war against pirates and slaves, and the character of the second war is not specifically stated; it is just represented as being a war fought by Augustus with the support of Italy and the west. The sequencing of chapters 24–5 is also disorientating, since the events in chapter 24 actually occurred only after those in chapter 25.

25.1 mare pacavi/I brought the sea under control   Augustus' claim to have brought peace to the seas was much proclaimed (see 3.1n. **terra et mari**; 13), but was not simply an exaggeration. Suetonius (*Aug.* 98.2) relates how, during the last few days of his lifetime, Augustus came across sailors from Alexandria sailing in the Bay of Naples. They made offerings of incense, declaring their gratitude that it was because of Augustus that they could sail the seas, and make their livelihoods through seaborne commerce. A similar sentiment still resonated in Alexandria in Caligula's time (Philo *Leg.* 21.146).

a praedonibus/from pirates   In 43 BC, during its struggle against Antony, the senate granted the official title 'commander of the fleet and coasts' to Sextus Pompey, son of Caesar's rival Pompey the Great (*praefectus classis et orae maritimae*: RRC 520–1 no. 511). On being proscribed by the triumvirs, Sextus Pompey seized Sicily and used his fleet in the western Mediterranean to impose a blockade on the supply of crucial grain supplies to Rome. As a result, by 39 BC he had provoked rioting at Rome, forcing the triumvirs to grant him recognition in a treaty which conceded to him control of Sicily, Sardinia, Corsica, and Achaea (Dio Cass. 48.31, 48.36–8; App. *B Civ.* 5.8.67–74; Vell. Pat. 2.77.1–2; Livy *Per.* 127–8; Plut. *Vit. Ant.* 32; Syme (1939) 189, 221; see 27.3n. **Siciliam et Sardiniam occupatas bello servili**). Dissent soon broke out over the terms of this treaty, however, and although he achieved naval victories over Octavian, Pompey was eventually defeated at Naulochus by Agrippa in 36 BC (Dio Cass. 49.1–11.1; App. *B Civ.* 5.9.77–10.92, 5.10.96–12.122; Suet. *Aug.* 16.1–3). He withdrew to the east, where he raised troops against Antony but was later killed (Dio Cass. 49.17–18.6, App. *B Civ.* 5.14.133–44; Livy *Per.* 129, 131; Syme (1939) 230–2). Given that his father Pompey had famously rid the Mediterranean of pirates within just forty days in 67 BC (Cic. *Leg. Man./De imp. Cn. Pomp.* 52–6; Livy *Per.* 99), there is an ironical flavour to Augustus dismissing his son as a pirate. In using such language, Augustus implicitly transforms his personal struggle for supremacy into a noble defence of Italy, and conceals the fact that Pompey was supported by several proscribed nobles, including even Livia's first husband, Tiberius Nero (Vell. Pat. 2.72.5; Tac. *Ann.* 5.1; Ridley (2003) 183–7). Nevertheless, such language is echoed in both the summary of Livy and Horace (Livy *Per.* 128, *cum Sex. Pompeius rursus latrociniis mare infestum redderet*; cf. Hor. *Epod.* 4.19), as well as much later by the Neronian poet Lucan (6.419–22), and is to be explained by the fact that Augustus could avoid having to declare war formally by claiming to be fighting against *praedones*. It was stated in Roman law that 'the "enemy" are those on whom we have publicly declared war, or who themselves have declared war on us; the rest are "robbers" or "bandits"' (Pompon. *Dig.* 50.16.118: *'hostes' hi sunt, qui nobis aut quibus nos publice bellum decrevimus: ceteri 'latrones' aut 'praedones' sunt.* Cf. Ulp. *Dig.* 49.15.24; Sattler (1960) 16–17).

eo bello/In this war   Coins were issued in celebration of Naulochus in 36 BC, depicting a galley on their obverse, with the legend IMP CAESAR, and on their reverse a Victory holding a wreath, palm branch, and rudder (*BM Coins, Rom. Rep.* II 581 no. 38 = Simon (1993) 89 no. 43). (For the honorific statue awarded to Octavian, see 3.1n. ***terra et mari***.)

servorum/slaves   In addition to dismissing his opponents as 'pirates' (25.1n. ***a praedonibus***), Augustus raises the spectre of this war having been in effect a slave revolt (see 27.3n. ***Siciliam et Sardiniam occupatas bello servili***). This official interpretation of the conflict was influential on contemporary and later sources (Hor. *Epod.* 9.7–10; Vell. Pat. 2.73.3; Flor. 2.18; Dio Cass. 48.19.4). Sextus Pompey had recruited slaves into his fleet: under the terms of the treaty struck between the triumvirs and Pompey in 39 BC, he undertook not to provide refuge for runaway slaves any more, and the slaves who had served in his fleet were to be granted their freedom (App. *B Civ.* 5.8.72). This was not to happen. Augustus records here how he handed over 30,000 slaves to their masters, but is silent about the fact that he also crucified a further 6,000, whose masters could not be identified (App. *B Civ.* 5.13.131; Dio Cass. 49.12.4–5; Oros. 6.18.33). By mentioning only his restoration of slaves to their masters, Augustus focuses on his protection of the rights of property owners (Ridley (2003) 81). In addition, Augustus is once again implicitly inviting comparison between his own actions and those of Gnaeus Pompey. As well as suppressing pirates in the Mediterranean, Pompey had played a role in quashing the infamous slave revolt led by Spartacus, executing 5,000 slaves in its final stages (Plut. *Vit. Pomp.* 21.2). Augustus far surpasses Pompey in capturing 30,000 slaves. In his account of the Sicilian war, therefore, we see Augustus rivalling and excelling Pompey in his wars against both pirates and slaves (Fugmann (1991) 311). What Augustus does not mention is that he himself recruited slaves in order to boost recruitment to his own forces: in 38 BC he freed and trained 20,000 slaves (Suet. *Aug.* 16.1; Dio Cass. 48.49.1).

arma contra rem publicam/arms against the state   This phrase is omitted altogether in the Greek version. Whereas the Latin original is rather ambiguous, and avoids stating who exactly the *praedones* were, the Greek version simply states that Augustus restored order to the seas by ridding them of runaway slaves who had turned to piracy.

25.2 iuravit in mea verba/swore an oath of allegiance to me   After 31 December 33 BC, the triumvirate officially lapsed (see 7.1n. *per continuos annos decem*), leaving Octavian to find a new mechanism through which to secure a legal mandate for his actions. It was probably unclear whether or not he could still lay claim to *imperium* (whereas the *imperium* of a magistrate had a fixed term, that of promagistrates only lapsed when they were relieved by a successor and re-entered the *pomerium* – Ferrary (2001) 121), nor could he bind the soldiers to him any longer by the standard individual military oath, the *sacramentum* (see 3.3n. *millia civium Romanorum sub sacramento meo fuerunt circiter quingenta*). His solution was to raise troops with the professed intention of protecting the state in a time of crisis (*tumultus*), exacting from them an oath (*coniuratio*). This was permissible for a private individual; he did not have to be a magistrate with *imperium*. Whether such an action would end up being condoned or condemned depended entirely upon subsequent events: Octavian was fortunate to emerge as victor, and so his *coniuratio* could be represented as having rescued the state. The oath was voluntary and collective (*sponte sua*), and was valid only for the duration of a specific war, with the soldiers being released from it at the war's conclusion (Linderski (1984) espec. 76, 77–80). No trace remains of quite how the oath was taken, but it seems likely that Antony also elicited a similar oath from his supporters in the east (Dio Cass. 50.6.6). In addition to raising troops against Antony in this way, however, the oath of loyalty appears to have been extended to civilians as well, perhaps to all adult male citizens in Italy and non-citizens in the western provinces. This oath, therefore, cannot be explained solely in terms of a military *coniuratio* (Herrmann (1968) 78–89). The distinction between civilian and military had earlier been obscured when senators, equestrians, and prominent plebeians from Rome had voluntarily joined in the oath-swearing ceremony being carried out by his soldiers for Antony at Tibur in 44 BC (App. *B Civ.* 3.7.46; cf. Dio Cass. 45.13.5). It would have been typical of Octavian to have modified an existing practice in his favour, but essentially a clear distinction between military oath and civilian oath of loyalty was no longer evident. In this way, he imposed obligations on civilians almost as if they were serving under him as soldiers (Campbell (1984) 19–23; Syme (1939) 284–5, 288–93; Ridley (2003) 187–92). The Greek translation ὤμοσεν εἰς τοὺς ἐμοὺς λόγους is a literal version of the Latin idiom (Adams (2003) 469).

Although, therefore, this oath certainly had a military flavour, it is likely that the swearing of an oath was not undertaken only by those who were to fight as Octavian's soldiers in his struggle against Antony. The oath of 32 BC foreshadows a later development, whereby Augustus used oath swearing as a way of reinforcing the loyalty of the provinces to himself and his heirs (Herrmann (1968) 120–1). The text of an oath for the well-being, honour, and victory of Augustus, Gaius and Lucius Caesars, and Agrippa Postumus, probably dating from 6/5 BC, from Conobaria (Baetica), shows that the provincials undertook to share the same friends and enemies, and to take up weapons on their behalf (González (1988) 113–14). This Baetican oath is similar to one attested at Samos (Herrmann (1968) 125–6), also from 6/5 BC, and to another from Phazimon (Paphlagonia) of 3 BC, taken by the whole of the province, by Romans and non-Romans alike (Herrmann (1968) 123–4; *ILS* 8781 = EJ no. 315 = LACTOR H37). The language of these oaths may reflect that employed in the oath of 32 BC (Brunt and Moore (1967) 67–8).

tota Italia sponte sua/The whole of Italy of its own accord   The unification of Italy was a relatively recent phenomenon, dating only from the end of the Social War, but the principle of evoking Italian support had long been adopted by Roman nobles (Syme (1939) 284–8). Augustus, however, had to look no further than his 'father' for a precedent: Julius Caesar took pains to represent himself as champion of the Italians after his crossing of the Rubicon, repeatedly referring to *tota Italia* (Caes. *B Civ.* 1.2.2, 6.3, 9.4, 35.1; cf. 1.15.1; Fugmann (1991) 314–15). Other passages in the *RGDA* also reveal the importance Augustus attributed to his relationship with Italy (see 9.2, 10.2, 16.1, 21.3), and the official image of his position in the lead-up to Actium finds vivid expression on the shield of Aeneas in Virgil (*Aen.* 8.678–84). If the oath was taken in the form of a *coniuratio*, then it was, strictly speaking, voluntary, but the exaction of this oath in 32 BC seems to have extended beyond a military context (see 25.2n. *iuravit in mea verba*). The fact that Bononia (Bologna) was exempted from having to take the oath raises questions about how voluntary it really was (Suet. *Aug.* 17.2, with Carter (1982) ad loc.). As Syme commented ((1939) 284), 'when an official document records voluntary manifestations of popular sentiment under a despotic government, a certain suspension of belief may safely be recommended'.

belli quo vici ad Actium ducem/as its commander for the war in which I conquered at Actium   As usual, Augustus does not mention his opponents (Antony and Cleopatra in this case) by name (cf. 1.1, 2, 10.2, 24.1). The battle of Actium was not really the decisive victory proclaimed here; that was represented rather by the capture of Alexandria the following year in 30 BC, and the deaths of Antony and Cleopatra. It was consequently the triumph at Alexandria that was celebrated on the final, climactic day of Octavian's triple triumph. Nevertheless, the idea of Actium as a crucial historical turning-point developed during the decade or so after the battle, and was firmly established by the end of Augustus' lifetime (see Gurval (1995)). The Greek version translates *ducem* as ἡγεμόνα, which it uses elsewhere as the equivalent of *princeps* (13, 30.1, 32.3).

Galliae, Hispaniae, Africa, Sicilia, Sardinia/The Gallic and Spanish provinces, Africa, Sicily, and Sardinia   Augustus alludes here to the western provinces assigned to him as triumvir under the treaty of Brundisium in 40 BC, along with Africa, which had initially been assigned to Lepidus, and Sicily, from which Sextus Pompey had been expelled (Dio Cass. 48.28.4; Syme (1939) 217). Dio Cassius (50.6.4) also includes Illyria in the list (Ridley (2003) 81). Dio had personal reasons for mentioning the province, since he had acted as governor in the region (Reinhold (1988) 97). Most likely, it was an area of disputed influence, lying on the boundary dividing east from west as distributed between Octavian and Antony (App. *B Civ.* 5.7.65; Plut. *Vit. Ant.* 61.5).

25.3 qui sub signis meis tum militaverint/who served under my standards at that time   Augustus gives the misleading impression that the 700 senators were actively on campaign with him, as also conveyed by Virgil's depiction of Actium on the shield of Aeneas, describing how Octavian was leading into battle 'Italians, with senators and people, the *Penates* and great gods' (Virg. *Aen.* 8.678–9; Ridley (2003) 192).

senatores plures quam DCC/more than 700 senators   At first sight, this implies that the whole senate was supporting Octavian, given that membership of the senate both in the late Republic and by the end of Augustus' lifetime normally totalled around 600. This, however, ignores the sudden mushrooming of senatorial numbers from the Caesarian period onwards, culminating in a membership of over 1,000 by 29 BC, which Augustus subsequently cut drastically (Suet. *Aug.* 35.1; see 8.2n. **senatum ter legi**). This statistic, therefore, hides the fact that Antony enjoyed the support of several hundred senators, including both of the consuls and other men of senior status; it is also likely that not all senators declared their loyalties straightaway (Dio Cass. 50.2.2–7, with Reinhold (1988) 89–90; cf. Dio Cass. 50.20.6). In fact, Antony probably enjoyed the support of considerably more than 300 senators at the start of 32 BC, given that the 700 supporters claimed here by Augustus presumably include senators who defected to him during 32 and 31 BC, as well as those who had not initially declared their loyalties (Wallmann (1976) 306–7; see 25.3n. ***consules facti sunt . . . LXXXIII***). At the start of 32 BC, both consuls were supporters of Antony, and one of them, C. Sosius, started the year by proposing measures against Octavian. The fact that these had to be blocked by a veto interposed by a tribune on the side of Octavian implies that the measures might otherwise have been passed by majority vote. The insecurity of Octavian's support in the senate is also suggested by the fact that he felt it necessary to appear in the senate a little later, amidst friends carrying concelaed daggers, in order to respond to Sosius (Dio Cass. 50.2.3–5; Wallmann (1976) 305). Antony could even convene a meeting of a rival senate at Ephesos (Dio Cass. 50.3.2). On their departure from Rome to join Antony, the consuls Cn. Domitius Ahenobarbus and C. Sosius were promptly replaced with suffect consuls who were loyal to Octavian, L. Cornelius Cinna and M. Valerius Messalla. The raw statistics cited by Augustus mask the insecurity of his position in 32 BC and the fact that many pro-Antonian senators only defected to him in the immediate lead-up to Actium (Syme (1939) 296; Vell. Pat. 2.84.1–2; Dio Cass. 50.13.5–7, 50.23.1).

consules facti sunt . . . LXXXIII/eighty-three were made consuls Seventy-eight out of these eighty-three consuls can be identified, of whom twenty-two were in fact initially supporters of Antony, who defected to Octavian before Actium (Groag (1941)).

ad eum diem quo scripta sunt/up until the day on which these words were written   Although Augustus is trying to give the impression that his followers in 31 BC had been of high status, all this really shows is that his supporters were well rewarded after his victory by political and religious preferment (Ridley (2003) 150). On the date of composition of the *RGDA*, see introduction pp. 42–3; 4.4, 7.2, 35.2, 20.3n. ***si vivus non perfecissem***.

ROME'S EMPIRE AND INFLUENCE THROUGHOUT THE WORLD (26–33)

A cursory glance at our evidence suggests that the disastrous elimination of the three legions led by Quinctilius Varus in the German forests in AD 9 appears to have persuaded Augustus to set limits on Rome's imperial expansion: at his death, he left advice for Tiberius not to expand the Roman empire any further (Dio Cass. 56.33.5; Tac. *Ann.* 1.11.4). This principle sits uneasily, however, with Augustus' own account of his achievements in the *RGDA* – a document issued at precisely the same moment as this advice to Tiberius – which illustrates instead how he claimed to have brought the whole world under Roman rule, emulating and surpassing the conquests of both Pompey and Alexander (see introduction pp. 36–7). This claim,

its justification during

direct rule has reached
…es to show how Rome's
areas directly ruled by
…natically represented as
…t – personal pronouns
…military achievements
…Roman rule should be
…n Virgil's *Aeneid* of an
…close to the sentiment
…gustus' world rule on a
…bably copies an official
…er than assuming that
…erialist ambitions in his
…*RGDA* and the advice
…probably be explained
…xpanding the sphere of
…t emperors (Whittaker

…ere personal names are
…e chapters are liberally
…lculated to inspire awe
…p. 37). Indeed, many of
…see 26.5n. *in Arabiam*
…erves that, as far as we
…st time in the *RGDA*
…ort the contention that
…vas actually equivalent
…94). Another point of
…ters 26–33 are without

…vnat matters is the 'list of
marvels', scattered around the world, rather than an historical sequence of
events.

ROME'S WORLD CONQUEST (26–7)

26.1 imperio nostro/to our authority   Translated here by the Greek
word ἡγεμονία (see 27.1, 30.1; introduction p. 27).

  fines auxi/I extended the territory   This opening statement sets the
tone for this section, with Augustus implying that Roman influence was
not confined only to areas ruled directly by Rome, but that it extended
well beyond territories formally recognized as provinces of Rome (Braunert

(1977) 217; Ridley (2003) 192–6). As well as new provinces, such as Galatia (25 BC) and Pannonia (AD 9), new prefectures were created, which were not regarded as provinces in their own right: Judaea was annexed to Syria (AD 6) and Paphlagonia was incorporated into Galatia (6 BC); Raetia and Moesia were governed by equestrian officers, the latter as an adjunct to the province of Macedonia. It is an exaggeration to claim that this was done for all provinces, however.

26.2 Gallias et Hispanias provincias/the Gallic and Spanish provinces
The Gallic and Spanish provinces were subdued and reorganized in the decade following Actium. Although Gallia Narbonensis (a province roughly corresponding to modern Languedoc and Provence) had long been under Roman control (under another name, Transalpina), it had only been thanks to Julius Caesar that the non-Mediterranean areas of Gaul had been conquered. Campaigns by C. Carrinas in 31–29/28–27? BC and by M. Valerius Messalla in 27 BC – both of whom won triumphs for their victories – prepared the way for Augustus to complete the process of conquest himself in his campaigns of 27–25 BC. He then reorganized what had been known as Gallia Comata into three provinces, the Tres Galliae: Aquitania, Belgica, and Lugdunensis.

The Iberian peninsula had been the first overseas area to which the Romans had extended their control in 218 BC, but some parts of it still proved intractable almost two hundred years later, especially in the mountainous areas of the north-west, and offered occasion for six triumphs to be won during a period of a few years by Cn. Domitius Calvinus in 36 BC, C. Norbanus Flaccus in 34 BC (*Fasti Triumphales Capitolini: Inscr. Ital.* XIII.i 87 = EJ p. 34), L. Marcius Philippus and Ap. Claudius Pulcher, both in 33 BC, C. Calvisius Sabinus in 28 BC (*Fasti Triumphales Barberini: Inscr. Ital.* XIII.i 343, 345 = EJ pp. 34–5), and Sex. Appuleius in 26 BC (*Fasti Triumphales Capitolini: Inscr. Ital.* XIII.i 87 = EJ p. 35; LACTOR N2b, N2d). Augustus himself was present in the region in 26–25 BC (*Fasti Feriarum Latinarum: Inscr. Ital.* XIII.i 151 = EJ p. 35), and he led a campaign against the Cantabri in 26 BC. During the next year's campaign in Asturia and Callaecia, however, he remained on his sickbed at Tarraco (*Fasti Feriarum Latinarum: Inscr. Ital.* XIII.i 151 = EJ p. 36). Nevertheless these campaigns were hailed as great victories: the gates of Janus were closed in 25 BC (see 13n. **ter . . . senatus claudendum esse censuit**), and Augustus was offered a triumph, which he declined (see 4.1n. **decernente pluris triumphos mihi senatu**; Flor. 2.33.48–53 = LACTOR N48). Nevertheless, there was then a revolt by the Cantabri and Astures as soon as Augustus had left Spain (Dio Cass. 53.29.1–2), and it was not until 19 BC that Agrippa managed with some difficulty to suppress the Cantabrian rebels (Livy 28.12.12 = LACTOR N47; Dio Cass. 54.11.2–5). Finally, Augustus returned once more in 16–13 BC, to preside over the reorganization of the provinces' boundaries.

Hispania had previously consisted of two provinces, Citerior and Ulterior. Hispania Ulterior was now split up into Baetica and Lusitania, resulting in the division of the peninsula into three provinces (Alföldy (1996) 449–52). The new province of Baetica set up a golden statue, probably representing a personification of the province itself, in Augustus' honour in the Augustan forum, celebrating his pacification of the region (*ILS* 103 = EJ no. 42 = LACTOR K28). The other Spanish provinces may have followed suit (Vell. Pat. 2.39.2; Alföldy (1992) 67–75).

Germaniam/Germany   Whereas Augustus could claim some personal involvement in the pacification of the Spanish and Gallic provinces, the same could not be said of Germany, despite their juxtaposition here. Successful campaigns in Germany were executed by Augustus' stepsons: military operations by Drusus the Elder and Tiberius in 12–8 BC resulted in imperatorial acclamations for Augustus and triumphal decorations for Drusus and Tiberius (see 4.1n. ***appellatus sum viciens et semel imperator***). These campaigns resulted in the conquest of much of Germany, even allowing for partisan exaggeration from Velleius (Vell. Pat. 2.97.3–4; cf. Dio Cass. 54.32–3, 55.1.2–5, 55.6.2–5). Subsequently, the Romans advanced further, conquering territory between the Rhine and the Elbe (Peter *HRRel.* II 96 Aufidius Bassus fr. 3), with Domitius Ahenobarbus crossing the Elbe in AD 1 and making peace with the Germans beyond the Elbe. He received triumphal decorations for this achievement (Tac. *Ann.* 4.44.2). Roman advances were consolidated by M. Vinicius in AD 1–4 and C. Sentius Saturninus with Tiberius in AD 4–6, but were interrupted by the Pannonian revolt, and brought to an abrupt halt by the Varus disaster in AD 9.

It is not surprising that Augustus is silent about the destruction of the three legions under Varus, since this could hardly be counted as among his *res gestae*, and the silence is not to be taken as an indication of a compositional date for the *RGDA*, nor of a lack of revision for an earlier layer of composition (Braccesi (1973) 32). Augustus is simply being selective in recording the high point of Roman success in Germany (Ridley (2003) 196–203): he can, therefore, boast that he pacified Germany as far as the Elbe (cf. Suet. *Aug.* 21.1), but omit to mention that the pacification did not last for very long. Augustus does, however, make clear that Germany was not yet a province, in contrast to the Spanish and Gallic provinces (Nenci (1958) 302).

qua includit Oceanus a Gadibus ad ostium Albis fluminis/where Ocean forms a boundary from Cadiz to the mouth of the River Elbe Augustus' definition of the territory conquered sets up an implicit comparison with Alexander the Great, and amounts to a claim to world conquest, given that the expanse of water known as Ocean was thought to flow around the edges of the inhabited world (Clarke (1999a) 308–12; cf Dion.

Hal. *Ant. Rom.* 1.3.3). Gades (Cadiz) was the location of the Pillars of Hercules, marking the westernmost extent of the Mediterranean before Ocean. Alexander was said to have made plans to conquer the Phoenicians at the Pillars of Hercules (Straits of Gibraltar), but was prevented from accomplishing this by his premature death (Curt. 10.1.17). Augustus, therefore, is demonstrating how his achievements have actually surpassed those of Alexander, with his conquests stretching further to the west (Levi (1947) 206; Nenci (1958) 290–7; Dion (1966) 253; Nicolet (1991b) 21–4; cf. 31.1n. **legationes saepe missae sunt**). Augustus' claim should not be taken as a statement that the Elbe was regarded as a frontier for Rome's empire, given that the Roman army crossed the river and set up an altar to Augustus on its north bank in AD 1 (Dio Cass. 55.10a.2; Whittaker (2000) 300); it was, rather, a 'means of communication with the interior' (Ridley (2003) 201).

pacavi/I brought under control   The verb *pacare* may almost be regarded as a slogan of the regime (cf. Vell. Pat. 2.90–91.1; Hellegouarc'h and Jodry (1980) 808–9); together with its cognate noun *pax*, it encompasses the idea of pacification through military victory (see 13n. **esset parta victoriis pax**).

26.3 Hadriano mari/to the Adriatic Sea   Augustus chooses a more Latinate form of the adjective, instead of the Greek-sounding *Hadriaticum mare* (see also 27.3; Gelsomino (1958) 149–50).

Alpes/the Alps   A series of wars were waged against various Alpine tribes, ostensibly to eliminate banditry in the mountain passes (see 26.3n. **nulli genti bello per iniuriam inlato**). Campaigns on the Italian side of the Alps by C. Antistius Vetus in 35/34 BC and by Messalla Corvinus in *c.* 28/27 BC were brought to a successful conclusion when, in 25 BC, Terentius Varro subdued the tribe of the Salassi, capturing and selling many thousands into slavery. Three thousand praetorian veterans were then settled in the newly established colony of Augusta Praetoria (Aosta) in order to consolidate his victory (see 28.2n. **Italia autem XXVIII colonias**). The foundation of this colony not only helped to secure peaceful conditions for northern Italy since it straddled the St Bernard Passes, but also gained control of the gold-rich river Duria (Strabo *Geography* 4.6.6–7 = LACTOR N11–12; Dio Cass. 53.25.3–5). Further campaigns in Raetia (the area of the modern German and Swiss Alps) by Augustus' stepsons Tiberius and Drusus in 15/14 BC were celebrated by Horace (Hor. *Carm.* 4.4, 4.14 = LACTOR G42, G44; cf. Strabo *Geography* 4.6.9 = LACTOR N14; Vell. Pat. 2.95.1–2; Dio Cass. 54.22). These resulted in a tenth imperatorial acclamation for Augustus (see 4.1n. **appellatus sum viciens et semel imperator**), as depicted on coins issued between 15 and 12 BC (*RIC* I²

p. 52 no. 164b = *BM Coins, Rom. Emp.* I p. 77 no. 447 = LACTOR N15).
Less celebrated was the campaigning by P. Silius Nerva in 16/15 BC, which
probably prepared the ground for Augustus' stepsons (Dio Cass. 54.20.1).
Three new Alpine districts were established: Alpes Maritimae, Alpes Gra-
iae, and Alpes Cottiae. Of these, the area known as the Alpes Cottiae came
under Rome's control in 8 BC, when its dynastic king was transformed into
equestrian prefect and Roman citizen, M. Iulius Cottius, to whom control
of the region was delegated. This transformation was commemorated by
the setting up by Cottius of an emphatically Roman triumphal arch in
honour of Augustus, still standing in modern Susa (*ILS* 94 = EJ no. 166 =
LACTOR M33). The final subjugation of the whole area was celebrated in
7/6 BC by setting up a massive victory monument, the *tropaeum Augusti*,
at La Turbie (near Monaco). Its inscription recorded the subjugation of all
the Alpine tribes, listing each one by name (Plin. *HN* 3.20.136–8 = EJ no.
40 = LACTOR N16; cf. *CIL* V 7817).

nulli genti bello per iniuriam inlato/but attacked no people unjustly
The ideology of waging a just war was an integral part of Roman mental-
ity, but often depended upon the subjective portrayal of non-Romans as
lawless brigands. By representing the Alpine tribes as bandits, the Romans
could justify their conquest of them, but what the Alpine tribes had been
doing – levying tolls in the mountain passes – was only what the Romans
themselves did (Brunt and Moore (1967) 71; Strabo *Geography* 4.6.6–7 =
LACTOR N11–12; see also Dio Cass. 54.22.1–2 for allegations of atrocities
by Raetians). Suetonius elaborates still further upon this claim, whilst also
echoing Augustus' own words, in describing Augustus as only waging wars
that were just and necessary, and in implying that he was reluctant to wage
war at all (*nec ulli genti sine iustis et necessariis causis bellum intulit, tantumque
afuit a cupiditate quoquo modo imperium vel bellicam gloriam augendi, Aug.*,
21.2); in doing so, he is influenced by contemporary Hadrianic attitudes.

26.4 classis mea/My fleet   This expression illustrates the way in which
Augustus appropriates the fleet, just as he does the army (cf. 30.2n. *exercitus
meus*; see also introduction p. 25).

per Oceanum/through Ocean   This striking claim to have navigated
Ocean continues the theme of the Roman empire being boundless (see
26.2n. *qua includit Oceanus a Gadibus ad ostium Albis fluminis*).

usque ad fines Cimbrorum/as far as the territory of the Cimbri
The Cimbri inhabited the area of the Jutland Peninsula, which divides the
North Sea from the Baltic Sea, with a southern border provided by the River
Elbe. During the period 12–9 BC, Drusus the Elder was the first Roman
to sail in this part of the North Sea (thought by the Romans to be part of

the Ocean encircling the edge of the world), setting out from the Rhine and reaching perhaps as far as the northern tip of the Jutland Peninsula (Denmark) (Suet. *Claud.* 1.2; Tac. *Germ.* 34.2; Dio Cass. 54.32.2; Plin. *HN* 2.67.167). It is likely that his aim was to sail from there to Scythia, in the mistaken belief that this would allow him to reach the Caspian Sea and India, but he was prevented by intemperate conditions (Nicolet (1991b) 22, 87; Dion (1966) espec. 257–61). During Tiberius' German campaign in AD 5, the Roman fleet sailed from the mouth of the Rhine through the North Sea in order to join forces with land troops by then sailing up the Elbe (Vell. Pat. 2.106.3; cf. Hellegouarc'h and Jodry (1980) 810–11). Although this passage of the *RGDA* is usually interpreted as referring to Tiberius' exploits (cf. Ridley (2003) 83; Woodman (1977) 145–6), Claude Nicolet has argued convincingly that it actually refers to those of his younger brother Drusus (Nicolet (1991b) n. 17: 91–4).

Charydes et Semnones/Charydes and Semnones These peoples lived to the south of the Cimbri, to the east of the Elbe river. The Greek version confuses the Charydes with the Chalyes, a tribe in the Black Sea region. The Semnones were the chief tribe of the group of German peoples known as the Suebi (Tac. *Germ.* 38–9).

alii Germanorum populi/other German peoples The Greek version uses ἔθνος here to translate *populus*, rather than δῆμος, in order to distinguish between the *populus Romanus* and a non-Roman nation (Wigtil (1982a) 633).

per legatos amicitiam meam et populi Romani petierunt/sent envoys to request my friendship and that of the Roman people In the case of the Cimbri, Strabo (*Geography* 7.2.1, 3) relates how they sent as a gift to Augustus their most sacred cauldron, used for collecting the blood of prisoners-of-war when their throats were cut, from which prophecies were elicited. Their embassy sought friendship from him, and an amnesty for previous offences (see 32.3). For Augustus' omission of the senate from his account of these foreign embassies, see introduction p. 25.

26.5 meo iussu et auspicio/Under my command and auspices This phrase recalls the traditional way of alluding to military *imperium* (cf. Plaut. *Amph.* 192; Livy 3.1, 10.7). For Augustus' insinuation of himself into a role as commander-in-chief of Rome's army, see introduction p. 25 and 4.2n. *per legatos meos auspicis meis*.

eodem fere tempore/at almost the same time This chronological expression is deliberately vague, giving a slightly misleading impression about the simultaneity of these two expeditions. The exact dating of the campaigns is uncertain, but it is likely that the Arabian campaign was launched first, and lasted from spring/summer 26 to autumn 25 BC. This campaign may not have been completed before an expedition was sent into Aethiopia (Strabo *Geography* 17.1.54), probably lasting for about six months, from autumn 25 BC into late spring 24 BC. A second campaign against the Aethiopians followed in 22 BC (Jameson (1968) 71–8). Augustus reverses the chronological sequence of events in order to mask the dismal failure of the Arabian expedition (see 26.5n. ***in Arabiam quae appellatur Eudaemon***; Jameson (1968) 81; Ridley (2003) 203–5). He also subsumes Arabia and Aethiopia into the theme of Roman conquests, even though Aethiopia may have been under Roman control for only two years, and Arabia not at all (Jameson (1968) 82) (see Map 5).

in Aethiopiam/into Aethiopia   The region known in antiquity as Aethiopia is less remote than the modern country of Ethiopia: it was the region to the south of Egypt, corresponding to modern northern Sudan. Roman interest in Aethiopia grew out of the annexation of Egypt: Cornelius Gallus, the first prefect of Egypt, boasted that he had received envoys from an Aethiopian king and offered him Roman protection (*ILS* 8995 = EJ no. 21 = LACTOR P5). P. Petronius, prefect of Egypt, fought against the Aethiopians twice. Firstly, he advanced into Aethiopia as far as Nabata (see 26.5n. ***Nabata***) in 25/24 BC, in response to an invasion of Egypt by the Aethiopians, who may, however, simply have been anticipating Roman aggression (Dio Cass. 54.5.4–6, with Rich (1990) ad loc.; Jameson (1968) 74–5). This expedition was more successful than the earlier one into Arabia: Petronius captured a handful of towns (Plin. *HN* 6.35.181–2), and the expedition ended with the surrender of Queen Candace (Candace, however, is not a personal name, but a title along the lines of 'queen mother': Shinnie (1978) 248) and the garrisoning of Premnis by Roman troops. Petronius sent a thousand Aethiopian prisoners-of-war to Rome as a token of his success. Secondly, a revolt by the Aethiopians, who attacked the Roman garrison, necessitated further military action by Petronius in about 22 BC, ending in an Aethiopian embassy suing for Roman friendship by approaching Augustus on Samos in the winter of 21/20 BC (Strabo *Geography* 17.1.54; Dio Cass. 54.7.4; Jameson (1968) 75). Ever since Homer (e.g. *Od.* 1.22–4), the Aethiopians had been regarded as living at the margins of the world: by recording this expedition, Augustus continues his theme of Rome's empire encompassing the known limits of the world.

in Arabiam quae appellatur Eudaemon/into the Arabia which is called Fortunate   Aelius Gallus, prefect of Egypt, launched an invasion along the coast of the Red Sea into Arabia from Egypt in 26/25 BC (Strabo *Geography* 16.4.22–4; Dio Cass. 53.29.3, with Rich (1990) ad loc.; Jameson

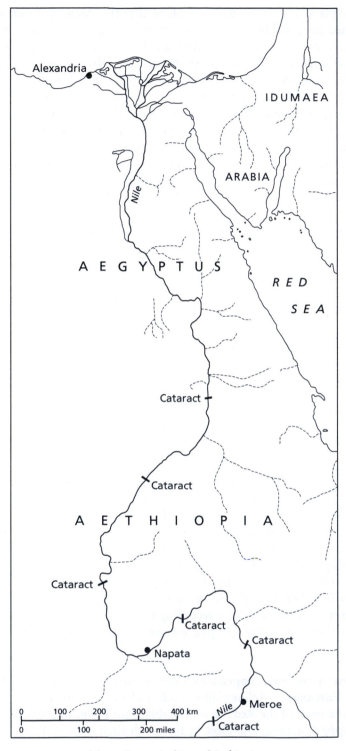

Map 5 Egypt, Arabia, and Aethiopia.

(1968) 76–8). Delayed by his mistaken decision to build warships, and reaching Leuke Kome by sea, when it would have been quicker to march overland, the army had to spend summer and winter there. The army then spent six months advancing as far as Mariba (see 26.5n. ***Mariba***), where it carried out a six-day siege, and then retreated because of a lack of water (Strabo *Geography* 16.4.24 = LACTOR N21), and arguably because Augustus had by now recalled Gallus, stripping him of his post as prefect (Jameson (1968) 76–7: but how could this have been done? – cf. Marek (1993) 142–3). Although the Elder Pliny, like Augustus, gives a positive account of the expedition (Plin. *HN* 6.32.160 = LACTOR N19, with a rare upbeat modern assessment by Sidebotham (1986) 598–9, cf. Marek (1993) 142 who contends that he did capture Mariba), this is belied by the account given by Strabo, who was a personal acquaintance of Gallus and had travelled with him extensively in Egypt, but who nevertheless had to acknowledge the failure of the expedition (Strabo *Geography* 2.5.12, 17.1.46).

The aims of the expedition are debated (Jameson (1968) 79–80; Marek (1993)). It may have been motivated by simple imperialism, or by the wish to gain control of a region noted for its wealth derived from trade in spices, and believed to contain quantities of gems, gold, and silver (Strabo *Geography* 16.4.22 = LACTOR N18; Bowersock (1983) 46–7; Sidebotham (1986) 592; criticized by Marek (1993) 125–38). Alternatively, it may have been part of a larger strategy, whereby Augustus desired to influence the Parthian succession, by supporting the pretender Tiridates II against Phraates IV (see 32.1n. ***Tiridates***; Ridley (2003) 127–8; Marek (1993) espec. 150–2). It is also possible, of course, that a combination of these factors may have led to the invasion. In any event, the expedition was a disaster: Augustus studiously mentions only the advance of his army into Arabia, and fails to mention its ignominious retreat, when many soldiers died through illness, exhaustion, and starvation (Strabo *Geography* 16.4.24 = LACTOR N22; Dio Cass. 53.29.3–8). Strabo himself acknowledged the expedition's failure, but blamed it on the treachery of the chief minister of Nabataea, Syllaeus; this appears to have been special pleading (Strabo *Geography* 16.4.23–4 = LACTOR N18, N22; Bowersock (1983) 47–8, 50–3; Sidebotham (1986) 594, 598), given that Syllaeus was subsequently entertained by Augustus at Rome, eventually to be executed for murder only in 6 BC.

Augustus differentiates here between Arabia Felix, the kingdom of the Sabaeans, in the south-west corner of the Arabian peninsula and Arabia, the kingdom of the Nabataeans (Bowersock (1983) 46). Augustus' unusual use of a Greek word in his paraphrase *quae appellatur Eudaemon* probably reflects the fact that the Latin name Arabia Felix had not yet entered Roman usage, and illustrates how unfamiliar this area would have been to Augustus' contemporaries (Gelsomino (1958) 150; Nicolet (1991b) 21). The region was thought to border on Ocean.

gentis utriusque/of both peoples This phrase is omitted in the Greek version (Vanotti (1975) 319).

Nabata/Nabata Nabata or Napata was about 85 miles downstream from the fourth cataract of the Nile; it had once been an important town in the Kingdom of Kush, but had been superseded as its capital by Meroe (see 26.5n. *Meroe*). Classical authors appear mistaken in identifying it as the royal residence, although it may have been a secondary residence (Strabo *Geography* 17.1.54 = LACTOR N34; Dio Cass. 54.5.5; Shinnie (1978) 248). After capturing the town, Petronius was forced to withdraw because of the hostile climatic conditions (Dio Cass. 54.5.5).

Meroe/Meroe Meroe (Begrawiya, about 70 miles downstream from the sixth cataract), is about 170 miles due south-east of Nabata. It was the capital of the Kingdom of Kush, acting as main royal residence and royal cemetery from about 300 BC (Shinnie (1978) 239). It was thought to be the southernmost point in the inhabitable world (Strabo *Geography* 2.5.7). A famous bronze head of Augustus (now in the British Museum) found in front of a small temple set up to commemorate the Aethiopian victory, with paintings depicting prisoners beneath the king's feet, was perhaps one of the statues looted by the Aethiopians from Egypt in 25/24 BC (Strabo *Geography* 17.1.54; Shinnie (1978) 247–8, 250; Walker and Burnett (1981) 22).

usque in fines Sabaeorum/as far as the territory of the Sabaei This phrase is omitted in the Greek version (Vanotti (1975) 319).

Mariba/Mariba Aelius Gallus did march this far, but then retreated after a six-day siege (see 26.5n. *in Arabiam quae appellatur Eudaemon*). This was probably the furthest south ever reached by Roman troops (Nicolet (1991b) 89 n. 4), and brings to a close the sequence of exotic place names which all evoke the ends of the earth. The remoteness of both Meroe and Mariba (Marib in Yemen) is mirrored by postponing the names of the towns until the ends of their clauses. (Marek (1993) 142 n. 83 draws attention to the parallel structure of Augustus' account of the army's advances into Arabia and Aethiopia (*in Aethiopiam usque ad oppidum Nabata . . . in Arabiam usque . . . ad oppidum Mariba*), which, he suggests, implies that Gallus was successful in capturing Mariba. This goes against the explicitly negative contemporary evidence of Strabo, however, who would have been only too pleased to be able to celebrate a success for his friend Gallus – see 26.5n. *in Arabiam quae appellatur Eudaemon* – and misses the point that Augustus would doubtless have been very happy for his readers to draw such an inference, false though it was.)

27.1 Aegyptum/Egypt The opening words of this chapter consist of two hexameter verses (*Aegyptum . . . eius*), setting a solemn epic tone for Augustus' account of these achievements (Hoeing (1908); cf. heading and 1.1n. *exercitum privato consilio*). Following the final defeat of Antony and Cleopatra at Alexandria in August 30 BC, Egypt was annexed and governed by a prefect of equestrian rank, who was directly responsible to Augustus himself, as his appointee (Tac. *Hist.* 1.11). The conquest of Egypt was celebrated as the grand climax to the triple triumph in 29 BC (see 4.1n. *tris egi curulis triumphos*), and was recorded in inscribed calendars as representing Octavian's rescuing of the state from grave danger (*Fasti Amit.*: *rem public(am) tristissim[o] periculo libera(vi)t* = EJ p. 49 = *Inscr. Ital.* XIII.ii 191, 489 = LACTOR C21; see 27.1n. *imperio populi Romani adieci*). This conquest opened up a valuable new source of grain for supplying Rome (Garnsey (1988) 231); to protect this from being seized by potential usurpers, who could then hold the populace of Rome to ransom by witholding grain supplies, Augustus established the rule that senators and distinguished equestrians were prohibited from entering the province without express permission (Tac. *Ann.* 2.59.3 = LACTOR M6; cf. Tac. *Hist.* 1.11 = LACTOR M8; Dio Cass. 51.17.1).

imperio populi Romani adieci/I added to the empire of the Roman people In this way, Augustus transforms what was really the final battle in his civil war against Antony into a war for the benefit of the Roman state (Ridley (2003) 152–4). His emphasis upon Egypt as now subject to the rule of the Roman people (for the word *imperium*, translated here by the Greek word ἡγεμονία, see 26.1, 30.1 and introduction pp. 27–8) is echoed in many different official media celebrating his victory. Gold and silver coins issued in 28/27 BC depicted animals associated with the Nile – the crocodile and hippopotamus – with the legend AEGVPTO CAPTA, 'Egypt captured' (*BM Coins, Rom. Emp.* I 106 nos. 650–5; *RIC* I² 61, 275 and 86 nos. 544–5; Simon (1993) 110–11 nos. 69a/b–70; LACTOR N31). Almost twenty years later, in 10/9 BC, the base of an obelisk brought back from Egypt was engraved with an inscription proclaiming once again the official interpretation of Alexandria's downfall, that Egypt 'had been reduced to the power of the Roman people', *Aegypto in potestatem populi Romani redacta* (*CIL* VI 702 = *ILS* 91 = EJ no. 14 = LACTOR K35; cf. *Fasti Praen.* = *Inscr. Ital.* XIII.ii 135). All this belies the fact that Egypt received special treatment, becoming to some extent the possession of the emperor (cf. Philo *In Flacc.* 19.158), who was viewed by the inhabitants of the country as a latter-day pharaoh (Reinhold (1988) 148–9). Augustus focuses upon Egypt's relationship to the people of Rome rather than to himself as a monarch, but it may be significant that he avoids referring to it as a province (Weber (1936) 201; cf. Braunert (1977) 209, who argues that the use of the verb *adieci* marks out Egypt's special position; cf. Vell. Pat. 2.94.4 for a parallel expression in describing Armenia – *redacta ea in potestatem populi Romani* – a client kingdom, not a province).

27.2 Armeniam maiorem/Greater Armenia   The mountainous region of Greater Armenia was situated to the north of Syria and Mesopotamia, to the east of the upper Euphrates as far as the Caspian Sea. It may have been considered to be of strategic importance to Rome, as it acted as a 'buffer state' adjacent to Parthia, blocking a possible route by which the Parthians might have launched an invasion of the Pontic region, even though they had earlier directed activity towards Syria through Mesopotamia (Sherwin-White (1984) 337–8). After it was made a client kingdom by Pompey (see 27.2n. *maiorum nostrorum exemplo*), Rome and Parthia contended with each other to influence the royal succession.

interfecto rege eius Artaxe/on the assassination of Artaxes its king Artaxes II (*PIR*² A1167, sometimes also 'Artaxias') had taken over from Artavasdes II (ruled *c.* 56/55–34 BC) who had been deposed in 34 BC by Antony and executed by Cleopatra in 31/30 BC in the aftermath of Actium (Strabo *Geography* 11.14.15; Dio Cass. 49.39.2–41.5, 51.5.5; Joseph. *AJ* 15.104–5; Plut. *Vit. Ant.* 50; Tac. *Ann.* 2.3.1; Livy *Per.* 131), but had been forced to take refuge in Parthia during Antony's attack on his country (Sullivan (1990) 290). Artaxes II (ruled *c.* 31–20 BC) subsequently took over the kingdom once Antony had moved out of the region in the build-up to Actium, and enjoyed Parthian support, but was killed by a pro-Roman faction of his kinsmen in 20 BC (Tac. *Ann.* 2.3.2), who asked Augustus for help (Dio Cass. 54.9.4–5; Chaumont (1976) 73–4; Sherwin-White (1984) 323). The kingdom was then handed over to his younger brother, Tigranes III (see 27.2n. *Tigrani, regis Artavasdis filio*).

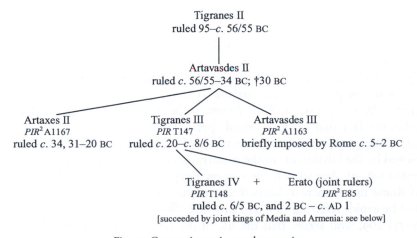

Fig. 22 Greater Armenia: royal succession.

cum possem facere provinciam/Although I could have made Greater Armenia a province   Augustus is disingenuous here: he was unlikely to have succeeded had he tried to make it a province, and failed even to settle affairs in it as a client kingdom, although he tried to mask his failure in the rest of his brief account (Ridley (2003) 205–8).

maiorum nostrorum exemplo/in accordance with the example set by our ancestors   Augustus is alluding to the precedent set by Pompey, who in 66 BC had made Armenia a client kingdom in the hands of Tigranes II (ruled 95–55 BC), after he had surrendered to him, having been a supporter of his father-in-law Mithridates VI Eupator of Pontus against Rome (Bedoukian (1968) 44–5; Chaumont (1976) 71–2). Augustus is also inviting a contrast between his actions and those of Antony, who had mounted a military campaign in 34 BC with the aim of annexing Armenia (Dio Cass. 49.44.4). Augustus represented his settlement of Tigranes III on the throne of Armenia as the submission of that kingdom to Rome. Coins issued in 19/18 BC bore the legends ARMENIA RECEPTA – alluding to the recovery of the kingdom as a Roman protectorate – or ARMENIA CAPTA (*BM Coins, Rom. Emp.* I 4–5 nos. 18–21, 8 nos. 43–4, 108–9 nos. 671–8; *RIC* I^2 62 nos. 290–2, 63 nos. 306–7, 83 nos. 514–17, 519–20, cf. 82 no. 513, 83 no. 518; Simon (1993) 113–15 nos. 72–7; Bedoukian (1978) 30). Nevertheless, although the reign of Tigranes III may have started in a pro-Roman atmosphere, it witnessed an increasing sympathy forming between Armenia and Parthia, in opposition to Rome, and his coins reflect this change (Bedoukian (1968) 56, (1978) 31).

Tigrani, regis Artavasdis filio/to Tigranes, son of King Artavasdes   Tigranes III (*PIR* T147) succeeded his elder brother Artaxes II (see 27.2n. **interfecto rege eius Artaxe**) in 20 BC, and possibly ruled until about 7 BC. He had lived at Rome for the previous ten years, and was installed by Tiberius, being crowned with a diadem by him (Vell. Pat. 2.122.1; Tac. *Ann.* 2.3.2; Suet. *Tib.* 9.1). When their father, Artavasdes II, was deposed by Antony, Tigranes and his brother Artavasdes had been imprisoned at Alexandria by Antony, where they were again captured – this time by Octavian – and transferred to Rome, where they were still detained on the grounds that their elder brother Artaxes II had killed some Roman citizens remaining in Armenia (Dio Cass. 51.16.2). Augustus' refusal to hand them over to Artaxes II provided him with a bargaining tool in dealing with the Armenian king, who remained in power for some years with Parthian support but, in the end, was killed by a pro-Roman faction, who invited Augustus to place Tigranes as a Roman nominee on the throne (Sherwin-White (1984) 325).

per Ti. Neronem/through the agency of Tiberius Nero   Although Augustus, along with several other sources, advertises Tiberius' involvement in installing Tigranes III in 20 BC (see 27.2n. *Tigrani, regis Artavasdis filio*), Tiberius appears to have shirked the task of settling Armenia for a second time which was assigned to him in 6 BC, when instead he retired to Rhodes for some years (Dio Cass. 55.9.4).

eandem gentem postea desciscentem et rebellantem domitam per Gaium filium meum/And when the same people later revolted and rebelled, they were subdued through the agency of Gaius, my son Tigranes III (see 27.2n. *Tigrani, regis Artavasdis filio*) ruled for only a few years, according to Tacitus (*Ann.* 2.3.2), but his reign appears to have come to an end only some time before 6 BC (Dio Cass. 55.9.4). Augustus refused to recognize his son and daughter, Tigranes IV and Erato, as rulers of Armenia, and tried to impose as Artavasdes III another of the sons of Artavasdes II whom Antony had captured, and whom Augustus had then kept in protective custody in Rome (see 27.2n. *Tigrani, regis Artavasdis filio*). His nephew Tigranes IV (*PIR* T148), however, who ruled jointly with his sister Erato enjoyed the support of Phraates V of Parthia in resisting this attempt to impose Artavasdes III (*PIR*² A1163) as ruler in Armenia. Artavasdes III was ejected at some expense to Rome (*non sine clade nostra deiectus*: Tac. *Ann.* 2.4.1, with Goodyear (1981) ad loc.), and probably died in *c.* 2/1 BC. Unsurprisingly, Augustus keeps his comments on this episode rather vague.

With Artavasdes III off the scene, Tigranes IV and Erato sought some accommodation with Rome. Once Tigranes IV had been killed in warfare by 'barbarians' – possibly Armenians resisting his conversion to a pro-Roman stance (Swan (2004) 129) – and Erato had abdicated in 1 BC/AD 1 (Dio Cass. 55.10a.5), Gaius Caesar arrived on the scene in the east to solve the succession crisis in Armenia, in an attempt to stop Parthia from retaining its dominant position there (Dio Cass. 55.10.18–19). He is variously said to have been on a mission to settle Egypt and Syria (Oros. 7.3.4; Vell. Pat. 2.101.1 – Syria only), Parthia, Arabia (Plin. *HN* 6.31.141), and Armenia (Tac. *Ann.* 2.4.1). Augustus now decided to unite the kingdoms of Greater Armenia and Media Atropatene (Azerbaijan), under the joint kingship of Ariobarzanes, who had been ruler of Media since 20 BC (see 27.2n. *regi Ariobarzani, regis Medorum Artabazi filio*), but some Armenians resisted this step. During the hostilities that ensued, Gaius was wounded on campaign at Artagira, and subsequently died, hardly the glorious suppression of a revolt claimed by Augustus here (Dio Cass. 55.10a.5–9; Flor. 2.32.42–5; Sherwin-White (1984) 325–6; see 14.1n. *quos iuvenes mihi eripuit fortuna*).

regi Ariobarzani, regis Medorum Artabazi filio/to King Ariobarzanes, son of Artabazus king of the Medes Ariobarzanes (*PIR*² A1044) had been installed as king of Media Atropatene by Augustus in

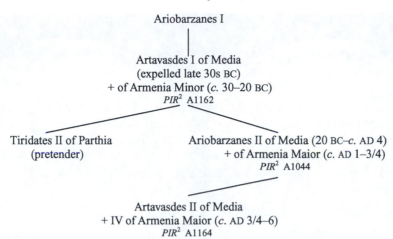

Ariobarzanes I

Artavasdes I of Media
(expelled late 30s BC)
+ of Armenia Minor (*c.* 30–20 BC)
*PIR*² A1162

Tiridates II of Parthia
(pretender)

Ariobarzanes II of Media (20 BC–*c.* AD 4)
+ of Armenia Maior (*c.* AD 1–3/4)
*PIR*² A1044

Artavasdes II of Media
+ IV of Armenia Maior (*c.* AD 3/4–6)
*PIR*² A1164

Fig. 23 Media Atropatene: royal succession (incorporating Greater Armenia from AD 3/4).
(Cf. Sullivan (1990) stemma 9.)

20 BC, when he freed Media from Armenian rule (Bedoukian (1978) 30; see
33n. *Ariobarzanem, regis Artavazdis filium*). Gaius installed him as king
of Greater Armenia too in about AD 1 (see 27.2n. **eandem gentem postea
desciscentem et rebellantem domitam per Gaium filium meum**). The
name Artabazes is a variant on Artavasdes (cf. at 33, Augustus describes the
same man as *regis Artavazdis filium*).

**post eius mortem filio eius, Artavasdi/after his death to his son,
Artavasdes** On the death of his father Ariobarzanes II (see 27.2n. *regi
Ariobarzani, regis Medorum Artabazi filio*), Artavasdes II of Media/IV
of Armenia (*PIR*² A1164) continued the joint kingship established by Gaius
for a few years, AD *c.* 3/4–6 (Dio Cass. 55.10a.7), but was killed by hostile
subjects (*quo interfecto*; Ridley (2003) 206), and was succeeded by Tigranes
V (see 27.2n. **Tigranem qui erat ex regio genere Armeniorum oriundus**). Coinage that may have been issued by Augustus depicts on one side a
laureate head of Augustus accompanied by the legend 'of god Caesar benefactor' (ΘΕΟΥ ΚΑΙΣΑΡΟΣ ΕΥΕΡΓΕΤΟΥ), and on the other a diademed
head of Artavasdes, with the legend 'of great king Artavasdes' (ΒΑΣΙΛΕΟΣ
ΜΕΓΑΛΟΥ ΑΡΤΑΥΑΖΔΟΥ) (Bedoukian (1968) 57–8, 66 no. 39, pl. XI,
(1978) 38) (Figure 24).

**Tigranem qui erat ex regio genere Armeniorum oriundus/Tigranes,
who was descended from the Armenian royal family** Tigranes V (*PIR*
T149) was grandson of King Herod the Great of Judaea via his father
Alexander, and grandson of King Archelaus of Cappadocia, who had mar-
ried an Armenian princess, via his mother Glaphyra (Joseph. *BJ* 1.28.1,
AJ 18.5.4). Augustus is probably being deliberately vague in describing his

Fig. 24 Laureate head of Augustus accompanied by the legend 'of god Caesar benefactor'; diademed head of Artavasdes, with the legend 'of great king Artavasdes' (coin: obverse and reverse, Bedoukian (1968) 66 no. 39, pl. XI). © The Trustees of the British Museum.

family background (in contrast to the specific details given for the other kings up to this point) in order to mask how tenuous Tigranes' family links with Armenia really were (Ridley (2003) 129), but implicitly recognizes that his attempt to impose non-Armenian, Median kings upon the Armenians had failed (Bedoukian (1978) 38). Tigranes himself tried to promote the idea that he was somehow a legitimate successor to the Artaxiad dynasty by issuing coins depicting Erato on their reverse, as well as coins depicting Augustus (Bedoukian (1971) 139 nos. 6–8, pl. XXXV, (1978) 38–9). He was the last of the kings whom Augustus attempted to impose upon the kingdom of Greater Armenia, after Artavasdes was killed in about AD 6 (see 27.2n. *post eius mortem filio eius, Artavasdi*), but he too ended up being expelled a year or so later, probably because, as a hellenized Jew, he was out of sympathy with Armenian culture and society. In short, Augustus' attempt to make Armenia a client kingdom of Rome failed, and probably created more serious problems (especially through the death of Gaius) than Augustus had hoped to solve in the first place. Tigranes was succeeded by Vonones I (ruled *c.* AD 11/12–15/16), who went on to be a thorn in the side of Tiberius. (On the turbulent course of events in Armenia and Media Atropatene, see in general Sherwin-White (1984) 323–8; Chaumont (1976) 73–83; on Vonones, see 33).

27.3 provincias omnis/all the provinces　　Augustus claims to have recovered control for Rome of the provinces, from Macedonia eastwards, granted to Antony under the terms of the Treaty of Brundisium in 40 BC (App. *B*

Civ. 5.7.65; Plut. *Vit. Ant.* 30.6; Dio Cass. 48.28.4). These included Macedonia, Achaea, Pontus, Bithynia, Asia, Cilicia, Syria, Cyprus, Crete, and Cyrene. Coins issued in 29/27 BC celebrated the recovery of the province of Asia, depicting Victory holding a wreath and palm branch, together with a *cista mystica*, and the legend ASIA RECEPTA (*BM Coins, Rom. Emp.* I 105 nos. 647–9; *RIC* I² 61 no. 276; Simon (1993) 120 no. 78).

trans Hadrianum mare/across the Adriatic Sea   For this choice of expression, see 26.3 **Hadriano mari**.

iam ex parte magna regibus ea possidentibus/which were at that stage mostly in the hands of kings   Antony had set up a system of client kingdoms, which involved some handing over of Roman provincial territory, but which mostly consisted of reallocating lands that had never been under direct Roman rule. In 37/36 BC he separated Lycaonia and Pamphylia from the Roman province of Cilicia and gave them to Amyntas, whom he had appointed king of Galatia (Dio Cass. 49.32.3, with Reinhold (1988) ad loc.). In addition to these territorial settlements, he nominated as kings Archelaus for Cappadocia, Polemo for Pontus, and Herod for Judaea. By establishing a new dynasty in each case, Antony tried to create a network of personal allegiances to him. He also made a series of territorial grants to Cleopatra and the children she had borne him, in an attempt to secure his own military position and as a punishment to rulers who had supported Parthia against him. There is some confusion about when specific territories were handed over to her, given a tendency in ancient sources – especially Dio and Plutarch – to lump together the grants of 37/36 and 34 BC, in an attempt to make Antony's actions seem all the more heinous; furthermore, the 'donations' of 34 BC (see below) were more about flamboyant spectacle than a real adjustment to territorial control. As far as we can judge, in 37/36 BC he gave to Cleopatra much of Arabia Nabataea, Phoenicia except Tyre and Sidon, Palestine, Crete, Cyrene, and Cyprus (Dio Cass. 49.32.4–5, with Reinhold (1988) ad loc.; Strabo *Geography* 14.6.6), Coele Syria, much of Cilicia, and part of Judaea (Joseph. *BJ* 1.18.5, *AJ* 15.3.8, 4.1; Plut. *Vit. Ant.* 36.3–4, with Pelling (1988) ad loc.). These gifts were measures calculated to harm Cleopatra's enemy, Herod (who leased back from her the lands taken from him), and to make available to her areas rich in timber to support her ship-building programme (Strabo *Geography* 14.5.3, 14.5.6).

The notorious celebration known as the 'Donations of Alexandria' followed the annexation of Greater Armenia in 34 BC (Dio Cass. 49.40.3–41.1). To Cleopatra herself and Caesarion, her son by Julius Caesar, Antony gave Cyprus and Coele Syria; for their elder son Alexander Helios (aged six), he proclaimed a kingdom consisting of Armenia, Media, and Parthia, even though he had not yet subdued the whole of this area (Livy *Per.* 131); to Alexander Helios' twin sister Cleopatra Selene, Antony assigned the Roman province of Cyrene, which thus can be properly counted among the Roman provinces recovered by Augustus (Reynolds and Lloyd (1996) 630–1), and is therefore singled out for specific mention by Augustus here; to their younger son Ptolemy Philadelphus (aged two), he handed over Phoenicia, Syria, and much of Cilicia (Dio Cass. 49.41.2–3, with Reinhold (1988) ad loc.; Plut. *Vit. Ant.* 54.4–9, with Pelling (1988) ad loc.). The ceremony was represented by Antony's enemies as a mock Roman triumph, and presented Octavian with an unmissable opportunity for portraying himself as going to war on behalf of Roman territories that had been alienated (Dio Cass. 49.40.3–4, with Reinhold ad loc.; Dio Cass. 50.1.5; Plut. *Vit. Ant.* 54–5.1; Vell. Pat. 2.82.4; Pelling (1996) 40–1). (In general, see Ridley (2003) 208–13; Syme (1939) 259–61, 270–3).

Siciliam et Sardiniam occupatas bello servili/Sicily and Sardinia which had been occupied at the time of the slave war   Sextus Pompey had been granted control of Sicily, Sardinia, Corsica, and Achaea by a treaty signed by the triumvirs, including Octavian himself (see 25.1n. *a praedonibus*). For the characterization of the struggle against Sextus Pompey as a slave war, see 25.1n. *servorum*.

COLONIAL FOUNDATIONS (28)

Up until 14 BC, Augustus founded colonies for the settlement of his veteran soldiers, as their reward on discharge (see 3.3n. *deduxi in colonias*). From 13 BC soldiers tended to receive monetary sums rather than land upon discharge, although this was not a fixed rule in practice (see 3.3n. *pro praemiis militiae*; for continued land allotments, see Brunt (1962) 83). Augustus has earlier described the expenditure involved in establishing colonies in Italy and abroad (see 16.1nn. *in consulatu meo quarto*; *summa sestertium circiter sexsiens milliens*; *deduxerunt colonias militum in Italia aut in provincis*). His emphasis here is on the geographical extent of his settlements. Colonies had an important role to play in consolidating Roman control of newly conquered territories and sometimes in securing an area's allegiance, with colonies being founded for the soldiers who had recently completed their military campaigns in those same areas. This was especially true of remote mountainous districts such as Pisidia and Lusitania. These new colonies often display regular grid layouts in their urban planning, as far as is possible within the local topography, and the colonists are often particularly keen to parade their loyalty to Rome and Augustus. The juxtaposition of this chapter with the previous one allows Augustus to draw an implicit contrast between his behaviour and Antony's, in listing his colonial foundations whereby he increased Rome's empire straight after his reference to Antony's alienation of territory (see 27.3n. *iam ex parte magna regibus ea possidentibus*).

It is often difficult to identify which colonies were founded by Augustus, especially in distinguishing them from Caesarian foundations, since a colony known as colonia Iulia might have been founded by either Augustus or Julius Caesar. Although he followed in Caesar's footsteps by establishing overseas colonies, Augustus' colonies were much more numerous and more distinctively military in character. The following comments aim to give an overall flavour of the nature of colonization in the different areas mentioned by Augustus rather than a definitive list of Augustan colonial foundations (cf. Vittinghoff (1952) 96–139). In addition to the veteran colonies with which Augustus is concerned here, he also made grants of colonial status to some existing urban centres in the provinces. This reflects the Roman preoccupation with urbanization and municipalization and their perceived links with civilization.

28.1 colonias in Africa/colonies in Africa   The two provinces of Africa Vetus and Nova had been thrown into disorder by the civil wars: Lepidus had built up a huge army there of sixteen legions, having been assigned the region as a triumvir. Colonization, alongside military campaigning, with three triumphs being awarded *ex Africa* between 34 and 28 BC (*Fasti Triumphales Capitolini: Inscr. Ital.* XIII.i 87 = EJ p. 34; *Fasti Triumphales Barberiniani = Inscr. Ital.* XIII.i 343–5 = EJ p. 35), had an important part to play in restoring order to the region, which was reorganized as a single province of Africa Proconsularis.

The most important colony in Africa was Iulia Carthago (Carthage), which became the administrative capital of Africa Proconsularis. Although it was planned and probably established with a first batch of settlers by Julius Caesar in 44 BC, Octavian played a further crucial role in supplementing the colony's population, perhaps in 36/35 BC (App. *Pun.* 20.136; Teutsch (1962) 101–6; Rives (1995) 21). It is possible that Statilius Taurus was sent by Octavian to settle veterans there (cf. Dio Cass. 49.14.6), at an opportune moment for appeasing his discontented troops with land, and just in time to settle the area after fighting between the governors of Africa Vetus and Nova (Whittaker (1996) 587–9, 605–8). Nearby colonies at Thuburbo Minus (Teboura) and Uthina (Oudna) may have been intended to provide Carthage with back-up support. Over twenty colonies were founded by Caesar and Augustus in the region, many of which were designed to control communication along the coastline (for other colonies in Africa Proconsularis, see Brunt (1971) 594–5; Whittaker (1996) 603–5). The colonies expressed their sense of allegiance to Augustus in different ways: he was celebrated as *conditor* ('founder') in an inscription at Sicca Veneria (*CIL* VIII 27568), whilst an altar set up at Carthage imitated Augustan monuments at Rome, with on one side a depiction of the cult statues from the temple of Mars the Avenger in the Augustan forum, and on another side the altar of Augustan Peace (Zanker (1988) 313–15; Rives (1995) 52–3).

Colonies in neighbouring Mauretania belong to a different context. Augustus founded twelve colonies in the client kingdom of Mauretania during the period of direct Roman rule in the region, 33–25 BC, after the death of King Bocchus and before Juba II assumed control (Plin. *HN* 5.1.2, 5.1.5, 5.1.20–1; Mackie (1983) 332–43). The colonies were intended to secure the region as a new province, before Augustus decided instead to make it a client kingdom in 25 BC. The colonies in the east were perhaps founded in order to provide support to the new king, Juba II, and to help secure the new kingdom's loyalty to Rome. Augustus does not specifically mention the colonies founded in Mauretania, perhaps because from 25 BC they were under the control of the governors of Baetica or Africa (Brunt (1971) 595–6).

Sicilia/Sicily   Sicily too had played its part during the civil wars, with demands made upon the island over several years (43–36 BC) to supply men and resources for Sextus Pompey's forces (Strabo *Geography* 6.2.4; see 25.1n. *a praedonibus*), and to act as a refuge for the proscribed (App. *B Civ.* 4.6.46). Following the battle of Naulochus in autumn 36 BC, Octavian took control of the province, levying indemnities upon cities that had supported Pompey (App. *B Civ.* 5.129) and confiscating land, some of which was then used for colonial foundations (Diod. Sic. 16.7.1; Dio Cass. 49.12.5; Wilson (1996) 435–7). During a visit to Sicily in 21 BC, Augustus carried out a reorganization of the province, establishing a handful of colonies at Syracusae (Syracuse), Catina (Catania), Tyndaris, Thermae Himeraeae (Termini Imerese), and possibly Tauromenium (Taormina) and Panormus (Palermo), unless these last two colonies were founded in 36 BC and 14 BC respectively (Dio Cass. 54.7.1; Wilson (1996) 437, with n. 12; Stone (1983) 22 n. 96; Brunt (1971) 597). All of these colonies were founded on the north and east coastline of the island, encouraging links to the Italian mainland (Wilson (1996) 439). These foundations went some way to restoring the fortunes of the island, much of which had been punished for its support of Pompey (Stone (1983)).

Macedonia/Macedonia   Following Actium, Octavian transferred veterans who had fought for Antony from Italy into colonies in Macedonia, including Philippi, Dyrrhachium (Dürres), Dium (Dion), and Cassandrea. These colonies were given 'Italian status', *ius Italicum*, which gave immunity from provincial taxation (Paulus *Dig.* 50.15.8.8), as a recompense for being moved from Italy (Brunt (1971) 598–9; Wilkes (1996) 573–4; see 16.1n. *in consulatu meo quarto*).

Augustus does not mention neighbouring Illyricum, where we know of a colony of veterans at Iader (Zadar) in 33 BC. Augustus' own involvement in the colony is attested to by an inscription hailing him as *parens coloniae* ('father of the colony'), in response to his giving the town its walls and towers (*CIL* III 13264). Less surprising is his omission of Pannonia, where the colony Iulia Emona was founded in AD 14, a contributory cause to the mutiny of the long-serving legionaries who were facing the prospect of being 'rewarded' with unproductive marshland instead of the expected cash gratuities (Keppie (1983) 209).

utraque Hispania/both Spains   Seven colonies in the peninsula can be attributed with confidence to Augustus – Astigi (Ecija) and Tucci (Martos) in Baetica; Ilici (Elche), Barcino (Barcelona), Caesaraugusta (Zaragoza), and Libisosa (Lezuza) in Tarraconensis; Emerita (Mérida) in Lusitania – but several more are distinct possibilities (Brunt (1971) 587, 590–3; Alföldy (1996) 456–7; Garcia y Bellido (1959) 474–502). At the time of these colonial foundations, the Spanish peninsula was still divided into only two provinces, Hispaniae Citerior and Ulterior (see 26.2n. ***Gallias et Hispanias provincias***); hence Augustus alludes to 'both Spains'. Following the premature declaration that the Cantabrian war had ended in 25 BC, Augustus founded a colony at Augusta Emerita in Lusitania for veterans of legions V Alauda and X Gemina (*PECS* 114; Dio Cass. 53.26.1). Once the task really had been completed, he then founded another at Caesaraugusta, probably between 16/13 BC, for veterans of IV Macedonica, VI Victrix, and X Gemina (*PECS* 181).

Achaia/Achaea   Patrae (Patras) had been destroyed in 146 BC, but was refounded some time after Actium as colonia Aroe Augusta Patrensis with veterans from legions X Fretensis and XII Fulminata and by an act of synoecism, by which local populations were relocated (*PECS* 681; Wilkes (1996) 573). It was the main port linking Greece to Italy. The establishment of the new colony had a dramatic effect upon the region. Large tracts of land on both sides of the Corinthian Gulf were expropriated for the benefit of the veteran settlers (see Strabo *Geography* 10.2.21 for their control of a productive fishing lake at Calydon). Existing settlements in the area were either destroyed and their inhabitants transplanted to the colony (Paus. 7.18.7 on the fate of Rhypes; cf. Strabo *Geography* 8.7.5), or they were made subject to the colony (Paus. 7.22.1 on Pharai, 7.22.6 on Triteia). The changes in the regional settlement pattern were also accompanied by religious ones, with cult objects being removed from now defunct centres and transported to the colony (Paus. 7.18.8–9 on Artemis Laphria; see 24.1n. ***ornamenta reposui***; Alcock (1993) 133–45).

Asia/Asia   Alexandria Troas (Tuzla) is the only certain example of an Augustan colony settled by veterans in the province of Asia (Brunt (1971) 600). Augustus' direct interest in building work in the colony is illustrated by a career inscription of C. Fabricius Tuscus 'prefect of the Apulan cohort and of the works which have been executed in the colony by Augustus' command' (EJ no. 368 = *AE* 1973.501 = LACTOR N27).

Syria/Syria   Berytus (Beirut in Lebanon) was founded on the coast of Phoenicia by Agrippa for veterans from the V Macedonica and VIII Augusta legions between about 16 and 14 BC (Strabo *Geography* 16.2.19; Brunt (1971) 601). The potential usefulness of colonies for emergency recruitment was demonstrated in 4 BC, when 1,500 armed recruits could be quickly raised from Berytus (Joseph. *BJ* 2.5.1).

Gallia Narbonensi/Gallia Narbonensis   Gallia Narbonensis (until 27 BC, Transalpina) had been Rome's province since 121 BC, with a colony founded at Narbo (Narbonne) in 118 BC. Although initially it had the function of protecting the route between Italy and Spain, military concerns were no longer pressing by the time of Augustus. Following Caesar's precedent, Augustus founded new colonies of the VII legion at Baeterrae (Béziers), of the II legion at Arausio (Orange), and of the VIII legion at Forum Iulii (Fréjus) some time during 40/28 BC (Brunt (1971) 589–90; Goudineau (1996) 477). The marble cadastres from Orange show how the best land in the colony's territory in the Rhône valley was allocated to the veterans, with the local Tricastini receiving only the leftover inferior tracts (Goudineau (1996) 478). Existing colonies also received new groups of veterans in 16/14 BC (Dio Cass. 54.23.7; see 16.1n. ***deduxerunt colonias militum in Italia aut in provincis***).

Pisidia/Pisidia   On the death of King Amyntas of Galatia at the hands of the Homanadenses in 25 BC, Pisidia in central Anatolia was annexed as part of the new province of Galatia (see introduction p. 7). A sequence of six veteran colonies (including Antioch, Comama, Cremna, Lystra, Olbasa, and Parlais) was founded in Pisidia in *c.* 25 BC, and later linked by the *via Sebaste* built in 6 BC. Other colonies were also founded at Iconium, Ninica, and Germa (see Map 3, Asia Minor). These colonies and their veteran settlers were entrusted with the task of securing Rome's grip on its newly annexed territory, amidst the still hostile Homanadenses, who were only finally vanquished towards the end of the first century BC (see introduction p. 13; Levick (1967) ch. 4, app. v; Brunt (1971) 600–1). In addition, colonists were settled within the existing cities of Apollonia, Attaleia, Isaura, and Neapolis (Mitchell (1979)).

28.2 Italia autem XXVIII colonias/Moreover Italy has twenty-eight colonies   The basis of Augustus' claim to have founded twenty-eight colonies in Italy is unclear, given that if he were to have included all the colonies in Italy founded or reinforced between 41 BC and AD 14, he would have reached a much higher total (perhaps fifty or more). Consequently, it is possible to draw up different lists of colonies, depending on the criteria selected. The most likely solution is a list including only colonies founded after Actium, on the grounds that earlier colonies were founded on the joint authority of the triumvirs (Keppie (1983) 76–7, 80–2; for different lists, see Mommsen (1883) 123; Gabba (1953) 109–10, Brunt (1971) 608–9; Carter (1982) 162). It seems likely that the programme of colonization after Actium was less contentious than that after Philippi. Colonies founded on the northern margins of Italy, notably at Augusta Praetoria Salassorum (Aosta), were military in character, designed to aid the pacification of recently conquered regions (see 26.3n. *Alpes*). The far south of Italy was the only area unaffected by colonization. In contrast to his foundation of colonies in the provinces, however, few of the colonies in Italy were new towns, but were existing municipalities to which a group of veterans was allocated as extra inhabitants (Keppie (1983) 1). Suetonius (*Aug.* 46.1) echoes Augustus' claim, and adds an analysis as to how Augustus took measures to enhance their prosperity and status.

RECOVERY OF MILITARY STANDARDS (29)

Every legion in the Roman army venerated its standards, principally its eagle (Jupiter's bird), which encapsulated the unit's sense of its own identity (Plin. *HN* 10.5.16). The eagle was made of silver or silver-gilt, and was housed in a chapel in the legionary headquarters along with the other standards (Dio Cass. 40.18.1). The eagle could act as a rallying point in battle (cf. Caes. *B Gall.* 4.25.3–5), might receive sacrifices after a victory (Joseph. *BJ* 6.316), and was anointed on holidays (Plin. *HN* 13.4.23). The anniversary day of the legion's foundation was celebrated as the *natalis aquilae*, the eagle's birthday. The loss of standards to the enemy was the ultimate disgrace for an army unit, which could result in the legion being disbanded (von Domaszewski (1895) 9–13; Watson (1969) 127–31).

29.1 signa militaria . . . reciperavi/I recovered several military standards It seems likely that in 29 BC M. Licinius Crassus regained standards lost to the Bastarnae by C. Antonius Hibrida in 62 BC (Dio Cass. 38.10.3, 51.26.5), but this is not mentioned here by Augustus. This probably reflects the fact that, as with his claim to *spolia opima* (see 19.2n. *Iovis Feretri*), Crassus' outstanding military successes were more of a challenge and embarassment to Augustus than ones which he could appropriate for himself.

ex Hispania et Gallia/from Spain and Gaul The occasions on which standards were lost and then recovered in Spain and Gaul are open to conjecture (Ridley (2003) 130). Standards may have been lost during an ambush in Spain in 39 BC (Dio Cass. 48.42.1), and then perhaps regained

Fig. 25 Long-haired bearded barbarian on his knees, holding out a military standard. *Denarius* issued at Rome 12 BC (coin: reverse, *RIC* I² 74 no. 416). © The Trustees of the British Museum.

during the Cantabrian wars. In Gaul, Augustus may have regained an eagle lost to the Eburones in 54 BC (Caes. *B Gall.* 5.37.4–7). *Denarii* issued at Rome in 12 BC depict on their reverse a long-haired bearded barbarian on his knees, holding out a military standard; these perhaps relate to the recovery of standards from Gaul (*BM Coins, Rom. Emp.* I 27, nos. 127–30; *RIC* I² 74 no. 416; Simon (1993) 121 no. 79)(see Figure 25).

a Dalmateis/from the Dalmatians   In 35/34 BC, Augustus recovered the military standards lost by A. Gabinius in 48 BC, and displayed them in the recently rebuilt *porticus Octavia* (see 19.1n. **porticum . . . Octaviam**; App. *Ill.* 3.12, 5.25, 5.28).

29.2 Parthos trium exercituum Romanorum spolia et signa reddere/the Parthians to give back to me spoils and standards of three Roman armies   The first disastrous defeat for the Romans at the hands of the Parthians was that of Crassus at Carrhae in 53 BC. Antony had subsequently attempted to retrieve the standards and prisoners seized by the Parthians from Crassus (Dio Cass. 49.24.5; Plut. *Vit. Ant.* 37.2, 40.6), but his legates were twice defeated, losing their standards too – L. Decidius Saxa in 40 BC (Dio Cass. 48.25), and Oppius Statianus in 36 BC (Plut. *Vit. Ant.* 38.5–6). Julius Caesar had intended to campaign against Parthia, but his plans were thwarted by his assassination (Dio Cass. 44.15.3–4; Suet. *Iul.* 79.3–80.1). The desire to escape the shame of Crassus' defeat in particular by recovering the standards was a theme in contemporary literature (cf. Prop. 3.4 = LACTOR G30; Hor. *Carm.* 3.5.2–12 = LACTOR G27) until in 20 BC Augustus recovered them by diplomacy (Suet. *Aug.* 21.3). He did so by a combination of good luck and effective posturing. The pretender to the Parthian throne, Tiridates II (see 32.1n. **Tiridates**), had kidnapped the son of the Parthian king Phraates IV, and delivered him into the hands of Augustus. In response to an embassy from Phraates IV, Augustus sent back this son in 23 BC, on condition that in exchange the Roman standards and prisoners should be returned by Phraates (Dio Cass. 53.33.1–2). Augustus then travelled to the east in 22 BC, and his presence, combined with that of Tiberius' army in neighbouring Armenia, where Tiberius was installing a new king (see 27.2n. **Tigrani, regis Artavasdis filio**), combined to persuade Phraates to complete his side of the bargain (Dio Cass. 54.8.1). All this took place against the background of Tiridates' potentially disruptive presence in Syria, with Augustus not promoting his claim to the Parthian kingship, but not quashing it either (Dio Cass. 51.18.2–3; Just. *Epit.* 42.5.6–12). Furthermore, if the interpretation is correct that Aelius Gallus' Arabian expedition had Parthia as its ultimate aim (Marek (1993); see 26.5n. **in Arabiam quae appellatur Eudaemon**), Phraates IV may have had good reason to fear Roman military intervention in the region (Sherwin-White (1984) 322–3; Campbell (1993) 220–3).

The recovery of the standards from the Parthians was widely celebrated in poetry (e.g. Ov. *Fast.* 5.579–96 = LACTOR K18, 6.465–8 = LACTOR N41; Prop. 4.6.79–84 = LACTOR G39; Hor. *Carm.* 4.15.6–8 = LACTOR G45), on coinage, and by monuments (Zanker (1988) 186–92; Galinsky (1996) 155–64; Rose (2005)). The famous Prima Porta statue of Augustus has a scene of the handing over of a Roman eagle standard by a barbarian to a Roman military officer in the centre of the cuirass (van der Vin (1981) 120–1) (see Figure 26). Horace's description of Phraates as submitting to Augustus on bended knee (*ius imperiumque Phraates / Caesaris accepit genibus minor.* Epist. 1.12.27–8 = LACTOR G34, written late 20 BC) was an image which was repeated on coins, and must have represented an officially approved view of the transaction (cf. the image evoked by Augustus' own words, *supplicesque amicitiam populi Romani petere coegi*). Coins issued from the Pergamum mint in 20/19 BC proclaim 'Parthian standards recovered', SIGNIS PARTHICIS RECEPTIS (*BM Coins, Rom. Emp.* I 110 nos. 679–81; cf. *RIC* I² 83 nos. 521–6; Simon (1993) 124 nos. 80–1), whilst coins minted at Rome in 18 BC depict a kneeling Parthian offering up a standard (*BM Coins, Rom. Emp.* I 3–4 nos. 10–17, 8 nos. 40–2, 11 nos. 56–9 = *RIC* I² 62 no. 287–9, 63 nos. 304–5, 64 nos. 314–15; Simon (1993) 124–5 nos. 82a–f; LACTOR N42) (see Figure 27). Military standards appeared on many coins minted in Rome, Asia Minor, Spain, Gaul, and Italy, probably during 19/18 BC (van der Vin (1981) 121–30; *BM Coins, Rom. Emp.* I 60 no. 332, 67–8 nos. 384–90, 71–3 nos. 410–25, 73–4 nos. 427–9, 114 no. 703 = *RIC* I² 44 no. 41, 46 no. 58, no. 60, 47 nos. 80–7, 48–9 nos. 103–21, 50 nos. 131–7, 82 nos. 508–10; Simon (1993) 125–9

Fig. 26 Cuirass of Prima Porta statue of Augustus.

nos. 84–95). Finally, the Parthian 'victory' may have been commemorated by modifications to the Actian arch in the Roman forum (see Rich (1998) 106–15).

in penetrali/in the innermost sanctum The standards would therefore have been placed next to the god's cult statue (Kockel (1995) 291).

in templo Martis Ultoris/in the temple of Mars the Avenger The standards were deposited in the temple of Mars the Avenger in the Augustan forum in 2 BC (see 21.1n *Martis Ultoris templum*); it is unclear where they were kept during the interim, but they were perhaps simply stored in another temple, possibly that of Jupiter Feretrius (cf. Hor. *Carm.* 4.15.6). The evidence of Dio Cassius (54.8.3) and some coins (minted in Spain) depicting a circular structure housing standards and labelled MARTIS VLTORIS has sometimes been used to support the proposition that a small shrine to Mars the Avenger was built on the Capitol to house the

Fig. 27 Standards recovered from the Parthians. *Denarius*, 18 BC (coin: LACTOR N42).

Fig. 28 Temple of Mars the Avenger. *Aureus, c.* 18 BC (coin: reverse, *RIC* I² 43 no. 28 = LACTOR K19).

standards recovered from the Parthians until the grand new temple to the god was completed in Augustus' new forum (see Figure 28) (Zanker (1988) 186–7; coins: *BM Coins, Rom. Emp.* I 58 no. 315, 60 no. 329, 65–6 nos. 366–75; Simon (1993) 128 no. 93; *RIC* I² 43 no. 28, 44 no. 39a, 46–7 nos. 68–74. Cf. Simon (1993) 127 no. 88, 129 no. 94; *BM Coins, Rom. Emp.* I 66 nos. 371–5, 67–8 nos. 384–9, 114 no. 704 (this last minted in Ephesus, otherwise all Spain); *RIC* I² 48 nos. 103–6, 49 nos. 114–17, 82 no. 507 (Pergamum)). It is unlikely, however, that this smaller shrine was ever actually constructed (Simpson (1977); Rich (1998) 79–97).

CONTROL OF THE DANUBE LANDS (30)

This chapter follows on from Augustus' reference to the recapture of standards from the Dalmatians (29.1), showing how his early success in the region was further consolidated.

30.1 Pannoniorum gentes/The Pannonian peoples   The area of the Balkans occupied by the Pannonian peoples was regarded as the dividing point between east and west, and was strategically important in buffering Italy against incursions by northern barbarians. It was in Rome's interests to control the overland route through the Danube region leading from Italy to the Greek east, the Pontic region, and beyond (Wilkes (1996) 545). As Syme memorably described it, this route linked Rome with Thessaloniki and Istanbul, via Zagreb and Belgrade, along the line of the Simplon–Orient Express (Syme (1971) 14).

ante me principem/before I became leader   This vague phrase (see 13n. *me principe*) allows for the implicit inclusion of Augustus' own earlier campaigns in Dalmatia in 35/34 BC, for which he celebrated a triumph (App. *Ill.* 3.15–5.28; Dio Cass. 49.36.1–2, 37; see 4.1n. *tris egi curulis triumphos*; 29.1n. *a Dalmateis*). These prepared the way for Tiberius' subjugation of the Pannonians (Scheid (2007) 78). The claim that he subdued 'Pannonian peoples, which before I became leader no army of the Roman people ever approached' remains rather contentious, however, given that it involves ignoring the achievements of L. Scipio, who conquered the Scordisci near the Danube in the late 80s BC (App. *Ill.* 1.5, unless the name L. Scipio is here a corruption of C. Curio – Kallet-Marx (1995) 361–4) and of C. Scribonius Curio, who reached the Danube in 75 BC and celebrated a triumph for his achievement in *c.* 72 BC (Eutr. 6.2.2; *Inscr. Ital.* XIII.i 564). Augustus showed a similar tendency in his autobiography to ignore successes of earlier Romans in this region, according to Appian (App. *Ill.* 3.15; Ridley (2003) 217). The accuracy of this claim can perhaps be salvaged, however, by making a clear distinction between the Pannonians in the interior between the rivers Save and Drave and Dalmatians in the coastal areas. Alternatively, the newly encountered peoples could be tribes futher to the south, beyond the river Save, such as the Mazaei, Ditiones, and Daesitiates (Syme (1971) 19–21; Wilkes (1969) 56, 65).

devictas per Ti. Neronem/once they were subdued through the agency of Tiberius Nero   Tiberius campaigned against the Pannonians during 12–9 BC, as a result of which he received triumphal honours (*ornamenta triumphalia*) and later an ovation and title of *imperator* (Dio Cass. 54.31.2–4, 55.2.4; Vell. Pat. 2.39.3, 96.2–3). His actions resulted in imperatorial salutations for Augustus in 12 and 10 BC (see 4.1n. *appellatus* *sum viciens et semel imperator*). Dio Cassius (54.34.3–4) is mistaken in presenting these campaigns as mere suppression of revolts, misled by the assumption that Augustus' earlier campaigns in the area in 35–33 BC had advanced further than they had. Tiberius' campaigns advanced Roman control considerably in the region to the south of the Danube, conquering the Breuci in the Save valley with the help of the Scordisci (Dio Cass. 54.31.3; Suet. *Tib.* 9.2; see 30.1n. **protulique fines Illyrici ad ripam fluminis Danuvi**; Wilkes (1969) 63–6; Syme (1971) 18–22; Rich (1990) 210; Scheid (2007) 78–9).

The fact that Augustus does not mention the revolt of Dalmatia and Pannonia in AD 6–9, which was suppressed by Tiberius, does create a misleading impression of the finality of the Pannonians' subjugation, but is not relevant to the date at which the *RGDA* was composed: it is quite reasonable for Augustus' account of his greatest achievements to include reference to the initial conquest of an area without also recounting its later revolt and reconquest (contra Brunt and Moore (1967) 73). He also does not mention the campaign by Sex. Appuleius in 8 BC, which probably completed the initial conquest of the Pannonians (Wilkes (1969) 66; Cassiod. *Chronicon*, ed. Migne (1865) col. 1227).

qui tum erat privignus et legatus meus/who at that time was my stepson and deputy The addition of this clause directs the reader away from assuming that Augustus is referring to Tiberius' suppression of the Pannonian revolt in AD 6–9, towards his initial conquest of the region in 12–9 BC, since Tiberius was adopted by Augustus in AD 4 (Ridley (2003) 85–8).

imperio populi Romani subieci/I made subject to the rule of the Roman people On the translation of *imperium* by the Greek word ἡγεμονία see 26.1, 27.1, introduction p. 27.

protulique fines Illyrici ad ripam fluminis Danuvi/I advanced the boundary of Illyricum to the bank of the river Danube In 12 BC Tiberius had advanced along the Save and Drave valleys to the Danube, with help from the Scordisci (see 30.1n. **devictas per Ti. Neronem**; Wilkes (1969) 65). During the revolt of AD 6–9 Tiberius had to reconsolidate the areas which he had initially conquered during 12–9 BC (Suet. *Tib.* 16–17). For this he was awarded a triumph, but he postponed celebrating it until AD 12, not wishing to celebrate a triumph so soon after the Varus disaster (Vell. Pat. 2.121.2; *Fasti Praen.* 23 Oct. – *Ti. Caesar curru triumphavit ex Ilurico* – *Inscr. Ital.* XIII.ii 135; disputed entry 16 Jan. – *Ti. Caesar ex Pa[nnonia . . . .]vit* – *Inscr. Ital.* XIII.ii 115, 399–400). Despite mentioning the *fines Illyrici*, it was not Augustus' intention to establish the Danube as a frontier for Rome's empire (Whittaker (2000) 301). This becomes clear in the very next section (30.2), where Augustus celebrates the fact that the army crossed the Danube and subdued Dacians beyond it. At some point soon after AD 9 Illyricum was subdivided into the two provinces of Dalmatia and Pannonia (Wilkes (1969) 46).

30.2 Dacorum transgressus exercitus/An army of Dacians which crossed over The Greek version translates *exercitus* as δύναμις rather than στράτευμα in order to distinguish the Dacian from the Roman army (Wigtil (1982a) 633). Incursions by Dacians upon Pannonia in 11 BC had resulted in the postponement of the senate's plan to shut the gates of Janus (Dio Cass. 54.36.2; see 13n. *ter . . . senatus claudendum esse censuit*), and later too, in AD 6, Dacians joined with Sarmatians in making incursions upon Moesia, eliciting action from Caecina Severus (Dio Cass. 55.30.4).

exercitus meus/my army Although arguably the result of the context, at least in part, with the need to distinguish the *exercitus* of Dacians from the *exercitus* of Romans, this phrase lays bare Augustus' appropriation of the army, recalling his reference to 'my fleet' (26.4). The Greek version retains the possessive adjective, despite already having made a clear distinction between Dacian δύναμις and Roman στράτευμα (see 30.2n. *Dacorum transgressus exercitus*).

Dacorum gentes imperia populi Romani perferre coegit/compelled the Dacian peoples to endure the commands of the Roman people Augustus does not claim to have conquered the Dacians, a cautious assessment which is reflected in other sources too (contra Ridley (2003) 217–18). The word *imperium* is translated only here as προστάγματα, and arguably implies a less comprehensive form of control than if it had been translated as ἡγεμονία (introduction p. 27). According to Strabo, the Dacians had come 'close to obeying' the Romans, but had not become completely submissive (*Geography* 7.3.13). Florus' account (2.28) of an expedition by Cn. Cornelius Lentulus Augur (*PIR²* C1379), in which he pushed back Dacians who had crossed over the Danube from the north, chimes in with what Augustus states here (Rich (1990) 201, 216–17; Syme (1971) 40–61, (1986) 287–92, very cautiously at 291 n. 65). So too does Suetonius' statement that Augustus checked Dacian incursions (*Aug.* 21.1 – *coercuit et Dacorum incursiones*). The date of Lentulus' expedition is unclear, possibly falling some time during the period 6 BC to AD 4. Florus states specifically that the Dacians were not subdued (*sic tum Dacia non victa*), but were pushed back across the river. Aelius Catus (*PIR²* A157) also shifted 50,000 Dacians from their lands beyond the Danube into Thrace/Lower Moesia, where they assumed a new identity as 'Moesians' (Strabo *Geography* 7.3.10). In claiming to have imposed his will upon the Dacians, Augustus implicitly betters the record of Julius Caesar, who only got as far as planning a campaign against the Dacians and Parthians when he was assassinated (Suet. *Iul.*

44.3, *Aug.* 8.2; App. *B Civ.* 2.16.110). The Dacians were finally subdued by Trajan's two Dacian campaigns in the early second century AD.

DIPLOMATIC SUCCESSES (31–3)

These chapters demonstrate how Rome exerted its influence well beyond the areas which it ruled directly, and illustrate how peaceful diplomacy had an important part to play in winning friends for Rome. The distinction between a request for friendship and submission through conquest was not always clearly preserved in the popular imagination, and Augustan poets allude to some of these peoples as if they had actually been conquered (cf. Hor. *Carm.* 3.8.23–4, Scythians). The theme of extending influence through friendship as well as through conquest provides another echo of Euhemerus' Zeus, supporting the view that the *RGDA* promoted the idea that Augustus deserved deification (Bosworth (1999); see introduction p. 41). Chapter 31 deals with embassies sent from faraway lands, chapter 32 with royal fugitives and hostages seeking protection from Rome, and chapter 33 with Rome's imposition of rulers upon foreign kingdoms. These chapters are liberally peppered with exotic geographical and personal names, as Augustus deliberately hops from one side of the world to another and back again, consolidating the impression created so far of the worldwide influence now exerted by Rome under his leadership (Nenci (1958) 299). Indians and Scythians were depicted in contemporary poetry as the archetypes of exotic peoples from the furthest east and north beyond Rome's sway, and Augustus derived a great deal of kudos from their embassies in particular (Virg. *G.* 2.170–2 = LACTOR G10, *Aen.* 6.791–5 = LACTOR G37; Hor. *Carm. Saec.* 55–6 = LACTOR L28, *Carm.* 4.14.41–4 = LACTOR G44). Several of the peoples listed here – Bastarnae, Scythians, Albanians, Hiberians – overlap with those listed by Pompey in an inscription celebrating his triumphs (Plin. *HN* 7.26.97–8), as Augustus invites a favourable assessment of his influence throughout the world in comparison with Pompey's conquests.

31.1 ad me ex India/to me from India　These opening words start off a sequence of anaphora, with the repetition of *ad me* (31.1, 32.1, 32.2), ending with *a me* (33), making the relationship between foreign potentates and Rome an emphatically personal one between themselves and Augustus himself (rather than the senate or people of Rome). By starting with the example of India, Augustus evokes the achievements of Alexander the Great, whose most celebrated conquest was India.

legationes saepe missae sunt/Embassies were often sent　The statement that embassies were often sent from India is probably an exaggeration: two embassies are known to have travelled great distances in order to meet

with Augustus, one to Tarraco in 25 BC (Oros. 6.21.19–20 = LACTOR
N39), the other to Samos in 20 BC (Dio Cass. 54.9.8–10). The first of these
was perhaps prompted by the Roman expedition into Arabia in 26/25 BC
(see 26.5; Sidebotham (1986) 602). Orosius makes explicit what remains
unstated by Augustus, namely the way in which he could be considered to
have emulated and even surpassed Alexander the Great: whereas Alexander
received embassies from the furthest west when he was in the east, the
opposite is true of Augustus, who was tracked down by an embassy from
the east (India) when he was at the western edge of the known world
(Tarraco). It is likely that Augustus is seeking to rival Alexander in his
presentation of the facts here (Nenci (1958) 296–8). Some detail is known
regarding the second embassy from Strabo: firstly, he mentions that an
embassy from King Pandion/Porus brought gifts to Augustus (*Geography*
15.1.4), and later he cites the evidence of Nicolaus of Damascus, who met
the Indian envoys at Antioch on their way to Augustus, and saw a letter
written in Greek from King Porus seeking friendship with Augustus and
offering safe passage through his country, as well as exotic curiosities being
taken as gifts for him, including huge snakes, a large turtle, and a man born
without arms (*Geography* 15.1.72–3 = LACTOR N40). The possibility of a
third embassy from India in 11 BC has been suggested, given the display at
Rome in that year of a tiger, a species of unimpeachable Indian origins, first
seen by the Romans only in 20 BC, when the Indian embassy brought tigers
as gifts (Sidebotham (1986) 601, with Plin. *HN* 8.25.65; Dio Cass. 54.9.8).
Embassies from India occurred against the background of trading contacts between southern India and Rome via the Red Sea, with pepper and
spices, perfumes, pearls and precious gems, ivory, and even parrots being
exported from India in exchange for Roman silver and gold coins, and
luxuries such as ornate glassware (Thorley (1969) 219–23; Raschke (1978)
650–76). Silk from China even made its way to Rome via north-west India
(Raschke (1978) 630–7). Such trade had begun during the Republic but
particularly flourished under Augustus, who inherited the contacts with
India developed by Ptolemaic Egypt (Schmitthenner (1979) 94–5, 103–6;
Thorley (1969) 209–13).

**non visae ante id tempus apud quemquam Romanorum ducem/such
as have not ever been seen before this time in the presence of any
Roman general**   By tacking this phrase onto the end of the sentence after
the main verb, Augustus further emphasizes the unparalleled nature of his
achievement. The motif of the approach of previously unknown peoples
is also found in accounts of embassies to Alexander the Great (Diod. Sic.
17.113.2, Gauls; Arr. *Anab.* 7.15.4; Nenci (1958) 304). Augustus' claim here
that embassies from India had never previously been seen becomes rather
garbled in later sources, apparently paraphrasing the *RGDA*, who claim
that Indians and Scythians had never before been seen by Romans (Suet.

Aug. 21.3 – *auditu modo cognitos*, with Carter (1982) ad loc.; Eutrop. 7.10 – *quibus antea Romanorum nomen incognitum fuerat*).

31.2 nostram amicitiam/our friendship This phrase reflects the centrality of Augustus to acts of diplomacy between Rome and distant kings, and is repeated in the next chapter, when referring to his dealings with the Parthian king (32.2 – *amicitiam nostram*). Presumably 'our' really means Augustus and the Roman people, as clearly spelled out earlier in the phrase 'my friendship and that of the Roman people' (*amicitiam meam et populi Romani*, 26.4; Braunert (1975) 46–7), and echoed in the formula used by Suetonius when mentioning the same embassies (*Aug.* 21.3, *pellexit ad amicitiam suam populique Rom. ultro per legatos petendam*). It contrasts with his account of the return of the standards by the Parthians, who are described as having sued for friendship with the Roman people (29.2).

Bastarnae Scythaeque et Sarmatarum qui sunt citra flumen Tanaim et ultra reges, Albanorumque rex et Hiberorum et Medorum/The Bastarnae and the Scythians, and kings of the Sarmatae who are on both sides of the river Don, and the king of the Albanians and of the Hiberians and of the Medes This list of distant peoples takes us across the Danube towards the Black Sea and beyond, as far east as the Caspian Sea. The Bastarnae, who inhabited the region above the mouth of the Danube, were defeated by Licinius Crassus in 29 BC after they had attacked Thracians who were allies of Rome (Dio Cass. 51.23.2–27.3; see 19.2n. ***Iovis Feretri***). Scythians from the area between the rivers Danube and Don sent envoys in 25 BC to Augustus at Tarraco (Oros. 6.21.19–20 = LACTOR N39). The Sarmatians dwelt further east on both banks of the Tanais (Don), which was thought to mark the boundary between Europe and Asia (Strabo *Geography* 2.5.31; Plin. *HN* 6.7.19, 8.24; cf. Hor. *Carm.* 3.10.1; see also 30.2n. ***Dacorum transgressus exercitus*** for their incursions upon Moesia). Beyond the eastern shores of the Black Sea lived the Hiberians in the area of modern Georgia, whilst the Albanians lived on the western shores of the Caspian Sea, to the north of Media Atropatene, in the area of modern Azerbaijan and Daghestan. Since their defeat by P. Canidius Crassus in 36 BC, the Hiberians had become subject-allies of Rome (Dio Cass. 49.24.1; Strabo *Geography* 6.4.2). For the Medes, neighbours of Armenia, modern Azerbaijan, see further 32.1–2, 33. The Greek version makes a mistake in translation, not realizing that *ultra* belongs with *Sarmatarum* (Reichmann (1943) 23). It is perhaps surprising that Augustus omits to mention the Chinese (*Seres*) anywhere in this chapter, even though they obviously belong to a different geographical region, if Florus is correct in including them in his list of the peoples who sued for friendship with Augustus (2.34.62; cf. Hor. *Carm.* 1.12.56, 4.15.23).

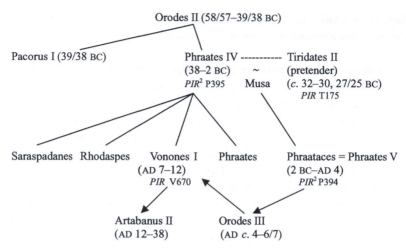

Fig. 29 Parthia: Arsacid royal succession. (Cf. Sullivan (1990) stemma no. 10.)

32.1 Tiridates/Tiridates   Tiridates II (*PIR* T175) laid claim to the throne of Parthia when Phraates IV had been driven out by his subjects in *c.* 32 BC, but then took refuge with Augustus in 30/29 BC (helpfully bringing with him the kidnapped son of his rival), after the deposed king regained his throne. In 27/26 BC he minted tetradrachms at Seleucia depicting himself as 'friend of the Romans', ΦΙΛΟΡΟΜΑΙΟΣ (*sic*), alongside more traditional Parthian titles: 'Of the king of kings, Arsaces, the beneficent, autocrat, friend of the Romans, (god) manifest, philhellene' (ΒΑΣΙΛΕΩΣ ΒΑΣΙΛΕΩΝ ΑΡΣΑΚΟΥ ΕΥΕΡΓΕΤΟΥ ΑΥΤΟΚΡΑΤΟΡ ΦΙΛΟΡΟΜΑΙΟ ΕΠΙΦΑΝΟΥΣ ΦΙΛΕΛΛΗΝΟΣ – Sellwood (1983) 292; Timpe (1975) 155–7). He then fled to Augustus for a second time in 26/25 BC (Dio Cass. 53.33.1, with Timpe (1975) 158–9, noting the conflation of two separate episodes in Justin's epitome), but Augustus avoided giving him open support. He did not hand him over to Phraates IV either, keeping him in nearby Syria, and the unstated threat from Rome that it might support Tiridates proved a useful bargaining tool in regaining the standards captured by the Parthians (Dio Cass. 51.18.2–3; Just. *Epit.* 42.5.6–12; see 29.2n. ***Parthos trium exercituum Romanorum spolia et signa reddere***). He disappears from the historical record once the affair of the standards is settled (Bivar (1983) 65–6; Sherwin-White (1984) 322–3).

Phrates regis Phratis filius/Phrates, son of king Phrates   The identity of this Phrates is unclear, but he may well be Phraates V (also known as Phraataces) (*PIR*[2] P394; discussed by Timpe (1975) 157–8), who was the son of Phraates IV and an Italian slave given to him by Augustus, Musa (Joseph. *AJ* 18.4.40). He ruled Parthia with his mother until AD 4 when he was deposed and fled to the Romans in Syria, and soon died in exile (Bivar (1983) 67–8; see 32.2n. ***Phrates***).

Medorum Artavasdes/Artavasdes king of the Medes   Artavasdes I (*PIR²* A1162), king of Media Atropatene (see Figure 23) had been an ally of Antony, with whose support he had made inroads upon the kingdom of Armenia under Artaxes II. In the aftermath of Actium, however, Artaxes II began to resume control of Greater Armenia with Parthian support (Dio Cass. 49.44.1–4; Sullivan (1990) 290, 298), and expelled Artavasdes, who took refuge with Octavian, was made king of Armenia Minor, and died in 20 BC (Dio Cass. 51.16.2, 54.9.2).

Adiabenorum Artaxares/Artaxares of the Adiabenians   The Adiabenians inhabited a region of northern Mesopotamia (Strabo *Geography* 16.1.19); this king is otherwise unknown.

Britannorum Dumnobellaunus et Tincomarus/Dumnobellaunus and Tincomarus of the Britons   Dumnobellaunus (also known as Dubnovellaunus) was king of the Trinovantes tribe, whose capital was at Camulodunum (Colchester), towards the end of the first century BC (Creighton (2000) 75). Tincomarus was king of the Atrebates to the south of the Thames in the area of modern Hampshire in the last decades of the first century BC. Until recently, his name was restored as Tin[commius], but new specimens of his coinage from the Alton hoard (Hampshire) now reveal his name in full (Cheesman (1998)). British chieftains sent embassies to Rome, where they made offerings on the Capitol, and paid high duties on goods imported and exported between Britain and northern Europe (Strabo *Geography* 4.5.3). There had been trading links with south-central England since the late second century BC. Coinage issued by some late Iron Age chieftains in southern England, notably Tincomarus, breaks from previous tradition in its use of Latin and style of writing, and in its choice of imagery. In this way, they bolstered their own authority by associating themselves with the power of Rome (Williams (2002) 136–7, 143–8; cf. Creighton (2000) 101–6 whose assumption that Tincomarus had been a hostage in Rome is unlikely, however). It is unclear whether or not Augustus made plans for an invasion of the island – various abortive campaigns are mentioned for 34, 27, and 26 BC (Dio Cass. 49.38.2, 53.22.5, 53.25.2) – but contemporary poets in works published up until about 23 BC reflect the expectation that he would launch a campaign in this furthest part of the world, beyond even Ocean itself (Virg. *G.* 3.25 = LACTOR G11; Prop. 2.27.5; Hor. *Carm.* 1.21.14–16, 1.35.29–30, 3.5.2–4 = LACTOR G27; Momigliano (1950) 39). Following the invasion by Julius Caesar in 54 BC, Britons had agreed to pay indemnities, but these had soon lapsed. Nevertheless, given the obeisance to Rome being offered by British chieftains attested by Strabo, Augustus may well have considered such an expedition not worth the expense and risk (Brunt (1990) 103–4).

Sugambrorum/of the Sugambri Augustus' brief reference to this king conceals a number of episodes that coloured dealings between the Sugambri and Romans. Under their leader Maelo (*PIR*² M65), the Sugambri on the right bank of the Rhine had defeated M. Lollius in 16 BC, with the loss of an eagle-standard (Dio Cass. 54.20.4–6; Strabo *Geography* 7.1.4; Suet. *Aug.* 23.1). Their territory was then invaded by Drusus in 12 BC (Vell. Pat. 2.97; Dio Cass. 54.32–3), and campaigns by Tiberius in 8 BC prompted them to send envoys to Augustus, which is presumably what Augustus is referring to here. On being arrested, these envoys then committed suicide (Dio Cass. 55.6.2–3). Vast numbers of the Sugambri were subsequently transported into Gaul (Suet. *Aug.* 21.1).

Marcomanorum Sueborum/of the Suebic Marcomanni The Marcomanni were a branch of the Suebi, a group of German peoples living in the area around the rivers Elbe and Main (Tac. *Germ.* 38, 42), who moved to Bohemia under pressure of campaigning by Drusus in *c.* 9/8 BC, and established a powerful kingdom there (Vell. Pat. 2.108; Dio Cass. 55.1.2; Tac. *Ann.* 2.62–3). The name of the king is not fully preserved on any of the inscriptions: only the letters -ros can be read in the Greek version at Ancyra.

32.2 Phrates/Phraates In about 10 BC (Syme (1978) 55), Phraates IV (*PIR*² P395, see Figure 29) entrusted to Augustus' custody his four legitimate sons (Saraspadanes, Rhodaspes, Vonones, and Phraates) and their families as hostages (Strabo *Geography* 6.4.2, 16.1.28 = LACTOR N44). His reasons for doing so were probably not quite as Augustus describes. In reality, distrustful of the loyalty of his own people (Tac. *Ann.* 2.1.2 = LACTOR N43), Phraates probably wanted the distant detention of these sons to remove potential foci of disaffection so as to secure the throne for himself in the first instance, and for his bastard son thereafter. Augustus' detention of his sons would have prevented them from ousting Phraates IV from his throne, in time-honoured tradition among the Parthians: Phraates IV himself, for example, had killed his own father Orodes II (Just. *Epit.* 42.4.16–5.1). He was also probably acting under pressure from his Italian concubine-turned-wife Musa, who was ambitious for her son to succeed to the throne (Joseph. *AJ* 18.4.39–42; see 32.1n. ***Phrates regis Phratis filius***). This son did in fact do so, as Phraates V, by murdering his father in *c.* 2 BC, taking advantage of the fact that the other sons were absent in Rome, and he assumed joint rule with his mother. The promise that his half-brothers would remain in Rome provided Augustus with a useful bargaining tool in persuading Phraates V not to interfere in Armenia in AD 1, when Gaius Caesar was attempting to impose a solution on that kingdom. Previously,

Phraates V had caused Rome some difficulties by supporting Tigranes IV and Erato in Armenia instead of Rome's nominee Artavasdes III (see 27.2n. ***eandem gentem postea desciscentem et rebellantem domitam per Gaium filium meum***; Brunt (1990) 462–4). Augustus made a point of displaying these hostages to the people of Rome at a show by leading them prominently to their seats near his own (Suet. *Aug.* 43.4). They were incorporated into the imperial court and were educated alongside Augustus' family and other foreign princes (Suet. *Aug.* 48.1): Augustus here refers to them as *pignora* ('pledges') rather than as *obsides* ('hostages'), giving a positive gloss to the fact that they were actually in detention at Rome, and could not return to Parthia without his consent (Nedergaard (1988) 108–9). Saraspadanes and Rhodaspes eventually died in Rome, as shown by an inscribed epitaph there (*ILS* 842 = EJ no. 183), but Vonones returned to rule as Augustus' nominee to the Parthian throne (see 33n. ***Vononem***).

32.3 plurimaeque aliae gentes/very many other peoples This is a very vague statement, and we can only hazard a guess at the peoples to whom Augustus is referring, such as the Cimbri who sent their sacred cauldron to Augustus (Strabo *Geography* 7.2.1, 3; see 26.4n. ***per legatos amicitiam meam et populi Romani petierunt***), and the Aethiopians, whose queen sent an embassy to Augustus on Samos suing for friendship in 21/20 BC in the wake of the expedition of P. Petronius (Strabo *Geography* 17.1.54 = LACTOR N34; see 26.5n. ***in Aethiopiam***).

33 gentes . . . reges/peoples . . . kings The syntax is inverted in the Greek version, with *gentes* (nominative case) becoming ἔθνη (accusative), and *reges* (accusative) becoming βασιλεῖς (nominative). Consequently, whereas in the Latin version people receive kings assigned to them by Augustus, in the Greek version the kings receive the people assigned to them. This is perhaps indicative of a different political outlook between the Greek east and Rome (Vanotti (1975) 320).

Vononem/Vonones After Phraates V (see 32.2n. ***Phrates***) was deposed in AD 4 (Joseph. *AJ* 18.2.4), the Parthians sent an embassy to Rome in order to ask Augustus to send back Vonones (*PIR* V670: see stemma of Arsacids, Figure 29), son of Phraates IV, as his successor (Strabo *Geography* 6.4.2; Joseph. *AJ* 18.2.4). He had spent many years in Rome as a hostage, and had been educated according to a Roman lifestyle. He too was deposed because of his Roman outlook, becoming instead king of Greater Armenia in AD *c*. 12 (Tac. *Ann.* 2.1–4; see 27.2n. ***Tigranem qui erat ex regio genere Armeniorum oriundus***). By AD *c*. 15, however, he fled to Syria, where he was imprisoned by the Roman governor.

Ariobarzanem, regis Artavazdis filium/Ariobarzanes, son of King Artavazdes Ariobarzanes (*PIR*² A1044) had been installed as king of Media Atropatene by Augustus in 20 BC, when he freed Media from Armenian rule (Bedoukian (1978) 30; see 27.2n. *regi Ariobarzani, regis Medorum Artabazi filio*, where Artabazi is a variant on Artavazdis). The same man was later installed as king of Greater Armenia, in *c.* AD 1 (see stemma for Media Atropatene, Figure 23).

THE PRE-EMINENCE OF AUGUSTUS (34–5)

These last two chapters invite contrasts and comparisons with the opening chapters of the *RGDA*. Between them, these chapters explicitly record Augustus' age at the start and end of his career. The virtues celebrated on the shield (*clupeus*), the award of which is recorded in chapter 34, are illustrated by actions recorded in the opening lines of the inscription: his treatment of the 'liberators' shows his *pietas* and *iustitia* (2), his attitude towards foreign peoples his *clementia* (3.1–2). His *virtus* emerges from the whole of chapters 1–3 (Hoben (1978) 1–8).

Chapter 34 is one of the most discussed of the whole inscription, but the recent publication of a new fragment from Pisidian Antioch renders much of the earlier analysis obsolete. Perhaps the most useful comment is by W. K. Lacey ((1996) 98), who observes that chapter 34 'is not a political or constitutional statement at all, but the capstone of Augustus' achievement', an account of his most distinguished honours which then culminates in chapter 35, which describes how Augustus has received the ultimate accolade of being named *pater patriae*.

34.1 in consulatu sexto et septimo/In my sixth and seventh consulships It is crucial to note that Augustus starts off his account by referring to a period of two years, 28–27 BC. What he describes with the words *rem publicam ex mea potestate in senatus populique Romani arbitrium transtuli* ('I transferred the state from my power into the control of the Roman senate and people'), therefore, was a process that took place gradually over an extended period of time (see 34.1n. *rem publicam . . . transtuli*).

postquam bella civilia exstinxeram/after I had put an end to civil wars Augustus' ending in 30 BC of a sequence of civil wars that had lasted more or less continuously for several decades, ever since the conflict between Sulla and Marius, was one of the most important factors in winning him public support. Poetry shows how desperately Italians longed for peace during the 30s BC (e.g. Hor. *Epod.* 7 = LACTOR G3, *Epod.* 16; Virg. *G.* 1.498–514 = LACTOR G9), and how gladly they welcomed its advent after the final defeat of Antony and Cleopatra (e.g. Hor. *Epod.* 9 = LACTOR G5, *Carm.* 1.37; Virg. *Aen.* 6.791–806 = LACTOR G37, 8.671–728 =

LACTOR G38). The extinguishing of civil wars by Augustus continued to be celebrated even under Tiberius, as shown by a decree produced by the senate in AD 20 alleging that Calpurnius Piso had attempted to stir up civil war ('He also tried to stir up civil war, though all the evils of civil war had long been buried by the divine nature of deified Augustus and by the virtues of Ti. Caesar Augustus' – *bellum etiam civile excitare conatus sit, iam pridem numine divi Aug(usti) virtutibusq(ue) Ti. Caesaris Aug(usti) omnibus civilis belli sepultis malis*, SCPP 45–7; Eck *et al.* (1996) 42), and by the echoing of such official language in Velleius (Vell. Pat. 2.89.2–3 = LACTOR E89.2–3). By clearly referring to the period after the battle at Actium and the capture of Alexandria, Augustus is acknowledging that his war against Antony was in reality a civil war, despite its representation at the time as being a conflict against the foreign power of Cleopatra (see 3.1n. **bella . . . civilia externaque**).

per consensum universorum potens rerum omnium/although by everyone's agreement I had power over everything Until the recent publication of a new inscribed fragment from Pisidian Antioch (Botteri (2003b); Lebek (2004); Drew-Bear and Scheid (2005) 233–6, foreshadowed by Krömer (1978)), this phrase was generally completed as *potitus rerum omnium*, following Mommsen's edition (1883) 144 (for a survey of previous interpretations, see Drew-Bear and Scheid (2005) 233–6; Ridley (2003) 220–7; Scheid (2007) 82–6). The new fragment reveals that Augustus is not making a claim about the way in which he came to acquire power, but is acknowledging the fact that he was in overall control of everything following the end of the civil wars (Botteri (2003b) 263). The word *per* should not be given a causal significance, but simply denotes the background circumstances ('un sens temporel concomitant', Drew-Bear and Scheid (2005) 236). This now reveals that the Greek version, ἐνκρατὴς γενόμενος, certainly has an aoristic meaning, equivalent to a present participle, rather than referring to something having happened in the past (Seyfarth (1957) 320–1). The punctuation adopted here results in the following sequence of events: the ending of the civil wars, having power over everything, transferring powers during 28–27 BC (cf. Botteri (2003b) 262; Drew-Bear and Scheid (2005) 233). By interpreting the participle *potens* as having a concessive meaning, we find that Augustus is making a claim that his transfer of powers was unexpected. The new text also resolves previous debate about whether *potiri* should signify 'take possession of' or 'be in possession of' (Seyfarth (1957) 311–18). In Tacitus' usage, the expression *rerum potiri* comes to denote the position of a *de facto* monarch, notably in his account of Tiberius' accession (*laetique interdum nuntii vulgabantur, donec provisis quae tempus monebat simul excessisse Augustum et rerum potiri Neronem fama eadem tulit*, Ann. 1.5.4 = LACTOR F5.4: 'optimistic reports were issued from time to time, until, with the

necessary preparations complete, the same rumour bore the news that
Augustus had died and that Nero was in charge'), where he perhaps deliberately echoes the *RGDA* for ironic effect, revealing that Tiberius immediately takes over Augustus' power, despite his ostensible hesitation in doing
so during the so-called 'accession debate' (Tac. *Ann.* 1.12–13 = LACTOR
F12–13).

The theme of universal consent was an important one in bolstering
Augustus' position, both initially and in later years (see 14.2; 35.1; cf. Vell.
Pat. 2.91.1). Under the Republic, the expression *consensus senatus* related to
a formal procedure, designating the 'opinion of the senate'. Augustus took
hold of this traditional expression and imbued it with a new significance
that transcended constitutional niceties (Instinsky (1940); Reinhold (2002)
63; Schäfer (1957) 325). The phrase had no legal significance; thus it is misleading to search for an explanation of Augustus' powers in constitutional
terms. He was the *de facto* leader after the end of the civil wars, but his
position as such was not made legitimate formally: as John Scheid ((2007)
86) comments, 'Le *consensus universorum* constituera l'un des fondements
du pouvoir impérial, et pour ainsi dire sa seule légitimité.' Indeed, his only
formal political office at this time was that of consul (Millar (1973) 62).
Instead, his control of affairs should be set against the background of the
outstanding honours decreed to him, and the many informal indications
of his supremacy (such as the way in which foreign embassies and client
kings sought out a meeting with him rather than with the senate). The
Greek translation, κατὰ τὰς εὐχάς, corresponds more closely to a picture
of informal acknowledgement of supremacy rather than to a formal voting
of powers (Instinsky (1940) 276–7).

rem publicam . . . transtuli/I transferred the state   Once we escape
from the assumption that Augustus is referring here to his 'restoration of
the Republic' on 13 January 27 BC (cf. Millar (1973) 63–7; Judge (1974)),
we can trace the way in which he 'transferred the state from my power
into the control of the Roman senate and people' gradually during the
course of 28–27 BC (cf. Vell. Pat. 2.89.3). In this context, the word *potestas* ('power') refers in a general way to the power wielded by Augustus
before 27 BC (contrast 34.3n. *auctoritate omnibus praestiti, potestatis
autem nihilo amplius habui* – Lintott (1999) 95 n. 5). Augustus did not
'restore the constitution of the Republic', but rather 'restored constitutional government' (Scheid (2007) 89). In a number of ways he aimed
to distance himself from his triumviral past. In 28 BC he annulled by
decree the illegal and unjust measures which the triumvirs had introduced
(Dio Cass. 53.2.5; Tac. *Ann.* 3.28.2, *sexto demum consulatu Caesar Augustus,
potentiae securus, quae triumviratu iusserat abolevit*). He 'restored laws and
rights to the Roman people', as commemorated on an *aureus* issued in
28 BC: LEGES ET IVRA P(opulo) R(omano) RESTITVIT (BM accession

Fig. 30 Restoration of constitutional government. *Aureus*, 28 BC (coin: obverse and reverse, BM CM 1995.4–1.1 = LACTOR H18).

no. CM 1995.4–1.1; Rich and Williams (1999); Simon (1993) 208–9; LAC-TOR H18) (see Figure 30). In February 28 BC, he recommended the traditional practice of handing over the *fasces*, symbols of office, to his fellow consul in alternate months (Dio Cass. 53.1.1). The principle of collegiality was an important one, underlining constitutional and religious propriety at Rome, and explains why Augustus emphasizes the role of colleagues elsewhere in the *RGDA* too (6.2; 8.2; 8.4; 10.2; 22.2; 34.3n. **quoque**). At the end of 28 BC, he took the usual oath on leaving his consular office that he

had done nothing contrary to the laws (Dio Cass. 53.1.1). His appointment
of a *praetor urbanus* in 28 BC would have signified a desire to ensure the
efficacy of the justice system (Dio Cass. 53.2.3). The year in which he ceased
to nominate lower magistrates, restoring elections, is unknown, but would
fit well into the same programme in 28 BC (Suet. *Aug.* 40.2, with Carter
(1982) ad loc.). Finally, a new *lex annalis* may have been passed, since the
rules governing minimum ages for holding magistracies are different under
Augustus from the Republic (Rich and Williams (1999) 200–1; Talbert
(1984) 17–18. It is perhaps more likely, however, that such a law was passed
c. 18 BC, since a year's remission was allowed for each child, echoing the
concerns of Augustus 'moral legislation' passed in that year: see 6.2n. **quae
tum per me geri senatus voluit, per tribuniciam potestatem perfeci**).
His first revision of the senate's membership in 29 BC marked an early stage
in his campaign to restore the government to working order (8.2). In addition to these political acts, he also took pains during 28 BC to encourage
the perception that normality was returning to other areas of Rome's life
too, notably religion, as illustrated by his restoration of eighty-two temples
during that same year (20.4; cf. Vell. Pat. 2.89.3–4, who links the political
and religious 'restorations').

After these several actions distancing himself from triumviral activities
and reintroducing the usual ceremonies that acted as symbols of constitutional normality, the stage was set for the handover of power in the senate
on 13 January 27 BC. At this meeting, he handed back control over the
provinces to the Roman people (Ov. *Fast.* 1.589, *redditaque est omnis populo
provincia nostro* = LACTOR H23; Strabo *Geography* 17.3.25 = LACTOR
H19, M2. Cf. a selection of recent work on the so-called 'first settlement':
Turpin (1994); Lacey (1996) ch. 3; Birley (2000) 724–9; Ferrary (2001) 108–
15; Cotton and Yakobson (2002) 204, 208–9; Gruen (2005) 34–5). What
Augustus does not mention here is that he subsequently took back control
of some provinces (Dio Cass. 53.12–16.3; Suet. *Aug.* 47).

The Greek version also supports the view that Augustus is not referring here to his 'restoration of the Republic' in a strictly constitutional
sense: elsewhere the Latin phrase *res publica* is translated into Greek
fairly literally as 'common affairs', τὰ κοινὰ πράγματα (or δημόσια)
(cf. 1.1, 1.3, 1.4), but here it is translated as κυριήα ('rights of ownership'),
which summons up an extraordinary image of Augustus' dominance in
the state, that fits in with the tendency of the Greek version to represent
Augustus' position at Rome as monarchical in character (Vanotti (1975)
309).

34.2 quo pro merito/For this service This phrase (notably the use of
quo) indicates that, according to Augustus, the honours described in 34.2
were awarded to him directly as a result of his actions described in 34.1.
By contrast, the Greek version does not dwell upon the idea of Augustus'

worthiness (Scheid (2007) 88). His use of a singular noun, *merito*, has bedevilled interpretations of this key chapter of the *RGDA*, misleading readers into assuming that his 'service' can be traced to a single occasion, namely his 'restoration of the Republic' on 13 January 27 BC (e.g. Adcock (1951) 133; cf. 34.1n. **rem publicam**). Nevertheless, this is not possible, given that Augustus starts his account of events by specifically alluding to a two-year period, 28–27 BC (34.1). Furthermore, the honours chosen by the senate (see below) seem more appropriate for Augustus' ending of the civil wars and revival of constitutional propriety than as a specific reward for his announcement on 13 January that he was returning the provinces to the government of senate and people.

Augustus appellatus sum/I was named Augustus   The name Augustus was granted in the senate on the proposal of L. Munatius Plancus (*PIR²* M728) (Vell. Pat. 2.91.1 = LACTOR E91.1, *quod cognomen illi iure Planci sententia consensus universi senatus populique Romani indidit*, with Hellegouarc'h and Jodry (1980) 813; cf. Suet. *Aug.* 7.2) on 16 January 27 BC (*Fast. Praen.* = *Inscr. Ital.* XIII.ii 115, 400: *Imp. Caesar [Augustus est a]ppell[a]tus* = LACTOR C7). This was the senate's additional response to the events of 13 January: although Augustus parades his new name in first place, it was in reality granted to him a few days later than the other honours (see 34.2nn. **laureis postes aedium mearum vestiti**; **coronaque civica**). Alternative dates for this grant are found in other sources. The close interrelationship of the events on the 13 and 16 January explains why Ovid (*Fast.* 1.589–90 = LACTOR H23) conflated the happenings from both days into his account of 13 January. Orosius' (6.20.8) dating to 6 January is the result of his desire to create a link to the date of Christ's epiphany.

The name 'Augustus' was chosen for its complex connotations: related to the Latin words *augur*, *augurium*, *auctoritas*, and *augeo*, it evoked the religious sphere of augury and auspices, as well as ideas of authority and increase (Ov. *Fast.* 1.608–16 = LACTOR H23; Suet. *Aug.* 7.2; Flor. 2.34.66; Dio Cass. 53.16.6–8; see 34.3n. **auctoritate omnibus praestiti, potestatis autem nihilo amplius habui**; Galinsky (1996) 16). Above all, it conveyed the idea of superhuman status: Livy tends to use the adjective *augustus* as a contrast to *humanus* in his early books, which he composed shortly after Augustus received the title (Taylor (1918)). Furthermore, it is this significance that is to the fore in the Greek translation of the name as σεβαστός ('revered'). The word *augustus* was not new, but had not been used as a name before: a famous phrase in the epic poet Ennius describes the original foundation of Rome by Romulus as being accompanied by an 'august augury' (*septingenti sunt, paulo plus aut minus, anni / augusto augurio postquam incluta condita Roma est*, Enn. *Ann.* 4.5 = Skutsch (1985) frs. 154–5). Its significance can be summarized as follows: 'An unprecedented name,

Fig. 31 Civic crown and laurels. Spanish mint, *c.* 19–18 BC (coin: obverse and reverse, *BM Coins, Rom. Emp.* I 58 no. 317). © The Trustees of the British Museum.

"Augustus" was pregnant with potent polyvalent implications: sanctity, heroization; divine election; mediation between gods and the Roman people; relationship with Romulus, who had founded Rome *augusto augurio*, in the famous phrase of the Roman poet Ennius; association with *auctoritas* and with the sense of "increase" in the root *aug-*, as well as augury' (Reinhold (2002) 64; cf. Ramage (1987) 100–4). In 8 BC, the month Sextilis was renamed Augustus (Censorinus *DN* 22; Macrob. *Sat.* 1.12.35 = LACTOR H35–6). The name of Romulus, which had also been in the running as an alternative *cognomen*, potentially had too many problematic connotations, notably of fratricide and royalty (Suet. *Aug.* 7.2; Flor. 2.34.66; Dio Cass. 53.16.7; Alföldi (1971) 37).

The granting of his honorific name was celebrated for years to come, for example on coinage minted in 19/18 BC, depicting the civic crown (see *corona civica*) around the text OB CIVIS SERVATOS on the reverse, and the legend CAESAR AVGVSTVS between two laurels on the obverse (Simon (1993) 138 no. 103 = *BM Coins, Rom. Emp.* I 58 no. 317; cf. Simon (1993) 138 no. 104; *BM Coins, Rom. Emp.* I 58 nos. 318–20, 63 nos. 351–2; *RIC* I² 43 nos. 26a and 33, 45 nos. 50–2) (see Figure 31).

laureis postes aedium mearum vestiti/the doorposts of my house were clothed with laurels   Two evergreen laurels, symbols of everlasting victory and peace (Plin. *HN* 15.39.127, 40.133), were placed on either side of the entrance to Augustus' house as one of the honours decreed on 13 January 27 BC by the senate (Dio Cass. 53.16.4); these were echoed by laurels carved in stone at Augustus' Mausoleum (see introduction p. 5). This combined the practice of adorning doorways with garlands in times of celebration

Fig. 32 Altar of Rome and Augustus. *Sestertius*, AD 9/14, Lugdunum mint (coin: reverse, *RIC* I² 231a = LACTOR M20).

(Alföldi (1973) 4–6) with the traditional display of triumphal spoils on a house façade (Plin. *HN* 35.2.7). The shrub was particularly associated with the god Apollo – not least via the myth of Daphne's metamorphosis (Ov. *Met.* 1.452–567, esp. 560–5) – whose temple was adjacent to Augustus' house on the Palatine (Plin. *HN* 15.40.134; Ov. *Tr.* 3.1.39–46). Traditionally, laurels grew on either side of various sacred buildings, including the *regia*, temple of Vesta, and the *curiae veteres* (Alföldi (1971) 37, (1973) 2; cf. Ov. *Fast.* 3.137–44). The overall effect was to imbue Augustus' house with a religious aura (Alföldi (1971) 68), and to associate him with the office of *pontifex maximus* even though he did not assume that role until well over a decade later (see 10.2n. ***pontifex maximus***).

In between the laurels was the civic crown (see 34.2n. ***coronaque civica***), and the entrance to Augustus' house was further adorned in 2 BC, when his title *pater patriae* was inscribed there (35.1). The two laurels were depicted on coins, along with the name CAESAR AVGVSTVS (see 34.2n. ***Augustus appellatus sum***), and were also a common motif on altars dedicated to the *Lares Augusti* in Rome (Hano (1986) 2367–9, pls. I.1, II.3–4, VIII.16, IX.18, XI.23; Alföldi (1973) 30–5), as well as on the imperial cult altar from Pompeii (Hano (1986) pl. VIII.17). As with the other honours mentioned in this chapter, depictions of the laurels spread into the provinces, and were often found in contexts associated with emperor worship, such as the altar to Rome and Augustus of the Three Gauls at Lugdunum (*BM Coins, Rom. Emp.* I 92–3 nos. 548–60, 94–6 nos. 565–88, pls. 20–1; *RIC* 57–8 nos. 229–48; LACTOR M20; von Hesberg (1978) 948–9 nos. 22–3; Alföldi (1973) 37–9 with further examples, pl. V.1) (see Figure 32). They became such common currency in popular consciousness that they even appear on oil lamps and seal rings (Alföldi (1973) 47–50, pls. XXII–XXIV). Following Augustus, laurels became regarded as insignia of imperial rank; they featured on coins issued by Vespasian (*BM Coins, Rom. Emp.* II 25 no. 133, *RIC* II 22 no. 72) and even continued to be associated with imperial residences on the Palatine in late antiquity (Alföldi (1973) 15, 17).

In 36 BC, Octavian had bought up properties on the Palatine in order to be able to extend his own house, the former home of the famous orator Hortensius (Vell. Pat. 2.81.3, with Woodman (1983) ad loc.; Suet. *Aug.* 72.1). Before he could do so, however, the area was struck by lightning, in response to which he declared it to be public property, a site for a temple of Apollo (Suet. *Aug.* 29.3; Dio Cass. 49.15.5). On his election as *pontifex maximus* (see 10.2n. **pontifex maximus**), he added an altar to Vesta to his house, and gave the *domus publica* to the Vestals (Ov. *Fast.* 4.949–52; Dio Cass. 54.27.3). Since he was required as *pontifex maximus* to live in a public property, he dedicated part of his house (Dio Cass. 54.27.3), and, after a fire in AD 3, he proclaimed the whole house public property (Dio Cass. 55.12.4–5). His house remained ostentatiously modest, but its entranceway would have left no viewer in doubt about the pre-eminence of its owner (Ov. *Tr.* 3.1.33–48, espec. 35, *'Iovis haec' dixi 'domus est?'* – '"Is this Jupiter's house?", I said'). (Cf. Iacopi (1995)).

coronaque civica/a civic crown　　The civic crown, a wreath of oak leaves, was originally awarded to an individual for saving the life of a fellow citizen (Alföldi (1971) 49–52; Plin. *HN* 22.4.8; Gell. *NA* 5.6.11). The saved citizen was from then on required to regard his saviour as his father, and was under an obligation to obey him (Polyb. 6.39.7; Cic. *Planc.* 30.72). By the late Republic, the significance of the civic crown had shifted, being now awarded to someone for a victory which had saved Rome. L. Gellius proposed the honour for Cicero for his suppression of Catiline (Cic. *Pis.* 3.6; Gell. *NA* 5.6.15), and a statue decorated with a civic crown was set up on the *rostra* in 45 BC in honour of Julius Caesar for ending the civil war (App. *B Civ.* 2.16.106; Dio Cass. 44.4.5; Weinstock (1971) 163–7). Similarly, the civic crown was awarded to Augustus for having saved the lives of citizens – OB CIVES SERVATOS (cf. Ov. *Tr.* 3.1.48, and coins cited below) – presumably by his victories and through his clemency in the civil wars (see 3.1, with Scheid (2007) 31; Val. Max. 2.8.7 = LACTOR H20; cf. Plin. *HN* 16.3.7, who comments wryly 'after the act of not killing a fellow-citizen began to seem like a virtue amidst the evil of civil wars' – *postquam civilium bellorum profano meritum coepit videri civem non occidere*), but the specific actions deserving the honour are left rather vague in Augustus' case (Dio Cass. 53.16.4). It probably reflects the general idea that Augustus was Rome's saviour rather than alluding to any specific circumstances (cf. *CIL* VI 873 = *ILS* 81 = EJ no. 17 = LACTOR H17, possibly an arch set up 'to commemorate the preservation of the state', *re publica conservata* in 29 BC; Vell. Pat. 2.60.1; Alföldi (1971) 68–72). The Greek version provides an explanatory periphrasis (Reichmann (1943) 22; Vanotti (1975) 320; Marrone (1977) 321–2). The award had been foreshadowed by the senate granting to Octavian the *corona obsidionalis*, a wreath of grass, an even higher award than the civic crown, on 13 September 30 BC, on report of Antony's death, in recognition of saving a whole army, and indeed the whole state, from grave danger (Plin. *HN* 22.6.13 = LACTOR H14; see 27.1n. **Aegyptum**). A passage in the *Fasti Praenestini* is traditionally restored as explaining the grant of the civic crown as being 'because he restored the Republic' – *corona querc[ea, uti super ianuam domus Imp. Caesaris] / Augusti poner[etur, senatus decrevit, quod rem publicam] / p. R. rest[it]u[it]* – but the crucial words are missing from the inscription (*Fast. Praen.* 13 January, *Inscr. Ital.* XIII.ii 113, 396–7 = LACTOR C5). Indeed, it is more likely that the gap in the inscription should read '[*quod leges et iura*] *p.R. rest[it][u[it]*' (Millar (2000) 6; cf. Judge (1974) 288–98; 34.1n. **rem publicam**).

The civic crown was a long-lasting, widespread motif on coins, variously appearing on coins issued immediately in 27 BC and afterwards in combination with the name CAESAR AVGVSTVS, the two laurels, and the legend OB CIVIS SERVATOS or CIVIBVS SERVATEIS (27 BC, Rome: Simon (1993) 136 no. 96 = *BM Coins, Rom. Emp.* I 106–7 nos. 656–8 = *RIC* I² 61 no. 277; 19/18 BC, Rome: Simon (1993) 137 nos. 101–2 = *BM Coins, Rom. Emp.* I 2 nos. 5–6, 7 no. 35, 10 no. 51 = *RIC* I² 62 nos. 278–9, no. 286, 63 no. 302, 64 no. 312; 18–17 BC, Spain: *BM Coins, Rom. Emp.* I 57 no. 314; cf. Simon (1993) 136 no. 99 = *BM Coins, Rom. Emp.* I 29 no. 134, 30 nos. 139–42, 31 nos. 147–51, 32 nos. 157–60, 33–4 nos. 165–8, nos. 171–3, 35–9 nos. 175–99 = *RIC* I² 65–6 nos. 323–36, 69–71 nos. 370–89 = LACTOR T28; 12 BC, Rome – above closed doors the legend OB C S, framing an oak wreath (not a laurel, as stated in *RIC*): Simon (1993) 136 no. 98 = *RIC* I² 74 no. 419 = *BM Coins, Rom. Emp.* I 26 no. 126 = LACTOR H32) (see Figure 33). Along with the other honours mentioned by Augustus in this chapter, the oak wreath was depicted on altars for the *Lares Augusti* (Hano (1986) 2369–70 pl. III^TER.7d, VIII.16, IX.19/20; Hölscher (1988) 392 no. 220, 398–400 no. 225). Augustus was depicted wearing the civic crown in different artistic media (Zanker (1988) 93–4). He appears on the *Gemma Augustea* being crowned with the wreath by the figure of Oikoumene (von Hesberg (1978) 982–3 no. 45; Zanker (1988) 231 fig. 182; Hölscher (1988) 371–2 no. 204; cf. Figure 12). The motif spread beyond Rome, to Pompeii (see 34.2n. **laureis postes aedium mearum vestiti**) and Ostia, where a marble sculpture of a round shield (presumably the *clipeus virtutis* – see 34.2n. **clupeus**) has in its middle the inscription *ob civis [ser]vatos* and is surrounded by a border composed of an oak-leaf wreath. This sculpture may originally have been on display in the temple of Rome and Augustus in Ostia's forum, and may date from the Julio-Claudian period after

Fig. 33 Honours at Augustus' house. *Aureus*, 12 BC (coin: *RIC* I² 74 no. 419 = LACTOR H32).

the death of Augustus. If this is correct, it illustrates the continuing cele-bration of Augustus' honours under his successors (Squarciapino (1982)). After Augustus, the honour became an imperial prerogative, although the *Augustalis* at Pompeii, C. Calventius Quietus, depicted it prominently on his tomb in the Flavian period (tomb south 20, Herculaneum Gate: Kockel (1983) 90–7, pls. 23b, 25e), in order to promote awareness of his close links to the emperor, whilst a house in the town, which may have belonged to an *Augustalis*, displays an oak wreath flanked by laurels above its doorway (Spinnazola (1953) 420 fig. 486, house II.v.4; Alföldi (1971) 71; Hano (1986) 2370; Zanker (1988) 277 fig. 219).

clupeus/shield By juxtaposing the shield with the laurels and civic crown, Augustus implies that it was awarded to him at the same time, but, as noted above in relation to the title 'Augustus' (see 34.2n. ***Augustus appellatus sum***), the chronology of honours is not straightforward. An intact copy of the shield in Luna marble, with a diameter of 96.5 cm, was found in a cryptoporticus in the *colonia* of Arelate (Arles), bearing the following inscription: *senatus / populusque Romanus / Imp. Caesari Divi f. Augusto / cos. VIII dedit clupeum / virtutis clementiae / iustitiae pietatis erga / deos patriamque* – 'The senate and people of Rome gave to Imperator Caesar Augustus, consul eight times, a shield of valour, clemency, justice, and piety towards gods and country' (Benoit (1952) 48–53 = *AE* 1952.165 = *ILS* 81 = EJ no. 22 = LACTOR H24; Hölscher (1988) 387–90 no. 216) (see Figure 34). It was perhaps originally displayed in a sanctuary for emperor worship (Benoit (1952) 55–8). This copy is explicitly dated to 26 BC, when Augustus was consul for the eighth time. Although it is

Fig. 34 Copy of the *clupeus virtutis* from Arles.

possible that the copy at Arles was set up later than that at Rome, perhaps in connection with a visit to the town by Augustus on his way back to Italy from Spain, it is also possible that the original shield at Rome was set up in 26, and not 27 BC. In support of this is the fact that Dio Cassius fails to mention the shield in his account of the honours granted to Augustus in January 27 BC (53.16.4–8), as well as the fact that the shield is said to be granted by the senate and people, not just by the senate, unlike the name 'Augustus'. Interesting implications arise if the shield was voted in 26 BC, when Augustus was absent from Rome, namely that Augustus' authority still needed reinforcing in 26 BC, despite all the unprecedented honours granted to him a year earlier (Seston (1954) 288–93; Lacey (1996) 93–4; von Hesberg and Panciera (1994) 115–18). Whatever the actual date of the shield being granted, however, it was commonly juxtaposed with laurels and civic crown on coins, illustrating that viewers were invited to regard them as the same package of honours, as suggested here too by Augustus.

The shield was much imitated in a variety of media. Firstly, a copy of the shield in marble, with a diameter of approximately 90 cm, has been attributed to Augustus' Mausoleum (*CIL* VI 40365; von Hesberg and Panciera (1994) 113–18). Also at Rome the shield is found, albeit less commonly than the laurels and civic crown, on altars relating to the cult of the *Lares Augusti*. The most famous of these is the 'Belvedere altar', which depicts a Victory holding up a shield which is supported by a pillar in between two laurels, accompanied by the inscription *senatus populusq / Romanus / Imp Caesari Divi f. Augusto / pontif maxum[o] / imp cos trib potest.* – 'The senate and people of Rome to Imperator Caesar Augustus,

Fig. 35 'Belvedere' altar.

son of the deified, chief priest, victorious commander, consul, holder of tribunician power' (see Figure 35) (for the significance of Victory, see 34.2 ***in curia Iulia***). Given that Augustus became *pontifex maximus* only in 12 BC, this shows that the motif continued to adorn new monuments for some years after the shield was initially granted (Hano (1986) 2370–2, pls. XI.23; Hölscher (1988) 394–6 no. 223 = *CIL* VI 876 = *ILS* 83 = EJ no. 23; cf. Hano (1986) pl. XI.25, altar of the *vicus Sandaliarius*). Elsewhere, the shield was celebrated on an inscribed altar found near the town of Potentia in Picenum, but now lost (*CIL* IX 5811 = *ILS* 82). This was apparently a monument set up by a local *sevir Augustalis* to commemorate the granting of the shield to Augustus. It depicted a Victory holding up a shield, and the following inscription: *s.p.q.R. / Augusto dedit / clupeum virtutis / [c]le[me]ntiae ius]t[itiae/ pietatis — / —?]*. Monuments in the provinces also displayed images of the shield, such as the altar of the *gens Augusta* at Carthage, which was carved with a relief depicting the seated goddess Roma holding out in her hand a statuette of a winged Victory carrying a round shield resting on a pillar (see Figure 36) (von Hesberg

Fig. 36 Altar of the *gens Augusta*, Carthage.

(1978) 946–7 fig. 21; Zanker (1988) 316 fig. 247). The shield appears in various guises on coins, either on its own (*BM Coins, Rom. Emp.* I 59 nos. 321–2, 60–1 nos. 333–9), in combination with a Victory (Spanish mint: Simon (1993) 139 no. 106; *BM Coins, Rom. Emp.* I 58 no. 316, 61 nos. 340–3, 70–1 nos. 403–9 = *RIC* I² 43 no. 31, 44–5 nos. 45–9, 46 nos. 61–2, 47–8 nos. 88–94), or together with the laurels or civic crown (*BM Coins, Rom. Emp.* I 63 nos. 353–56, 67 nos. 381–3 = *RIC* I² 43 no. 30, 44 nos. 34–6, nos. 42–3, 45 no. 52, 47 nos. 78–9) (see Figure 37). The shield remained a potent symbol of imperial power, appearing on coins issued by Tiberius to commemorate Augustus (*BM Coins, Rom. Emp.* I 140 no. 141; *RIC* I² 99 no. 77), and also on coins minted in Spain in AD 68 (*BM Coins, Rom. Emp.* I 304 no. 57, 305, nos. 59–60; *RIC* I² 212 nos. 110, 116). Finally the shield appears in a different context on a cameo now in Vienna, which depicts Augustus in a chariot being pulled across the sea in triumph by four tritons, with the shield in the front of the chariot (Hölscher (1967) pl. 1.12).

Fig. 37 Shield of virtues. *Denarius, c.* 19 BC, Spanish mint (coin: reverse, *RIC* I² 44 no. 42b
= LACTOR H25).

in curia Iulia/in the Julian senate house The shield was placed
alongside the statue of Victory which Octavian had dedicated in the senate
house to celebrate his victory in Egypt (Dio Cass. 51.22.1–2, with Reinhold
(1988) ad loc.), and coins and other momuments frequently juxtapose
Victory and the shield (see 34.2n. *clupeus*; Hölscher (1967) 102–5). The
Greek version simplifies the reference to the location, translating it just as
'council chamber' (cf. 35.1; Marrone (1977) 319).

**virtutis clementiaeque iustitiae et pietatis caussa/because of my val-
our, clemency, justice, and piety** Although there existed a canon of
four virtues (wisdom, justice, fortitude, moderation) promoted by Greek
philosophers since Plato, the shield did not simply adopt this traditional
standard, but presented a new set of virtues which set Augustus apart as
pre-eminent in society, and perhaps held out a promise of future apotheosis
(Classen (1991) 22–4; Seston (1954) 293; Hölscher (1967) 106–8; Wallace-
Hadrill (1981a) 300–7). A careful use of conjunctions creates two balancing
pairs of virtues: *virtus* and *clementia, iustitia* and *pietas*. These virtues went
on to occupy a prominent place in Augustan art and literature, notably in
Horace's 'Roman Odes', *Carm.* 3.1–6 (Ryberg (1966) espec. 234; Nisbet and
Rudd (2004) 22, 30, 38–9 on *virtus* and *iustitia*; Hölscher (1988) 359–60).
The first of these virtues, *virtus*, primarily evokes the quality of valour
on the battlefield (Ramage (1987) 46), and the focus on military success
would have been visually complemented by the shield's juxtaposition with
the statue of Victory in the senate house. When juxtaposed with laurels,
the idea of military triumph would likewise have been strongly evoked
(see 34.2n *laureis postes aedium mearum vestiti*). Conversely, setting the

shield next to the civic crown would have brought to the fore the other qualities, particularly clemency and justice. The inscription on the marble copy of the shield at Arles removes the careful way in which Augustus balances the pairs of virtues in his account, whilst offering more detail on the nature of his *pietas* (Seston (1954) 287). The Greek version has a different emphasis: instead of stating, like the Latin, that the shield was given to Augustus because of his virtues, it simply states that the shield testified to his virtues (Wigtil (1982a) 635).

testatum est/the fact was declared that The use of the impersonal passive verb form here lends an impression of objectivity to Augustus' recital of his own virtues (Ramage (1987) 26).

34.3 post id tempus/After this time Augustus represents the honours granted to him as providing testimony to his pre-eminence (Seston (1954) 289). The Greek version does not translate the phrase *post id tempus*, thus removing any sense of chronological or causal relationship between Augustus' primacy and honours granted to him by the senate. He did not, therefore, according to the Greek version, excel in *auctoritas* only once he had received the honours (Vanotti (1975) 320–31).

auctoritate omnibus praestiti, potestatis autem nihilo amplius habui/I excelled everyone in influence, but I had no more power The word *potestas* here designates legitimate power derived from holding political office (contrast 34.1n. **rem publicam . . . transtuli**), whereas *auctoritas* refers to personal prestige, which would be both non-transferable and potentially unlimited in scope (cf. extensive discussion by Galinsky (1996) 10–41). Hence Augustus was the *princeps*, or leader, of the Roman state, but not in a way that was defined constitutionally (see 13n. **me principe**; 8.5n. **ipse multarum rerum exempla imitanda posteris tradidi**), as Meyer Reinhold ((2002) 63–4) has clearly explained: 'This "authority" did not, in the Roman sense, connote legitimated power, the right to command, but rather esteem for preeminent status and soundness of judgment, and recognized priority in consultation. It signified a unique ethical–political relationship between himself and all others that was nontransferable. Since this quality was not constitutionally defined, its scope was unlimited; it was a fuzzy concept that enabled Augustus to act as author–initiator and to take unrestricted action in a wide range of matters.' As Karl Galinsky remarks ((1996) 12), 'Augustus makes it clear that he does not want to be just a functionary or magistrate but that he aims to provide a higher kind of moral leadership.'

The contrast between *auctoritas* and *potestas* was not new: traditionally, the senate operated only by making recommendations, by expressing its *auctoritas* (the 'sense of the meeting'), not by passing legislation. The impact of *auctoritas* could also emerge in an individual's case, as when Q. Metellus Celer successfully forbade the revival of games in 61 BC, even though he did not possess the formal right to do so (Cic. *Pis.* 4.8, *atque id quod nondum potestate poterat obtinuit auctoritate*, 'and he achieved through his influence what he could not yet achieve through his formal power'; Galinsky (1996) 16; Ramage (1987) 41–54). This phrase provides a neat conclusion to the chapter, which started with the statement about transferring the state *ex mea potestate* (Adcock (1952)), and implicitly evokes again the impact of the *consensus universorum*, which now, however, confirms *auctoritas* rather than *potestas* (Galinsky (1996) 14).

quoque/in each   This word is omitted in the Greek version, perhaps because the Latin is potentially ambiguous between *quŏque* ('also') and *quōque* ('in each') (Vanotti (1975) 321). At first sight, the omission of an apex (the usual way of marking a long vowel in inscriptions) might appear to solve the problem, and indicate that *quŏque* is intended (Hohl (1947) 104), but apices are used arbitrarily in the rest of this chapter. For instance, we find long vowels marked where they should not be, in *clúpei* and *civíca*. This may be explained if long vowels were not marked in the Latin text from which the stonecutter was working (Adcock (1952) 11). To judge from its context, the word is more likely to be *quōque* (Adcock (1952) 10–11; Hurlet (1997) 354–6), and refers in the first place to those who acted as consuls alongside Augustus, and then to Agrippa and Tiberius who are referred to as his colleagues earlier in the inscription (6.2, 8.2, 8.4). This statement obscures the fact that Augustus often held powers separately from their office, such as tribunician power when not a tribune, consular power when not a consul, and censorial power when not a censor. Besides, even if Augustus did have colleagues, it is doubtful that they felt that they possessed power equal to Augustus'; a more accurate assessment of Augustus' position in the state may be found in Ovid, who stated *res est publica Caesar*, 'the state is Caesar' (*Tr.* 4.4.15; cf. Wirszubski (1960) 109–18).

35.1 senatus et equester ordo populusque Romanus universus/the Roman senate and equestrian order and people all together   The new prominence of the equestrian order in Roman society under Augustus (Nicolet (1984); Rowe (2002) ch. 2) is reflected by this striking modification of the traditional phrase *senatus populusque Romanus*. Ovid too, himself an equestrian, mentions the *equites* specifically in his account of how the title was granted (*sancte pater patriae, tibi plebs, tibi curia nomen / hoc dedit, hoc dedimus nos tibi nomen, eques, Fast.* 2.127–8 = LACTOR H38). Suetonius' account of how the title came to be granted has a rather different emphasis. According to the biographer (*Aug.* 58), a deputation from the *plebs* to Augustus at Antium offered him the title, but he declined; a popular acclamation in the theatre at Rome, however, was followed by a speech in the senate by M. Valerius Messalla Corvinus (*PIR* V90; Syme (1986) ch. 15) in which he acclaimed Augustus as *pater patriae* (not by a decree, as Dio Cass. 55.10.10); this gives no part to the equestrians specifically (cf. *Fasti Praen.* below), although it leaves open the possibility that they took part in the acclamation at the theatre. The biographer claims to record the precise words of Messalla's speech and Augustus' emotional reply in the senate. All sources, however, agree on the fact that the title was the result of consensus between *plebs* and senate (Alföldi (1971) 93–4), unlike the honours bestowed in January 27 BC, which emanated from the senate alone (34.2).

patrem patriae/father of the fatherland   The *Fasti Praenestini* offer the date 5 February as the occasion on which Augustus was acclaimed as *pater patriae* by the senate and people (*Inscr. Ital.* XIII.ii 119, 407 = EJ p. 47 = LACTOR C13, *feriae ex s.c. quod eo die Imperator Caesar Augustus, pontifex maximus, trib. potest. xxi, cos. xiii, a senatu populoque Romano pater patriae appellatus*). For some years previously, however, Augustus had already been called *pater* ('father') or *parens* ('parent') (Alföldi (1971) 92–3), as recorded in various inscriptions from Italy and the provinces (*CIL* X 823, Pompeii, 10 BC; *CIL* III 6803 = *ILS* 101, Pisidian Antioch; *CIL* XII 136 = *ILS* 6755, Sion, Narbonensis, 8/7 BC; *CIL* II 2107 = *ILS* 96, Urgavo, Baetica, 6 BC). Coins had been issued in 19/18 BC naming him as PARENT(I) CONS(ERVATORI) SVO; the triumphal images accompanying this legend indicate that the primary connotation of the title was as the saviour of Rome through military victories (Figure 38) (Simon (1993) 126 no. 86 = *BM Coins, Rom. Emp.* I 69–70 nos. 397–402 = *RIC* I² 48 nos. 96–101). A similar assimilation of the roles of father and saviour is also found in poetry (Hor. *Carm.* 3.24.25–32; cf. Ov. *Tr.* 2.574; Alföldi (1971) 48). This fits in with previous examples of leading Romans who had been called 'father' of Rome, all of whom had rescued the state from various crises of internal revolution or external warfare (Alföldi (1971) 47–9). For example, Camillus had rescued Rome from the Gauls (Livy 5.49.7, *Romulus ac parens patriae conditorque alter urbis . . . appellabatur*), Marius from the Cimbri (Cic. *Rab. Post.* 10.27, *C. Marium . . . vere patrem patriae, parentem . . . vestrae libertatis atque huiusce rei publicae possumus dicere*), and Cicero from Catiline (Cic. *Pis.* 3.6, *me Q. Catulus, princeps huius ordinis et auctor publici consili, frequentissimo senatu parentem patriae nominavit*, cf. *Att.* 9.10.3 = Shackleton Bailey (1968) no. 177, for the combination of *parens* and *conservator*). Such individuals were also regarded as successors to Romulus, re-founding Rome at a time of

Fig. 38 Augustus as *parens* and *conservator*, 19/18 BC, Spanish mint (coin, *RIC* I² 48 nos. 96–101). © The Trustees of the British Museum.

crisis (Alföldi (1971) 28–36; Camillus, 'second founder', Plut. *Vit. Cam.* 1.1; Marius, the 'third founder' of Rome: Plut. *Vit. Mar.* 27.5, Livy *Per.* 68, with Alföldi (1971) 29; Cicero mocked as 'Romulus from Arpinum' – 'Sallust' *Inv. In Cic.* 7.1). Most recently, Julius Caesar had been hailed as *parens patriae* in 45/44 BC (Livy *Per.* 116; Suet. *Iul.* 76.1; Flor. 2.13.91), in recognition of his clemency after his victory in the civil war (App. *B Civ.* 2.20.144; Alföldi (1971) 86–8; Weinstock (1971) 200–5).

The official bestowal of the title was commemorated on coinage issued in the same year at the Lugdunum mint (Simon (1993) 93 no. 60 – CAESAR AVGVSTVS DIVI F PATER PATRIAE = *RIC* I² 55 no. 204). It became an important part of imperial titulature for most later emperors, although not in the case of Tiberius, whose reluctance to accept the title is reflected in the fact that later emperors generally assumed the title only after having ruled for a number of years: there was evidently an underlying feeling that an emperor had to earn the title (Rich (1990) 152). The title *pater patriae* evoked the connotations of the father figure in Roman society, reflecting not only the affection and responsibility a father feels towards his children, familiar to modern society, but also the obedience required by Roman law from children to their father, as enshrined in the principle of *patria potestas*, paternal power (Alföldi (1971) 42–6; Saller (1994) ch. 5; Dio Cass. 53.18.3; Sen. *Clem.* 1.14.2). The motif of being a *pater* underscored important elements in Roman political life, with senators being known as *patres conscripti*. The concept of being a father figure also provided an ideal for Roman relations with provincials, with Cicero advising his brother that he should aspire to be the *parens* of Asia when acting as the province's governor (*Q. Fr.* 1.10.31). For Strabo, the task of administrating the Roman empire was so complex that it needed Augustus to act as a father figure with absolute authority (Strabo *Geography* 6.4.2, 'It would be difficult to administer such a great empire other than by entrusting it to one man as a father': χαλεπὸν δὲ ἄλλως διοικεῖν τὴν τηλικαύτην ἡγεμονίαν ἢ ἑνὶ ἐπιτρέψαντας ὡς πατρί).

Given both the prominence given to this episode in the *RGDA*, and Augustus' initial reaction in the senate as recorded by Suetonius (*Aug.* 58.2), Augustus clearly put great value on having been acclaimed as *pater patriae*. This may have been partly the result of an appreciation of the historical and legendary precedents evoked by the title. For Livy, the title is one of the motifs linking Romulus, Camillus, and Augustus as the three most important figures in the history of Rome, with Camillus occurring at the halfway point between the other two (for other similarities between Augustus and Camillus, see 20.4n. *duo et octoginta templa deum*; Edwards (1996) ch. 2). Camillus is acclaimed as 'Romulus and father of his country and second founder of the city', *Romulus ac parens patriae conditorque alter urbis* (Livy 5.49.7), whilst Augustus encouraged the idea that he himself was a new Romulus, and re-founder of Rome (Scott (1925)). The significance of the title *pater patriae* for Augustus was not limited to precedent, however: it also encouraged the development of a parallel between Augustus and Jupiter, with the former's elevated position being the human equivalent to the latter's pre-eminence in heaven (Ov. *Fast.* 2.131–2, *hoc tu per terras, quod in aethere Iuppiter alto, / nomen habes: hominum tu pater, ille deum* – 'this name you have on earth, which Jupiter has in high heaven: you are father of men, he of the gods'). Overall, we must appreciate that the grant of this title to Augustus was not simply just another meaningless honour, but that it had multiple legal and religious resonances and evoked ideas of someone acting as a saviour, patron, and god (Alföldi (1971) 138; Ramage (1987) 104–10).

in curia Iulia/in the Julian senate house   On the Greek translation of this phrase, see 34.2n. *in curia Iulia*.

in foro Aug. sub quadrigis/in the Augustan forum under the chariot This reveals that a triumphal four-horse chariot stood in his forum. It has not been located in excavations, probably lying somewhere beneath the via dei Fori Imperiali; it was perhaps in the centre of the forum, opposite the entrance to the temple of Mars the Avenger. It has sometimes been suggested that this statue base was inscribed with an account of Augustus' achievements, on analogy with the other *elogia* in the Augustan forum, a prototype *RGDA*, but this relies on an idiosyncratic interpretation of a brief statement in Velleius (Vell. Pat. 2.39.2; Braccesi (1973), with criticism by Nicolet (1991b) 41–3; cf. Alföldy (1992) 67–75; see 21.1n. **forumque Augustum**).

35.2 annum agebam septuagensumum sextum/I was in my seventy-sixth year   This statement gives us a period for the composition of the *RGDA* from on or after his birthday on 23 September AD 13 to before his death on 19 August AD 14 (introduction pp. 42–3).

APPENDIX – SUMMARY OF AUGUSTUS' EXPENDITURE

In contrast to the rest of the *RGDA*, the Appendix does not purport to originate with Augustus himself: it is written in the third person and was probably composed in the Greek east for a provincial audience (see introduction p. 19). This is suggested by the use of *denarii* as the monetary unit, and by the shift in emphasis from the main text of the *RGDA*. Section 4 of the Appendix mentions towns stricken by fire and earthquake, which are not mentioned explicitly in the main text of the *RGDA*, but which may well refer to events in the provinces, notably Asia (see App. 4n. **donata pecunia colonis, municipiis, oppidis**; 17.1n. **quater**).

App. 1 denarium sexiens milliens/600,000,000 denarii   The sum of 600 million denarii is equivalent to 2,400 million sesterces. This total sum does not match exactly the total reached by adding up all of the individual sums listed in the main text of the *RGDA* (Wolters (1988)). This discrepancy can be explained in a variety of ways. Firstly, the final section of the Appendix alludes to acts of generosity which are not mentioned in the main text; in addition, even in the main text Augustus does not always specify the sums spent, for example in chapter 18. The simplest explanation, however, is that the total in the Appendix is simply a rounded up figure.

App. 2 opera fecit nova/He built new works   Augustus' building projects are presented with a different emphasis here, commenting first on his new buildings, and then on buildings which he rebuilt (chs. 19–21).

deum Penatium/the *Penates*   The Greek translation explains them here as 'state gods', in contrast to 19.2, where they are translated as 'household gods'.

pulvinar ad circum/*pulvinar* at the Circus   The Greek version lists the buildings in a different order from the Latin, transposing the *lupercal* into between the temples of Jupiter Feretrius and Apollo, and omitting altogether the *pulvinar*. The Greek version omits the topographical precision of the phrase *trans Tiberim* in referring to the *nemus Caesarum*. It does, however, insert a new entry altogether, the 'porticoes on the Palatine', and redesignates the *porticus Octavia* as the 'portico on the Flaminian circus'.

App. 3 refecit Capitolium/He restored the Capitoline temple   See chapter 20.

App. 4 impensa praestita in spectacula/Expenses supplied for theatrical shows   See chapters 22–3.

donata pecunia colonis, municipiis, oppidis/money given to colonies, municipalities, and towns   These gifts, along with the gifts to individual senators, are not mentioned in the *RGDA*. The Greek version makes a distinction between gifts of money to the colonies and municipalities of Italy, and others to towns in the provinces stricken by earthquakes. In Italy, Naples was rebuilt by Augustus after earthquake and fire had destroyed it, and the town promptly decreed a Greek-style festival of athletics and music in his honour in 2 BC, the quadrennial *Italika Romaia Sebasta Isolympia*, which Augustus attended shortly before his death (Strabo *Geography* 5.4.7; Dio Cass. 55.10.9; Suet. *Aug.* 98.5). Augustus followed in the steps of Hellenistic kings in helping to rebuild towns that suffered from earthquakes (Suet. *Aug.* 47): on record are subventions to Laodicea and Tralles (Strabo *Geography* 12.8.18), Paphos (Dio Cass. 54.23.7), and the province of Asia (Dio Cass. 54.30.3). A decree was passed by Cos in honour of Augustus as its second founder in recognition of his rebuilding of the town following an earthquake (Dittenberger and Purgold (1896) no. 53).

amicis senatoribusque/to friends and senators   Dio Cassius (53.2.2) suggests that in 28 BC it was necessary for Octavian to make gifts of money to senators, given a shortage of men willing to undertake the expense of the office of aedile. In addition, a couple of individual senators are known to have received significant sums from Augustus. M. Hortensius Hortalus (*PIR*² H210), grandson of the orator Hortensius, received 1 million sesterces from him, allegedly as an inducement to him to marry and have children, and later tried, unsuccessfully, to win a top-up from Tiberius in AD 16 (Tac. *Ann.* 2.37–8), whilst the suffect consul of 16 BC, L. Tarius Rufus (*PIR* T14), was given the huge sum of 100 million sesterces (Plin. *HN* 18.7.37 = LACTOR T17).

senatoribusque, quorum census explevit/and to senators, whose census qualification he topped up   The first occasion on which we hear of Augustus augmenting the personal wealth of individual senators comes in 28 BC, when Augustus made gifts of money to some senators, according to

Dio Cassius (53.2.1, with Rich (1990) ad loc.). The need for this probably arose from his first revision of the senate's membership in the previous year, when senators needed to meet a census requirement of 400,000 sesterces. In 18 BC, during his second revision of the membership of the senate, Augustus again had to supplement the wealth of some senators of good character in order to prevent them from failing to meet the new requirement introduced that year for senators to possess 1 million sesterces (Dio Cass. 54.17.3–4; see 8.2n. ***senatum ter legi***). Augustus next made gifts to over eighty young senators and *equites* in AD 4 (Dio Cass. 55.13.6). Clearly, the sums involved in these gifts overall were quite considerable, but Augustus' generosity was closely linked to his revision of the senate's membership (Suet. *Aug.* 41.1). These gifts were not so much personal gifts to private individuals as an attempt by Augustus to consolidate his attempts to bolster the senatorial order (Nicolet (1984) 94–5).

Appendix

This appendix tabulates differences between this commentary's composite text and that presented by Scheid (2007) 4–25.

LATIN TEXT

	Cooley	Scheid
Heading	Rom[a]ni	Rom(ani)
2	[interfecer]unt	[trucidaver]unt
3.1	[b]ella	[be]lla
3.3	p[raemis mil]itiae	p[raemis milit]iae
5.2	periclo praesenti	peric(u)lo [p]raesenti
5.2	[liberarim]	[liberarem]
6.1	[Maximo] e[t]	[Maximo et]
7.2	[p]rinceps s[enatus fui. . .]	[p]rinceps s[enatus. . . fui]
7.3	[XVvir]um sacris	[XVvir]um [sac]ris
8.4	[et te]rtium	[et ter]tium
8.4	[tr]iginta septem millia	[tr]iginta et septem millia
9.1	[senatus decrevit]	[decrevit senatus]
9.1	vivo me	vivo m[e]
10.2	Valgio consulibu[s]	Valgio consulibus
11	[Fortunae] Red[ucis]	[Fortunae R]ed[ucis]
11	facere [iussit]	facere [decrevit]
12.1	tribunorum [plebis]	tribunorum [plebi]
12.1	Lu[c]retio	Lu[creti]o
12.1	principibus viris	princi[pi]bus viris
12.1	mis[s]a e[st]	[mi]s[s]a [est]
12.2	Qui[nctilio]	Qui[ntilio]
12.2	facer[e iussit]	facer[e decrevit]
17.1	prae<e>rant	prae(e)rant
18	[ab illo anno]	[ab eo anno]
18	[ve]ct[i]g[alia]	[vecti]g[alia]
19.2	Iunonis	Iunonis (typographical error)
20.5	[munivi]	[refeci]
22.1	quinquiens	quinquens (typographical error)
22.1	millia	milla (typographical error)
22.2	deinceps	deincep[s]
22.2	[co]n[s]ules	[consu]les
23	spectaculum	spectaclum

	Cooley	Scheid
25.1	praedonibus	praedonib[u]s
25.2	bel[li]	be[lli]
25.3	cir[c]iter	ci[rc]iter
26.1	provinc[iarum]	prov[inciarum]
26.5	[magn]aeque	[maxim]aeque
27.2	privignus	priv[ig]nus
28.2	XXVIII colonias	X[XVIII colo]nias
30.2	Danu\<v>ium	Dan]u\<v>ium (typographical error)
32	confugerunt [r]eges	confug[erunt r]eges
34.2	pop[ulumq]ue	po[pulumq]ue

GREEK TEXT

	Cooley	Scheid
1.2	με [ψη]φίσ[μασ]ι	[με ψηφίσμασ]ι
1.2	Πά[νσ]α\<ι>	Πά[νσ]α(ι)
1.2	καὶ [Αὔλωι Ἱρτίω]ι ὑπ[ά]το[ι]ς	[καὶ Αὔλωι Ἱρτίωι ὑ]π[ά]το[ι]ς
1.2	ὑπατευσάντων τὸ	ὑπατ[ευσά]ν[των τ]ὸ
1.2	σ[υ]μ[β]ουλεύειν	σ[υμβου]λεύειν
1.2	ῥάβδους	ῥάβδου[ς]
1.3	με[τὰ] τῶ[ν] ὑ[π]άτων	με[τὰ τῶν ὑπά]των
1.3	ἀντιστρατήγωι ὄντ[ι]	ἀντιστρατήγω[ι ὄντι]
1.4	ὕπατον ἀπ[έδειξ]εν	ὕπα[τον ἀπέδειξ]εν
1.4	ἔχοντα ἀρχὴν ἐπὶ τῆι	ἔχον[τα ἀρχὴν ἐπὶ] τῆι
1.4	πραγμάτ[ων] ε[ἴ]λατο	πρα[γμάτων] εἴλατ[ο]
2	φονεύσαντ[α]ς	[φονεύ]σ[αν]τ[α]ς
3.1	[γῆ]ν	[γῆν]
3.1	[ὀθνείου]ς ἐν	[ὀθνείους] ἐν
3.1	πολλ[άκις]	πολ[λάκις]
3.1	[νει]κήσας	[νεικ]ήσας
3.3	ἀποικίας	ἀπο[ι]κίας
3.3	ἀπ[έπεμψα εἰς τὰ]ς ἰδίας π[ό]λεις	ἀ[πέπεμψα εἰς τὰς] ἰδία[ς πόλεις]
3.3	ἐκπλ[ηρωθέντων τῶν] ἐνι[αυτῶν τῆς] στρατε[ίας] μυριάδας	ἐκ[πληρωθέντων τῶν ἐνιαυτῶν τῆς] στρατε[ίας μυριάδα]ς
3.3	ὀλ[ίγω]ι π[λείοις ἢ τριάκοντα καὶ] αὐτο[ῖ]ς πᾶσ[ιν]	ὀ[λίγωι πλείους ἢ τριάκοντα καὶ αὐτοῖς πᾶσιν]
3.3	ἐμ[έρισ]α ἢ	[ἐμέρισα ἢ]
3.3	ἔδωκ[α]	[ἔδωκα]
3.4	ναῦς εἷ[λον	[ναῦς εἷλον]
3.4	ἢ τ[ριήρεις ἐγένοντο]	[ἢ τριήρεις ἐγένοντο]
4.1	[ἀ]πὸ τ[ῶ]ν ῥ[ά]βδων τὴν δάφνην ἀπ[έθηκα]	[ἀπὸ τῶν ῥάβδ]ων τὴν [δάφνην ἀπέθηκα]
4.1	τὰς εὐχάς, ἃς ἐν τῶ[ι]	[τὰ]ς εὐχάς, [ἃς ἐν] τῶ[ι]
4.1	ἐν τῶ[ι] πολέμωι	ἐν τῶ[ι πολέμωι]

	Cooley	Scheid
4.2	[ἢ] τὰς τῶν [πρεσβευτῶν]	[ἢ τὰς τῶν πρεσβευτῶν]
4.2	[κατ]ὰ θά[λασσα]ν	[κατὰ θάλασσαν]
4.3	[πρ]οήχθησαν	[προήχθ]ησαν
4.4	ὑπάτευον	[ὑπάτ]ε[υ]ον
5.2	παρη<ι>τησάμην	παρη(ι)τησάμην
6.1	ἵνα ἐπιμελητὴς	ἵν[α ἐπιμελη]τὴς
6.1	ἐ[πὶ μ]εγίστηι ἐ[ξ]ουσίαι μόνος	ἐ[πὶ με]γίστηι [ἐξ]ουσ[ίαι μ]ό[νος]
8.2	τετρακόσια[ι] ἑξήκοντα	τετρακό[σιαι ἑ]ξήκοντα
8.2	μυρ[ι]άδες [καὶ] τρισχίλιαι	μυρ[ιάδες καὶ τρισχίλιαι]
8.3	ἐξ[ουσίαι]	ἐξ[ουσίαι] (typographical error)
9.2	ὁμοθυμαδὸν	ὁμοθυμαδ[ὸν]
10.1	νό[μωι] ἐκυρώθη	νό[μωι ἐκ]υρώθη
12.1	ἄρξαντες [σ]ὺν	ἄρξαντε[ς σ]ὺν
12.1	ὑπάτου	ὑπ[ά]του
14.1	καταχθ[ῶ]σιν	κα[τ]αχθ[ῶ]σιν
14.1	μετέχωσιν	[με]τέχωσιν
15.2	τρισὶ	τρισ[ὶ]
15.3	πλεῖον	πλ[εῖ]ον
17.1	κατήνενκα	κατήνενκ[α]
19.1	ἱπποδρόμωι	ἱπποδρόμω[ι]
20.5	Ῥώμης εἰς Ἀρίμινον	Ῥώμης [εἰς Ἀρίμινον]
21.3	π[ολιτει]ῶν	πο[λιτει]ῶν
22.1	τ[ρὶ]ς μονομαχίας	[τρὶς μ]ονομαχίας
22.1	υἱ[ί]ωνῶν	[υἱ]ωνῶν
22.1	[π]αρέσχον	[π]αρέσ[χ]ον
22.2	δεκαπέντε ἀνδ[ρ]ῶν	δεκαπέντε [ἀνδρ]ῶν
22.3	ἢ υἱων[ῶν	καὶ υἱων[ῶν (typographical error)
23	Τι[βέριδος]	Τε[βέριδος]
25.2	Σι[κελία]	Σ[ικελία]
25.3	τότε	τό]τε
25.3	ἐν	[ἐ]ν
25.3	ὀ[γδοή]κοντα	ὀ[γδοήκ]οντα
26.1	ἡγεμονία<ι>	ἡγεμονία(ι)
26.2	εἰρήνη<ι>	εἰρήνη(ι)
26.4	ἠ<ι>τήσαντο	ἠ(ι)τήσαντο
26.5	Μερόη<ι>	Μερόη(ι)
27.2	Ἀρταουάσδη<ι>	Ἀρταουάσδη(ι)
27.3	Σαρδὼ{ι} προκατειλημ<μ>ένας	Σαρδὼ ⌈ι⌉ προκατειλημ(μ)ένας
28.1	ἑκατέρα<ι>	ἑκατέρα(ι)
28.1	Συρία<ι>	Συρία(ι)
30.2	ἐπειτάδε	ἐπετάδε (?typographical error)
34.2	πρόπυλά	πρόπυλ[ά]
34.2	Ῥω[μα]ίων	Ῥω[μ]αίων
34.2	κα[ὶ δ]ικαιοσύνην	καὶ [δ]ικαιοσύνην
App.3	θέ[ατ]ρον	θέ[ατ]ρον (typographical error)

Bibliography

BIBLIOGRAPHICAL NOTE

It may be helpful to draw attention to recent editions of the *RGDA*. The most recent edition, by Scheid (2007), presents in detail the four inscribed texts upon which we rely for our reconstructions of the original inscription outside Augustus' Mausoleum at Rome. He includes separate majuscule texts of all four inscriptions, with full apparatus criticus, as well as a composite text that juxtaposes Greek and Latin on facing pages, with translation below into French of the Latin text. Given Scheid's careful work re-examining the inscriptions and his inclusion of the new fragments from Antioch, his edition is the best place to go for an up-to-date presentation of the texts of the *RGDA* and their problems. For students who wish to read the Latin inscriptions themselves, both Damon (1995) and Wallace (2000) offer editions of the Latin text accompanied by vocabulary and grammatical notes. LACTOR 17, *The Age of Augustus*, opens with a translation and brief notes of the Latin text (Section A).

Ramage (1987) 117–57 provides a survey of scholarship on the *RGDA*, selectively for the period 1883–1940, and extensively for 1941–87; Scheid (2007) lxxviii–lxxxiv provides a brief analysis of earlier editions of the texts.

Adams, J. N. (2003) *Bilingualism and the Latin Language* (Cambridge University Press)

Adcock, F. E. (1951) 'The interpretation of *Res Gestae Divi Augusti*, 34. I', *CQ* n.s.1: 130–5

(1952) 'A note on *Res Gestae divi Augusti* 34,3', *JRS* 42: 10–12

Aigner, H. (1979) 'Bermerkungen zu Kapitel 17 der Res Gestae divi Augusti', *GB* 8: 173–83

Alcock, S. E. (1993) *Graecia Capta. The Landscapes of Roman Greece* (Cambridge University Press)

Alföldi, A. (1971) *Der Vater des Vaterlandes im römischen Denken*, Libelli 261 (Darmstadt: Wissenschaftliche Buchgesellschaft)

(1973) *Die zwei Lorbeerbäume des Augustus* (Bonn: Rudolf Habelt)

Alföldy, G. (1972) 'Die Ablehnung der Diktatur durch Augustus', *Gymnasium* 79: 1–12

(1991) 'Augustus und die Inschriften: Tradition und Innovation. Die Geburt der imperialen Epigraphik', *Gymnasium* 98: 289–324

(1992) *Studi sull'epigrafia augustea e tiberiana di Roma*, Vetera 8 (Rome: Quasar)

(1996) 'Spain', in Bowman *et al.*, eds., 449–63

Ameling, W. (1994) 'Augustus und Agrippa', *Chiron* 24: 1–28

Andreussi, M. (1996a) 'Iuno Regina', in *LTUR* III: 125–6

    (1996b) 'Iuppiter Libertas, aedes', in *LTUR* III: 144

Arundell, F. V. J. (1834) *Discoveries in Asia Minor; Including a Description of the Ruins of Several Ancient Cities, and Especially Antioch of Pisidia*, 2 vols. (London: Richard Bentley)

Ashby, T. (1935) *The Aqueducts of Ancient Rome*, ed. I. A. Richmond (Oxford: Clarendon Press)

Ashby, T. and Fell, R. A. L. (1921) 'The Via Flaminia', *JRS* 11: 125–90

Astin, A. E. (1963) 'Augustus and "censoria potestas"', *Latomus* 22: 226–35

Bagnall, R. S. and Derow, P. (2004) *The Hellenistic Period. Historical Sources in Translation*, 2nd edn. (Oxford: Blackwell)

Bardon, H. (1968) *Les empereurs et les lettres latines d'Auguste à Hadrien* (Paris: Les Belles Lettres)

Barnes, T. D. (1974) 'The victories of Augustus', *JRS* 64: 21–6

Barton, T. (1995) 'Augustus and capricorn: Astrological polyvalency and imperial rhetoric', *JRS* 85: 33–51

Beacham, R. (2005) 'The emperor as impresario: Producing the pageantry of power' in Galinsky, ed., 151–74

Beard, M., North, J., and Price, S. (1998) *Religions of Rome* I. *A History* (Cambridge University Press)

Bedoukian, P. Z. (1968) 'A classification of the coins of the Artaxiad dynasty of Armenia', *ANSMusN* 14: 41–68

    (1971) 'Coinage of the later Artaxiads', *ANSMusN* 17: 137–9

    (1978) *Coinage of the Artaxiads of Armenia* (London: Royal Numismatic Society)

Benoit, F. (1952) 'Le sanctuaire d'Auguste et les cryptoportiques d'Arles', *RA* 39: 31–67

Benton, T. (2000) 'Epigraphy and fascism', in *The Afterlife of Inscriptions. Reusing, Rediscovering, Reinventing, and Revitalizing Ancient Inscriptions*, ed. A. E. Cooley, Bulletin of the Institute of Classical Studies Supplement 75 (London: Institute of Classical Studies) 163–92

Béranger, J. (1958) 'L'accession d'Auguste et l'idéologie du "privatus"', *Palaeologia* 7: 1–11 (reprinted in (1973) *Principatus. Etudes de notions et d'histoire politiques dans l'Antiquité gréco-romaine*, Université de Lausanne, Publications de la Faculté de Lettres 20 (Geneva: Librairie Droz) 243–58

Berchem, D. van (1939) *Les distributions de blé et d'argent à la plebe romaine sous l'empire* (Geneva: Georg; repr. New York: Arno Press, 1975)

Birley, A. R. (2000) 'Q. Lucretius Vespillo (cos. ord. 19)', *Chiron* 30: 711–48

Bivar, A. D. H. (1983) 'The political history of Iran under the Arsacids', in *The Cambridge History of Iran* III.1. *The Seleucid, Parthian and Sasanian Periods*, ed. E. Yarshater (Cambridge University Press) 21–99

Bondanella, P. (1987) *The Eternal City. Roman Images in the Modern World* (Chapel Hill and London: University of North Carolina Press)

Bonnefond, M. (1987) 'Transferts de functions et mutation idéologique: Le Capitole et le Forum d'Auguste', in *L'Urbs. Espace urbain et histoire*, Coll.EFR 98 (Rome: Ecole française de Rome) 251–78

Bosworth, B. (1999) 'Augustus, the *Res Gestae* and Hellenistic theories of apotheosis', *JRS* 89: 1–18

Botteri, P. (2001) 'Missione in Turchia: Il *monumentum Ancyranum*', *QS* 54: 133–48

(2003a) 'Ancyra, Antiochia e Apollonia: La rappresentazione delle *Res Gestae Divi Augusti*', in *The Representation and Perception of Roman Imperial Power*, eds. L. de Blois *et al.* (Amsterdam: Gieben) 240–9

(2003b) 'L'integrazione Mommseniana a *Res Gestae divi Augusti* 34, 1 *"potitus rerum omnium"* e il testo greco', *ZPE* 144: 261–7

Bowersock, G. (1965) *Augustus and the Greek World* (Oxford: Clarendon Press)

(1983) *Roman Arabia* (Cambridge, Mass.: Harvard University Press)

(1984) 'Augustus and the East: The problem of the succession', in Millar and Segal, eds., 169–88

(1990) 'The Pontificate of Augustus', in *Between Republic and Empire. Interpretations of Augustus and his Principate*, eds. K. A. Raaflaub and M. Toher (Berkeley: University of California Press) 380–94

Bowman, A. K., Champlin, E., and Lintott, A. eds. (1996) *The Cambridge Ancient History* X. *The Augustan Empire, 43 B.C.–A.D. 69*, 2nd edn. (Cambridge University Press)

Braccesi, L. (1973) 'Un'ipotesi sull'elaborazione delle "Res Gestae divi Augusti"', *GIF* 25: 25–40

Braund, D. C. (1985) *Augustus to Nero. A Sourcebook on Roman History 31 BC–AD 68* (London and Sydney: Croom Helm)

Braunert, H. (1974) 'Zum Eingangssatz des *res gestae Divi Augusti*', *Chiron* 4: 343–58

(1975) 'Die Gesellschaft des römischen Reiches im Urteil des Augustus', in Lefèvre, ed., 9–54

(1977) '*Omnium provinciarum populi Romani . . . fines auxi.* Ein Entwurf' *Chiron* 7: 207–17

Brosius, M. ed. and trans. (2000) *The Persian Empire from Cyrus II to Artaxerxes I*, LACTOR 16 (London: LACTOR)

Brunt, P. A. (1962) 'The army and the land in the Roman revolution', *JRS* 52: 69–86

(1963) Review of H. D. Meyer, *Die Aussenpolitik des Augustus und die augusteische Dichtung*, *JRS* 53: 170–6

(1966) 'The "Fiscus" and its development', *JRS* 56: 75–91

(1971) *Italian Manpower 225 BC–AD 14* (Oxford: Clarendon Press)

(1984) 'The role of the Senate in the Augustan regime', *CQ* 34: 423–44

(1990) *Roman Imperial Themes* (Oxford: Clarendon Press)

Brunt, P. A. and Moore, J. M. (1967) *Res Gestae Divi Augusti. The Achievements of the Divine Augustus* (Oxford University Press)

Buchner, E. (1976) 'Solarium Augusti und Ara Pacis', *MDAI(R)* 83: 319–65

Buckler, W. H., Calder, W. M., and Guthrie, W. K. C. (1933) *Monumenta Asiae Minoris Antiqua* IV. *Monuments and Documents from Eastern Asia and Western Galatia* (Manchester University Press) [= *MAMA*]

Burian, J. (1991) 'Die Errichtung des Prinzipats und der Tatenbericht des Augustus', *Klio* 73: 420–31

Burrell, B. (2004) Neokoroi. *Greek Cities and Roman Emperors*, Cincinnati Classical Studies (Leiden: Brill)

Burstein, S. M. (1985) *The Hellenistic Age from the battle of Ipsos to the death of Kleopatra VII*, Translated Documents of Greece and Rome 3 (Cambridge University Press)

Cagnetta, M. (1976) 'Il mito di Augusto e la "rivoluzione" fascista', *QS* 2.4: 139–81

Caldelli, M. L. (1993) *L'Agon Capitolinus. Storia e protagonisti dall'istituzione dom-izianea al IV secolo*, Studi pubblicati dall'Istituto italiano per la storia antica 54 (Rome: Istituto italiano per la storia antica)

Campbell, B. (1993) 'War and diplomacy: Rome and Parthia, 31 BC–AD 235', in *War and Society in the Roman World*, eds. J. Rich and G. Shipley (London and New York: Routledge) 213–40

    (2000) *The Writings of the Roman Land Surveyors. Introduction, Text, Translation and Commentary*, *JRS* Monograph no. 9 (London: Society for the Promotion of Roman Studies)

Campbell, J. B. (1984) *The Emperor and the Roman Army 31 BC–AD 235* (Oxford: Clarendon Press)

Carter, J. M. (1982) Suetonius. Divus Augustus (Bristol Classical Press)

Catalogo della mostra archeologica nelle Terme di Diocleziano (1911) (Bergamo: Istituto italiano d'arti grafiche)

Cecchelli, C. (1925/6) 'L'Ara della Pace sul Campidoglio', *Capitolium* 1: 65–71

Champlin, E. (1989) 'The testament of Augustus', *RhM* 132: 154–65

Chaniotis, A. (2005) *War in the Hellenistic World. A Social and Cultural History* (Oxford: Blackwell)

Chaumont, M.-L. (1976) 'L'Arménie entre Rome et l'Iran. 1. De l'avènement d'Auguste à l'avènement de Dioclétien', *ANRW* II.9.1: 71–194

Cheesman, C. E. A. (1998) 'Tincomarus Commi Filius', *Britannia* 29: 309–15

Ciancio Rossetto, P. (1999a) 'Pulvinar ad Circum Maximum', in *LTUR* IV: 169–70

    (1999b) 'Theatrum Marcelli', in *LTUR* V: 31–5

Claridge, A. (1998) *Rome. An Oxford Archaeological Guide* (Oxford University Press)

Clarke, K. (1999a) *Between Geography and History. Hellenistic Constructions of the Roman World*, Oxford Classical Monographs (Oxford: Clarendon Press)

    (1999b) 'Universal perspectives in historiography', in *The Limits of Histori-ography. Genre and Narrative in Ancient Historical Texts*, ed. C. S. Kraus, *Mnemosyne* suppl. 191 (Leiden: Brill) 249–79

Classen, C. J. (1991) 'Virtutes imperatoriae', *Arctos* 25: 17–39

Coarelli, F. (1995) 'Fortuna Redux, ara', in *LTUR* II: 275

    (1996a) 'Iuventas, Aedes', in *LTUR* III: 163

    (1996b) 'Lares, Aedes', in *LTUR* III: 174

    (1996c) 'Lupercal', in *LTUR* III: 198–9

    (1999a) 'Quirinus, Aedes', in *LTUR* IV: 185–7

    (1999b) 'Sepulcrum: A. Hirtius', in *LTUR* IV: 290

Coleman, K. M. (1993) 'Launching into history: Aquatic displays in the early Empire', *JRS* 83: 48–74

Cooley, A. E. (1998) 'The moralizing message of the *senatus consultum de Cn. Pisone Patre*', *G&R* 45: 199–212

    (2000) 'Inscribing history at Rome', in *The Afterlife of Inscriptions*, ed. A. E. Cooley, BICS Supplement 75 (London) 7–20

    (2006) 'Beyond Rome and Latium: Roman religion in the age of Augustus', in *Religion in Republican Italy*, eds. C. E. Schultz and P. B. Harvey, Jr, *YClS* 33 (Cambridge University Press) 228–52

    (2007) 'The publication of Roman official documents in the Greek East', in *Literacy and the State in the Ancient Mediterranean*, eds. K. Lomas,

R. D. Whitehouse and J. B. Wilkins, Accordia Specialist Studies on the Mediterranean 7 (London: Accordia Research Institute, University of London) 203–18

Cooley, M. G. L. ed. (2003) *The Age of Augustus*, LACTOR 17 (London: LACTOR) [= LACTOR]

Corbier, M. (1974) *L'Aerarium Saturni et l'Aerarium Militare. Administration et prosopographie sénatoriale*, Coll.EFR no. 24 (Rome: Ecole française de Rome)
(2006) *Donner à voir, donner à lire. Mémoire et communication dans la Rome ancienne* (Paris: CNRS Editions)

Cotton, H. M. and Yakobson, A. (2002) '*Arcanum Imperii*: The powers of Augustus', in *Philosophy and Power in the Graeco-Roman World. Essays in Honour of Miriam Griffin*, eds. G. Clark and T. Rajak (Oxford University Press) 193–209

Crawford, M. H. (1974) *Roman Republican Coinage* I (Cambridge University Press) [= *RRC*]
ed. (1996) *Roman Statutes*, *BICS* Suppl. 64 (London: Institute of Classical Studies)

Creighton, J. (2000) *Coins and Power in Late Iron Age Britain* (Cambridge University Press)

Cremonesi, F. (1925/6) 'Per la resurrezione della Roma imperiale', *Capitolium* 1: 393–402

Crook, J. A. (1996) 'Political history, 30 B.C. to A.D. 14', 'Augustus: power, authority, achievement' in Bowman *et al.*, eds., 70–112, 113–46

Cumont, F. (1932/3) 'L'adoration des Mages et l'art triumphal de Rome', *MPAA* 3: 81–105

Damon, C. (1995) *Res Gestae Divi Augusti*, Bryn Mawr Latin Commentaries (Bryn Mawr, Pa.: Thomas Library, Bryn Mawr College)

Davies, P. J. E. (2000) *Death and the Emperor. Roman Imperial Funerary Monuments from Augustus to Marcus Aurelius* (Cambridge University Press)

Davis, P. J. (1999) '"Since my part has been well played": Conflicting evaluations of Augustus', *Ramus* 28.1: 1–15

Degrassi, A. (1937) *Inscriptiones Italiae* XIII.iii. *Elogia* (Rome: Libreria dello Stato) [= *Inscr. Ital.* XIII.iii]
(1947) *Inscriptiones Italiae* XIII.i. *Fasti Consulares et Triumphales* (Rome: Libreria dello Stato) [= *Inscr. Ital.* XIII.i]
(1952) *I fasti consolari dell'impero romano dal 30 avanti Cristo al 613 dopo Cristo* (Rome: Edizioni di storia e letteratura)
(1957) *Inscriptiones Latinae Liberae Rei Publicae*, Biblioteca di studi superiori 23 (Florence: 'La Nuova Italia' Editrice) [= *ILLRP*]
(1963) *Inscriptiones Italiae* XIII.ii. *Fasti Anni Numani et Iuliani* (Rome: Istituto Poligrafico dello Stato) [= *Inscr. Ital.* XIII.ii]

De Maria, S. (1988) *Gli archi onorari di Roma e dell'Italia romana* (Rome: Bretschneider)

Demougin, S. (1988) *L'ordre équestre sous les Julio-Claudiens*, Coll.EFR no. 108 (Rome: Ecole française de Rome)

Dessau, H. (1906) 'Livius und Augustus', *Hermes* 41: 142–51
(1928) 'Mommsen und das Monumentum Ancyranum', *Klio* 22: 261–83

Diesner, H.-J. (1985) 'Augustus und sein Tatenbericht', *Klio* 67: 35–42

Dignas, B. (2002) *Economy of the Sacred in Hellenistic and Roman Asia Minor* (Oxford University Press)

Dion, R. (1966) 'Explication d'un passage des "Res gestae divi Augusti"', in *Mélanges d'archéologie, d'épigraphie et d'histoire offerts à Jérome Carcopino*, eds. J. Heurgon *et al.* (Paris: Hachette) 249–69

Dittenberger, W. and Purgold, K. (1896) *Die Inschriften von Olympia* (Berlin: A. Asher & Co.)

Domaszewski, A. von (1895) *Die Religion des römischen Heeres* (Trier: Fr. Lintz'schen)

Drew-Bear, T. and Scheid, J. (2005) 'La copie des *Res Gestae* d'Antioche de Pisidie', *ZPE* 154: 217–60

Drummond, A. (1995) *Law, Politics and Power. Sallust and the Execution of the Catilinarian Conspirators*, Historia Einzelschriften 93 (Stuttgart: Franz Steiner)

Duncan-Jones, R. (1982) *The economy of the Roman Empire. Quantitative studies*, 2nd edn. (Cambridge University Press)

Eck, W. (2003) *The Age of Augustus*, trans. D. L. Schneider (Oxford: Blackwell)

Eck, W., Caballos, A., and Fernández, F. (1996) *Das Senatus Consultum de Cn. Pisone Patre*, Vestigia 48 (Munich: Beck)

Eder, W. (2005) 'Augustus and the power of tradition', in Galinsky, ed., 13–32

Edwards, C. (1996) *Writing Rome. Textual Approaches to the City* (Cambridge University Press)

Ehrenberg, V. (1925) 'Monumentum Antiochenum', *Klio* 19: 189–213

Ehrenberg, V. and Jones, A. H. M. (1976) *Documents Illustrating the Reigns of Augustus and Tiberius*, 2nd edn. (Oxford: Clarendon Press) [= EJ]

Ehrhardt, C. (1986) 'Two quotations by Augustus Caesar', *LCM* 11.8: 132–3

Elsner, J. (1996) 'Inventing *imperium*: Texts and the propaganda of monuments in Augustan Rome', in *Art and Text in Roman Culture*, ed. J. Elsner (Cambridge University Press) 32–53

Ensslin, W. (1932) 'Zu den Res gestae divi Augusti', *RhM* 81: 335–65

Evans, J. D. (1992) *The Art of Persuasion. Political Propaganda from Aeneas to Brutus* (Ann Arbor: University of Michigan Press)

Ferrary, J.-L. (2001) 'À propos des pouvoirs d'Auguste', *CCG* 12: 101–54

Flower, H. I. (1996) *Ancestor Masks and Aristocratic Power in Roman Culture* (Oxford: Clarendon Press)

Frank, T. (1919) 'The Columna Rostrata of C. Duilius', *CPh* 14.1: 74–82

Fugmann, J. (1991) 'Mare a praedonibus pacavi (*R.G.* 25,1). Zum Gedanken der aemulatio in den Res Gestae des Augustus', *Historia* 40: 307–17

Gabba, E. (1953) 'Sulle colonie triumvirali di Antonio in Italia', *PP* 8: 101–10

Gagé, J. (1935) *Res Gestae Divi Augusti ex Monumentis Ancyrano et Antiocheno Latinis Ancyrano et Apolloniensi Graecis* (Paris: Les Belles Lettres)

(1939) 'Le genre littéraire des "res gestae" triomphales et ses thèmes', *REL* 17: 33–4

Galinsky, K. (1996) *Augustan Culture. An Interpretive Introduction* (Princeton University Press)

ed. (2005) *The Cambridge Companion to the Age of Augustus* (Cambridge University Press)

Ganzert, J. and Kockel, V. (1988) 'Augustusforum und Mars-Ultor-Tempel', in *Kaiser Augustus und die verlorene Republik* (Berlin: Antikenmuseum Berlin) 149–99

Garcia y Bellido, A. (1959) 'Las colonias romanas de Hispania', *AHDE* 447–512

Garnsey, P. (1988) *Famine and Food Supply in the Graeco-Roman World. Responses to Risk and Crisis* (Cambridge University Press)

Gelsomino, R. (1958) 'I grecismi di Augusto. Atti e documenti pubblici', *Maia* 10: 148–56

Giglioli, G. Q. (1927/8) 'Il museo dell'impero romano', *Capitolium* 3: 8–14
  (1928/9) 'Origine e sviluppo del museo dell'impero di Roma', *Capitolium* 4: 303–12

Giovannini, A. (1983) Consulare Imperium, Schweizerische Beiträge zur Altertumswissenschaft 16 (Basel: Friedrich Reinhardt)
  ed. (2000) *La Révolution Romaine après Ronald Syme. Bilans et perspectives* (Geneva: Fondation Hardt)

Girardet, K. M. (1995) 'Per continuos annos decem (res gestae divi Augusti 7.1). Zur Frage nach dem Endtermin des Triumvirats', *Chiron* 25: 147–61
  (2000) 'Imperium "maius". Politische und Verfassungsrechtliche Aspekte. Versuch einer Klärung', in Giovannini, ed., 167–236

Giuliani, C. F. and Verduchi, P. (1993) 'Basilica Iulia', in *LTUR* I: 177–9

González, J. (1988) 'The first oath *pro salute Augusti* found in Baetica', *ZPE* 72: 113–27

Goodyear, F. R. D. (1972) *The Annals of Tacitus. I. Annals 1.1–54*, Cambridge Classical Texts and Commentaries 15 (Cambridge University Press)
  (1981) *The Annals of Tacitus. II. Annals 1.55–81 and Annals 2*, Cambridge Classical Texts and Commentaries 23 (Cambridge University Press)

Gordon, A. E. (1968) 'Notes on the *Res Gestae* of Augustus', *California Studies in Classical Antiquity* 1: 125–38
  (1983) *Illustrated Introduction to Latin Epigraphy* (Berkeley, Los Angeles, London: University of California Press)

Gordon, R. (1990) 'From Republic to Principate: Priesthood, religion and ideology', and 'The Veil of Power: Emperors, sacrificers and benefactors', in *Pagan Priests. Religion and Power in the Ancient World*, eds. M. Beard and J. North (London: Duckworth) 179–98, 201–31

Goudineau, C. (1996) 'Gaul', in Bowman, *et al.*, eds., 464–502

Gradel, I. (2002) *Emperor Worship and Roman Religion*, Oxford Classical Monographs (Oxford: Clarendon Press)

Groag, E. (1941) 'Zur senatorischen Gefolgschaft des Caesar im actischen Krieg', in *Laureae Aquincenses Memoriae Valentini Kvzsinszky Dicatae* II, Dissertationes Pannonicae ser. 2 no. 11 (Budapest) 30–9

Groag, E. *et al.*, eds. (1933–) *Prosopographia imperii romani saec. I. II. III*, 2nd edn. (Berlin and Leipzig: Walter de Gruyter) [= *PIR²*]

Gros, P. (1993) 'Apollo Palatinus', in *LTUR* I: 54–7
  (1996) 'Iulius, divus, Aedes', in *LTUR* III: 116–19
  (1999) 'Theatrum Pompei', in *LTUR* V: 35–8

Grueber, H. A. (1910) *Coins of the Roman Republic in the British Museum* II (London: British Museum) [= *BM Coins, Rom. Rep.*]

Gruen, E. (2005) 'Augustus and the making of the Principate', in Galinsky, ed., 33–51

Gurval, R. A. (1995) *Actium and Augustus. The Politics and Emotions of Civil War* (Ann Arbor: University of Michigan Press)

Güterbock, H. G. (1989) 'The Temple of Augustus in the 1930's', in *Anatolia and the Ancient Near East. Studies in Honor of Tahsin Özgüç*, eds. K. Emre *et al.* (Ankara) 155–7

Güven, S. (1998) 'Displaying the *Res Gestae* of Augustus: A monument of imperial image for all', *JSAH* 57.1: 30–45

Halfmann, H. (1986) 'Zur Datierung und Deutung der Priesterliste am Augustus-Roma-Tempel in Ankara', *Chiron* 16: 35–42

Hallett, J. (1985) 'Queens, *princeps* and women of the Augustan élite: Propertius' Cornelia-elegy and the *Res Gestae Divi Augusti*', in *The Age of Augustus. Conference held at Brown University Providence Rhode Island 1982*, ed. R. Winkes, Archaeologia Transatlantica 5 (Louvain-La-Neuve and Providence, RI: Université Catholique de Louvain and Brown University) 73–88

Hamilton, W. J. (1842) *Researches in Asia Minor, Pontus, and Armenia; With Some Account of their Antiquities and Geology*, 2 vols. (London: John Murray)

Hanell, K. (1960) 'Das Opfer des Augustus an der Ara Pacis: Eine archäologische und historische Untersuchung', *ORom* 2: 33–120

Hano, M. (1986) 'A l'origine du culte impérial: Les autels des Lares Augusti. Recherches sur les thèmes iconographiques et leur signification', *ANRW* II.16.3: 2333–81

Harrer, G. A. (1937) 'Jean Gagé, Res Gestae Divi Augusti' (review), *AJPh* 58.2: 247–50

Harrison, S. J. (1989) 'Augustus, the poets, and the *spolia opima*', *CQ* 39.2: 408–14

Haselberger, L. *et al.* (2002) *Mapping Augustan Rome, JRA* suppl. 50 (Portsmouth, RI: Journal of Roman Archaeology)

Hellegouarc'h, J. and Jodry, C. (1980) 'Les *Res Gestae* d'Auguste et l'*Historia Romana* de Velleius Paterculus', *Latomus* 39: 803–16

Herbert-Brown, G. (1994) *Ovid and the Fasti. An Historical Study* (Oxford: Clarendon Press)

Herrmann, P. (1968) *Der römische Kaiserreid. Untersuchungen zu seiner Herkunft und Entwicklung*, Hypomnemata vol. 20 (Göttingen: Vandenhoeck & Ruprecht)

Hesberg, H. von (1978) 'Archäologische Denkmäler zum römischen Kaiserkult', *ANRW* II.16.2: 911–95

(1996) 'Mausoleum Augusti: das Monument', in *LTUR* III: 234–7

Hesberg, H. von and S. Panciera (1994) *Das Mausoleum des Augustus. Der Bau und seine Inschriften* (Munich: Bayerische Akademie der Wissenschaften)

Heuss, A. (1975) 'Zeitgeschichte als Ideologie: Komposition und Gedankenführung des Res gestae divi Augusti', in Lefèvre, ed., 55–95

Hill, P. V. (1989) *The Monuments of Ancient Rome as Coin Types* (London: Seaby)

Hoben, W. (1978) 'Caesar-Nachfolge und Caesar-Abkehr in den Res gestae divi Augusti', *Gymnasium* 85: 1–19

Hoeing, C. (1908) 'Notes on the *Monumentum Ancyranum*', *ClPh* 3: 87–90

Hoffmann, W. (1969) 'Der Widerstreit von Tradition und Gegenwart im Tatenbericht des Augustus', *Gymnasium* 76: 17–33

Hohl, E. (1937) 'Zu den Testamenten des Augustus', *Klio* 30: 323–42

(1947) 'Das Selbstzeugnis des Augustus über seine Stellung im Staat', *MH* 4: 101–15

Holloway, R. R. (1966) 'The tomb of Augustus and the princes of Troy', *AJA* 70: 171–3

Hölscher, T. (1967) Victoria Romana. *Archäologische Untersuchungen zur Geschichte und Wesensart der römischen Siegesgöttin von den Anfängen bis zum Ende des 3. Jhrs. n. Chr.* (Mainz am Rhein: Philipp von Zabern)

(1984) 'Actium und Salamis', *JDAI* 99: 187–214

(1988) 'Historische Reliefs', in *Kaiser Augustus und die verlorene Republik* (Berlin: Antikenmuseum Berlin) 351–400

Hornblower, S. and Spawforth, A. (1996) *The Oxford Classical Dictionary*, 3rd edn. (Oxford University Press) [= *OCD³*]

Huet, V. (1996) 'Stories one might tell of Roman art: Reading Trajan's Column and the Tiberius Cup', in *Art and Text in Roman Culture*, ed. J. Elsner (Cambridge University Press) 8–31

Humann, K. and Puchstein, O. (1890) *Reisen in Kleinasien und Nordsyrien* (Berlin: Dietrich Reimer)

Humphrey, J. (1986) *Roman Circuses. Arenas for Chariot Racing* (Berkeley and Los Angeles: University of California Press)

Hurlet, F. (1997) *Les collègues du prince sous Auguste et Tibère*, Coll. EFR no. 227 (Rome: Ecole française de Rome)

Huttner, U. (1997) 'Hercules und Augustus', *Chiron* 27: 369–91

Iacopi, I. (1995) 'Domus: Augustus (Palatium)', in *LTUR* II: 46–8

Instinsky, H. U. (1940) 'Consensus universorum', *Hermes* 75: 265–78

Jameson, S. (1968) 'Chronology of the campaigns of Aelius Gallus and C. Petronius', *JRS* 58: 71–84

Jones, A. H. M. (1951) 'The imperium of Augustus', *JRS* 41: 112–19 (reprinted in 1968, 1–17)

(1968) *Studies in Roman Government and Law* (Oxford: Blackwell)

Judge, E. A. (1974) '"Res publica restituta": A modern illusion?', in *Polis and Imperium. Studies in Honour of Edward Togo Salmon*, ed. J. A. S. Evans (Toronto: Hakkert) 279–311

Kaimio, J. (1979) *The Romans and the Greek Language*, Commentationes Humanarum Litterarum 64 (Helsinki: Societas Scientiarum Fennica)

Kallet-Marx, R. M. (1995) *Hegemony to Empire. The Development of the Roman Imperium in the East from 148 to 62 BC* (Berkeley and Los Angeles: University of California Press)

Keppie, L. (1983) *Colonisation and Veteran Settlement in Italy 47–14 BC* (London: British School at Rome)

(1984) *The Making of the Roman Army from Republic to Empire* (London: Batsford)

King, C. W. (1885) *Handbook of Engraved Gems*, 2nd edn. (London: George Bell)

Kinneir, J. M. (1818) *Journey through Asia Minor, Armenia, and Koordistan in the Years 1813 and 1814 with Remarks on the Marches of Alexander and Retreat of the Ten Thousand* (London: John Murray)

Klebs, E. *et al.* (1897/8) *Prosopographia imperii Romani saec. i.ii.iii.* (Berlin: Academia scientiarum regiae Borvssicae) [= *PIR*]

Kleiner, D. E. E. (1992) *Roman Sculpture* (New Haven, Conn. and London: Yale University Press)

(2005) 'Semblance and storytelling in Augustan Rome', in Galinsky, ed., 197–233

Kockel, V. (1983) *Die Grabbauten vor dem Herkulaner Tor in Pompeji* (Mainz am Rhein: Philipp von Zabern)

(1995) 'Forum Augustum', in *LTUR* II: 289–95

Konrad, C. F. (1996) 'Notes on Roman Also-Rans', in Linderski, ed. (1996a) 103–43

Kornemann, E. (1933) 'Monumentum Ancyranum', in *Paulys Realencyclopädie der classischen Altertumswissenschaft*, ed. G. Wissowa (Stuttgart: Alfred Druckenmüller) 211–31

Koster, S. (1978) 'Das "präskript" der Res Gestae Divi Augusti', *Historia* 27: 241–6

Kostof, S. (1978) 'The Emperor and the Duce: The planning of Piazzale Augusto Imperatore in Rome', in *Art and Architecture in the Service of Politics*, eds. H. A. Millon and L. Nochlin (Cambridge Mass. and London: MIT Press) 270–325

Kraft, K. (1967) 'Der Sinn des Mausoleums des Augustus', *Historia* 16: 189–206

Krencker, D. and Schede, M. (1936) *Der Tempel in Ankara* (Berlin and Leipzig: Walter de Gruyter)

Krömer, D. (1978) 'Textkritisches zu Augustus und Tiberius (*Res gestae* c. 34 – Tac. *Ann.* 6,30,3)', *ZPE* 28: 127–43

Kuttner, A. L. (1995) *Dynasty and Empire in the Age of Augustus. The Case of the Boscoreale Cups* (Berkeley: University of California Press)

Lacey, W. K. (1996) *Augustus and the Principate. The Evolution of the System*, ARCA Classical and Medieval Texts, Papers and Monographs 35 (Leeds: Francis Cairns)

Lauffer, S. (1982) 'Annos undeviginti natus', in *Althistorische Studien Hermann Bengston zum 70. Geburtstag dargebracht von Kollegen und Schülern*, ed. H. Heinen, Historia Einzelschriften 40 (Wiesbaden: Franz Steiner Verlag) 174–7

Lauter, H. (1982) 'Zwei Bemerkungen zur Basilica Iulia', *MDAI(R)* 89: 447–51

Lauton, A. (1949) 'Zur Sprache des Augustus im Monumentum Ancyranum', *WS* 64: 107–23

Lebek, W. D. (2004) '*Res Gestae divi Augusti* 34,1: Rudolf Kassels *potens rerum omnium* und ein neues Fragment des Monumentum Antiochenum', *ZPE* 146: 60

Lefèvre, E., ed. (1975) *Monumentum Chiloniense. Studien zur augusteischen Zeit* (Amsterdam: Verlag Adolf M. Hakkert)

Lehmann, G. A. (2004) 'Der Beginn der *Res Gestae* des Augustus und das politische *exemplum* des Cn. Pompeius Magnus', *ZPE* 148: 151–62

Levi, M. A. (1947) 'La composizione delle "Res gestae divi Augusti"', *RFIC* 25: 189–210

Levick, B. (1967) *Roman Colonies in Southern Asia Minor* (Oxford: Clarendon Press)

(1972) 'Atrox fortuna', *CR* ns. 22: 309–11

Lewis, M. W. H. (1955) *The Official Priests of Rome under the Julio-Claudians*, American Academy in Rome, Papers and Monographs 16 (Rome: American Academy in Rome)

Liebeschuetz, J. H. W. G. (1979) *Continuity and Change in Roman Religion* (Oxford: Clarendon Press)

Linderski, J. (1984) 'Rome, Aphrodisias and the *Res Gestae*: The *genera militiae* and the status of Octavian', *JRS* 74: 74–80

ed. (1996a) Imperium sine fine: *T. Robert S. Broughton and the Roman Republic*, Historia Einzelschriften 105 (Stuttgart: Franz Steiner)

(1996b) 'Q. Scipio Imperator', in Linderski, ed. (1996a), 145–85

Lintott, A. (1999) *The Constitution of the Roman Republic* (Oxford: Clarendon Press)

Lo Cascio, E. (1994) 'The size of the Roman population: Beloch and the meaning of the Augustan census figures', *JRS* 84: 23–40

Lucas, P. (1712) *Voyage du sieur Paul Lucas fait par ordre du roy dans la Grèce, l'Asie Mineure, la Macedoine et l'Afrique* (Paris: Nicolas Simart)

Luce, T. J. (1990) 'Livy, Augustus, and the Forum Augustum', in *Between Republic and Empire. Interpretations of Augustus and His Principate*, eds. K. A. Raaflaub and M. Toher (Berkeley and Los Angeles: University of California Press) 123–38

Macciocca, M. (1996) 'Mausoleum Augusti: Le sepolture', in *LTUR* III: 237–9
    (1999) 'Sepulcrum: C. Vibius Pansa', in *LTUR* IV: 302

Mackie, N. (1983) 'Augustan colonies in Mauretania', *Historia* 32: 332–58

Malcovati, E. (1944) *Imperatoris Caesaris Augusti Operum Fragmenta* (Turin: Paravia)

Mannsperger, D. (1973) 'Apollon gegen Dionysos: Numismatische Beiträge zu Octavians Rolle als Vindex Libertatis', *Gymnasium* 80: 381–404
    (1982) 'Annos undeviginti natus: Das Münzsymbol für Octavians Eintritt in die Politik', in *Praestant Interna. Festschrift für Ulrich Hausmann*, eds. B. von Freytag gen. Löringhoff, D. Mannsperger, F. Prayon (Tübingen: Ernst Wasmuth) 331–7

Marek, C. (1993) 'Die Expedition des Aelius Gallus nach Arabia im Jahre 25 v. Chr.', *Chiron* 23: 121–56

Marrone, G. C. (1977) 'Sulla traduzione in alcune epigrafi bilingui latino-greche del periodo augusteo', in *Contributi di storia antica in onore di Albino Garzetti* (Genova: Istituto di storia antica e scienze ausiliarie) 315–30

Martels, Z. R. W. M. von (1991) 'The discovery of the inscription of the *Res Gestae divi Augusti*', *RPL* 14: 147–56

Mattingly, H. (1923) *Coins of the Roman Empire in the British Museum* I. *Augustus to Vitellius* (London: British Museum) [= *BM Coins, Rom. Emp.* I]
    (1930) *Coins of the Roman Empire in the British Museum* II. *Vespasian to Domitian* (London: British Museum) [= *BM Coins, Rom. Emp.* II]

Mattingly, H. and Sydenham, E. A. (1926) *The Roman Imperial Coinage* II. *Vespasian to Hadrian* (London: Spink) [= *RIC* II]

Medina Lasansky, D. (2004) *The Renaissance Perfected. Architecture, Spectacle, and Tourism in Fascist Italy* (University Park, Penn.: Pennsylvania State University Press)

Meuwese, A. P. M. (1920) *De Rerum Gestarum Divi Augusti Versione Graeca* (Buscoduci: C. N. Teulings)
    (1926) 'De versione graeca Monumenti Ancyrani quaestiones', *Mnemosyne* 54: 224–33

Migne, J.-P. (1865) *Patrologiae Latinae* vol. 69 (Paris)

Miles, G. (1988) '*Maiores, conditores*, and Livy's perspective on the past', *TAPhA* 118: 185–208

Millar, F. (1963) 'The fiscus in the first two centuries', *JRS* 53: 29–42
    (1973) 'Triumvirate and Principate', *JRS* 63: 50–67
    (1984) 'State and subject: The impact of monarchy', in Millar and Segal, eds., 37–60

(1992) *The Emperor in the Roman World (31 B.C.–A.D. 337)*, 2nd edn. (London: Duckworth)

(2000) 'The first revolution: Imperator Caesar, 36–28 BC', in Giovannini, ed., 1–38

Millar, F. and Segal, E., eds. (1984) *Caesar Augustus. Seven Aspects* (Oxford: Clarendon Press)

Mitchell, S. (1976) 'Requisitioned transport in the Roman Empire: A new inscription from Pisidia', *JRS* 66: 106–31

(1979) 'Iconium and Ninica: Two double communities in Roman Asia Minor', *Historia* 28: 409–38

(1986) 'Galatia under Tiberius', *Chiron* 16: 17–33

(1993) *Anatolia. Land, Men, and Gods in Asia Minor* I. *The Celts and the Impact of Roman Rule* (Oxford: Clarendon Press)

(2005) 'The treaty between Rome and Lycia of 46 BC', in *Papyri Graecae Schøyen* I, ed. R. Pintaudi (Florence: Edizione Gonnelli) 163–258

(2008) *The Imperial Temple at Ankara and the* Res Gestae *of the Emperor Augustus. A Historical Guide* (Ankara: Museum of Anatolian Civilizations)

Mitchell, S. and Waelkens, M. (1998) *Pisidian Antioch. The Site and its Monuments* (London: Duckworth with the Classical Press of Wales)

Momigliano, A. (1942) '"Terra Marique"', *JRS* 32: 53–64

(1950) '*Panegyricus Messallae* and '*Panegyricus Vespasiani*': Two references to Britain', *JRS* 40: 39–42

Mommsen, T. (1883) *Res gestae divi Augusti. Ex monumentis ancyrano et apolloniensi* (Berlin: Weidmannsche)

(1906) 'Der Rechenschaftsbericht des Augustus', in *Gesammelte Schriften* IV. Historische Schriften I (Berlin: Weidmannsche) 247–58 (first published 1887)

(1907) 'Sui modi usati da' Romani nel conservare e pubblicare le leggi ed i senatusconsulti', in *Gesammelte Schriften* III. *Juristische Schriften* (Berlin: Weidmannsche) 290–313

Moretti, G. (1938) 'Lo scavo e la ricostruzione dell'Ara Pacis Augustae', *Capitolium* 13: 479–90

Mostra augustea della romanità (1938) 4th edn. (Rome: C. Colombo)

Mulè, F. P. (1934) '"La parola al piccone"', *Capitolium* 10: 465–8

Muñoz, A. (1938) 'La sistemazione del Mausoleo di Augusto', *Capitolium* 13: 491–508

Murray, W. M. and Petsas, P. M. (1989) *Octavian's Campsite Memorial for the Actium War*, *TAPhA* 79.4 (Philadelphia, Pa.: American Philosophical Society)

Mussolini, B. (1942) *Discorsi*, preface by B. Giuliano (Bologna: N. Zanichelli)

Nedergaard, E. (1988) 'The four sons of Phraates IV in Rome', *ActaHyp* 1: 102–15

Nenci, G. (1958) 'L'*imitatio Alexandri* nelle *Res Gestae Divi Augusti*', in *Introduzione alle guerre persiane e altri saggi di storia antica* (Pisa: Goliardica Editrice) 283–308

Newby, Z. (2005) *Greek Athletics in the Roman World. Victory and Virtue*, Oxford Studies in Ancient Culture and Representation (Oxford University Press)

Nicolet, C. (1980) *The World of the Citizen in Republican Rome*, trans. P. S. Falla (London: Batsford)

(1984) 'Augustus, government, and the propertied classes', in Millar and Segal, eds., 89–128

(1991a) 'Les fastes d'Ostie et les recensements augustéens', in *Epigrafia. Actes du Colloque international d'épigraphie latine en mémoire de Attilio Degrassi* (Rome: Université de Roma – La Sapienza, Ecole française de Rome) 119–31

(1991b) *Space, Geography, and Politics in the Early Roman Empire* (Ann Arbor: University of Michigan Press)

Nisbet, R. G. M. and Rudd, N. (2004) *A Commentary on Horace, Odes, Book III* (Oxford University Press)

Nissen, H. (1886) 'Die litterarische Bedeutung des Monumentum Ancyranum', *RhM* 41: 481–99

Pallottino, M. (1937) 'La mostra augustea della romanità', *Capitolium* 12: 519–28

Panciera, S. (2003) 'Umano, sovrumano o divino? Le divinità augustee e l'imperatore a Roma', in *The Representation and Perception of Roman Imperial Power*, eds. L. de Blois *et al.* (Amsterdam: J. C. Gieben) 215–39

Papi, E. (1996) 'Nemus Caesarum', in *LTUR* IV: 340

Parsi-Magdelain, B. (1964) 'La cura legum et morum', *RD* (4th ser.) 42: 373–412

Patterson, J. R. (1999) 'Via Flaminia', in *LTUR* V: 135–7

Pavis D'Escurac, H. (1976) *La Préfecture de l'Annone Service Administratif Impérial d'Auguste à Constantin*, BEFAR 126 (Rome: Ecole Française de Rome)

Pekáry, T. (1975) 'Statuae meae . . . argenteae steterunt in urbe XXC circiter, quas ipse sustuli: Interpretationen zu Res gestae divi Augusti 24', in Lefèvre, ed., 96–108

Pelling, C. B. R. (1988) *Plutarch. Life of Antony* (Cambridge University Press)
   (1996) 'The triumviral period', in Bowman *et al.*, eds., 1–69

Pensabene, P. (1996) 'Magna Mater, aedes', in *LTUR* III: 206–8

Perrot, G. and Guillaume, E. (1862) *Exploration archéologique de la Galatie et de la Bithynie* (Paris: Librairie de Firmin Didot Frères)

Peter, H. (1906) *Historicorum Romanorum Reliquiae* II (Leipzig: Teubner)

Pleket, H. W. (1958) *The Greek Inscriptions in the 'Rijksmuseum van Oudheden' at Leyden* (Leiden: Brill)

Pococke, R. (1745) *A Description of the East and Some Other Countries* vol. II, part II. *Observations on the Islands of the Archipelago, Asia Minor, Thrace, Greece and some other parts of Europe* (London: W. Bowyer)

Polverini, L. (1978) 'La prima manifestazione agonistica di carattere periodico a Roma', in *Scritti storico-epigrafici in memoria di Marcello Zambelli*, ed. L. Gasperini, Università di Macerata, Pubblicazioni della Facoltà di Lettere e Filosofia 5 (Rome: Centro editoriale internazionale) 325–32

Potter, D. (1998) 'Senatus consultum de Cn. Pisone', *JRA* 11: 437–57

Premerstein, von A. (1927a) 'Erwiderung' (response to Robinson 1927), *Philologische Wochenschrift* 47.20: 604–5
   (1927b) 'Res gestae divi Augusti' (Review of E. Diehl's 4th edn. 1925 and Robinson 1926b), *Philologische Wochenschrift* 47.2: 43–50
   (1932) 'Gliederung und Aufstellung der Res gestae divi Augusti in Rom und im pisidischen Antiochia', *Klio* 25: 197–225

Purcell, N. (1995) 'Forum Romanum (The Republican Period)', in *LTUR* II: 325–36

Quartermaine, L. (1995) '"Slouching towards Rome": Mussolini's imperial vision', in *Urban Society in Roman Italy*, eds. T. J. Cornell and K. Lomas (London: UCL Press) 203–15

Raaflaub, K. (1987) 'Die Militärreformen des Augustus und die politische Problematik des frühen Prinzipats', in *Saeculum Augustum* I. *Herrschaft und Gesellschaft*, ed. G. Binder, Wege der Forschung vol. 266 (Darmstadt: Wissenschaftliche Buchgesellschaft) 246–307

Ramage, E. S. (1987) *The Nature and Purpose of Augustus' 'Res Gestae'*, Historia Einzelschriften no. 54 (Stuttgart: Franz Steiner)

(1988) 'The date of Augustus' Res Gestae', *Chiron* 18: 71–82

Ramsay, W. M. (1916) 'Colonia Caesarea (Pisidian Antioch) in the Augustan age', *JRS* 6: 83–134

(1922) 'Studies in the Roman Province Galatia', *JRS* 12: 147–86

(1928) 'Zum Streit um das Monumentum Antiochenum. 2', *Klio* 22: 172–3

Ramsay, W. M. and von Premerstein, A. (1927a) *Monumentum Antiochenum. Die neugefundene Aufzeichnung der Res Gestae divi Augusti im pisidischen Antiochia*, *Klio* Beiheft 19 (Leipzig: Dieterich)

(1927b) 'Zum Streit um das Monumentum Antiochenum', *Klio* 21: 435–6

Raschke, M. G. (1978) 'New studies in Roman commerce with the East', *ANRW* II.9.2: 604–1361

Rathbone, D. W. (1996) 'The imperial finances', in Bowman *et al.*, eds., 309–23

Reeder, J. C. (1992) 'Typology and ideology in the Mausoleum of Augustus: Tumulus and tholos', *ClAnt* 11.2: 265–307

Regard, P. F. (1924) 'La version grecque du Monument d'Ancyre', *REA* 26: 147–61

Rehak, P. (2001) 'Aeneas or Numa? Rethinking the Meaning of the Ara Pacis Augustae', *ABull* 83. 2: 190–208

Reichmann, V. (1943) *Römische Literatur in griechischer Übersetzung*, *Philologus* Suppl. vol. 34.3 (Leipzig: Dieterich)

Reinhold, M. (1988) *From Republic to Principate. An Historical Commentary on Cassius Dio's* Roman History Books *49–52 (36–29 BC)*, American Philological Association 34 (Atlanta, Ga.: Scholars Press)

(2002) 'Augustus's conception of himself', in *Studies in Classical History and Society*, American Philological Association, American Classical Studies 45 (Oxford University Press), 59–69 (originally published in *Thought Quarterly* 55 (1980) 1–18)

Reynolds, J. (1982) *Aphrodisias and Rome*, *JRS* Monograph no. 1 (London: Society for the Promotion of Roman Studies)

Reynolds, J. and Lloyd, J. (1996) 'Cyrene', in Bowman *et al.*, eds., 619–40

Riccobono, S. (1941) *Fontes Iuris Romani Antejustiniani*, 2nd edn. (Florence: Barbèra) [= *FIRA*²]

Rich, J. W. (1990) *Cassius Dio. The Augustan Settlement (Roman History 53–55.9)* (Warminster: Aris & Phillips)

(1996) 'Augustus and the spolia opima', *Chiron* 26: 85–127

(1998) 'Augustus's Parthian honours, the temple of Mars Ultor and the arch in the forum Romanum', *PBSR* 66: 71–128

(2003) 'Augustus, war and peace', in *The Representation and Perception of Roman Imperial Power*, eds. L. de Blois *et al.* (Amsterdam: J. C. Gieben) 329–57

Rich, J. W. and J. H. C. Williams (1999) '*Leges et ivra p.R. restituit*: A new aureus of Octavian and the settlement of 28–27 BC', *NC* 159: 169–213

Richardson, J. (2003) 'Imperium Romanum between Republic and Empire' in *The Representation and Perception of Roman Imperial Power* eds. L. de Blois *et al.* (Amsterdam: J. C. Gieben) 137–47

Richardson Jr, L. (1978) '*Honos et Virtus* and the *Sacra Via*', *AJA* 82: 240–6

Rickman, G. (1980) *The Corn Supply of Ancient Rome* (Oxford: Clarendon Press)

Ridley, R. (1986) 'Augusti manes volitant per aura: The archaeology of Rome under the Fascists', *Xenia* 11: 19–46

   (1988) '*Res gestae divi Augusti*: The problem of chronology', in *Hestíasis. Studi di tarda antichità offerti a Salvatore Calderone* II, Università degli Studi di Messina, Studi Tardoantichi II (Messina: Sicania) 265–91

   (2003) *The Emperor's Retrospect. Augustus' Res Gestae in Epigraphy, Historiography and Commentary* (Leuven and Dudley, Mass.: Peeters)

Rives, J. B. (1995) *Religion and Authority in Roman Carthage from Augustus to Constantine* (Oxford: Clarendon Press)

Robinson, D. M. (1924) 'A preliminary report on the excavations at Pisidian Antioch and at Sizma', *AJA* 28: 435–44

   (1926a) 'The Res Gestae divi Augusti as recorded on the Monumentum Antiochenum', *AJPh* 47.1: 1–54

   (1926b) 'Roman sculptures from Colonia Caesarea (Pisidian Antioch)', *ABull* 9.1: 5–69

   (1926c) 'Two new heads of Augustus', *AJA* 30.2: 125–36

   (1927) 'Entgegnung' (response to von Premerstein 1927a), *Philologische Wochenschrift* 47.20: 603–4

   (1928) 'Zum Streit um das Monumentum Antiochenum. 1', *Klio* 22: 169–72

Robinson, O. F. (1992) *Ancient Rome. City Planning and Administration* (London and New York: Routledge)

Rogers, R. S. (1947) 'The Roman emperors as heirs and legatees', *TAPhA* 78: 140–58

Rose, C. B. (2005) 'The Parthians in Augustan Rome', *AJA* 109.1: 21–75

Rowe, G. (2002) *Princes and Political Cultures. The New Tiberian Senatorial Decrees* (Ann Arbor: University of Michigan Press)

   (in press) 'The elaboration and diffusion of the text of the *Monumentum Ephesenum*', in *The Customs Law of Asia*, eds. M. Cottier *et al.*, Oxford Studies in Ancient Documents (Oxford University Press)

Roxan, M. M. (1985) *Roman Military Diplomas 1978–1984* (London: Institute of Archaeology)

Ryberg, I. S. (1966) '*Clupeus virtutis*', in *The Classical Tradition. Literary and Historical Studies in Honor of Harry Caplan*, ed. L. Wallach (Ithaca, NY: Cornell University Press) 232–8

Sablayrolles, R. (1981) 'Espace urbain et propaganda politique: L'organisation du centre de Rome par Auguste (*Res Gestae* 19 à 21)', *Pallas* 28: 59–77

Saller, R. P. (1994) *Patriarchy, Property and Death in the Roman Family* (Cambridge University Press)

Santirocco, M. (1995) 'Horace and Augustan ideology', *Arethusa* 28: 225–43

Sattler, P. (1960) *Augustus und der Senat. Untersuchungen zur römischen Innenpolitik zwischen 30 und 17 v. Christus* (Göttingen: Vandenhoeck & Ruprecht)

Schäfer, M. (1957) 'Cicero und der Prinzipat des Augustus', *Gymnasium* 64: 310–35

Schede, M. and Schultz, H. S. (1937) *Ankara und Augustus* (Berlin: Walter de Gruyter)

Scheer, T. S. (1995) 'Res Gestae Divi Augusti 24: Die Restituierung göttlichen Eigentums in Kleinasien durch Augustus', in *Rom und der griechische Osten.*

Festschrift für Hatto H. Schmitt zum 65. Geburtstag, eds. Ch. Schubert and K. Brodersen (Stuttgart: Franz Steiner) 209–23

Scheid, J. (1998) *Recherches archéologiques à la Magliana: Commentarii Fratrum Arvalium qui supersunt: Les copies épigraphiques des protocoles annuels de la confrérie arvale: 21 av.–304 ap. J.-C.* (Rome: Ecole française de Rome and Soprintendenza archeologica di Roma)

   (1999) 'Auguste et le grand pontificat: Politique et droit sacré au début du Principat', *RD* 77: 1–19

   (2000) 'Ronald Syme et la religion des Romains', in Giovannini, ed., 39–72

   (2003) *An Introduction to Roman Religion*, trans. J. Lloyd (Bloomington and Indianapolis: Indiana University Press)

   (2005) 'Augustus and Roman religion: Continuity, conservatism, and innovation', in Galinsky, ed., 175–93

   (2007) *Res Gestae Divi Augusti. Hauts faits du divin Auguste* (Paris: Les Belles Lettres)

Schmitthenner, W. (1973) *Oktavian und das Testament Cäsars. Eine Untersuchung zu den politischen Anfängen des Augustus*, 2nd edn. (Munich: Beck)

   (1979) 'Rome and India: Aspects of universal history during the Principate', *JRS* 69: 90–106

Schnegg-Köhler, B. (2002) *Die augusteischen Säkularspiele*, Archiv für Religionsgeschichte 4 (Munich and Leipzig: Saur)

Schütz, M. (1990) 'Zur Sonnenuhr des Augustus auf dem Marsfeld', *Gymnasium* 97: 432–57

Scobie, A. (1990) *Hitler's State Architecture. The Impact of Classical Antiquity* (University Park, Pa. and London: Pennsylvania State University Press)

Scott, K. (1925) 'The identification of Augustus with Romulus-Quirinus', *TAPhA* 56: 82–105

   (1932) 'Chapter IX of the Res Gestae and the Ruler Cult', *CPh* 27.3: 284–7

Seager, R. (1972) '*Factio*: Some observations', *JRS* 62: 53–8

Sellwood, D. (1983) 'Parthian coins', in *The Cambridge History of Iran* III.1. The Seleucid, Parthian and Sasanian Periods, ed. E. Yarshater (Cambridge University Press) 279–98

Seston, W. (1954) 'Le *clipeus virtutis* d'Arles et la composition des *Res Gestae Divi Augusti*', *CRAI*: 286–97

Seyfarth, W. (1957) 'Potitus rerum omnium: Ein Beitrag zur Deutung der RGDA, Kapitel 34', *Philologus* 101: 305–23

Shackleton Bailey, D. R. (1968) *Cicero's Letters to Atticus IV. 49 BC* (Cambridge University Press)

Sherk, R. K. (1969) *Roman Documents from the Greek East* (Baltimore, Md.: Johns Hopkins Press) [= *RDGE*]

   (1984) *Rome and the Greek East to the Death of Augustus*, Translated Documents of Greece and Rome 4 (Cambridge University Press) [= *RGE*]

   (1988) *The Roman Empire. Augustus to Hadrian*, Translated Documents of Greece and Rome 6 (Cambridge University Press)

Sherwin-White, A. N. (1984) *Roman Foreign Policy in the East 168 BC to AD 1* (London: Duckworth)

Shinnie, P. L. (1978) 'The Nilotic Sudan and Ethiopia, *c.* 660 BC to *c.* AD 600', in *The Cambridge History of Africa* II. From *c.* 500 BC to AD 1050, ed. J. D. Fage (Cambridge University Press) 210–71

Sidebotham, S. E. (1986) 'Aelius Gallus and Arabia', *Latomus* 45: 590–602

Silverio, A. M. L. (1983) 'La mostra augustea della romanità', in *Dalla mostra al museo. Dalla Mostra archeologica del 1911 al Museo della civiltà romana*, Roma Capitale 1870–1911 4 (Venice: Marsilio Editori) 77–90

Simon, B. (1993) *Die Selbstdarstellung des Augustus in Münzprägung und in den Res Gestae*, Antiquates 4 (Hamburg: Kovač)

Simon, E. (1967) *Ara Pacis Augustae*, Monumenta Artis Antiquae 1 (Tübingen: Ernst Wasmuth)

Simpson, C. J. (1977) 'The date of dedication of the Temple of Mars Ultor', *JRS* 67: 91–4

Skard, E. (1955) 'Zu Monumentum Ancyranum', *SO* 31: 119–21

Skutsch, O. (1985) *The* Annals *of Q. Ennius* (Oxford: Clarendon Press)

Smith, R. R. R. (1988) '*Simulacra gentium*: The *ethne* from the Sebasteion at Aphrodisias', *JRS* 78: 50–77

Speidel, M. A. (2000) 'Geld und Macht: Die Neuordnung des staatlichen Finanzwesens unter Augustus', in Giovannini, ed., 113–66

Spinazzola, V. (1953) *Pompei alla luce degli scavi nuovi di via dell'Abbondanza (anni 1910–1923)* I (Rome: Libreria dello stato)

Squarciapino, M. F. (1982) 'Corona civica e clupeus virtutis da Ostia', in *Miscellanea Archaeologica Tobias Dohrn dedicata*, eds. H. Blanck and S. Steingräber, Archaeologica 26 (Rome: Bretschneider) 45–52

Steinby, E. M. ed. (1993) *Lexicon Topographicum Urbis Romae* I. A–C (Rome: Edizioni Quasar) [= *LTUR* I]

    (1995) *Lexicon Topographicum Urbis Romae* II. D–G (Rome: Edizioni Quasar) [= *LTUR* II]

    (1996) *Lexicon Topographicum Urbis Romae* III. H–O (Rome: Edizioni Quasar) [= *LTUR* III]

    (1999a) *Lexicon Topographicum Urbis Romae* IV. P–S (Rome: Edizioni Quasar) [= *LTUR* IV]

    (1999b) *Lexicon Topographicum Urbis Romae* V. T–Z (Rome: Edizioni Quasar) [= *LTUR* V]

Stewart, P. (2003) *Statues in Roman Society. Representation and Response*, Oxford Studies in Ancient Culture and Representation (Oxford University Press)

Stillwell, R. (1976) *The Princeton Encyclopedia of Classical Sites* (Princeton University Press) [= *PECS*]

Stone, M. (1999) 'A flexible Rome: Fascism and the cult of *romanità*', in *Roman Presences. Receptions of Rome in European Culture, 1789–1945*, ed., C. Edwards (Cambridge University Press) 205–20

Stone III, S. C. (1983) 'Sextus Pompey, Octavian and Sicily', *AJA* 87.1: 11–22

Stylow, A. U. and Corzo Pérez, S. (1999) 'Eine neue Kopie des senatus consultum de Cn. Pisone patre', *Chiron* 29: 23–8

Sullivan, R. D. (1990) *Near Eastern Royalty and Rome, 100–30 BC*, Phoenix suppl. no. 24 (Toronto: University of Toronto Press)

Sutherland, C. H. V. (1984) *The Roman Imperial Coinage. From 31 BC to AD 69*, 2nd revised edn. (London: Spink) [= *RIC* I²]

Swan, P. M. (2004) *The Augustan Succession. An Historical Commentary on Cassius Dio's Roman History Books 55–56 (9 B.C.–A.D.14)* (Oxford University Press)

Syme, R. (1939) *The Roman Revolution* (Oxford: Clarendon Press)

(1958) 'Imperator Caesar: A study in nomenclature', *Historia* 7: 172–88 (repr. in (1979) *Roman Papers* I, ed. E. Badian (Oxford: Clarendon Press) 361–77)

(1959) 'Livy and Augustus', *HSPh* 64: 27–87 (repr. in (1979) *Roman Papers* I, ed. E. Badian (Oxford: Clarendon Press) 400–54)

(1971) *Danubian Papers* (Bucharest: Association Internationale d'Études du Sud-Est Européen)

(1973) 'The *Titulus Tiburtinus*', in *Akten des VI. Internationalen Kongresses für griechische und lateinische Epigraphik, Vestigia* 17 (Munich: Beck) (repr. in (1984) *Roman Papers* III, ed. A. R. Birley (Oxford: Clarendon Press) 869–84)

(1974) 'The crisis of 2 B.C.', *SBAW* 7: 3–34 (repr. in (1984) *Roman Papers* III, ed. A. R. Birley (Oxford: Clarendon Press) 912–36)

(1978) 'Mendacity in Velleius', *AJPh* 99: 45–63 (repr. in (1984) *Roman Papers* III, ed. A. R. Birley (Oxford: Clarendon Press) 1090–104)

(1979a) 'Problems about Janus', *AJPh* 100: 188–212 (repr. in (1984) *Roman Papers* III, ed. A. R. Birley (Oxford: Clarendon Press) 1179–97)

(1979b) 'Some imperatorial salutations', *Phoenix* 33: 308–29 (repr. in (1984) *Roman Papers* III, ed. A. R. Birley (Oxford: Clarendon Press) 1198–219)

(1986) *The Augustan Aristocracy* (Oxford: Clarendon Press)

Tagliamonte, G. (1993) 'Capitolium', in *LTUR* I: 226–31

Talbert, R. J. A. (1984) *The Senate of Imperial Rome* (Princeton University Press)

Taylor, L. R. (1918) 'Livy and the name Augustus', *CR* 32.7/8: 158–61

(1942) 'The Election of the Pontifex Maximus in the Late Republic', *CPh* 37: 421–4

Teutsch, L. (1962) *Das Städtewesen in Nordafrika in der Zeit von C. Gracchus bis zum Tode des Kaisers Augustus* (Berlin: Walter de Gruyter)

Thomas, E. and Witschel, C. (1992) 'Constructing reconstruction: Claim and reality of Roman rebuilding inscriptions from the Latin West', *PBSR* 47: 135–77

Thorley, J. (1969) 'The development of trade between the Roman Empire and the East under Augustus', *G&R* 16.2: 209–23

Timpe, D. (1975) 'Zur augusteischen Partherpolitik zwischen 30 und 20 v. Chr.', *WJA* 1: 155–69

Torelli, M. (1982) *Typology and Structure of Roman Historical Reliefs* (Ann Arbor: University of Michigan Press)

(1999) 'Pax Augusta, ara', in *LTUR* IV: 70–4

Tortorici, E. (1993) 'Curia Iulia', in *LTUR* I: 332–3

Turpin, W. (1994) 'Res Gestae 34.1 and the settlement of 27 BC', *CQ* 44.2: 427–37

Urban, R. (1979) 'Tacitus und die Res gestae divi Augusti: Die Auseinandersetzung des Historikers mit der offiziellen Darstellung', *Gymnasium* 86: 59–74

Vanotti, G. (1975) 'Il testo greco delle "Res Gestae Divi Augusti": Appunti per una interpretazione politica', *GIF* 27: 306–25

(1997) '*Heghemon* nel testo greco delle *res gestae*', *Klio* 79.2: 362–71

Vassileiou, A. (1984a) 'Caius ou Lucius Caesar proclamé *princeps juventutis* par l'ordre équestre', in *Hommages à Lucien Lerat* II, ed. H. Walter, Centres de recherches d'histoire ancienne vol. 55, Annales littéraires de l'Université de Besançon 294 (Paris: Les Belles Lettres) 827–39

(1984b) 'Sur les dates de naissance de Drusus, de Caius et Lucius Caesar', *RPh* 58: 45–52

Vendittelli, L. (1996) 'Minerva, aedes (Aventinus)', in *LTUR* III: 254

Versnel, H. S. (1970) *Triumphus. An Inquiry into the Origin, Development and Meaning of the Roman Triumph* (Leiden: Brill)

Veyne, P. (1990) *Bread and Circuses. Historical Sociology and Political Pluralism* (London: Penguin)

Viereck, P. (1888) *Sermo Graecus Quo Senatus Populusque Romanus Magistratusque Populi Romani Usque Ad Tiberii Caesaris Aetatem In Scriptis Publicis Usi Sunt Examinatur* (Gottingen: Vandenhoeck & Ruprecht)

Ville, G. (1981) *La gladiature en occident des origines à la mort de Domitien* (Rome: Ecole française de Rome)

Vin, J. P. A. van der (1981) 'The return of Roman ensigns from Parthia', *BABesch* 56: 117–39

Virlouvet, C. (1995) *Tessera frumentaria. Les procedures de la distribution du blé public à Rome*, BEFAR no. 286 (Rome: Ecole française de Rome)

Viscogliosi, A. (1993) 'Apollo, aedes in circo', in *LTUR* I: 49–54

  (1999) 'Porticus Octavia', in *LTUR* IV: 139–41

Vittinghoff, F. (1952) *Römische Kolonisation und Bürgerrechtspolitik* (Wiesbaden: Akademie der Wissenschaften und der Literatur)

Volkmann, H. (1954/5) 'Bemerkungen zu den Res Gestae divi Augusti', *Historia* 3: 81–86

Vollenweider, M.-L. (1964) 'Principes iuventutis', *Schweizer Münzblätter* 13/14: 76–81

Wagenvoort, H. (1936) 'Princeps' *Philologus* 45: 206–21, 323–45

Walker, S. and Burnett, A. (1981) *The Image of Augustus* (London: British Museum)

Wallace, R. E. (2000) *Res Gestae Divi Augusti* (Wauconda, Ill.: Bolchazy-Carducci Publishers)

Wallace-Hadrill, A. (1981a) 'The emperor and his virtues', *Historia* 30: 298–323

  (1981b) 'Family and inheritance in the Augustan marriage-laws', *PCPhS* 27: 58–80

  (1986) 'Image and authority in the coinage of Augustus', *JRS* 76: 66–87

  (2005) '*Mutatas Formas*: The Augustan transformation of Roman knowledge', in Galinsky, ed., 55–84

Wallmann, P. (1976) 'Zur Zusammensetzung und Haltung des Senats im Jahre 32 v. Chr.', *Historia* 25: 305–12

Walser, G. (1955) 'Der Kaiser als Vindex libertatis', *Historia* 4: 353–67

Watson, G. R. (1969) *The Roman Soldier* (London: Thames and Hudson)

Weber, W. (1936) *Princeps. Studien zur Geschichte des Augustus* (Stuttgart: Kohlhammer)

Weinstock, S. (1971) *Divus Julius* (Oxford: Clarendon Press)

Whittaker, C. R. (1996) 'Roman Africa: Augustus to Vespasian', in Bowman *et al.*, eds., 586–618

  (2000) 'Frontiers', in *The Cambridge Ancient History* XI. *The High Empire, AD 70–192*, eds. A. K. Bowman, P. Garnsey, D. Rathbone, 2nd edn. (Cambridge University Press) 293–319

Wiedemann, T. (1986) 'The *fetiales*: A reconsideration', *CQ* 36.2: 478–90

  (1992) *Emperors and Gladiators* (London and New York: Routledge)

Wigtil, D. N. (1982a) 'The ideology of the Greek "Res Gestae"', *ANRW* II.30.1 (Berlin and New York: Walter de Gruyter) 624–38

  (1982b) 'The translator of the Greek *Res Gestae* of Augustus', *AJPh* 103: 189–94

Wilamowitz-Möllendorff, U. von (1886) 'Res Gestae Divi Augusti', *Hermes* 21: 623–7

Wilkes, J. J. (1969) *Dalmatia* (London: Routledge and Kegan Paul)

(1996) 'The Danubian and Balkan provinces', in Bowman *et al.*, eds., 545–85

Williams, G. (1962) 'Poetry in the moral climate of Augustan Rome', *JRS* 52: 28–46

Williams, J. H. C. (2001) '"Spoiling the Egyptians": Octavian and Cleopatra', in *Cleopatra of Egypt from History to Myth*, eds. S. Walker and P. Higgs (London: British Museum Press) 190–9

(2002) 'Pottery stamps, coin designs, and writing in late Iron Age Britain', in *Becoming Roman, Writing Latin? Literacy and Epigraphy in the Roman West*, ed. A. E. Cooley, *JRA* Suppl. 48 (Portsmouth RI: Journal of Roman Archaeology), 135–49

Williamson, C. (1987) 'Monuments of bronze: Roman legal documents on bronze tablets', *ClAnt* 6: 160–83

Wilson, R. J. A. (1996) 'Sicily, Sardinia, Corsica', in Bowman *et al.*, eds., 434–48

Wirszubski, C. (1960) *Libertas as a Political Idea at Rome during the Late Republic and Early Principate* (Cambridge University Press)

Wiseman, T. P. (1994) *Historiography and Imagination. Eight Essays on Roman Culture* (University of Exeter Press)

Wolters, R. (1988) 'Zum Anhang der Res Gestae divi Augusti', *ZPE* 75: 197–206

Woodman, A. J. (1977) *Velleius Paterculus. The Tiberian Narrative (2.94–131)*, Cambridge Classical Texts and Commentaries 19 (Cambridge University Press)

(1983) *Velleius Paterculus. The Caesarian and Augustan Narrative (2.41–93)*, Cambridge Classical Texts and Commentaries 25 (Cambridge University Press)

Yavetz, Z. (1969) Plebs *and* Princeps (Oxford: Clarendon Press)

(1984) 'The *Res Gestae* and Augustus' public image', in Millar and Segal, eds., 1–36

Zachos, K. (2003) 'The *tropaeum* of Augustus at Nikopolis', *JRA* 16.1: 64–92

(2007) *Nicopolis B. Proceedings of the Second International Nicopolis Symposium* (Preveza: Actia Nicopolis Foundation)

Zanker, P. (1988) *The Power of Images in the Age of Augustus*, trans. A. Shapiro (Ann Arbor: University of Michigan Press)

Zeri, A. (2006) 'L'ara pacis Augustae da Morpurgo a Meier', *Forma Urbis* 11.5: 4–25

Index locorum

General index